PHILIP'S

MODERN SCHOOL ·ATLAS·

In association with Heinemann Educational

George Philip Limited
Michelin House, 81 Fulham Road
London SW3 6RB

Heinemann Educational
Halley Court, Jordan Hill
Oxford OX2 8EJ

CONTENTS

Published in Great Britain in 1994
by George Philip Limited,
an imprint of Reed Consumer Books Limited,
Michelin House, 81 Fulham Road,
London SW3 6RB

Cartography by Philip's

Ninetieth edition
© 1994 Reed International Books Limited

Reprinted 1995

ISBN 0-540-05815-7 Paperback edition
ISBN 0-540-05795-9 Hardback edition

Printed in Italy

BRITISH ISLES MAPS

A separate map key is provided on the first page of the World Maps section.

SETTLEMENTS

◼ **LONDON**   ▣ **GLASGOW**   ▣ **BRADFORD**   ⊡ Brighton   ● Gateshead

◉ Aylesbury   ◎ Sligo   ⊙ Selkirk   ○ Burford   ○ Lampeter

Settlement symbols and type styles vary according to the population and importance of towns

▧ Built up areas   ▫ London Boroughs

ADMINISTRATION

—— International boundaries

W A L E S   Country names

—— National boundaries

K E N T   Administrative area names

····· Administrative boundaries

EXMOOR   National park names

COMMUNICATIONS

═══ Motorways
=== *under construction*

━━ Main passenger railways
▬▬▬ *under construction*
⌐----⌐ *in tunnels*

—— Major roads
——— *under construction*
⌐----⌐ *in tunnels*

—— Other passenger railways
——— *under construction*
⌐----⌐ *in tunnels*

—— Other important roads
——— *under construction*
⌐----⌐ *in tunnels*

····· Canals
····· *in tunnels*

⊕ Major airports   ⊕ Other airports

PHYSICAL FEATURES

〜 Perennial rivers

▲ 444   Elevations in metres

▨ Tidal flats

△ 1342   Elevations-highest in county (or region in Scotland) in metres

◗ Lakes or reservoirs

▾ 38   Depths below sea level in metres

⬭ Reservoirs under construction

ELEVATION AND DEPTH TINTS

Height of Land above Sea Level	Land below Sea Level	Depth of Sea

in metres	1000	750	500	400	200	100	0							
								150	300	600	1500	3000	6000	in feet
in feet	3000	2250	1500	1200	600	300								
							0	20	50	100	200	500	1000	2000
														in metres

SHETLAND ISLANDS on same scale

Muckle Flugga
Herma Ness
Haroldswick
Bluemull Sd.
Baltasound
Balta
Unst
Whale Firth
Uyeasound
Mu Ness
Ramna Stacks
Cullivoe
Belmont
Pt. of Fethaland
Gutcher
Fetlar
Colgrave Sd.
The Faither
North Roe
Mid Yell
The Snap
Ramna Hill 453
Yell Sound
Yell
Esha Ness
Ulsta
Burravoe
Hillswick
Lunna Ness
Sullom
St. Magnus Bay
Brae
Out Skerries
Muckle Roe
SHETLAND
Skaw Taing
Papa Stour
Vidlin
Whalsay
Sd. of Papa
Sandness
Aith
Symbister
South Nesting B.
Walls
Score Hd.
Bressay
Easter Skeld
Lerwick
I. of Noss
Gruting Voe
Scalloway
Hamnavoe
Bard Hd.
West Burra
Kettla Ness
293
Helli Ness
Hoswick
Mousa
St. Ninian's I.
Northpunds
Scousburgh
Boddam
Fitful Hd.
B. of Quendale
Sumburgh Hd.

NORTHERN SCOTLAND

Butt of Lewis (Rubha Robhanais)
Port of Ness (Port Nis)
South Dell
Barve
Ness
Cellar Hd.
Barvas (Barabhas)
North Tolsta
Tolsta Hd.
Shawbost
Carloway (Carlabhagh)
Ben Mholach 291
Back
Broad Bay
Newmarket
Tiumpan Hd.
Gallan Hd.
Great Bernera
Uig
L. Roag
Stornoway (Steornabhaigh)
Melbost
Portaguiran
Callanish
Bayble
Eye Peninsula
Aird Brenish
Gorynahine
Chicken Hd.
Brenish 575
Gisla
Crossbost
Lewis
L. Langavat
Balallan
L. Erisort
Cromore
Scarp
Kintarvie
Gravir
Husinish Pt.
North
L. Shell
Kebock Hd.
Gasker
Husinish (Huisinis)
Ardvourlied
Lemreway
Seaforth
Beinn Mhor 571
Harris
Clisham 799
West L. Tarbert
Ardhasig
WESTERN
Taransay
Tarbert (Tairbeart)
East L. Tarbert
Sd. of Taransay
Scalpay
Sd. of Shiant
Toe Hd.
Scarastavore
South Harris
Shiant Is.
Pabbay
Leverburgh (An T-ob)
Sd. of Pabbay
Berneray
Rodel (Roghadal)
Renish Pt.
ISLES
Haskeir Is.
Rubha Hunish
Griminish Pt.
Sollas
Kilmaluag
Lochmaddy (Loch Nam Madadh)
Vaternish Pt.
Staffin
North Uist
L. Maddy
Paible
Clachan
Uig
L. Snizort
Trotternish
Monach Is.
Carinish
L. Eport
Dunvegan Hd.
The Storr 719
Baleshare
Eaval 347
Stein
Grimsay
Ronay
Lusta
Sound of Monach
Gramsdale
Milovaig
Carbost
Sound of Raasay
Benbecula
Creagony
Wiay
Lephin
Dunvegan
Roskhill
Portree
Ardivachar Pt.
Bach nam Faoleann
Healaval Bheag 488
Raasay
L. Bee
Neist Pt.
Bracadale
Toscaig
Howmore
Hecla 605
L. Bracadale
Coillore
Harport
Scanser
Rubha Ardvule
Glamaig
Ben Mhor 620
Carbost
Drynoch
South Uist
Fernilea
Sligachan
L. Eynort
Minginish
Daliburgh
Cuillin Hills 1009
Bla Bheinn 928
Lochboisdale (Loch Baghasdail)
Glenbrittle
L. Boisdale
Rubh'an Dunain
Kilbride
Sd. of Eriskay
Soay Sd.
Elgol
Sound of Barra
Soay
Eriskay
Cuillin Sd.
Greian Hd.
Canna 183
Barra
Sanday
Castlebay
Heaval 384
Bruernish Pt.
Rhum (Rum)
Vatersay
810
Sandray
Kinloch
Pabbay
Sound of Rhum
Eigg
Mingulay
394
Berneray
Sd. of Eigg
Barra Hd.
268
Muck
124
Pt. of Ardnamurchan
Ardnamurchan
Kilchoan
Ben Hiant 527
Coll
Sorisdale
Clabhach
Mingary
Tobermory
Arinagour

West from Greenwich

North Minch
L. Inchar
L. Laxford
C. W
115
Kinloc
Handa I.
Laxford Br.
Scour
Eddrachillis Bay
Pt. of Stoer
Kylestro
Drumbeg
Unap
Stoer
Assynt
Rubha Coigeach 167
Enard B.
L. Assy
Reiff
Lochinver
Inverkirkaig
Summer Is.
Achiltibuie
L. Lurgainn
Coigach
L. Broom
Little Minch
Greenstone Pt.
Gruinard B.
Ullap
Mellon Charles
Aultbea
Ardessie
Ardcharnich
Ari Teallach 1062
L. na Sealga
Melvaig
Longa I.
L. Ewe
Poolewe
Gairloch
Kerrysdale
Port Henderson
L. Gairloch 179
Sloch 981
We
Red Point
Talladale
Kinlochewe
Diabaig
L. Maree
L. Torridon
Liathach 1053
Fasag
Achnasheen
Rona
Torridon
Shieldaig
Achnashellach
Applecross Forest
Inner Sound
316
Coulags
Strathc
Monar For
Applecross
Carron
1052 L. M
Kishorn
Lochcarron
Ling
Toscaig
Stromemore
Narrows
Crowlin Is.
L. Carron
Plockton
Stromeferry
Cann M
1182
Kyle of Lochalsh
Auchtertyre
Bihaig
L. Mullardoc
Kyleakin
Dornie
Breakish
L. Alsh
Broadford
Kylerhea
Gleneig
Shiel Bridge
Five Sisters 1068
A'Chralaig 1120
Chuan
Eilean Iarmain
The Saddle 1012
Glen Shiel
Teangue
Arnisdale
Sd. of Sleat
L. Hourn
L. Quoich
Jayne Tom
Armadale
Ardvasar
Knoydart
1040 Sgurr na Cichu
Pt. of Sleat
Inverie
Glen G
Mallaig
L. Nevis
Morar
310
L. Arkaig
Tarbet
Culvain 383
Arisaig
L. Morar
Kinlochmoidart
Kinfoche
Corpach
Rhois-Bheinn 882
Lochailort
Glenfinnan
L. Eil
Shona I.
Fort William
L. Moidart
Moidart
Kinlochmoidart
Ardgour
Salen
888
Acharacle
Sunart
Strontian
Corran
Onich
Kinloch
L. Sunart
Kungarrloch
L. Leven
Ballachulish

Outer Hebrides   **Inner Hebrides**   **Skye**   **HIGHL**   **Sea of the Hebrides**

Projection : Conical with two standard parallels

ft m
3000 1000
2250 750
1500 500
1200 400
600 200
300 100
0 0
20 60
50 150
100 300
200 600
m ft

ORKNEY ISLANDS
on same scale

1:1 000 000

20 miles

30 km

CARTOGRAPHY BY PHILIP'S. COPYRIGHT REED INTERNATIONAL BOOKS LTD

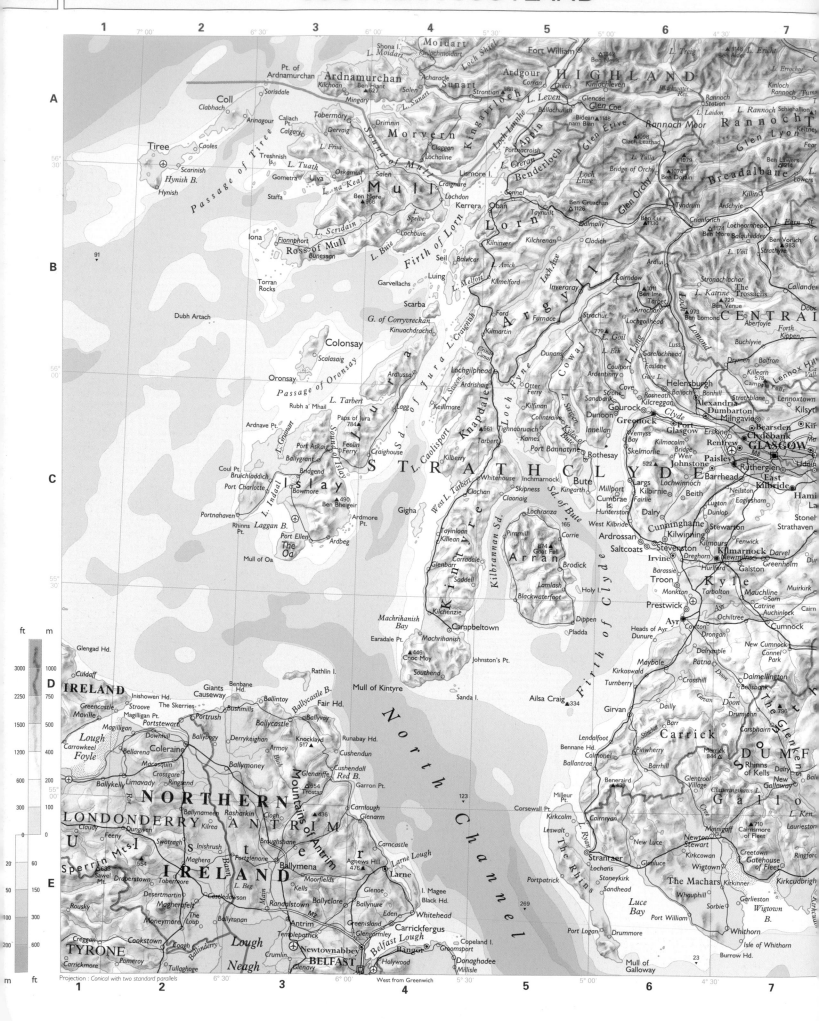

1:1 000 000

20 miles

30 km

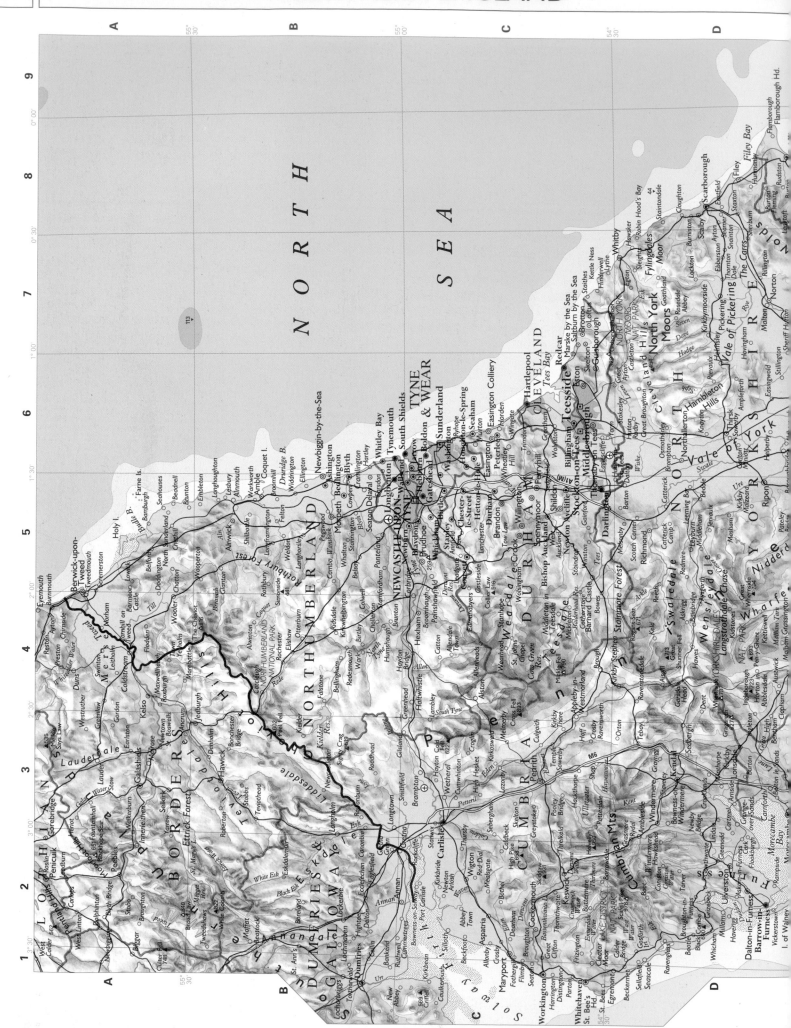

Great Ouse

The Wash

Mouth of the Humber

HOLDERNESS

HUMBERSIDE

KINGSTON UPON HULL

Grimsby · Cleethorpes

LINCOLNSHIRE

Lincolnshire Wolds

The Fens

King's Lynn

March · Wisbech

CAMBRIDGESHIRE

Scunthorpe

Gainsborough

Lincoln

Boston

Spalding

Peterborough

Cambridge

YORKSHIRE

York · Leeds

WEST YORKSHIRE

Harrogate

Bradford · Halifax · Huddersfield

SOUTH YORKSHIRE

Sheffield · Rotherham · Barnsley · Doncaster

Pontefract · Wakefield

NOTTINGHAMSHIRE

Worksop · Mansfield · NOTTINGHAM

Newark-on-Trent

Grantham

LINCOLN

RUTLAND

Oakham · Uppingham

NORTHAMPTONSHIRE

Northampton · Kettering · Corby · Wellingborough

Rugby

LANCASHIRE

Blackpool · Fleetwood · Cleveleys · Lytham St. Anne's

Preston · Blackburn · Burnley · Nelson · Colne

Forest of Bowland · Bleasdale Moors

GREATER MANCHESTER

MANCHESTER · Bolton · Bury · Oldham · Rochdale · Stockport · Salford

MERSEYSIDE

LIVERPOOL · Birkenhead · Wallasey · Southport · St. Helens · Bootle · Crosby

Liverpool Bay

CHESHIRE

Chester · Crewe · Northwich · Macclesfield · Congleton · Nantwich

DERBYSHIRE

DERBY · Chesterfield · Matlock · Buxton · Belper · Ashbourne

PEAK DISTRICT NATIONAL PARK

Dove Dale

STAFFORDSHIRE

STOKE-ON-TRENT · The Potteries · Newcastle-under-Lyme · Stafford · Stone · Uttoxeter · Leek · Cannock · Burton upon Trent

Cannock Chase

WEST MIDLANDS

BIRMINGHAM · WOLVERHAMPTON · COVENTRY · Walsall · West Bromwich · Dudley · Solihull · Sutton Coldfield · Smethwick

WARWICKSHIRE

Nuneaton · Bedworth · Kenilworth · Leamington Spa · Royal · Warwick · Redditch

HEREFORD AND WORCESTER

Kidderminster · Stourport-on-Severn · Bromsgrove · Droitwich · Bewdley

SHROPSHIRE

Shrewsbury · Telford · Wellington · Oswestry · Bridgnorth · Whitchurch · Market Drayton · Ludlow · Church Stretton

The Wrekin · Wenlock Edge · The Long Mynd · Clee Hills · Clun Forest

CLWYD

Wrexham · Rhyl · Prestatyn · Mold · Flint · Denbigh · Ruthin · Llangollen · St. Asaph

Clwydian Ra.

POWYS

Welshpool · Newtown · Llanidloes · Llandrindod Wells · Knighton · Presteigne

River Severn · River Trent · River Witham · River Nene · River Derwent · River Dee · River Mersey · River Ribble · River Ouse

Sherwood Forest

Rockingham Forest

Wyre Forest

Marston Moor

Forest of Bowland

CARTOGRAPHY BY PHILIP'S. COPYRIGHT REED INTERNATIONAL BOOKS LTD

West from Greenwich

Projection: Conical with two standard parallels

1:1 000 000

10   0   10   20 miles
10   0   10   20   30 km

m   750   500   400   200   100   0
ft   2250   1500   1200   600   300   0
ft   60   50   20   0   20   50   100
m   150   300

Grid references: 7 8 9 10 11 12

LINCOLNSHIRE
NORFOLK
CAMBRIDGESHIRE
SUFFOLK
BEDFORDSHIRE
HERTFORDSHIRE
ESSEX
GREATER LONDON
SURREY
KENT
WEST SUSSEX
EAST SUSSEX
FRANCE

The Wash
The Fens
Breckland
NORFOLK BROADS NAT. PARK
North Downs
The Weald
South Downs
Thames Estuary
Strait of Dover
Rye Bay

Major places: Grantham, Boston, King's Lynn, Cromer, Sheringham, Norwich, Great Yarmouth, Lowestoft, Peterborough, Wisbech, March, Ely, Thetford, Diss, Beccles, Cambridge, Newmarket, Bury St. Edmunds, Stowmarket, Ipswich, Felixstowe, Harwich, Bedford, Milton Keynes, Luton, Stevenage, Colchester, Clacton-on-Sea, Harlow, Chelmsford, Southend-on-Sea, LONDON, Basildon, Brentwood, Gravesend, Rochester, Chatham, Gillingham, Maidstone, Margate, Broadstairs, Ramsgate, Canterbury, Deal, Dover, Folkestone, Hythe, Ashford, Tonbridge, Royal Tunbridge Wells, Guildford, Crawley, Horsham, Haywards Heath, Burgess Hill, Brighton, Hove, Worthing, Eastbourne, Hastings, Bexhill, Lewes, Newhaven, Chichester, Bognor Regis, Calais, Boulogne-sur-Mer

East from Greenwich

CARTOGRAPHY BY PHILIP'S. COPYRIGHT REED INTERNATIONAL BOOKS LTD

1:1 000 000

0   10   20 miles
0   10   20   30 km

IRISH SEA

St. George's Channel

Cardigan Bay

Caernarfon Bay

Tremadog Bay

LIVERPOOL

Liverpool Bay

CHESHIRE

STAFFS.

SHROPSHIRE

HEREFORD AND WORCESTER

Malvern Hills

GWENT

DYFED

POWYS

GWYNEDD

CLWYD

Anglesey

SNOWDONIA NATIONAL PARK

BRECON BEACONS NATIONAL PARK

PEMBROKESHIRE COAST NATIONAL PARK

Black Mountains

Brecon Beacons

Cambrian Mountains

Berwyn Mts.

Clwydian Ra.

St. Helens Warrington Widnes Runcorn Birkenhead Wallasey Hoylake West Kirby Chester Ellesmere Port Northwich Nantwich Crewe Sandbach

Holyhead Amlwch Beaumaris Bangor Caernarfon Pwllheli Criccieth Porthmadog Blaenau Ffestiniog Harlech Barmouth Dolgellau Tywyn Machynlleth Aberystwyth

Llandudno Colwyn Bay Abergele Rhyl Prestatyn Denbigh Ruthin Wrexham Llangollen Bala Corwen Mold

Welshpool Newtown Llanidloes Rhayader Builth Wells Llandrindod Wells Radnor Knighton Presteigne

Shrewsbury Wellington Telford Bridgnorth Kidderminster Stourport-on-Severn Bewdley Droitwich WORCESTER Bromyard Leominster Ludlow Church Stretton Whitchurch

Hereford Ross-on-Wye Ledbury Monmouth Abergavenny Pontypool

Aberaeron New Quay Cardigan Fishguard Haverfordwest Milford Haven Newport Carmarthen Llandovery Lampeter Llanelli

Cader Idris Snowdon Plynlimon Pumlumon Fawr Mynydd Eppynt Mynydd Preseli Forest Fawr

The Skerries Carmel Hd. Holyhead B. Bardsey I. St. Tudwal's Is. Great Ormes Hd. Strumble Hd. St. David's Hd. Ramsey I. Skomer I. Skokholm I. Grassholm I. St. Ann's Hd.

M53 M56 M6 M5 M50 M4

CHANNEL ISLANDS
on same scale

FRANCE

C. de la Hague · St. Anne · Les Pleux · Barneville-Carteret · Carteret

Aldernay · Passage de la Déroute

Jersey · St. Peter Port · Guernsey · CHANNEL ISLANDS

Grosnez Pt. · St. Ouens Bay · St. Brelade · St. Helier · St. Peter · St. Martin · Rozel · St. Peter · Gorey · la Rocque Pt.

St. Sampson · Herm · Sark · Torteval

CARTOGRAPHY BY PHILIP'S. COPYRIGHT REED INTERNATIONAL BOOKS LTD

SCILLY ISLES
on same scale

Isles of Scilly · Tresco · Bryher · St. Martin's · St. Mary's · Hugh Town · St. Agnes · Broad Sd. · Crow Sound · St. Mary's Sd.

Gurnard's Hd. · 252 · Pendeen · C. Cornwall · Penzance · Newlyn · St. Just · Sennen · St. Buryan · Land's End · St. Levan · Wolf Rock

Main regions
AVON · SOUTH GLAMORGAN · SOMERSET · DORSET · DEVON · CORNWALL · Dartmoor National Park · Exmoor National Park

Waters
Bristol Channel · Bridgwater Bay · Barnstaple or Bideford Bay · Lyme Bay · Tor Bay · Start Bay · Falmouth Bay · Mount's Bay · Gerrans Bay · Veryan B. · St. Austell B.

Selected places
BRISTOL · CARDIFF · Newport · Bath · Weston-super-Mare · Bridgwater · Taunton · Tiverton · Exeter · PLYMOUTH · Torquay · Paignton · Brixham · Newton Abbot · Dawlish · Teignmouth · Exmouth · Sidmouth · Seaton · Lyme Regis · Bridport · Weymouth · Portland Bill · Dorchester · Yeovil · Wells · Glastonbury · Street · Frome · Warminster · Barnstaple · Bideford · Ilfracombe · Lynton · Minehead · Watchet · Truro · Falmouth · Penryn · Helston · Redruth · Camborne · Hayle · St. Ives · Newquay · Padstow · Wadebridge · Bodmin · Bude · Launceston · Okehampton · Tavistock · Liskeard · Looe · Fowey · St. Austell · Mevagissey · Lizard Pt.

Projection: Conical with two standard parallels

1:1 000 000

West from Greenwich

m / ft elevation scale: 3000 · 2250 · 1500 · 1200 · 600 · 300 · 150 · 0
1000 · 750 · 500 · 400 · 200 · 100 · 60 · 0

ATLANTIC

OCEAN

Projection : Conical with two standard parallels

West from Greenwich

Inishtrahull

Glengad Hd.
Culdaff
Greencastle
Moville
Magilligan Pt.
Inishowen Hd.
The Skerries
Giants Causeway
Benbane Hd.
Bushmills
Ballintoy
Ballycastle B.
Fair Hd.
Ballyvoy

Machrihanish Bay
Machrihanish
Earadale Pt.
Southend
Cnoc Moy ▲446
Kilchenzie
Campbeltown
Dippen
Arran
Pladda
Heads of Ayr
Dunure
Ayr
Coylton
Ochiltree
Drongan
New Cumnock
Cumnock

Lough Foyle
Carrowkeel
Magilligan
Downhill
Portstewart
Portrush
Bellarena
Macosquin
Downhill
Ballybogy
Derrykeighan
Armoy
Knocklayd 517 ▲
Runabay Hd.
Cushendun
Mull of Kintyre
Sanda I.
Johnston's Pt.
Ailsa Craig ▲334
Girvan
Maybole
Dalrymple
Patna
Dailly
Crosshill
Dalmellington
Bellsbank
L. Doon
Drumjohn
Connel Park
Carsphairn
The Glenkens

STRATHCLYDE

Firth of Clyde

Kirkoswald
Turnberry
Barr
Straiton
Pinwherry
Barrhill
844 ▲ Merrick
796 ▲

Carrick
Lendalfoot
Bennane Hd.
Colmonel
Ballantrae
Benderaird ▲439
Glentrool Village
Clatteringshaws L.
Rhinns of Kells
New Galloway
710 ▲

Milleur Pt.
Corsewall Pt.
Kirkcolm
Leswalt
Cairnryan
L. Ryan
Stranraer
Lochans
Portpatrick
Stoneykirk
Sandhead
Port Logan
Drummore
Mull of Galloway
The Rhins

DUMFRIES & GALLOWAY
New Luce
Glenluce
Kirkcowan
Wigtown
Creetown
Gatehouse of Fleet
Minnigaff
Newton Stewart
Cairnsmore of Fleet ▲710

The Machars
Whauphill
Garlieston
Sorbie
Wigtown B.
Whithorn
Isle of Whithorn
Burrow Hd.

23

Luce Bay
Port William

269

Portrush

ONDONDERRY

Coleraine
Ballymoney
Ballybogy
Finvoy
Dunloy
Newtown Crommelin
▲554 Trostan
Glenariffe
Red B.
Garron Pt.
Carnlough
Glenarm
123
Ringsend
Garvagh
Kilrea
Rasharkin
Clogh
Broughshane
▲436
Carncastle
Agnews Hill ▲476

North Channel

SPERRIN Mts.
▲683 Sawel Mt.
▲554
Draperstown
Tobermore
Maghera
Inishrush
Ballymena
Moorfields
Kells
Ballyclare
Glenoe
Larne
Larne Lough
Glynn
Whitehead
I. Magee
Black Hd.

Desertmartin
Magherafelt
Bellaghy
Ahoghill
L. Beg
Randalstown
Antrim
Templepatrick
Eden
Greenisland
Carrickfergus
Copeland I.
Groomsport

Moneymore
Castledawson
Ballyronan
The Loup
Toome
M2
Glengormley
Newtownabbey
Legoniel
Holywood
Bangor
Donaghadee
Millisle

HERN IRELAND
RONE
Cookstown
Coagh
Stewartstown
Lough Neagh
Crumlin
Glenavy
BELFAST
Dunmurry
Dundonald
Newtownards
Greyabbey
Ballywalter

TRONE
Carrickmore
Pomeroy
Tullyhogue
Coalisland
Ulster
Lisburn
Moira
Hillsborough
Comber
Saintfield
Kircubbin
Portavogie

Sixmilecross
Donaghmore
Dungannon
Aghalee
Drumbeg
Lurgan
Carryduff
Killyleagh
Crossgar
Portaferry
Strangford

Granville
Moy
Charlemont
Portadown
Craigavon
M1
Dromore
Ballynahinch
Downpatrick
Ardglass
Ballyquintin Pt.

Ballygawley
Benburb
Gilford
Banbridge
Dromara
Clough
Killard Pt.

▲372
Emyvale
Aughnacloy
Caledon
ARMAGH
Armagh
Tandragee
Loughbrickland
Katesbridge
Ballyroney
Dundrum B.
Killough
St. John's Pt.
17

Slieve Beagh ▲202
Tedavnet
Glaslough
Middletown
Keady
Markethill
Mountnorris
Poyntz Pass
Rathfriland
Castlewellan
Newcastle
Slieve Donard ▲852

Monaghan
Smithborough
MONAGHAN
Newbliss
Ballybay
Bessbrook
Newtown Hamilton
Hilltown
Mayobridge
Mourne Mts.
Annalong
125

Drum
Rockcorry
Castleblaney
Cullyhanna
Crossmaglen
Newry
Meigh
Slieve Gullion ▲577
Warrenpoint
Rostrevor
▲744
Kilkeel
Greencastle
Cranfield Pt.

Cootehill
Forkhill
Slieve Foye ▲590
Carlingford
Greenore
Ballagan Pt.
Carlingford Lough

Shercock
Carrickmacross
Inishkeen
Louth
Kilcurry
Dundalk (Dún Dealgan)
Dromiskin

Bailieborough
Stradone
Kingscourt
Dunany Pt.
Dundalk Bay

Ballyjamesduff
Virginia
L. Ramor
Mullagh
Castletown
Collon
Castlebellingham
Annagassan

▲278 Canbane East
Nobber
Drumconrath
Ardee
Dee
Dunleer
Clogherhead
Clogher Hd.
Termonfeckin
164

Crossakiel
Ceanannus Mor (Kells)
Rathkenny
Newtown Monasterboice
Drogheda (Droichead Atha)
Mornington
Laytown
Julianstown

MEATH
Athboy
Trim
An Uaimh (Navan)
Slane
Boyne
Duleek
Ardcath
Balbriggan
Skerries

Delvin
Stonyford
Tremblestown
Summerhill
Dunshaughlin
Naul
Lusk
Rush
Lambay I.

Killucan
Ballivor
Rathmolyon
Ashbourne
Ratoath
Ballyboghil
Donabate
Portmarnock

Downs
Royal Canal
Dunboyne
Clonee
Swords
Cloghran
Malahide
Ireland's Eye
The Skerries
Carmel Hd.
Cemaes
Amlwch

Edenderry
Carbury
Johnstown Bridge
Kilcock
Maynooth
Lucan
Glasnevin
Finglas
Howth
Howth Hd.
Wylfa Hd.
Llanfechell
Parys Mt. ▲128

Killane
Timahoe
Clonard
Cloncurry
Donadea
Celbridge
DUBLIN
Clontarf
ANGLESEY
Holyhead B.
L. Alaw
Llanerchymedd

Allenwood
Ballinagh
Carbury
Leixlip
Lucan
Clondalkin
Dundrum
DUBLIN (Baile Atha Cliath)
Blackrock
Dun Laoghaire (Dúnleary)
Holyhead 220 ▲
Holy I.
Valley
Bodedern
Gwalchmai
Llangefni

ISLE OF MAN
Pt. of Ayre
Andreas
Bride
Ballaugh
Sulby
Ramsey B.
Ramsey
Maughold
Maughold Hd.
Kirk Michael
Snaefell ▲620
Laxey
Peel
St. John's
Onchan
Glenmaye
Foxdale
South Barrule ▲483
Douglas
Bradda Hd.
Port Erin
Colby
Ballasalla
Port St. Mary
Castletown
Calf of Man
Langness
45

NETHAM
Clonmel
Killann
Timahoe
MEATH
Clane
Rathcoole
Tallaght

IRISH SEA

CARTOGRAPHY BY PHILIP'S. COPYRIGHT REED INTERNATIONAL BOOKS LTD

1:1 000 000

10   0   20 miles
10   0   10   20   30 km

55° 00'
54° 30'
54° 00'
53° 30'

7°00'   7   6°30'   8   6°00'   9   5°30'   10   5°00'   11   4°30'   12   13

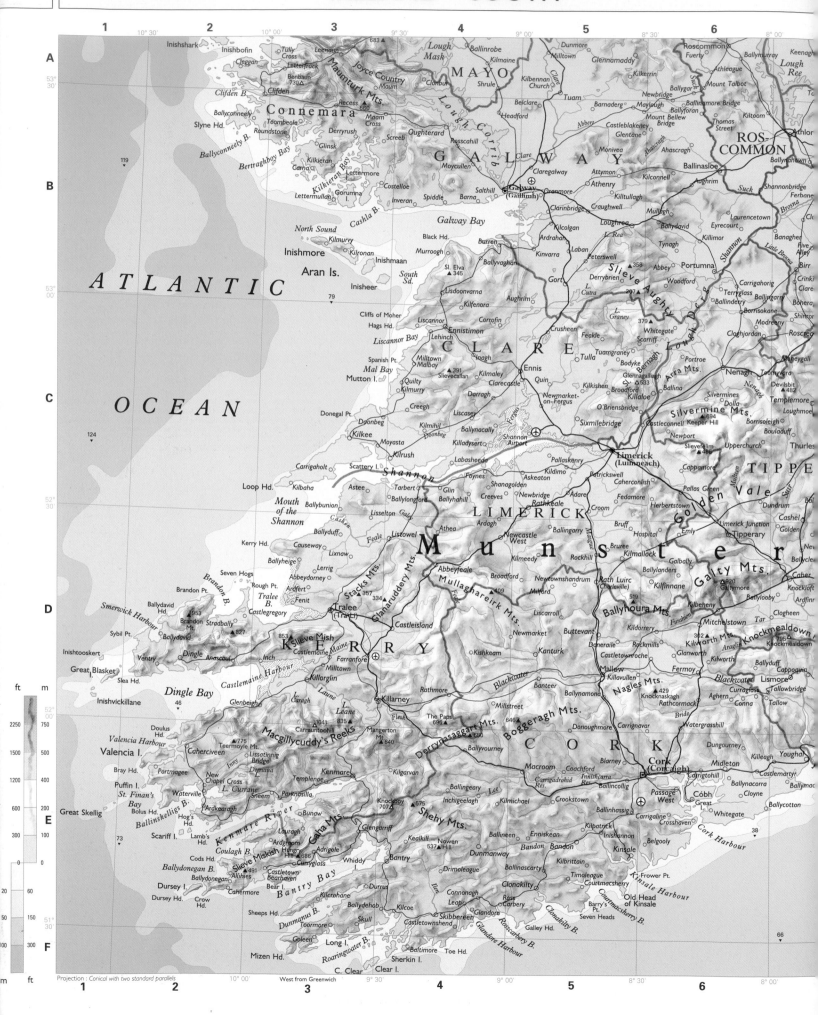

ATLANTIC OCEAN

Projection : Conical with two standard parallels

West from Greenwich

IRISH

SEA

St. George's Channel

CELTIC

SEA

WALES

1:1 000 000

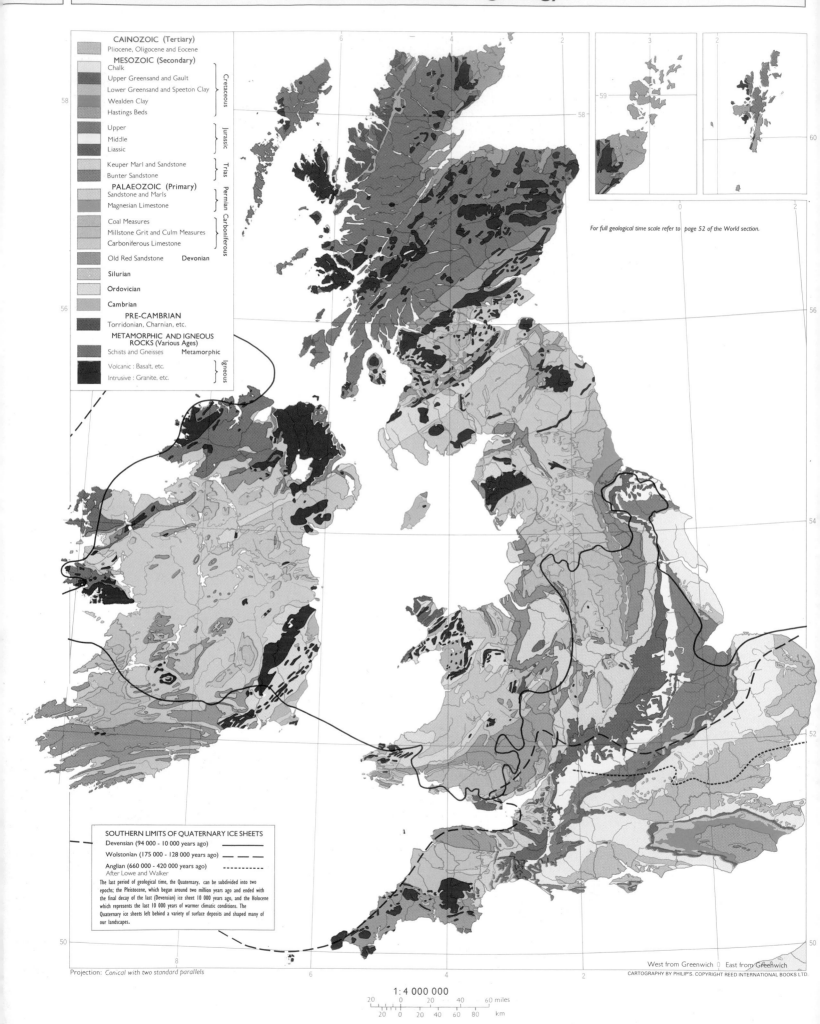

CAINOZOIC (Tertiary)
Pliocene, Oligocene and Eocene

MESOZOIC (Secondary)
Chalk
Upper Greensand and Gault
Lower Greensand and Speeton Clay — *Cretaceous*
Wealden Clay
Hastings Beds

Upper
Middle — *Jurassic*
Liassic

Keuper Marl and Sandstone — *Trias*
Bunter Sandstone

PALAEOZOIC (Primary)
Sandstone and Marls — *Permian*
Magnesian Limestone

Coal Measures
Millstone Grit and Culm Measures — *Carboniferous*
Carboniferous Limestone

Old Red Sandstone — Devonian

Silurian

Ordovician

Cambrian

PRE-CAMBRIAN
Torridonian, Charnian, etc.

METAMORPHIC AND IGNEOUS ROCKS (Various Ages)
Schists and Gneisses — Metamorphic

Volcanic : Basalt, etc. — *Igneous*
Intrusive : Granite, etc.

For full geological time scale refer to page 52 of the World section.

SOUTHERN LIMITS OF QUATERNARY ICE SHEETS
Devensian (94 000 - 10 000 years ago) ————————
Wolstonian (175 000 - 128 000 years ago) — — — —
Anglian (660 000 - 420 000 years ago) ·················
After Lowe and Walker

The last period of geological time, the Quaternary, can be subdivided into two epochs; the Pleistocene, which began around two million years ago and ended with the final decay of the last (Devensian) ice sheet 10 000 years ago, and the Holocene which represents the last 10 000 years of warmer climatic conditions. The Quaternary ice sheets left behind a variety of surface deposits and shaped many of our landscapes.

Projection: *Conical with two standard parallels*

West from Greenwich 0 East from Greenwich

CARTOGRAPHY BY PHILIP'S. COPYRIGHT REED INTERNATIONAL BOOKS LTD.

1 : 4 000 000

20   0   20   40   60 miles
20 0   20   40   60   80 km

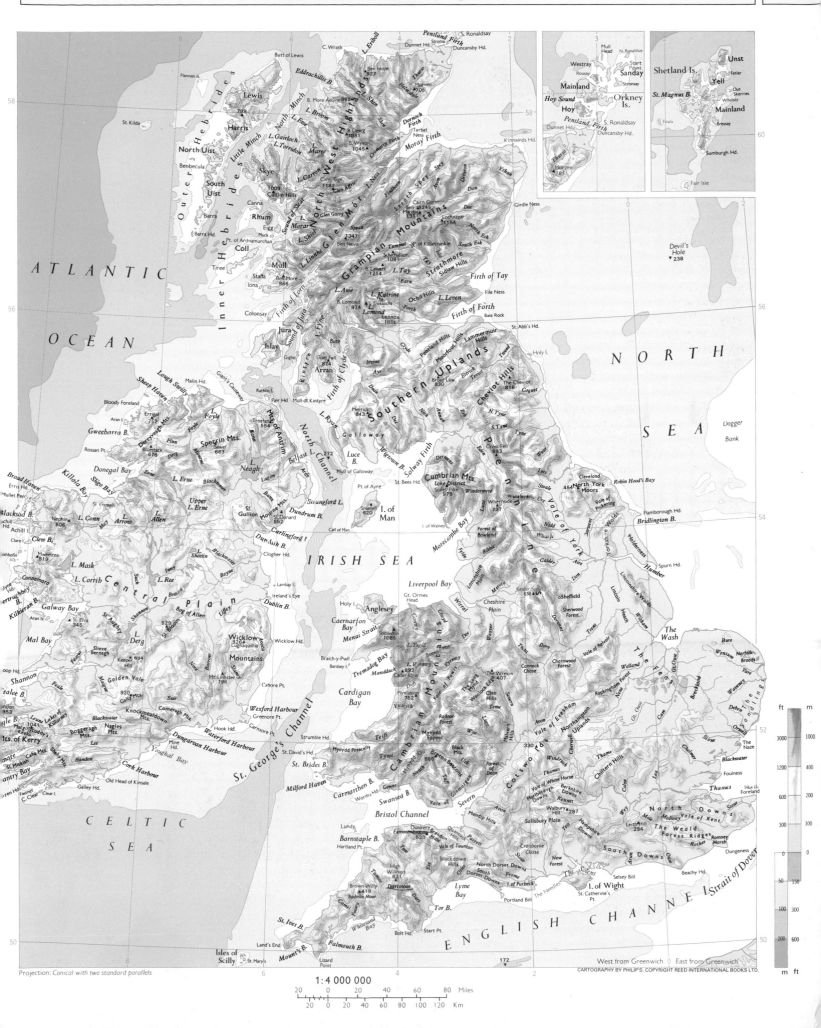

Projection: Conical with two standard parallels

1 : 4 000 000

West from Greenwich   East from Greenwich
CARTOGRAPHY BY PHILIP'S. COPYRIGHT REED INTERNATIONAL BOOKS LTD.

JANUARY TEMPERATURE
Actual surface temperature

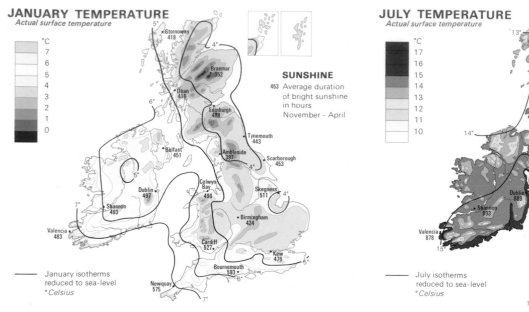

°C
7
6
5
4
3
2
1
0

SUNSHINE
453 Average duration of bright sunshine in hours November - April

Stornoway 418
Braemar 352
Oban 416
Edinburgh 488
Tynemouth 443
Belfast 451
Ambleside 397
Scarborough 453
Colwyn Bay 496
Skegness 511
Dublin 497
Birmingham 424
Shannon 493
Valencia 483
Cardiff 527
Kew 476
Bournemouth 593
Newquay 575

— January isotherms reduced to sea-level °*Celsius*

JULY TEMPERATURE
Actual surface temperature

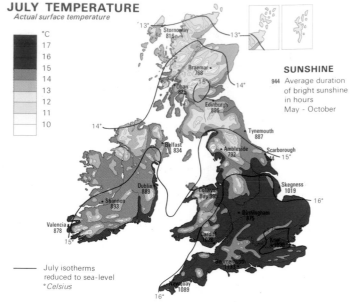

°C
17
16
15
14
13
12
11
10

SUNSHINE
944 Average duration of bright sunshine in hours May - October

Stornoway 816
Braemar 768
Oban 825
Edinburgh 896
Tynemouth 887
Belfast 834
Ambleside 792
Scarborough
Dublin 889
Colwyn Bay 995
Skegness 1019
Shannon 893
Valencia 878
Cardiff 1076
Kew
Bournemouth 1143
Newquay 1089

— July isotherms reduced to sea-level °*Celsius*

ANNUAL RAINFALL

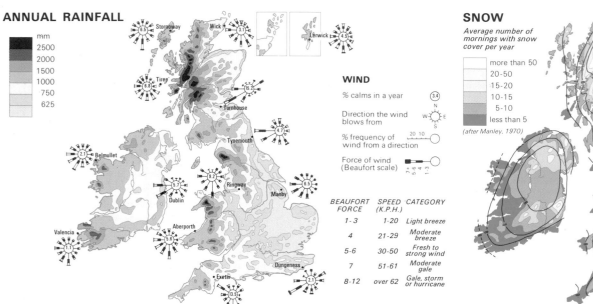

mm
2500
2000
1500
1000
750
625

Stornoway 6.5
Wick 3.1
Lerwick 4.5
Tiree 6.8
Turnhouse 15.2
Belmullet 2.1
Tynemouth 4.7
Dublin 5.7
9.2
Ringway
Manby 6.5
Valencia 1.1
Aberporth 5.6
Dungeness 2.1
Exeter 13.5

WIND

% calms in a year — (3.4)
N W E S

Direction the wind blows from

% frequency of wind from a direction — 20 10

Force of wind (Beaufort scale)

BEAUFORT FORCE	SPEED (K.P.H.)	CATEGORY
1 - 3	1 - 20	Light breeze
4	21 - 29	Moderate breeze
5 - 6	30 - 50	Fresh to strong wind
7	51 - 61	Moderate gale
8 - 12	over 62	Gale, storm or hurricane

SNOW
Average number of mornings with snow cover per year

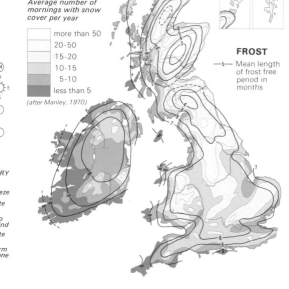

more than 50
20 - 50
15 - 20
10 - 15
5 - 10
less than 5

(after Manley, 1970)

FROST
—5— Mean length of frost free period in months

VARIABILITY OF RAIN
The percentage frequency with which rainfall varies from the normal rainfall regime in an area: the higher the percentage figure, the more variable the rainfall.

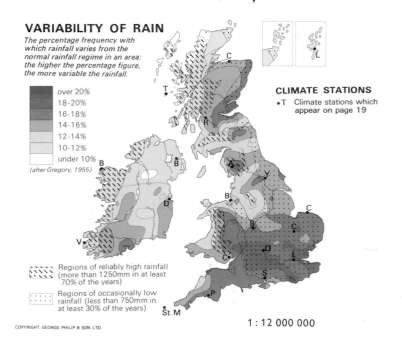

over 20%
18 - 20%
16 - 18%
14 - 16%
12 - 14%
10 - 12%
under 10%

(after Gregory, 1955)

CLIMATE STATIONS
• T Climate stations which appear on page 19

Regions of reliably high rainfall (more than 1250mm in at least 70% of the years)

Regions of occasionally low rainfall (less than 750mm in at least 30% of the years)

SYNOPTIC CHART FOR A TYPICAL WINTER DEPRESSION
21st January 1971

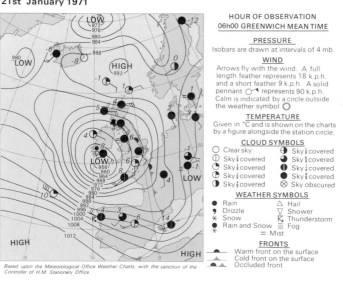

HOUR OF OBSERVATION
06h00 GREENWICH MEAN TIME

PRESSURE
Isobars are drawn at intervals of 4 mb.

WIND
Arrows fly with the wind. A full length feather represents 18 k.p.h. and a short feather 9 k.p.h. A solid pennant represents 90 k.p.h. Calm is indicated by a circle outside the weather symbol

TEMPERATURE
Given in °C and is shown on the charts by a figure alongside the station circle.

CLOUD SYMBOLS
○ Clear sky
◐ Sky ¾ covered
◖ Sky ¼ covered
● Sky covered
⊗ Sky obscured

WEATHER SYMBOLS
● Rain   △ Hail
, Drizzle   ▽ Shower
✳ Snow   Ⓚ Thunderstorm
✶ Rain and Snow   ≡ Fog
≡ Mist

FRONTS
Warm front on the surface
Cold front on the surface
Occluded front

Based upon the Meteorological Office Weather Charts, with the sanction of the Controller of H.M. Stationery Office

COPYRIGHT. GEORGE PHILIP & SON, LTD.

1 : 12 000 000

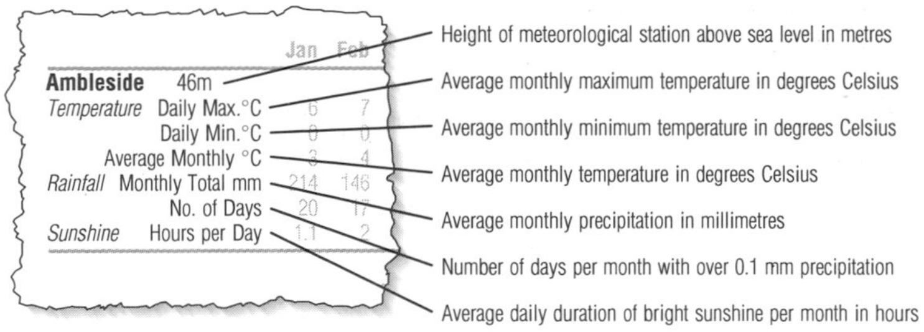

Jan Feb
Ambleside 46m
Temperature Daily Max.°C 6 7
Daily Min.°C 0 0
Average Monthly °C 3 4
Rainfall Monthly Total mm 214 146
No. of Days 20 17
Sunshine Hours per Day 1.1 2
Height of meteorological station above sea level in metres
Average monthly maximum temperature in degrees Celsius
Average monthly minimum temperature in degrees Celsius
Average monthly temperature in degrees Celsius
Average monthly precipitation in millimetres
Number of days per month with over 0.1 mm precipitation
Average daily duration of bright sunshine per month in hours

	Jan	Feb	Mar	Apr	May	June	July	Aug	Sep	Oct	Nov	Dec	Year
Ambleside 46m													
Temperature Daily Max.°C	6	7	9	12	16	19	20	19	17	13	9	7	13
Daily Min.°C	0	0	2	4	6	9	11	11	9	6	3	1	5
Average Monthly °C	3	4	6	8	11	14	15	15	13	10	6	4	9
Rainfall Monthly Total mm	214	146	112	101	90	111	134	139	184	196	209	215	1851
No. of Days	20	17	15	15	14	15	18	17	18	19	19	21	208
Sunshine Hours per Day	1.1	2	3.2	4.5	6	5.7	4.5	4.2	3.3	2.2	1.4	1	3.3
Belfast 4m													
Temperature Daily Max.°C	6	7	9	12	15	18	18	18	16	13	9	7	12
Daily Min.°C	2	2	3	4	6	9	11	11	9	7	4	3	6
Average Monthly °C	4	4	6	8	11	13	15	15	13	10	7	5	9
Rainfall Monthly Total mm	80	52	50	48	52	68	94	77	80	83	72	90	845
No. of Days	20	17	16	16	15	16	19	17	18	19	19	21	213
Sunshine Hours per Day	1.5	2.3	3.4	5	6.3	6	4.4	4.4	3.6	2.6	1.8	1.1	3.5
Belmullet 9m													
Temperature Daily Max.°C	8	9	10	12	14	16	17	17	16	14	10	9	12
Daily Min.°C	3	4	4	6	8	10	11	11	10	8	5	4	7
Average Monthly °C	5	6	7	9	11	13	14	14	13	11	8	6	10
Rainfall Monthly Total mm	108	64	82	70	75	80	76	95	108	116	127	131	1132
No. of Days	18	13	16	15	14	12	14	17	16	18	20	22	195
Sunshine Hours per Day	1.9	2.5	3.4	5.2	7	6	4.6	5.1	3.9	2.9	1.9	1.3	3.8
Birkenhead 60m													
Temperature Daily Max.°C	6	6	9	11	15	17	19	19	16	13	9	7	12
Daily Min.°C	2	2	3	5	8	11	13	13	11	8	5	3	7
Average Monthly °C	4	4	6	8	11	14	16	16	14	10	7	5	10
Rainfall Monthly Total mm	64	46	40	41	55	55	67	80	66	71	76	65	726
No. of Days	18	13	13	13	13	13	15	15	15	17	17	19	181
Sunshine Hours per Day	1.6	2.4	3.5	5.3	6.3	6.7	5.7	5.4	4.2	2.9	1.8	1.3	3.9
Birmingham 163m													
Temperature Daily Max.°C	5	6	9	12	16	19	20	20	17	13	9	6	13
Daily Min.°C	2	2	3	5	7	10	12	12	10	7	5	3	7
Average Monthly °C	3	4	6	8	11	15	16	16	14	10	7	5	10
Rainfall Monthly Total mm	74	54	50	53	64	50	69	69	61	69	84	67	764
No. of Days	17	15	13	13	14	13	15	14	14	15	17	18	178
Sunshine Hours per Day	1.4	2.1	3.2	4.6	5.4	6	5.4	5.1	3.9	2.8	1.6	1.2	3.6
Cambridge 12m													
Temperature Daily Max.°C	6	7	11	14	17	21	22	22	19	15	10	7	14
Daily Min.°C	1	1	2	4	7	10	12	12	10	6	4	2	6
Average Monthly °C	3	4	6	9	12	15	17	17	14	10	7	5	10
Rainfall Monthly Total mm	49	35	36	37	45	45	58	55	51	51	54	41	558
No. of Days	15	13	10	11	11	11	12	12	11	13	14	14	147
Sunshine Hours per Day	1.7	2.5	3.8	5.1	6.2	6.7	6	5.7	4.6	3.4	1.9	1.4	4.1
Cardiff 62m													
Temperature Daily Max.°C	7	7	10	13	16	19	20	21	18	14	10	8	14
Daily Min.°C	2	2	3	5	8	11	12	13	11	8	5	3	7
Average Monthly °C	4	5	7	9	12	15	16	17	14	11	8	6	10
Rainfall Monthly Total mm	108	72	63	65	76	63	89	97	99	109	116	108	1065
No. of Days	18	14	13	13	13	13	14	15	16	16	17	18	180
Sunshine Hours per Day	1.7	2.7	4	5.6	6.4	6.9	6.2	6	4.7	3.4	1.9	1.5	4.3
Craibstone 91m													
Temperature Daily Max.°C	5	6	8	10	13	16	18	17	15	12	8	6	11
Daily Min.°C	0	0	2	3	5	8	10	10	8	6	3	1	5
Average Monthly °C	3	3	5	7	9	12	14	13	12	9	6	4	8
Rainfall Monthly Total mm	78	55	53	51	63	54	95	75	67	92	93	80	856
No. of Days	19	16	15	15	14	14	18	15	16	18	19	18	197
Sunshine Hours per Day	1.8	2.9	3.5	4.9	5.9	6.1	5.1	4.8	4.3	3.1	2	1.5	3.8
Cromer 54m													
Temperature Daily Max.°C	6	7	9	12	15	18	21	20	18	14	10	8	13
Daily Min.°C	1	1	3	5	7	10	12	13	11	8	5	3	7
Average Monthly °C	4	4	6	8	11	14	16	16	15	11	7	5	10
Rainfall Monthly Total mm	58	46	37	39	48	39	63	56	54	61	64	53	618
No. of Days	18	16	13	13	11	11	13	12	14	16	18	18	173
Sunshine Hours per Day	1.8	2.6	4	5.4	6.4	6.8	6.3	5.8	5	3.6	2	1.9	4.3
Dublin 47m													
Temperature Daily Max.°C	8	8	10	13	15	18	20	19	17	14	10	8	14
Daily Min.°C	1	2	3	4	6	9	11	11	9	6	4	3	6
Average Monthly °C	4	5	7	8	11	14	15	15	13	10	7	6	10
Rainfall Monthly Total mm	67	55	51	45	60	57	70	74	72	70	67	74	762
No. of Days	13	10	10	11	10	11	13	12	12	11	12	14	139
Sunshine Hours per Day	1.9	2.5	3.4	5	6.2	6	4.8	4.9	3.9	3.2	2.1	1.6	3.8

	Jan	Feb	Mar	Apr	May	June	July	Aug	Sep	Oct	Nov	Dec	Year
Durham 102m													
Temperature Daily Max.°C	6	6	9	12	15	18	20	19	17	13	9	7	13
Daily Min.°C	0	0	1	3	6	9	11	10	9	6	3	2	5
Average Monthly °C	3	3	5	7	10	13	15	15	13	9	6	4	9
Rainfall Monthly Total mm	59	51	38	38	51	49	61	67	60	63	66	55	658
No. of Days	17	15	14	13	13	14	15	14	14	16	17	17	179
Sunshine Hours per Day	1.7	2.5	3.3	4.6	5.4	6	5.1	4.8	4.1	3	1.9	1.4	3.6
Lerwick 82m													
Temperature Daily Max.°C	5	5	6	8	11	13	14	14	13	10	8	6	9
Daily Min.°C	1	1	2	3	5	7	10	10	8	6	4	3	5
Average Monthly °C	3	3	4	5	8	10	12	12	11	8	6	4	7
Rainfall Monthly Total mm	109	87	69	68	52	55	72	71	87	104	111	118	1003
No. of Days	25	22	20	21	15	15	17	17	19	23	24	25	243
Sunshine Hours per Day	0.8	1.8	2.9	4.4	5.3	5.3	4	3.8	3.5	2.2	2.2	0.5	3
London (Kew) 5m													
Temperature Daily Max.°C	6	7	10	13	17	20	22	21	19	14	10	7	14
Daily Min.°C	2	2	3	6	8	12	14	13	11	8	5	4	7
Average Monthly °C	4	5	7	9	12	16	18	17	15	11	8	5	11
Rainfall Monthly Total mm	54	40	37	37	46	45	57	59	49	57	64	48	593
No. of Days	15	13	11	12	12	11	12	11	13	13	15	15	153
Sunshine Hours per Day	1.5	2.3	3.6	5.3	6.4	7.1	6.4	6.1	4.7	3.2	1.8	1.3	4.1
Oxford 63m													
Temperature Daily Max.°C	7	7	11	14	17	20	22	22	19	14	10	8	14
Daily Min.°C	1	1	2	5	7	10	12	12	10	7	4	2	6
Average Monthly °C	4	4	6	9	12	15	17	17	14	11	7	5	10
Rainfall Monthly Total mm	61	44	43	41	55	52	55	60	59	64	69	57	660
No. of Days	13	10	9	9	10	9	10	10	10	11	12	13	126
Sunshine Hours per Day	1.7	2.6	3.9	5.3	6.1	6.6	5.9	5.7	4.4	3.2	2.1	1.6	4.1
Plymouth 27m													
Temperature Daily Max.°C	8	8	10	12	15	18	19	19	18	15	11	9	14
Daily Min.°C	4	4	5	6	8	11	13	13	12	9	7	5	8
Average Monthly °C	6	6	7	9	12	15	16	16	15	12	9	7	11
Rainfall Monthly Total mm	99	74	69	53	63	53	70	77	78	91	113	110	950
No. of Days	19	15	14	12	12	12	14	14	15	16	17	18	178
Sunshine Hours per Day	1.9	2.9	4.3	6.1	7.1	7.4	6.4	6.4	5.1	3.7	2.2	1.7	4.6
Renfrew 6m													
Temperature Daily Max.°C	5	7	9	12	15	18	19	19	16	13	9	7	12
Daily Min.°C	1	1	2	4	6	9	11	11	9	6	4	2	6
Average Monthly °C	3	4	6	8	11	14	15	15	13	9	7	4	9
Rainfall Monthly Total mm	111	85	69	67	63	70	97	93	102	119	106	127	1109
No. of Days	19	16	15	15	14	15	17	17	17	18	18	20	201
Sunshine Hours per Day	1.1	2.1	2.9	4.7	6	6.1	5.1	4.4	3.7	2.3	1.4	0.8	3.4
St Helier 9m													
Temperature Daily Max.°C	9	8	11	13	16	19	21	21	19	16	12	10	15
Daily Min.°C	5	4	6	7	10	13	15	15	14	11	8	6	9
Average Monthly °C	7	6	8	10	13	16	18	18	17	13	10	8	12
Rainfall Monthly Total mm	89	68	57	43	44	39	48	67	69	77	101	99	801
No. of Days	19	15	13	12	11	10	11	12	15	15	17	19	169
Sunshine Hours per Day	2.3	3.1	5	6.7	7.8	8.5	7.8	7.6	5.6	4.1	2.5	1.8	5.3
St Mary's 50m													
Temperature Daily Max.°C	9	9	11	12	14	17	19	19	18	15	12	10	14
Daily Min.°C	6	6	7	7	9	12	13	14	13	11	9	7	9
Average Monthly °C	8	7	9	10	12	14	16	16	15	13	10	9	12
Rainfall Monthly Total mm	91	71	69	46	56	49	61	64	67	80	96	94	844
No. of Days	22	17	16	13	14	14	16	15	16	17	19	21	200
Sunshine Hours per Day	2	2.9	4.2	6.4	7.6	7.6	6.7	6.7	5.2	3.9	2.5	1.8	4.8
Southampton 20m													
Temperature Daily Max.°C	7	8	11	14	17	20	22	22	19	15	11	8	15
Daily Min.°C	2	2	3	5	8	11	13	13	11	7	5	3	7
Average Monthly °C	5	5	7	10	13	16	17	17	15	11	8	6	11
Rainfall Monthly Total mm	83	56	52	45	56	49	60	69	70	86	94	84	804
No. of Days	17	13	13	12	12	12	13	13	14	14	16	17	166
Sunshine Hours per Day	1.8	2.6	4	5.7	6.7	7.2	6.5	6.4	4.9	3.6	2.2	1.6	4.5
Tiree 9m													
Temperature Daily Max.°C	7	7	9	10	13	15	16	16	15	12	10	8	12
Daily Min.°C	4	3	4	5	7	10	11	11	10	8	6	5	7
Average Monthly °C	5	5	6	8	10	12	14	14	13	10	8	6	9
Rainfall Monthly Total mm	117	77	67	64	55	70	91	90	118	129	122	128	1128
No. of Days	23	19	17	17	15	16	20	18	20	23	22	24	234
Sunshine Hours per Day	1.3	2.6	3.7	5.7	7.5	6.8	5.2	5.3	4.2	2.6	1.6	0.9	4
Valencia 9m													
Temperature Daily Max.°C	9	9	11	13	15	17	18	18	17	14	12	10	14
Daily Min.°C	5	4	5	6	8	11	12	13	11	9	7	6	8
Average Monthly °C	7	7	8	9	11	0	15	15	14	12	9	8	11
Rainfall Monthly Total mm	165	107	103	75	86	81	107	95	122	140	151	168	1400
No. of Days	20	15	14	13	13	13	15	15	16	17	18	21	190
Sunshine Hours per Day	1.6	2.5	3.5	5.2	6.5	5.9	4.7	4.9	3.8	2.8	2	1.3	3.7
York 17m													
Temperature Daily Max.°C	6	7	10	13	16	19	21	21	18	14	10	7	13
Daily Min.°C	1	1	2	4	7	10	12	12	10	7	4	2	6
Average Monthly °C	3	4	6	9	12	15	17	16	14	10	7	5	10
Rainfall Monthly Total mm	59	46	37	41	50	50	62	68	55	56	65	50	639
No. of Days	17	15	13	13	13	14	15	14	14	15	17	17	177
Sunshine Hours per Day	1.3	2.1	3.2	4.7	6.1	6.4	5.6	5.1	4.1	2.8	1.6	1.1	3.7

WATER SUPPLY

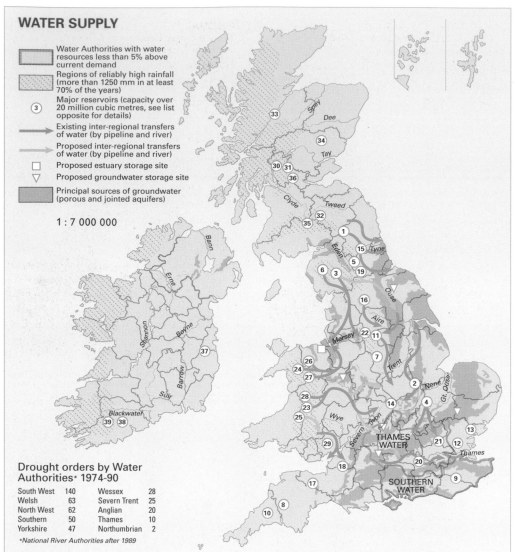

Water Authorities with water resources less than 5% above current demand

Regions of reliably high rainfall (more than 1250 mm in at least 70% of the years)

③ Major reservoirs (capacity over 20 million cubic metres, see list opposite for details)

→ Existing inter-regional transfers of water (by pipeline and river)

→ Proposed inter-regional transfers of water (by pipeline and river)

☐ Proposed estuary storage site

▽ Proposed groundwater storage site

Principal sources of groundwater (porous and jointed aquifers)

1 : 7 000 000

Drought orders by Water Authorities* 1974-90

South West	140	Wessex	28
Welsh	63	Severn Trent	25
North West	62	Anglian	20
Southern	50	Thames	10
Yorkshire	47	Northumbrian	2

*National River Authorities after 1989

Major reservoirs (with capacity in million m³)

England			Wales	
1	Kielder Res.	198	23 Elan Valley	9
2	Rutland Water	123	24 Llyn Celyn	7
3	Haweswater	85	25 Llyn Brianne	6
4	Grafham Water	59	26 Llyn Brenig	6
5	Cow Green Res.	41	27 Llyn Vyrnwy	6
6	Thirlmere	41	28 Llyn Clywedog	4
7	Carsington Res.	36	29 Llandegfedd Res.	
8	Roadford Res.	35		
9	Bewl Water Res.	31	**Scotland**	
10	Colliford Lake	29	30 Loch Lomond	8
11	Ladybower Res.	28	31 Loch Katrine	6
12	Hanningfield Res.	27	32 Megget Res.	6
13	Abberton Res.	25	33 Loch Ness	2
14	Draycote Water	23	34 Backwater Res.	2
15	Derwent Res.	22	35 Daer Res.	2
16	Grimwith Res.	22	36 Carron Valley Res.	2
17	Wimbleball Lake	21		
18	Chew Valley Lake	20	**Ireland**	
19	Balderhead Res.	20	37 Poulaphouca Res.	16
20	Thames Valley (linked reservoirs)		38 Inishcarra Res.	5
21	Lea Valley (linked reservoirs)		39 Carrigadrohid Res.	
22	Longdendale (linked reservoirs)			

Average daily domestic water use in England and Wales (1990)

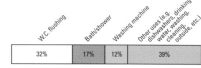

W.C. flushing	Bath/shower	Washing machine	Other uses (e.g. dishwashers, drinking water, washing, cleaning, outside, etc.)
32%	17%	12%	39%

Water abstractions in England and Wales (199 35 249 megalitres per day* of which:

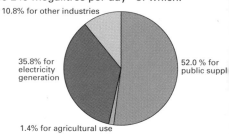

10.8% for other industries

35.8% for electricity generation

52.0 % for public suppl

1.4% for agricultural use

*average daily domestic consumption per head 136 litres.

WATER ABSTRACTIONS   1 : 12 000 000

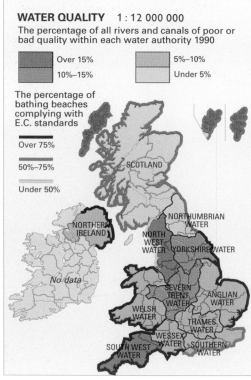

THAMES WATER   Water authority

6.8   Number of households supplied (in millions)

1883 (16%)   Water supply* in megalitres per day (with percentage of total abstraction from groundwater in brackets)

*Piped mains water, excluding water abstracted for agricultural and industrial use

SCOTLAND
5.1 | 2248 (0%)

N. IRELAND
1.6 | 666 (0%)

NORTHUMBRIAN WATER
1.3 | 1060 (9%)

NORTH WEST WATER
6.8 | 1883 (16%)

YORKSHIRE WATER
4.0 | 1498 (13%)

SEVERN TRENT WATER
6.8 | 2421 (20%)

ANGLIAN WATER
3.8 | 1928 (43%)

WELSH WATER
2.7 | 2671 (1%)

THAMES WATER
7.0 | 3827 (39%)

WESSEX WATER
1.1 | 798 (51%)

SOUTHERN WATER
2.0 | 1621 (50%)

SOUTH WEST WATER
1.4 | 630 (9%)

WATER QUALITY   1 : 12 000 000

The percentage of all rivers and canals of poor or bad quality within each water authority 1990

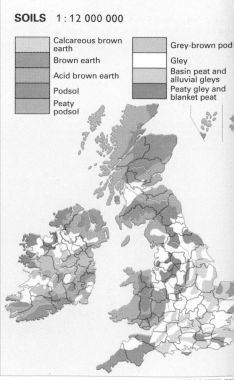

	Over 15%		5%–10%
	10%–15%		Under 5%

The percentage of bathing beaches complying with E.C. standards

Over 75%

50%–75%

Under 50%

No data

SOILS   1 : 12 000 000

	Calcareous brown earth		Grey-brown pod
	Brown earth		Gley
	Acid brown earth		Basin peat and alluvial gleys
	Podsol		Peaty gley and blanket peat
	Peaty podsol		

COPYRIGHT GEORGE PHIL

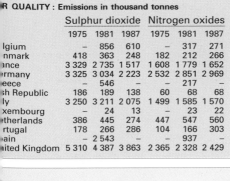

R QUALITY : Emissions in thousand tonnes

	Sulphur dioxide			Nitrogen oxides		
	1975	1981	1987	1975	1981	1987
lgium	–	856	610	–	317	271
nmark	418	363	248	182	212	266
ance	3 329	2 735	1 517	1 608	1 779	1 652
rmany	3 325	3 034	2 223	2 532	2 851	2 969
eece	–	546	–	–	217	–
sh Republic	186	189	138	60	68	68
ly	3 250	3 211	2 075	1 499	1 585	1 570
xembourg	–	24	13	–	23	22
therlands	386	445	274	447	547	560
rtugal	178	266	286	104	166	303
ain	–	2 543	–	–	937	–
ited Kingdom	5 310	4 387	3 863	2 365	2 328	2 429

FORESTRY   1 : 12 000 000

The percentage of the total area covered by woodland and forest

- Over 20%
- 15%-20%
- 10%-15%
- 5%-10%
- Under 5%

△ 50%-80% coniferous
△ Over 80% coniferous

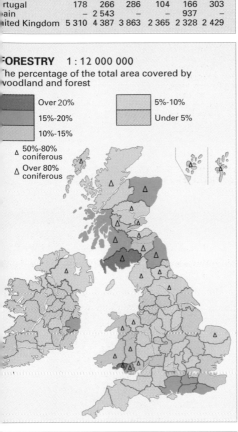

NATURAL VEGETATION   1 : 12 000 000

The plant cover associated with a particular environment if it is unaffected by human activity

- Oak
- Beech and Oak
- Ash and Oak
- Birch and Oakwood
- Scots Pine
- Heath, moorland, water meadows, fen, bog and marsh

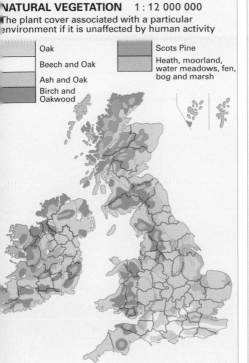

ACID RAIN   1 : 12 000 000

Average acidity of precipitation in the U.K. (pH scale)

- 4.29 and under (most acidic)
- 4.30-4.39
- 4.40-4.49
- 4.50-4.59
- 4.60-4.69
- 4.70-4.79
- 4.80 and over (least acidic)

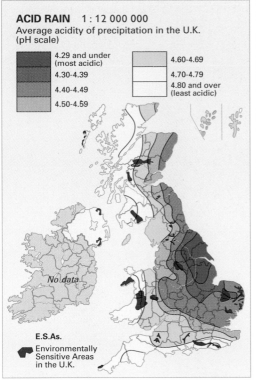

No data

E.S.As.
Environmentally Sensitive Areas in the U.K.

AIR QUALITY   1 : 12 000 000

Hourly average of tropospheric ozone (O_3) exceeding 100 parts per billion (summer 1990)*

- Over 45
- 30-45
- 15-30
- Under 15

Ground-level concentrations of smoke in the U.K., by region

U.K. average: 12 micrograms per m³

- Less than the U.K. average
- More than the U.K. average
- Over 3x the U.K. average

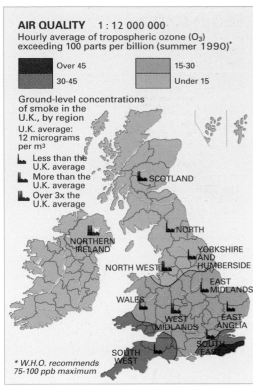

SCOTLAND
NORTH
NORTHERN IRELAND
YORKSHIRE AND HUMBERSIDE
NORTH WEST
EAST MIDLANDS
WALES
WEST MIDLANDS
EAST ANGLIA
SOUTH EAST
SOUTH WEST

* W.H.O. recommends 75-100 ppb maximum

CONSERVATION

- National Parks
- Areas of Outstanding Natural Beauty
- National Scenic Areas
- Forest Parks and Special Protected Areas
- Green Belts (and the urban areas they surround)
- Heritage Coast (England and Wales)/Coastal Conservation Zones (Scotland)
- * World Heritage Sites in the U.K.

(also designated but not shown, St. Kilda, Outer Hebrides and Henderson Island, South Pacific Ocean)

1 : 7 000 000

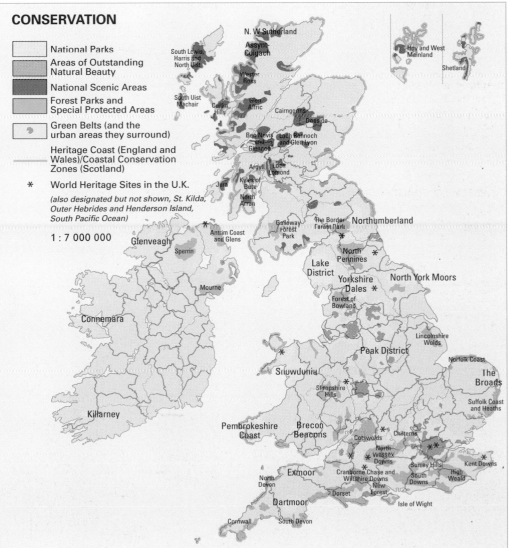

N. W. Sutherland
Assynt-Coigach
South Lewis, Harris and North Uist
Hoy and West Mainland
Shetland
Wester Ross
South Uist Machair
Cuillin Hills
Glen Affric
Cairngorms
Deeside
Ben Nevis and Glencoe
Loch Rannoch and Glen Lyon
Argyll
Loch Lomond
Jura
Kyles of Bute
North Arran
Galloway Forest Park
The Border Forest Park
Northumberland
Glenveagh
Antrim Coast and Glens
Sperrin
Lake District
North Pennines
Yorkshire Dales
North York Moors
Mourne
Forest of Bowland
Connemara
Lincolnshire Wolds
Peak District
Norfolk Coast
Snowdonia
The Broads
Shropshire Hills
Suffolk Coast and Heaths
Killarney
Pembrokeshire Coast
Brecon Beacons
Cotswolds
Chilterns
North Wessex Downs
Surrey Hills
Kent Downs
Exmoor
Cranborne Chase and Wiltshire Downs
South Downs
High Weald
North Devon
New Forest
Dorset
Dartmoor
Isle of Wight
Cornwall
South Devon

TYPES OF FARM

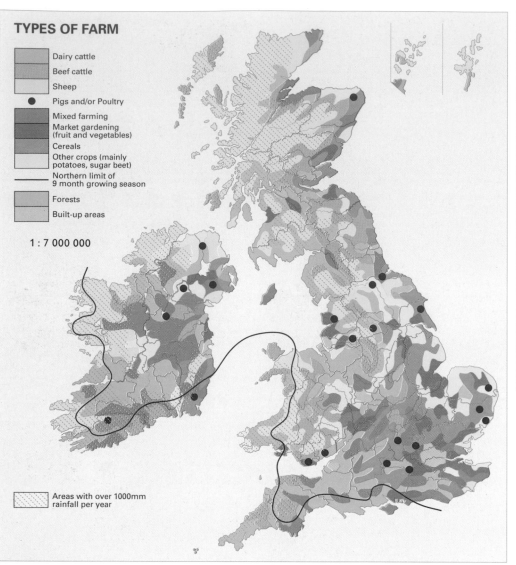

- Dairy cattle
- Beef cattle
- Sheep
- ● Pigs and/or Poultry
- Mixed farming
- Market gardening (fruit and vegetables)
- Cereals
- Other crops (mainly potatoes, sugar beet)
- Northern limit of 9 month growing season
- Forests
- Built-up areas

1 : 7 000 000

Areas with over 1000mm rainfall per year

LAND UNDER AGRICULTURE 1 : 12 000 000
The percentage of the total land area used for farming

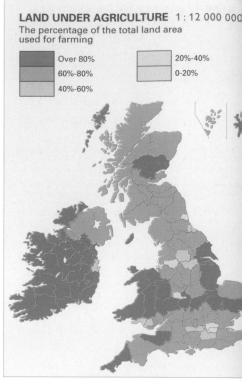

- Over 80%
- 60%-80%
- 40%-60%
- 20%-40%
- 0-20%

AGRICULTURAL LAND USE 1990 (U.K. only)

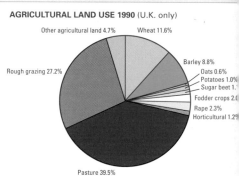

- Other agricultural land 4.7%
- Wheat 11.6%
- Barley 8.8%
- Oats 0.6%
- Potatoes 1.0%
- Sugar beet 1.
- Fodder crops 2.0
- Rape 2.3%
- Horticultural 1.2%
- Rough grazing 27.2%
- Pasture 39.5%

WHEAT 1 : 12 000 000
The percentage of the total farmland used for growing wheat

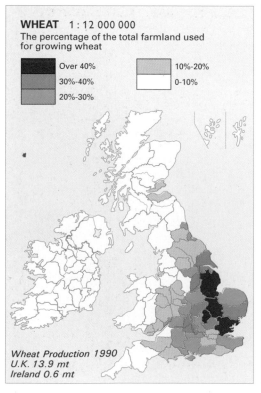

- Over 40%
- 30%-40%
- 20%-30%
- 10%-20%
- 0-10%

Wheat Production 1990
U.K. 13.9 mt
Ireland 0.6 mt

BARLEY 1 : 12 000 000
The percentage of the total farmland used for growing barley

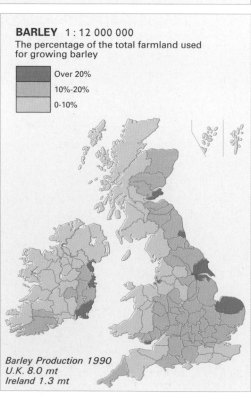

- Over 20%
- 10%-20%
- 0-10%

Barley Production 1990
U.K. 8.0 mt
Ireland 1.3 mt

PASTURE 1 : 12 000 000
The percentage of the total farmland used for grazing livestock

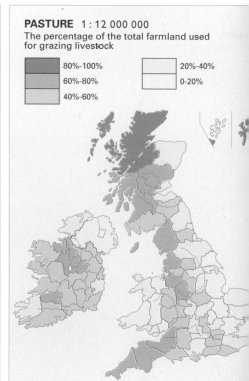

- 80%-100%
- 60%-80%
- 40%-60%
- 20%-40%
- 0-20%

NUMBER AND SIZE OF AGRICULTURAL HOLDINGS IN THE U.K.

Average size of holdings (hectares)

	1940	1980	1989
England & Wales	33.8	60.2	57.9
Scotland	81.8	96.2	195.9
Northern Ireland	13.7	24.2	25.2

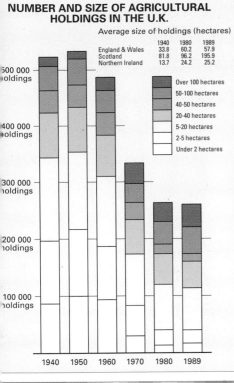

- Over 100 hectares
- 50-100 hectares
- 40-50 hectares
- 20-40 hectares
- 5-20 hectares
- 2-5 hectares
- Under 2 hectares

500 000 holdings
400 000 holdings
300 000 holdings
200 000 holdings
100 000 holdings

1940 1950 1960 1970 1980 1989

POTATOES   1 : 12 000 000

The percentage of the total farmland used for growing potatoes

- Over 3%
- 2%-3%
- 1%-2%
- Under 1%

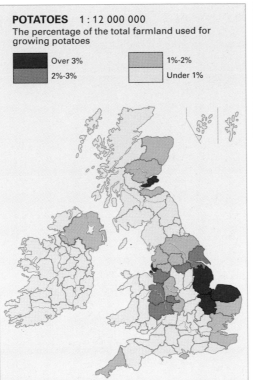

MARKET GARDENING   1 : 12 000 000

The percentage of the total farmland used for market gardening

- Over 5%
- 2.5%-5%
- 1.0%-2.5%
- Under 1%

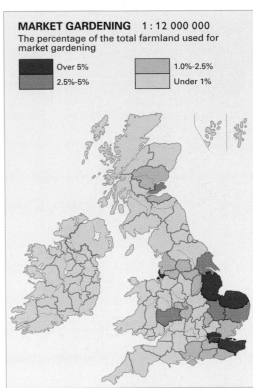

FISHING

Quantities of fish landed at major ports (port districts in Scotland) in 1989

('000 tonnes)
100
50
10
5

Type of fish landed
- Demersal (Deep Sea Fish)
- Pelagic (Shallow Water Fish)
- Shellfish

Fishing Regions
IV North Sea
VIa West Scotland
VIIa Irish Sea
VIIb South & West Ireland
VIId English Channel
VIIf Bristol Channel

Fish landed according to region of capture (1989)
- Demersal
- Pelagic

1 fish represents 10 000 caught

Region boundary

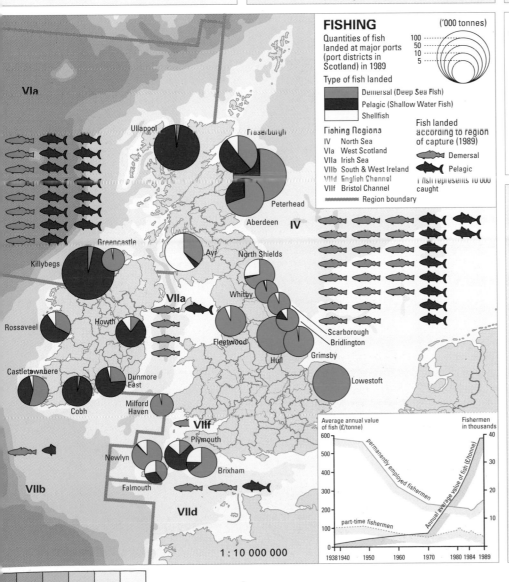

1 : 10 000 000

1000 500 200 100 50 m

Average annual value of fish (£/tonne)
Fishermen in thousands

permanently employed fishermen
part-time fishermen
Annual average value of fish (£/tonne)

600 500 400 300 200 100
40 30 20 10

1938 1940 1950 1960 1970 1980 1984 1989

VALUE OF AGRICULTURAL OUTPUT (U.K. only)

£ billion

- Farm crops
- Horticulture
- Livestock
- Livestock Products

12 10 8 6 4 2 0

1970 1980 1990

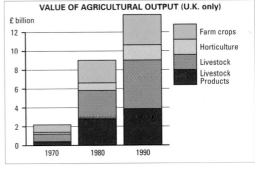

AGRICULTURAL LAND & LIVESTOCK, 1970-90 (U.K. only)

Agricultural land (thousand ha)   Livestock (thousands)

1970 (19 123): 26.7%, 41.1%, 32.2%
1970 (46 749): 26.7%, 17.2%, 56.1%

1980 (18 953): 28.3%, 40.6%, 31.1%
1980 (52 687): 25.6%, 15.0%, 59.4%

1990 (18 542): 30.0%, 40.0%, 30.0%
1990 (63 307): 18.9%, 11.7%, 69.4%

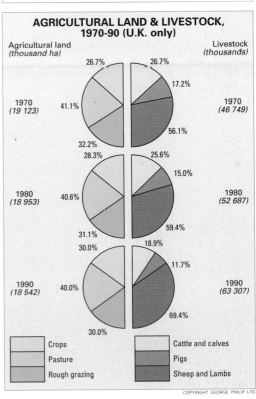

- Crops
- Pasture
- Rough grazing
- Cattle and calves
- Pigs
- Sheep and Lambs

COPYRIGHT GEORGE PHILIP LTD.

EMPLOYMENT IN MANUFACTURING

The percentage of the workforce employed in manufacturing in 1989

- Over 30%
- 25%-30%
- 20%-25%
- 15%-20%
- 12.5%-15%
- Under 12.5%

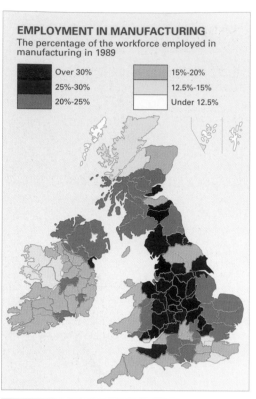

CHANGE IN MANUFACTURING EMPLOYMENT

The percentage change in the number of people employed in manufacturing 1980-89*

- Over 10% gain
- 0-10% gain
- 0-10% loss
- 10%-20% loss
- 20%-30% loss
- Over 30% loss

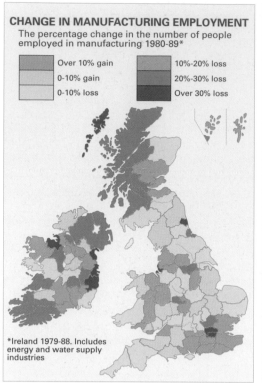

*Ireland 1979-88. Includes energy and water supply industries

LOCATION OF MANUFACTURING INDUSTR

Heavy Industry
- ▲ Chemicals
- ■ Iron and Steel
- ● Motor vehicles

Light Industry
- ◆ Electrical Engineering

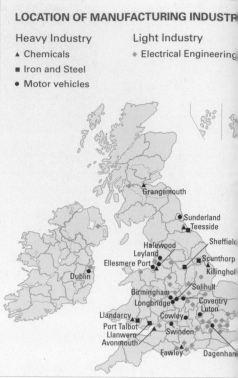

Grangemouth
Sunderland
Teesside
Halewood
Leyland
Sheffield
Ellesmere Port
Scunthorp
Killinghol
Dublin
Birmingham
Solihull
Longbridge
Coventry
Llandarcy
Cowley
Luton
Port Talbot
Swindon
Llanwern
Avonmouth
Fawley
Dagenham

EMPLOYMENT IN AGRICULTURE

The percentage of the workforce employed in agriculture in 1989

- Over 25%
- 10%-25%
- 2.5%-10%
- 1%-2.5%
- 0-1%

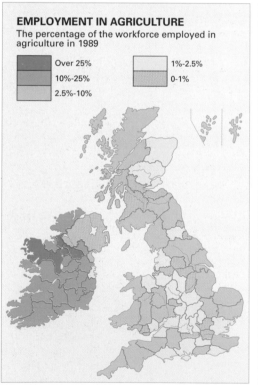

EMPLOYMENT IN SERVICES

The percentage of the workforce employed in the service industry in 1989

- Over 80%
- 70%-80%
- 60%-70%
- 50%-60%
- Less than 50%

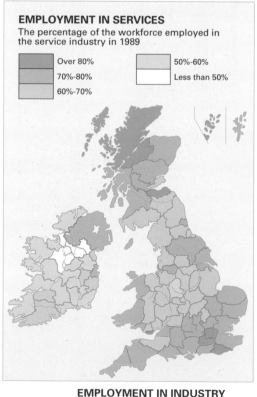

ASSISTED AREAS

These are areas in which extra financial support is focused to encourage economic growth

- Development areas in the U.K.
- Intermediate areas in the U.K.

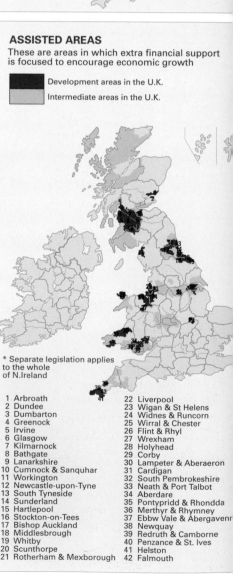

* Separate legislation applies to the whole of N.Ireland

1 Arbroath	22 Liverpool
2 Dundee	23 Wigan & St Helens
3 Dumbarton	24 Widnes & Runcorn
4 Greenock	25 Wirral & Chester
5 Irvine	26 Flint & Rhyl
6 Glasgow	27 Wrexham
7 Kilmarnock	28 Holyhead
8 Bathgate	29 Corby
9 Lanarkshire	30 Lampeter & Aberaeron
10 Cumnock & Sanquhar	31 Cardigan
11 Workington	32 South Pembrokeshire
12 Newcastle-upon-Tyne	33 Neath & Port Talbot
13 South Tyneside	34 Aberdare
14 Sunderland	35 Pontypridd & Rhondda
15 Hartlepool	36 Merthyr & Rhymney
16 Stockton-on-Tees	37 Ebbw Vale & Abergavenn
17 Bishop Auckland	38 Newquay
18 Middlesbrough	39 Redruth & Camborne
19 Whitby	40 Penzance & St. Ives
20 Scunthorpe	41 Helston
21 Rotherham & Mexborough	42 Falmouth

EMPLOYMENT IN INDUSTRY

Employment in the U.K. by industry

- Services
- Transport
- Manufacturing
- Mining & energy supply
- Agriculture, forestry and fishing

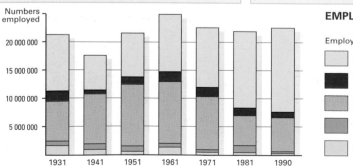

Numbers employed

20 000 000
15 000 000
10 000 000
5 000 000

1931 1941 1951 1961 1971 1981 1990

1 : 12 000 000

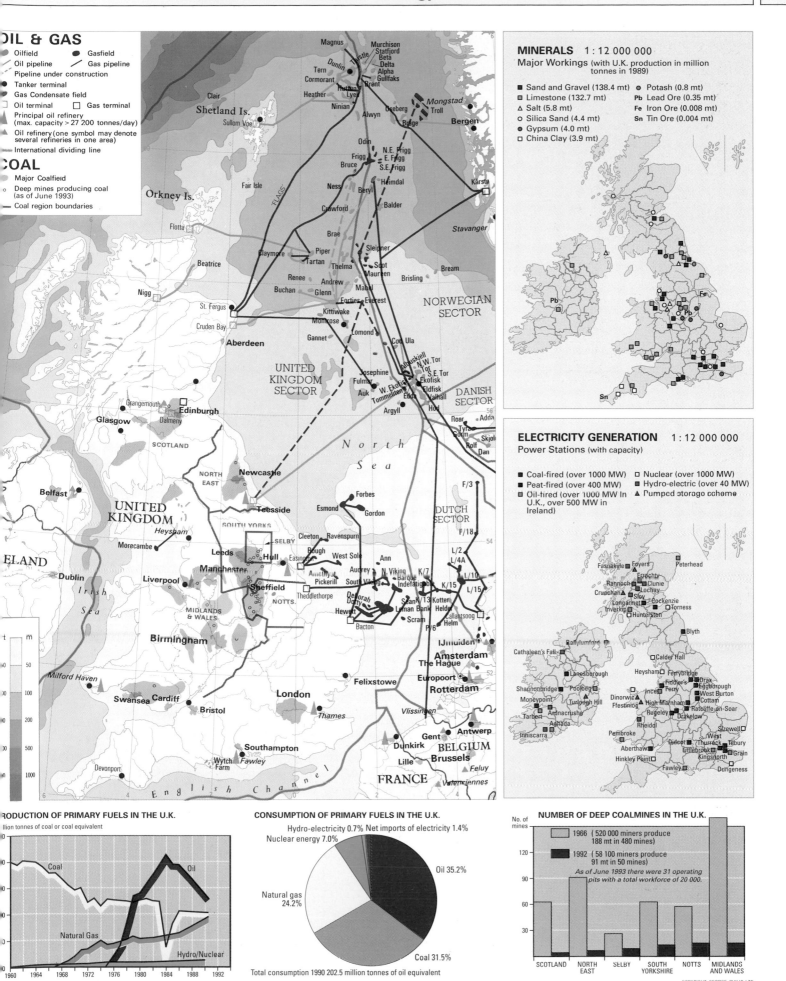

OIL & GAS

- ■ Oilfield
- ● Gasfield
- Oil pipeline
- Gas pipeline
- Pipeline under construction
- ▲ Tanker terminal
- Gas Condensate field
- □ Oil terminal □ Gas terminal
- ■ Principal oil refinery (max. capacity > 27 200 tonnes/day)
- ◇ Oil refinery (one symbol may denote several refineries in one area)
- International dividing line

COAL

- Major Coalfield
- ● Deep mines producing coal (as of June 1993)
- Coal region boundaries

MINERALS 1 : 12 000 000

Major Workings (with U.K. production in million tonnes in 1989)

- ■ Sand and Gravel (138.4 mt)   ◉ Potash (0.8 mt)
- ■ Limestone (132.7 mt)   Pb Lead Ore (0.35 mt)
- △ Salt (5.8 mt)   Fe Iron Ore (0.008 mt)
- ○ Silica Sand (4.4 mt)   Sn Tin Ore (0.004 mt)
- ◉ Gypsum (4.0 mt)
- □ China Clay (3.9 mt)

ELECTRICITY GENERATION 1 : 12 000 000

Power Stations (with capacity)

- ■ Coal-fired (over 1000 MW)   □ Nuclear (over 1000 MW)
- ■ Peat-fired (over 400 MW)   ■ Hydro-electric (over 40 MW)
- ■ Oil-fired (over 1000 MW in U.K., over 500 MW in Ireland)   ▲ Pumped storage scheme

PRODUCTION OF PRIMARY FUELS IN THE U.K.

million tonnes of coal or coal equivalent

Coal
Oil
Natural Gas
Hydro/Nuclear

1960 1964 1968 1972 1976 1980 1984 1988 1992

CONSUMPTION OF PRIMARY FUELS IN THE U.K.

Hydro-electricity 0.7% Net imports of electricity 1.4%
Nuclear energy 7.0%
Oil 35.2%
Natural gas 24.2%
Coal 31.5%

Total consumption 1990 202.5 million tonnes of oil equivalent

NUMBER OF DEEP COALMINES IN THE U.K.

No. of mines

- 1966 (520 000 miners produce 188 mt in 480 mines)
- 1992 (58 100 miners produce 91 mt in 50 mines)

As of June 1993 there were 31 operating pits with a total workforce of 20 000.

120
90
60
30

SCOTLAND | NORTH EAST | SELBY | SOUTH YORKSHIRE | NOTTS | MIDLANDS AND WALES

ROADS AND FERRIES

— M6 — Motorways
—— Main primary routes

Average 24 hour flow of vehicles at a selected point on a motorway. Figures are given in thousands

----- Principal ferry routes
--Oslo-- Long haul sea ferry destinations

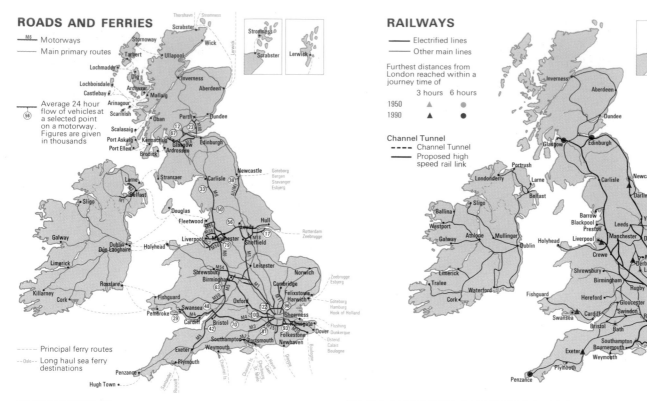

RAILWAYS

—— Electrified lines
—— Other main lines

Furthest distances from London reached within a journey time of

	3 hours	6 hours
1950	▲	●
1990	▲	●

Channel Tunnel
- - - Channel Tunnel
—— Proposed high speed rail link

CHANNEL TUNNEL

Estimated journey times between London-Brussels and London-Paris

Hours

1990/1 Best time achievable using existing networks
1994 Opening of Channel Tunnel
1996 Estimated completion date of new line in Belgium
2000 Estimated completion date of high speed rail link

London – Brussels
London – Paris

MEANS OF TRANSPORTATION WITHIN THE U.K.

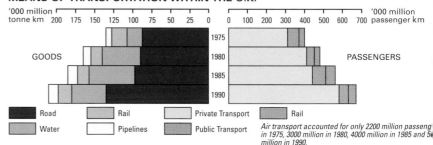

'000 million tonne km   200 175 150 125 100 75 50 25 0   GOODS

0 100 200 300 400 500 600 700 '000 million passenger km   PASSENGERS

1975
1980
1985
1990

Road
Water
Rail
Pipelines
Private Transport
Public Transport
Rail

Air transport accounted for only 2200 million passeng in 1975, 3000 million in 1980, 4000 million in 1985 and 5 million in 1990.

PORTS

Goods traffic by port group
Foreign and domestic traffic
million tonnes

Fuel
Other goods

Ports handling over 1 million tonnes of goods traffic
million tonnes
■ 50-60
□ 40-50
◉ 30-40
◎ 20-30
• 10-20
· 1-10

● Ports where fuel represents over 75% of all goods handled
Hull Ports handling over 1 million tonnes of unitized traffic
— Port group boundaries

The total figure for the Irish Rep. does not include domestic traffic

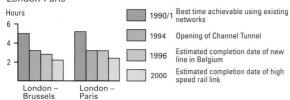

AIRPORTS

Passenger traffic
'000 passengers

International
Domestic

· Selected airports with less than 200 000 passengers

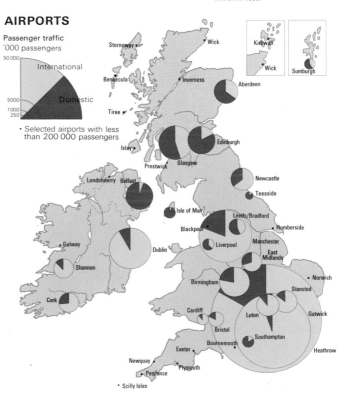

1 : 10 000 000

The DISTRICTS of Northern Ireland have been numbered and can be identified by reference to this table.

1	Londonderry	14	Craigavon
2	Limavady	15	Armagh
3	Coleraine	16	Newry & Mourne
4	Ballymoney	17	Banbridge
5	Moyle	18	Down
6	Larne	19	Lisburn
7	Ballymena	20	Antrim
8	Magherafelt	21	Newtownabbey
9	Cookstown	22	Carrickfergus
10	Strabane	23	North Down
11	Omagh	24	Ards
12	Fermanagh	25	Castlereagh
13	Dungannon	26	Belfast

ORKNEY

HIGHLAND

SHETLAND

° Norwich   Administrative headquarters
MERSEYSIDE   Metropolitan counties
Antrim   Former Northern Ireland counties

Projection: *Conical with two standard parallels*

West from Greenwich | East from Greenwich
COPYRIGHT. GEORGE PHILIP & SON. LTD.

1 : 4 000 000

POPULATION DENSITY 1891   1 : 12 000 000

See map at right for reference to colours

Density in 1891 by country :
U.K. 142 people per km²
Ireland 49 people per km²

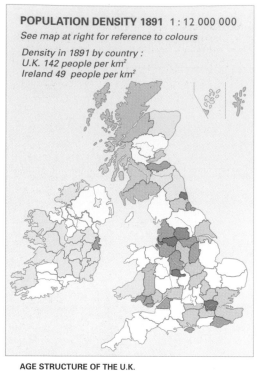

POPULATION DENSITY 1991

Persons per km²

- Over 1000
- 500–1000
- 200–500
- 100–200
- 50–100
- 25–50
- Under 25

The density for the whole of the U.K. is 223 people per km², the density for Ireland is 51.

1 : 7 000 000

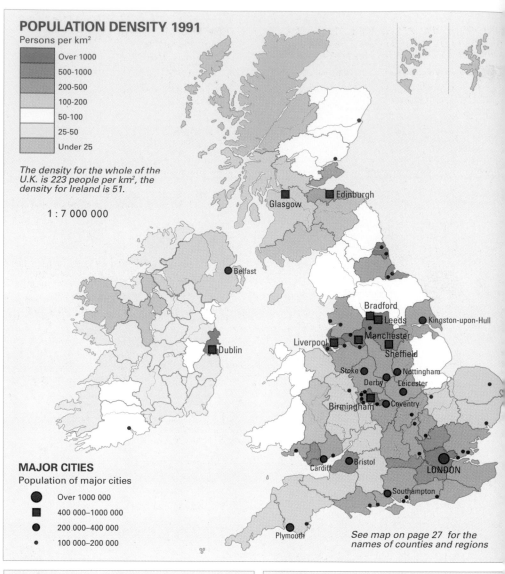

Glasgow
Edinburgh
Belfast
Bradford
Leeds
Kingston-upon-Hull
Liverpool
Manchester
Sheffield
Dublin
Stoke
Nottingham
Derby
Leicester
Birmingham
Coventry
Cardiff
Bristol
LONDON
Southampton
Plymouth

MAJOR CITIES

Population of major cities

- ● Over 1 000 000
- ■ 400 000–1 000 000
- ● 200 000–400 000
- • 100 000–200 000

See map on page 27 for the names of counties and regions

AGE STRUCTURE OF THE U.K.

The bars represent the percentage of males and the percentage of females in the age group shown

□ 1901   □ 1990   — Projected 2150

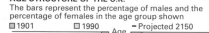

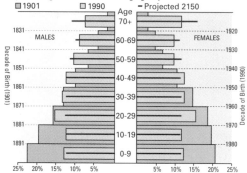

MALES   FEMALES

Age: 70+, 60–69, 50–59, 40–49, 30–39, 20–29, 10–19, 0–9

Decade of Birth (1901): 1831, 1841, 1851, 1861, 1871, 1881, 1891

Decade of Birth (1990): 1920, 1930, 1940, 1950, 1960, 1970, 1980

25% 20% 15% 10% 5%   5% 10% 15% 20% 25%

YOUNG PEOPLE   1 : 12 000 000

The percentage of the population under 15 years old in 1990 (Ireland 1986)

- Over 30%
- 25%–30%
- 20%–25%
- 19%–20%
- 18%–19%
- Under 18%

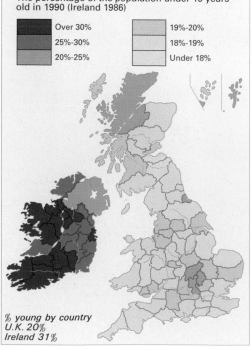

% young by country
U.K. 20%
Ireland 31%

OLD PEOPLE   1 : 12 000 000

The percentage of the population over pensionable age* in 1989

- Over 20%
- 17.5%–20%
- 15%–17.5%
- 12.5%–15%
- 10%–12.5%
- Under 10%

* Pensionable age is 65 for males, 60 for females

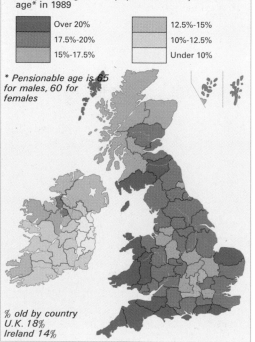

% old by country
U.K. 18%
Ireland 14%

URBANIZATION   1 : 12 000 000

The percentage of the population living in towns and cities (latest available year)

- Over 90%
- 80%–90%
- 70%–80%
- 60%–70%
- 50%–60%
- Under 50%

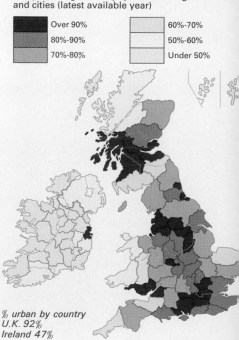

% urban by country
U.K. 92%
Ireland 47%

NATURAL POPULATION CHANGE

The difference between the number of births and the number of deaths per thousand inhabitants in 1990

- Over 10 more births
- 5-10 more births
- 2.5-5 more births
- 0-2.5 more births
- 0-2.5 more deaths
- Over 2.5 more deaths

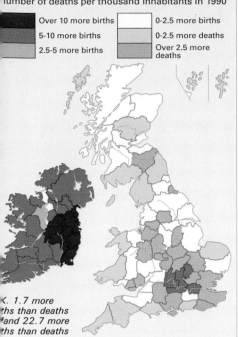

K. 1.7 more
ths than deaths
and 22.7 more
ths than deaths

ETHNIC GROUP

Ethnic minority groups

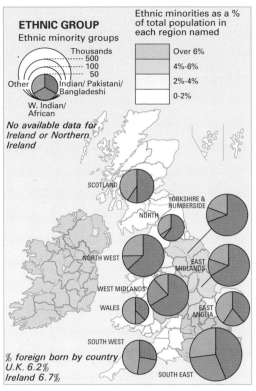

Thousands
500
100
50

Other — Indian/ Pakistani/ Bangladeshi
W. Indian/ African

Ethnic minorities as a % of total population in each region named

- Over 6%
- 4%-6%
- 2%-4%
- 0-2%

No available data for Ireland or Northern Ireland

SCOTLAND
YORKSHIRE & HUMBERSIDE
NORTH
NORTH WEST
EAST MIDLANDS
WEST MIDLANDS
WALES
EAST ANGLIA
SOUTH WEST
SOUTH EAST

% foreign born by country
U.K. 6.2%
Ireland 6.7%

MIGRATION 1 : 12 000 000

The difference between the number moving in and the number moving away (per 1000 inhabitants)*

- Over 15 moved in
- 10-15 moved in
- 5-10 moved in
- 0-5 moved in
- 0-5 moved away
- 5-10 moved away

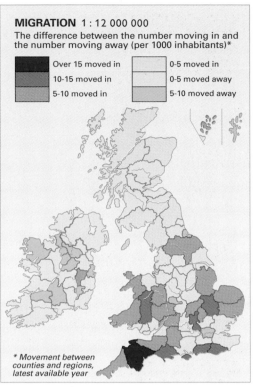

* Movement between counties and regions, latest available year

U.K. VITAL STATISTICS 1900-2000

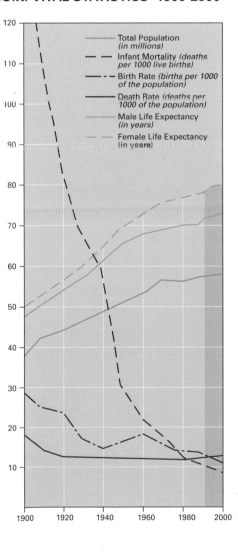

- Total Population (in millions)
- Infant Mortality (deaths per 1000 live births)
- Birth Rate (births per 1000 of the population)
- Death Rate (deaths per 1000 of the population)
- Male Life Expectancy (in years)
- Female Life Expectancy (in years)

POPULATION CHANGE 1961-1991

The percentage change in the number of people between 1961 and 1991

- Over 30% gain
- 25%-30% gain
- 20%-25% gain
- 15%-20% gain
- 10%-15% gain
- 5%-10% gain
- 0-5% gain

- 0-5% loss
- 5%-10% loss
- Over 10% loss

1 : 7 000 000

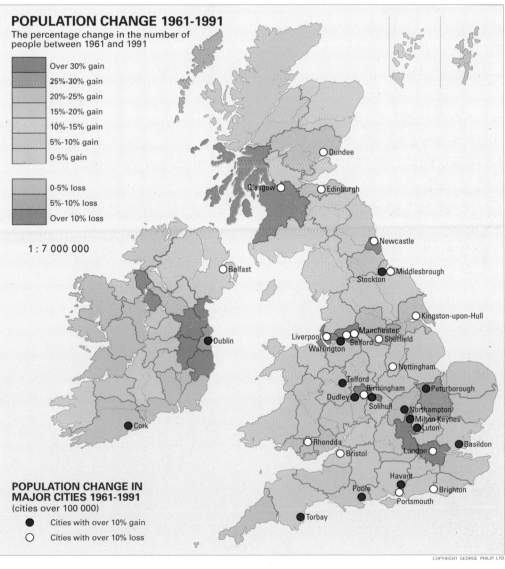

Dundee
Glasgow
Edinburgh
Newcastle
Belfast
Middlesbrough
Stockton
Kingston-upon-Hull
Manchester
Liverpool
Salford
Sheffield
Warrington
Dublin
Nottingham
Telford
Birmingham
Peterborough
Dudley
Solihull
Northampton
Milton Keynes
Luton
Cork
Rhondda
Basildon
Bristol
London
Havant
Poole
Brighton
Portsmouth
Torbay

POPULATION CHANGE IN MAJOR CITIES 1961-1991
(cities over 100 000)

- ● Cities with over 10% gain
- ○ Cities with over 10% loss

BRITISH ISLES: *standards of living*

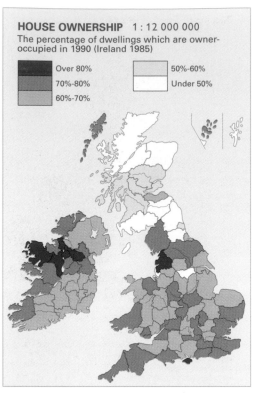

HOUSE OWNERSHIP 1 : 12 000 000
The percentage of dwellings which are owner-occupied in 1990 (Ireland 1985)

Over 80%	50%-60%
70%-80%	Under 50%
60%-70%	

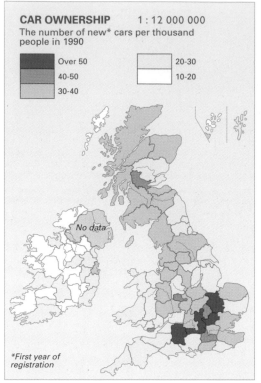

CAR OWNERSHIP 1 : 12 000 000
The number of new* cars per thousand people in 1990

Over 50	20-30
40-50	10-20
30-40	

No data

*First year of registration

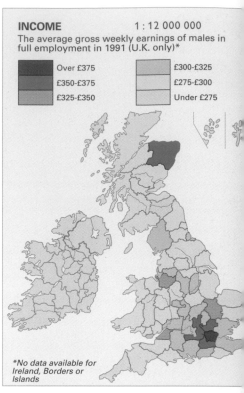

INCOME 1 : 12 000 000
The average gross weekly earnings of males in full employment in 1991 (U.K. only)*

Over £375	£300-£325
£350-£375	£275-£300
£325-£350	Under £275

*No data available for Ireland, Borders or Islands

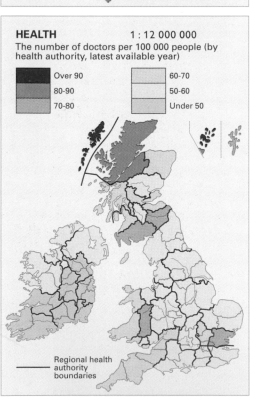

HEALTH 1 : 12 000 000
The number of doctors per 100 000 people (by health authority, latest available year)

Over 90	60-70
80-90	50-60
70-80	Under 50

Regional health authority boundaries

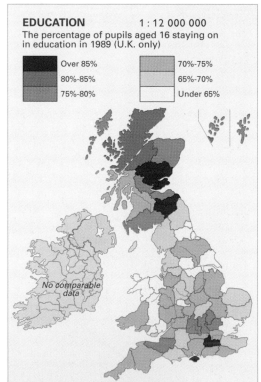

EDUCATION 1 : 12 000 000
The percentage of pupils aged 16 staying on in education in 1989 (U.K. only)

Over 85%	70%-75%
80%-85%	65%-70%
75%-80%	Under 65%

No comparable data

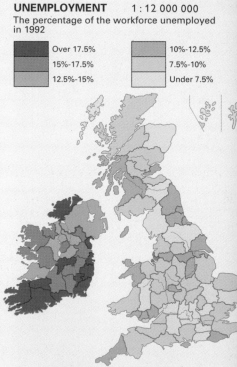

UNEMPLOYMENT 1 : 12 000 000
The percentage of the workforce unemployed in 1992

Over 17.5%	10%-12.5%
15%-17.5%	7.5%-10%
12.5%-15%	Under 7.5%

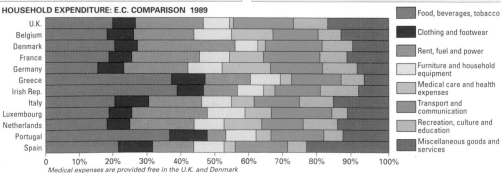

HOUSEHOLD EXPENDITURE: E.C. COMPARISON 1989

U.K.
Belgium
Denmark
France
Germany
Greece
Irish Rep.
Italy
Luxembourg
Netherlands
Portugal
Spain

0 10% 20% 30% 40% 50% 60% 70% 80% 90% 100%
Medical expenses are provided free in the U.K. and Denmark

Food, beverages, tobacco	
Clothing and footwear	
Rent, fuel and power	
Furniture and household equipment	
Medical care and health expenses	
Transport and communication	
Recreation, culture and education	
Miscellaneous goods and services	

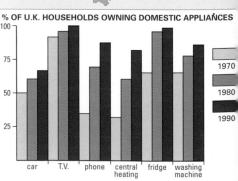

% OF U.K. HOUSEHOLDS OWNING DOMESTIC APPLIANCES

100
75
50
25

car   T.V.   phone   central   fridge   washing
                     heating   machine

1970
1980
1990

U.K. TRADE
TOP TEN TRADING PARTNERS 1990

e container represents 1% of the total value of imports or 1% of the total value of exports

IMPORTS — **EXPORTS**

Total Imports 1990 £126billion	Total Exports 1990 £104billion

IMPORTS:
- Germany £19.9b
- U.S.A. £14.4b
- France £11.7b
- Netherlands £10.5b
- Japan £6.7b
- Italy £6.7b
- Belgium/Lux. £5.7b
- Irish Republic £4.5b
- Switzerland £4.2b
- Norway £4.2b

EXPORTS:
- Germany £13.1b
- U.S.A. £13.0b
- France £10.9b
- Netherlands £7.5b
- Belgium/Lux. £5.6b
- Italy £5.6b
- Irish Republic £5.3b
- Spain £3.7b
- Sweden £2.7b
- Japan £2.6b

TYPE OF GOODS
- Machinery and Transport Equipment
- • Road Vehicles
- Other manufactured Goods
- Chemicals
- Food and Live Animals
- Mineral fuels, Lubricants, etc.
- Other Goods

U.K. TOTAL FOREIGN TRADE 1970-1990 (£ million)

	Imports	Exports		Imports	Exports
70	£9 051m	£8 063m	1982	£56 940m	£55 538m
74	£23 117m	£16 494m	1986	£84 790m	£78 331m
78	£40 969m	£37 308m	1990	£126 165m	£103 91m

TOURISM
TOP 20 TOURIST ATTRACTIONS (U.K. 1991)

● Theme Park ○ Country Park
● Museum ● Historic Property

	Visitors
● Blackpool Pleasure Beach	6 500 000
● British Museum, London	5 061 287
● National Gallery, London	4 280 139
○ Strathclyde Country Park	4 220 000
● Palace Pier, Brighton	3 500 000
● Pleasure Beach, Gt. Yarmouth	2 500 000
● Madame Tussauds, London	2 248 956
● Eastbourne Pier	2 200 000
● Alton Towers, Staffs.	1 968 000
● Tower of London	1 923 520
● Tate Gallery, London	1 816 421
● Pleasureland, Southport	1 750 000
● Natural History Museum, London	1 571 681
● St. Pauls Cathedral, London	1 500 000
● Chessington World of Adventures, Surrey	1 410 000
● Science Museum, London	1 327 503
○ Bradgate Park, Leics.	1 300 000
● Blackpool Tower	1 300 000
● Frontierland, Morecambe	1 300 000
○ Sandwell Valley Country Park	1 250 000

FOREIGN VISITORS TO THE U.K.

Nature of visit
- Business
- Leisure

Country of origin
- North America
- Western Europe
- Other

No. of visits (millions)

1970 1980 1990

INCOME FROM TOURISM

The percentage of total U.K. income from tourism by region in 1990

- Over 25%
- 10%-25%
- 5%-10%
- 2.5%-5%
- 0-2.5%

Total income from tourism
U.K. 1990 £10.2 billion
Ireland 1990 £7.7 billion

Regions: SCOTLAND, NORTHERN IRELAND, NORTHUMBRIA, CUMBRIA, YORKSHIRE AND HUMBERSIDE, NORTH WEST, EAST MIDLANDS, HEART OF ENGLAND, EAST ANGLIA, WALES, THAMES AND CHILTERNS, LONDON, WEST COUNTRY, SOUTHERN, SOUTH EAST

VISITS ABROAD BY U.K. RESIDENTS

Top 10 destinations visited, 1990

No. of U.K. visitors ('000)
0 1000 2000 3000 4000 5000 6000 7000

- France
- Spain
- Irish Rep.
- U.S.A.
- Germany
- Greece
- Netherlands
- Italy
- Portugal
- Belgium

Total visits by area, 1990

North America	2 349 000
Western Europe E.C.	22 032 000
Western Europe non E.C.	3 786 000
Rest of World	3 016 000

DEPENDENCE ON TRADE WITH THE U.K.

Trade with the U.K. as a percentage of each country's total trade

- Over 10%
- 7.5%-10%
- 5.0%-7.5%
- 2.5%-5.0%
- 1.0%-2.5%
- Under 1.0%

CHANGES IN TRADE WITH THE U.K.

Percentage change in exports and imports for selected countries 1985-1990

Change
- 1000%
- 500%
- 100%
- 50%

Increase 1985-1990

Exports to U.K. Imports from U.K.

Decrease 1985-1990

World map labels: CANADA, U.S.A., MEXICO, JAMAICA, ECUADOR, ARGENTINA, NORWAY, ALGERIA, NIGERIA, SAUDI ARABIA, KENYA, SOUTH AFRICA, Former U.S.S.R., IRAN, INDIA, JAPAN, SINGAPORE, MALAYSIA, INDONESIA, AUSTRALIA

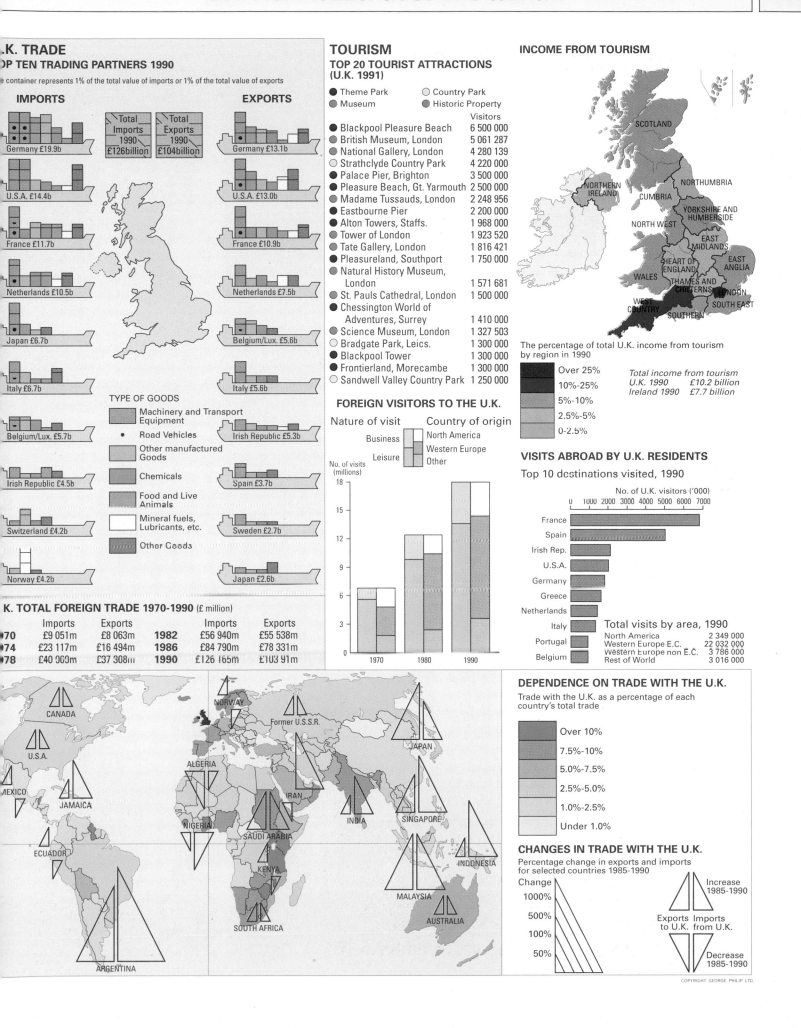

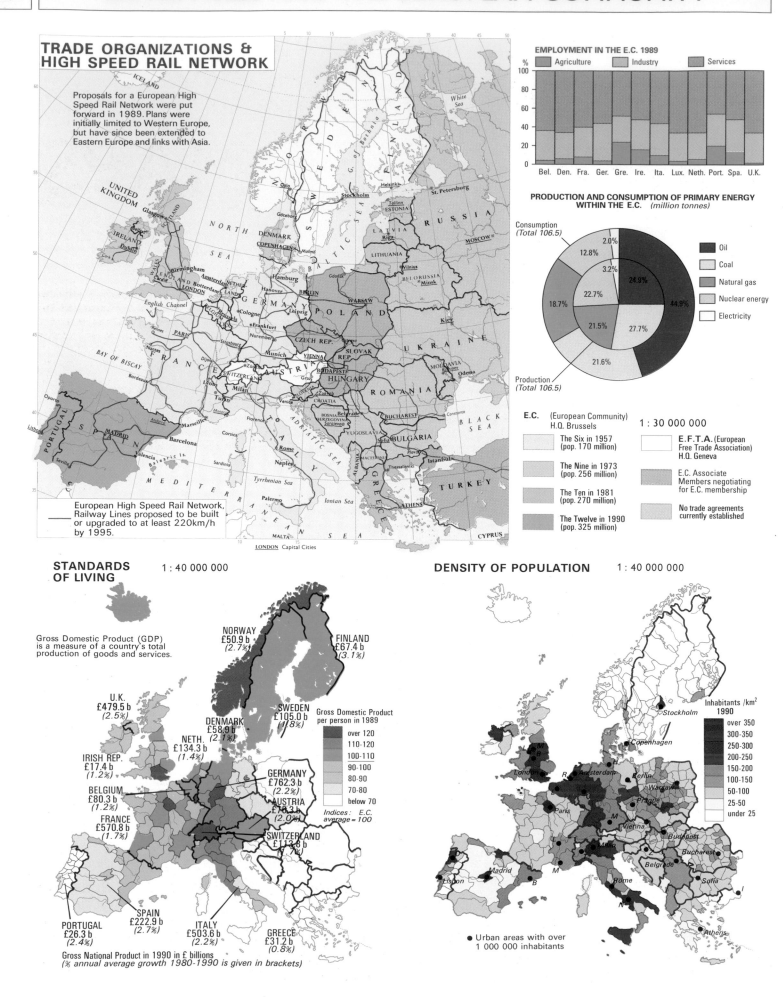

TRADE ORGANIZATIONS & HIGH SPEED RAIL NETWORK

Proposals for a European High Speed Rail Network were put forward in 1989. Plans were initially limited to Western Europe, but have since been extended to Eastern Europe and links with Asia.

European High Speed Rail Network, Railway Lines proposed to be built or upgraded to at least 220km/h by 1995.

LONDON Capital Cities

EMPLOYMENT IN THE E.C. 1989

Agriculture   Industry   Services

Bel. Den. Fra. Ger. Gre. Ire. Ita. Lux. Neth. Port. Spa. U.K.

PRODUCTION AND CONSUMPTION OF PRIMARY ENERGY WITHIN THE E.C.   (million tonnes)

Consumption (Total 106.5)

2.0%
12.8%
3.2%
24.9%
22.7%
44.9%
18.7%
21.5%
27.7%
21.6%

Production (Total 106.5)

Oil
Coal
Natural gas
Nuclear energy
Electricity

E.C. (European Community) H.Q. Brussels

1 : 30 000 000

The Six in 1957 (pop. 170 million)
The Nine in 1973 (pop. 256 million)
The Ten in 1981 (pop. 270 million)
The Twelve in 1990 (pop. 325 million)

E.F.T.A. (European Free Trade Association) H.Q. Geneva
E.C. Associate Members negotiating for E.C. membership
No trade agreements currently established

STANDARDS OF LIVING   1 : 40 000 000

Gross Domestic Product (GDP) is a measure of a country's total production of goods and services.

NORWAY £50.9 b (2.7%)
FINLAND £67.4 b (3.1%)
U.K. £479.5 b (2.5%)
SWEDEN £105.0 b (1.8%)
DENMARK £58.9 b (2.1%)
NETH. £134.3 b (1.4%)
IRISH REP. £17.4 b (1.2%)
GERMANY £762.3 b (2.2%)
BELGIUM £80.3 b (1.2%)
AUSTRIA £103.6 b (2.0%)
FRANCE £570.8 b (1.7%)
SWITZERLAND £112.8 b (1.7%)
PORTUGAL £26.3 b (2.4%)
SPAIN £222.9 b (2.7%)
ITALY £503.6 b (2.2%)
GREECE £31.2 b (0.8%)

Gross Domestic Product per person in 1989
over 120
110-120
100-110
90-100
80-90
70-80
below 70
Indices : E.C. average = 100

Gross National Product in 1990 in £ billions (% annual average growth 1980-1990 is given in brackets)

DENSITY OF POPULATION   1 : 40 000 000

Inhabitants /km² 1990
over 350
300-350
250-300
200-250
150-200
100-150
50-100
25-50
under 25

Stockholm, Copenhagen, London, Amsterdam, Berlin, Warsaw, Prague, Paris, Vienna, Budapest, Bucharest, Madrid, Milan, Belgrade, Rome, Lisbon, Sofia, Athens

● Urban areas with over 1 000 000 inhabitants

INDEX TO BRITISH ISLES MAPS

This index lists the major placenames which appear on the large-scale maps of the British Isles (pages *2–15* with the yellow band). Placenames for the rest of the world can be found in the World Index, with the turquoise band.

The first number beside each name in the index gives the map page on which that feature or place will be found. The letter and figure immediately after the page number give the grid square within which the feature is situated. The letter represents the latitude and the figure the longitude. In some cases the feature may fall within the specified square, while the name is outside. This is usually the case only with very large features. Rivers are indexed to their mouths or confluence.

The 'geographical co-ordinates' which follow the letter-figure references give the latitude and longitude of each place. The first co-ordinate indicates latitude – the distance north of the Equator. The second co-ordinate indicates longitude – the distance east or west of the Greenwich Meridian. Both latitude and longitude are measured in degrees and minutes (there are 60 minutes in a degree).

Thus the entry in the index for Runcorn reads:

Runcorn............ **7 F3** 53 20N 2 44W

This indicates that Runcorn appears on map page 7 in grid square F3 at latitude 53 degrees, 20 minutes north and at longitude 2 degrees, 44 minutes west. To find Runcorn by using the geographical co-ordinates, look at the edges of the map. The degrees of latitude are indicated by blue figures on the left-hand edge of the map and the degrees of longitude are marked on the bottom edge of the map. Runcorn will be found where lines extended from the two points on the map edge would cross on the map.

An open square □ indicates that the name refers to an administrative unit such as a county or region; rivers are indicated by an arrow ⟶. Names composed of a proper name (Wight) and a description (Isle of) are positioned alphabetically by the proper name. All names beginning St. are alphabetized under Saint. A list of abbreviations used can be found in the World Index at the end of the atlas.

A

Abberton Res.	**9 C10**	51 50N	0 52 E
Abbeyfeale	**14 D4**	52 23N	9 20W
Aberaeron	**10 C5**	52 15N	4 16W
Aberayron = Aberaeron	**10 C5**	52 15N	4 16W
Abercarn	**10 D7**	51 39N	3 9W
Aberchirder	**3 G12**	57 34N	2 40W
Aberdare	**10 D7**	51 43N	3 27W
Aberdeen	**3 H13**	57 9N	2 6W
Aberdovey = Aberdyfi	**10 B5**	52 33N	4 3W
Aberdyfi	**10 B5**	52 33N	4 3W
Aberfeldy	**5 A8**	56 37N	3 50W
Abergavenny	**10 D7**	51 49N	3 1W
Abergele	**10 A6**	53 17N	3 35W
Abersychan	**10 D7**	51 44N	3 3W
Abertillery	**10 D7**	51 44N	3 9W
Aberystwyth	**10 C5**	52 25N	4 6W
Abingdon	**8 C6**	51 40N	1 17W
Aboyne	**3 H12**	57 4N	2 48W
Accrington	**7 E4**	53 46N	2 22W
Achill Hd.	**12 D1**	53 59N	10 15W
Achill I.	**12 D1**	53 58N	10 5W
A'Chralaig	**2 H7**	57 11N	5 10W
Adlington	**7 E3**	53 36N	2 36W
Adwick le Street	**7 E6**	53 35N	1 12W
Agnews Hill	**13 B10**	54 51N	5 55W
Ailsa Craig	**4 D5**	55 15N	5 7W
Ainsdale	**7 E2**	53 37N	3 2W
Aird Brenish	**2 F3**	58 8N	7 8W
Airdrie	**5 C8**	55 53N	3 57W
Aire ⟶	**7 E7**	53 42N	0 55W
Alcester	**8 B5**	52 13N	1 52W
Aldbrough	**7 E8**	53 50N	0 7W
Aldeburgh	**9 B12**	52 9N	1 35 E
Alderley Edge	**7 F4**	53 18N	2 15W
Alderney	**11 H9**	49 42N	2 12W
Aldershot	**9 D7**	51 15N	0 43W
Aldridge	**7 G5**	52 36N	1 55W
Alexandria	**4 C6**	55 59N	4 40W
Alford, *Gramp.*	**3 H12**	57 13N	2 42W
Alford, *Lincs.*	**7 F9**	53 16N	0 10 E
Alfreton	**7 F6**	53 6N	1 22W
Allen, Bog of	**15 B9**	53 15N	7 0W
Allen, L.	**12 C5**	54 12N	8 5W
Alloa	**5 B8**	56 7N	3 49W
Alness	**3 G9**	57 41N	4 15W
Alnmouth	**6 B5**	55 24N	1 37W
Alnwick	**6 B5**	55 25N	1 42W
Alsager	**7 F4**	53 7N	2 20W
Alsh, L.	**2 H6**	57 15N	5 39W
Alston	**6 C4**	54 48N	2 26W
Alton	**9 D7**	51 8N	0 59W
Altrincham	**7 F4**	53 25N	2 21W
Alva	**5 B8**	56 9N	3 49W
Alyth	**5 A9**	56 38N	3 15W
Amble	**6 B5**	55 20N	1 36W
Ambleside	**6 D3**	54 26N	2 58W
Amersham	**9 C7**	51 40N	0 38W
Amesbury	**8 D5**	51 10N	1 46W
Amlwch	**10 A5**	53 24N	4 21W
Ammanford	**10 D5**	51 48N	4 0W
Ampthill	**9 B8**	52 3N	0 30W
An Teallach	**2 G7**	57 49N	5 18W
An Uaimh	**13 D8**	53 39N	6 40W
Andover	**8 D6**	51 13N	1 29W
Anglesey	**10 A5**	53 17N	4 20W
Angus, Braes of	**3 J11**	56 51N	3 10W
Annagh Hd.	**12 C1**	54 15N	10 5W
Annalee ⟶	**13 C7**	54 3N	7 15W
Annan	**5 E9**	54 57N	3 17W
Annan ⟶	**5 E9**	54 58N	3 18W
Annandale	**5 D9**	55 10N	3 25W
Anstey	**7 G6**	52 41N	1 14W
Anstruther	**5 B10**	56 14N	2 40W
Antrim	**13 B9**	54 43N	6 13W
Antrim □	**13 B9**	54 55N	6 20W
Antrim, Mts. of	**13 B9**	54 57N	6 8W
Appin	**4 A5**	56 37N	5 20W
Appleby-in-Westmorland	**6 C4**	54 35N	2 29W
Appledore	**11 E5**	51 3N	4 12W
Aran Fawddwy	**10 B6**	52 48N	3 40W
Aran I.	**12 B4**	55 0N	8 30W
Aran Is.	**14 B3**	53 5N	9 42W
Arbroath	**5 A10**	56 34N	2 35W
Arbury Hill	**8 B6**	52 13N	1 12W
Ardee	**13 D8**	53 51N	6 32W
Arderin	**15 B7**	53 3N	7 40W
Ardgour	**4 A5**	56 45N	5 25W
Ardivachar Pt.	**2 H3**	57 23N	7 25W
Ardmore Hd.	**15 E7**	51 58N	7 43W
Ardmore Pt.	**4 C3**	55 40N	6 2W
Ardnamurchan	**4 A4**	56 43N	6 0W
Ardnamurchan, Pt. of	**4 A3**	56 44N	6 14W
Ardnave Pt.	**4 C3**	55 54N	6 20W
Ardrossan	**4 C6**	55 39N	4 50W
Ards Pen.	**13 B10**	54 30N	5 30W
Arenig Fawr	**10 B6**	52 56N	3 45W
Argyll	**4 B5**	56 14N	5 10W
Arisaig	**2 J6**	56 55N	5 50W
Arisaig, Sd. of	**2 J6**	56 50N	5 50W
Arkaig, L.	**2 J7**	56 58N	5 10W
Arklow	**15 C10**	52 48N	6 10W
Arklow Hd.	**15 C10**	52 46N	6 10W
Armadale	**5 C8**	55 54N	3 42W
Armagh	**13 C8**	54 22N	6 40W
Armagh □	**13 C8**	54 18N	6 37W
Armthorpe	**7 E6**	53 32N	1 3W
Arnold	**7 F6**	53 2N	1 8W
Arran	**4 C5**	55 34N	5 12W
Arrow, L.	**12 C5**	54 3N	8 20W
Arun ⟶	**9 E7**	50 48N	0 33W
Arundel	**9 E7**	50 52N	0 32W
Ascot	**9 D7**	51 24N	0 41W
Ash	**9 D7**	51 14N	0 43W
Ashbourne	**7 F5**	53 2N	1 44W
Ashburton	**11 F6**	50 31N	3 45W
Ashby de la Zouch	**7 G6**	52 45N	1 29W
Ashdown Forest	**9 D9**	51 4N	0 2 E
Ashford	**9 D10**	51 8N	0 53 E
Ashington	**6 B5**	55 12N	1 35W
Ashton-in-Makerfield	**7 F3**	53 29N	2 39W
Ashton under Lyne	**7 F4**	53 30N	2 8W
Aspatria	**6 C2**	54 45N	3 20W
Assynt	**2 F7**	58 20N	5 10W
Athboy	**13 D8**	53 37N	6 55W
Athenry	**14 B5**	53 18N	8 45W
Atherstone	**7 G5**	52 35N	1 32W
Atherton	**7 E3**	53 32N	2 30W
Athlone	**14 B7**	53 26N	7 57W
Atholl, Forest of	**3 J10**	56 51N	3 50W
Athy	**15 C9**	53 0N	7 0W
Attleborough	**9 A11**	52 32N	1 1 E
Auchterarder	**5 B8**	56 18N	3 43W
Auchtermuchty	**5 B9**	56 18N	3 15W
Aughnacloy	**13 C8**	54 25N	6 58W
Aviemore	**3 H10**	57 11N	3 50W
Avoca	**15 C10**	52 52N	6 13W
Avoca ⟶	**15 C10**	52 48N	6 9W
Avon □	**8 D3**	51 30N	2 40W
Avon ⟶, *Avon*	**8 D3**	51 30N	2 43W
Avon ⟶, *Hants.*	**8 E5**	50 44N	1 45W
Avon ⟶, *Warks.*	**8 C4**	51 57N	2 9W
Avonmouth	**8 C3**	51 30N	2 42W
Awe, L.	**4 B5**	56 15N	5 15W
Axe Edge	**7 F5**	53 14N	1 59W
Axminster	**11 F7**	50 47N	3 1W
Aylesbury	**9 C7**	51 48N	0 49W
Aylsham	**9 A11**	52 48N	1 16 E
Ayr	**4 D6**	55 28N	4 37W
Ayr ⟶	**4 D6**	55 29N	4 40W
Ayr, Heads of	**4 D6**	55 25N	4 43W
Ayr, Pt. of	**10 A7**	53 21N	3 19W
Ayre, Pt. of	**3 E12**	58 55N	2 43W

B

Bacton	**9 A11**	52 50N	1 29 E
Bacup	**7 E4**	53 42N	2 12W
Badenoch	**3 J9**	56 59N	4 15W
Bagenalstown = Muine Bheag	**15 C9**	52 42N	6 57W
Baggy Pt.	**11 E5**	51 11N	4 12W
Bagh nam Faoileann	**2 H3**	57 22N	7 13W
Baginbun Hd.	**15 D9**	52 10N	6 50W
Bagshot	**9 D7**	51 22N	0 41W
Baildon	**7 E5**	53 52N	1 46W
Baile Atha Cliath = Dublin	**15 B10**	53 20N	6 18W
Bakewell	**7 F5**	53 13N	1 40W
Bala	**10 B6**	52 54N	3 36W
Bala, L.	**10 B6**	52 53N	3 38W
Balbriggan	**13 D9**	53 35N	6 10W
Baldock	**9 C8**	51 59N	0 11W
Ballachulish	**4 A5**	56 40N	5 10W
Ballagan Pt.	**13 D9**	54 0N	6 6W
Ballaghaderreen	**12 D4**	53 55N	8 35W
Ballater	**3 H11**	57 2N	3 2W
Ballina, *Mayo*	**12 C3**	54 7N	9 10W
Ballina, *Tipp.*	**14 C6**	52 49N	8 27W
Ballinasloe	**14 B6**	53 20N	8 12W
Ballinderry ⟶	**13 B8**	54 40N	6 32W
Ballinrobe	**12 D3**	53 36N	9 13W
Ballinskelligs B.	**14 E2**	51 46N	10 11W
Ballybunion	**14 C3**	52 30N	9 40W
Ballycastle	**13 A9**	55 12N	6 15W
Ballyclare	**13 B10**	54 46N	6 0W
Ballyconneely B.	**14 B2**	53 23N	10 8W
Ballydavid Hd.	**14 D2**	52 15N	10 20W
Ballydonegan B.	**14 E2**	51 38N	10 6W
Ballyhaunis	**12 D4**	53 47N	8 47W
Ballyhoura Mts.	**14 D5**	52 18N	8 33W
Ballymena	**13 B9**	54 53N	6 18W
Ballymoney	**13 A8**	55 5N	6 30W
Ballymote	**12 C4**	54 5N	8 31W
Ballynahinch	**13 C10**	54 24N	5 55W
Ballyquintin Pt.	**13 C11**	54 20N	5 30W
Ballyshannon	**12 B5**	54 30N	8 10W
Balmoral Forest	**3 J11**	57 0N	3 15W
Baltimore	**14 F4**	51 29N	9 22W
Bamber Bridge	**7 E3**	53 44N	2 39W
Bamburgh	**6 A5**	55 36N	1 42W
Banbridge	**13 C9**	54 21N	6 17W
Banbury	**8 B6**	52 4N	1 21W
Banchory	**3 H13**	57 3N	2 30W
Bandon	**14 E5**	51 44N	8 45W
Bandon ⟶	**14 E5**	51 40N	8 41W
Banff	**3 G12**	57 40N	2 32W
Bangor, *Down*	**13 B10**	54 40N	5 40W
Bangor, *Gwynedd*	**10 A5**	53 13N	4 9W
Bann ⟶, *Down*	**13 C8**	54 30N	6 31W
Bann ⟶, *L'derry.*	**13 A8**	55 10N	6 40W
Bannockburn	**5 B8**	56 5N	3 55W
Bannow B.	**15 D9**	52 13N	6 48W
Banstead	**9 D8**	51 19N	0 10W
Bantry	**14 E4**	51 40N	9 28W
Bantry B.	**14 E3**	51 35N	9 50W
Bard Hd.	**2 B15**	60 6N	1 5W
Bardsey Sd.	**10 B4**	52 47N	4 46W
Bargoed	**10 D7**	51 42N	3 22W
Barking and Dagenham	**9 C9**	51 31N	0 10 E
Barmouth	**10 B5**	52 44N	4 3W
Barnard Castle	**6 C5**	54 33N	1 55W
Barnet	**9 C8**	51 37N	0 15W
Barnoldswick	**7 E4**	53 55N	2 11W
Barns Ness	**5 C11**	55 59N	2 27W
Barnsley	**7 E6**	53 33N	1 29W
Barnstaple	**11 E5**	51 5N	4 3W
Barnstaple B.	**11 E5**	51 5N	4 20W
Barra	**2 J3**	57 0N	7 30W
Barra Hd.	**2 J2**	56 47N	7 40W
Barrhead	**4 C7**	55 48N	4 23W
Barrow ⟶	**15 D9**	52 14N	6 58W
Barrow-in-Furness	**6 D2**	54 8N	3 15W
Barrow upon Humber	**7 E8**	53 41N	0 22W
Barrowford	**7 E4**	53 51N	2 14W
Barry	**8 E7**	51 23N	3 19W
Barry I.	**8 E7**	51 23N	3 17W
Barry's Pt.	**14 E5**	51 36N	8 40W
Barton upon Humber	**7 E8**	53 41N	0 27W
Basildon	**9 C9**	51 34N	0 29 E
Basingstoke	**8 D6**	51 15N	1 5W
Bass Rock	**5 B10**	56 5N	2 40W
Bath	**8 D4**	51 22N	2 22W
Bathgate	**5 C8**	55 54N	3 38W
Batley	**7 E5**	53 43N	1 38W
Battle	**9 E9**	50 55N	0 30 E
Beachy Hd.	**9 E9**	50 44N	0 16 E
Beaconsfield	**9 C7**	51 36N	0 39W
Beaminster	**8 E3**	50 48N	2 44W
Bearsden	**4 C7**	55 55N	4 21W
Beauly	**3 H9**	57 29N	4 27W
Beauly ⟶	**3 H9**	57 26N	4 28W
Beauly Firth	**3 H9**	57 30N	4 20W
Beaumaris	**10 A5**	53 16N	4 7W
Bebington	**7 F2**	53 23N	3 1W
Beccles	**9 B12**	52 27N	1 33 E
Bedford	**9 B8**	52 8N	0 29W
Bedford Level	**9 A8**	52 35N	0 15W
Bedfordshire □	**9 B8**	52 4N	0 28W
Bedlington	**6 B5**	55 8N	1 35W
Bedwas	**11 D7**	51 36N	3 10W
Bedworth	**8 D6**	52 28N	1 29W
Bee, L.	**2 H3**	57 22N	7 21W
Beeston	**7 G6**	52 55N	1 11W
Beighton	**7 F6**	53 21N	1 21W
Beinn a' Ghlo	**3 J10**	56 51N	3 42W
Beinn Mhor	**2 G4**	57 59N	6 39W
Beith	**4 C6**	55 45N	4 38W
Belfast	**13 B10**	54 35N	5 56W
Belfast L.	**13 B10**	54 40N	5 50W
Belmullet	**12 C2**	54 13N	9 58W
Belper	**7 F6**	53 2N	1 29W
Belturbet	**12 C7**	54 6N	7 28W
Bembridge	**8 E6**	50 41N	1 4W
Ben Alder	**3 J9**	56 50N	4 30W
Ben Avon	**3 H11**	57 6N	3 28W
Ben Bheigeir	**4 C3**	55 43N	6 6W
Ben Chonzie	**5 B8**	56 27N	4 0W
Ben Cruachan	**4 B5**	56 26N	5 8W
Ben Dearg, *Highl.*	**3 G8**	57 47N	4 58W
Ben Dearg, *Tayside*	**3 J10**	56 52N	3 52W
Ben Dhorain	**3 F10**	58 7N	3 50W
Ben Dorain	**4 A6**	56 32N	4 42W
Ben Eighie	**2 G7**	57 37N	5 30W
Ben Hee	**3 F8**	58 16N	4 43W
Ben Hiant	**4 A3**	56 42N	6 1W

35

Dalton-in-Furness Humber

Dalton-in-Furness	**6 D2**	54 9N	3 10W
Danbury	**9 C10**	51 43N	0 34 E
Darlington	**6 C5**	54 33N	1 33W
Dart →	**11 G6**	50 24N	3 36W
Dartford	**9 D9**	51 26N	0 15 E
Dartmoor	**11 F6**	50 36N	4 0W
Dartmouth	**11 G6**	50 21N	3 35W
Darton	**7 E5**	53 36N	1 32W
Darvel	**4 C7**	55 37N	4 20W
Darwen	**7 E4**	53 42N	2 29W
Daventry	**8 B6**	52 16N	1 10W
Dawlish	**11 F7**	50 34N	3 28W
Dawros Hd.	**12 B4**	54 48N	8 32W
Deal	**9 D11**	51 13N	1 25 E
Dean, Forest of	**8 C3**	51 50N	2 35W
Dearne	**7 E6**	53 32N	1 17W
Dee →, *Clwyd*	**10 A7**	53 15N	3 7W
Dee →, *Gramp.*	**3 H13**	57 4N	2 7W
Deer Sd.	**3 E12**	58 58N	2 50W
Denbigh	**10 A7**	53 12N	3 26W
Denby Dale	**7 E5**	53 35N	1 40W
Dennis Hd.	**3 D13**	59 23N	2 26W
Denny	**5 B8**	56 1N	3 55W
Denton	**7 F4**	53 26N	2 10W
Derby	**7 G6**	52 27N	1 28W
Derbyshire □	**7 F5**	53 0N	1 30W
Derg, L.	**14 C6**	53 0N	8 20W
Derravaragh, L.	**12 D7**	53 38N	7 22W
Derry = Londonderry	**12 B7**	55 0N	7 23W
Derry →	**15 C9**	52 43N	6 35W
Derrynasaggart Mts.	**14 E4**	51 58N	9 15W
Derwent →, *Derby*	**7 G6**	52 53N	1 17W
Derwent →, *N. Yorks.*	**7 E7**	53 45N	0 57W
Desborough	**9 B7**	52 27N	0 50W
Deveron →	**3 G12**	57 40N	2 31W
Devilsbit	**14 C7**	52 50N	7 58W
Devizes	**8 D5**	51 21N	2 0W
Devon □	**8 F6**	50 50N	3 40W
Devonport	**11 G5**	50 23N	4 11W
Dewsbury	**7 E5**	53 42N	1 38W
Didcot	**8 C6**	51 36N	1 14W
Dinas Hd.	**10 C4**	52 2N	4 56W
Dingle	**14 D2**	52 9N	10 17W
Dingle B.	**14 D2**	52 3N	10 20W
Dingwall	**3 G9**	57 36N	4 26W
Dinnington	**7 F6**	53 21N	1 12W
Diss	**9 B11**	52 23N	1 6 E
Ditchling Beacon	**9 E8**	50 49N	0 7W
Dizzard Pt.	**11 F4**	50 46N	4 38W
Dodman Pt.	**11 G4**	50 13N	4 49W
Dolgellau	**10 B6**	52 44N	3 53W
Dolgelley = Dolgellau	**10 B6**	52 44N	3 53W
Dollar	**5 B8**	56 9N	3 41W
Don →, *Gramp.*	**3 H13**	57 14N	2 5W
Don →, *S. Yorks.*	**7 E7**	53 41N	0 51W
Donaghadee	**13 B10**	54 38N	5 32W
Doncaster	**7 E6**	53 31N	1 9W
Donegal	**12 B5**	54 39N	8 8W
Donegal □	**12 B6**	54 53N	8 0W
Donegal B.	**12 B4**	54 30N	8 35W
Donegal Harbour	**12 B5**	54 35N	8 15W
Donna Nook	**7 F9**	53 29N	0 9 E
Dooega Hd.	**12 D1**	53 54N	10 3W
Doon, L.	**4 D7**	55 15N	4 22W
Dorchester	**11 F4**	50 42N	2 28W
Dorking	**9 D8**	51 14N	0 20W
Dornoch	**3 G9**	57 52N	4 5W
Dornoch Firth	**3 G10**	57 52N	4 0W
Dorridge	**8 B5**	52 22N	1 45W
Dorset □	**8 E4**	50 48N	2 25W
Douglas	**13 C13**	54 9N	4 29W
Doulus Hd.	**14 E2**	51 57N	10 19W
Doune	**4 B7**	56 12N	4 3W
Dounreay	**3 E10**	58 34N	3 44W
Dove →	**7 G5**	52 51N	1 36W
Dover	**9 D11**	51 7N	1 19 E
Dovey = Dyfi →	**10 B6**	52 32N	4 0W
Down □	**13 C10**	54 20N	5 47W
Downham Market	**9 A9**	52 36N	0 22 E
Downpatrick	**13 C10**	54 20N	5 43W
Downpatrick Hd.	**12 C3**	54 20N	9 21W
Driffield	**7 D8**	54 1N	0 25W
Drogheda	**13 D9**	53 45N	6 20W
Droichead Atha = Drogheda	**13 D9**	53 45N	6 20W
Droichead Nua	**15 B9**	53 11N	6 50W
Droitwich	**8 B4**	52 16N	2 10W
Dromore	**12 B7**	54 31N	7 28W
Dronfield	**7 F6**	53 18N	1 29W
Druridge B.	**6 B5**	55 16N	1 32W
Drygarn Fawr	**10 C6**	52 13N	3 39W
Dublin	**15 B10**	53 20N	6 18W
Dublin □	**15 B10**	53 24N	6 20W
Dudley	**8 A4**	52 30N	2 5W
Dufftown	**3 H11**	57 26N	3 9W
Dukinfield	**7 F4**	53 29N	2 5W
Dulas B.	**10 A5**	53 22N	4 16W
Dumbarton	**4 C6**	55 58N	4 35W
Dumfries	**5 D8**	55 4N	3 37W
Dumfries & Galloway □	**5 D8**	55 5N	4 0W
Dún Dealgan = Dundalk	**13 C9**	54 1N	6 25W
Dun Laoghaire	**15 B10**	53 17N	6 9W
Dunaff Hd.	**12 A6**	55 18N	7 30W
Dunany Pt.	**13 D9**	53 51N	6 15W
Dunbar	**5 C10**	56 0N	2 32W
Dunblane	**5 B8**	56 10N	3 58W
Duncansby Hd.	**3 E12**	58 39N	3 0W
Dundalk	**13 C9**	54 1N	6 25W
Dundalk B.	**13 D9**	53 55N	6 15W
Dundee	**5 B10**	56 29N	3 0W
Dundrum	**13 C10**	54 17N	5 50W
Dunfermline	**5 B9**	56 5N	3 28W
Dungannon	**13 B8**	54 30N	6 47W
Dungarvan	**15 D7**	52 6N	7 40W
Dungarvan Harbour	**15 D7**	52 5N	7 35W
Dungeness	**9 E10**	50 54N	0 59 E
Dunipace	**5 B8**	56 4N	3 55W
Dunkeld	**5 A8**	56 34N	3 36W
Dunkery Beacon	**8 D1**	51 15N	3 37W
Dúnleary = Dun Laoghaire	**15 B10**	53 17N	6 9W
Dunmanway	**14 E4**	51 43N	9 8W
Dunnet B.	**3 E11**	58 37N	3 23W
Dunoon	**4 C6**	55 57N	4 56W
Duns	**5 C11**	55 47N	2 20W
Dunstable	**9 C7**	51 53N	0 31W
Dunster	**8 D2**	51 11N	3 28W
Dunvegan Hd.	**2 G4**	57 30N	6 42W
Durham	**6 C5**	54 47N	1 34W
Durham □	**6 C5**	54 42N	1 45W
Durlston Hd.	**8 E5**	50 35N	1 58W
Durness	**3 E8**	58 34N	4 45W
Dursley	**8 C4**	51 41N	2 21W
Dury Voe	**2 B15**	60 20N	1 8W
Dyce	**3 H13**	57 12N	2 11W
Dyfed □	**10 D5**	52 0N	4 30W
Dyfi →	**10 B6**	52 32N	4 0W
Dymchurch	**9 D11**	51 2N	1 0 E

E

Ealing	**9 C8**	51 30N	0 19W
Earadale Pt.	**4 D4**	55 24N	5 50W
Earby	**7 E4**	53 55N	2 8W
Earl Shilton	**7 G6**	52 35N	1 20W
Earlsferry	**5 B10**	56 11N	2 50W
Earn →	**5 B9**	56 20N	3 19W
Earn, L.	**4 B7**	56 23N	4 14W
Easington	**6 C6**	54 50N	1 24W
Easington Colliery	**6 C6**	54 49N	1 19W
East Cowes	**8 E6**	50 45N	1 17W
East Dereham	**9 A10**	52 40N	0 57 E
East Grinstead	**9 D9**	51 8N	0 0 E
East Kilbride	**4 C7**	55 46N	4 10W
East Linton	**5 C10**	56 0N	2 40W
East Retford = Retford	**7 F7**	53 19N	0 55W
East Sussex □	**9 E9**	51 0N	0 20 E
East Wittering	**9 E7**	50 46N	0 53W
Eastbourne	**9 E9**	50 46N	0 18 E
Easter Ross	**3 G8**	57 50N	4 35W
Eastleigh	**8 E6**	50 58N	1 21W
Eastwood	**7 F6**	53 2N	1 17W
Eaval	**2 G3**	57 33N	7 12W
Ebbw Vale	**10 D7**	51 47N	3 12W
Eccleshall	**7 G4**	52 52N	2 14W
Eckington	**7 F6**	53 19N	1 21W
Eday Sd.	**3 D12**	59 12N	2 45W
Eddrachillis B.	**2 F7**	58 16N	5 10W
Eddystone	**11 G5**	50 11N	4 16W
Eden →	**6 C2**	54 57N	3 2W
Edenbridge	**9 D9**	51 12N	0 4 E
Edenderry	**15 B8**	53 21N	7 3W
Edge Hill	**8 B6**	52 7N	1 28W
Edinburgh	**5 C9**	55 57N	3 12W
Egham	**9 D7**	51 25N	0 33W
Egremont	**6 D1**	54 28N	3 33W
Eigg	**2 J5**	56 54N	6 10W
Eil, L.	**2 J7**	56 50N	5 15W
Eishort, L.	**2 H5**	57 9N	6 0W
Elan →	**10 C6**	52 17N	3 30W
Elan Valley Reservoirs	**10 C6**	52 12N	3 42W
Elgin	**3 G11**	57 39N	3 20W
Elie	**5 B10**	56 11N	2 50W
Elland	**7 E5**	53 41N	1 49W
Ellesmere Port	**7 F3**	53 17N	2 55W
Ellon	**3 H13**	57 21N	2 5W
Ely	**9 B9**	52 24N	0 16 E
Emsworth	**9 E7**	50 51N	0 56W
Enard B.	**2 F7**	58 5N	5 20W
Enfield	**9 C8**	51 39N	0 4W
Ennell, L.	**12 E7**	53 29N	7 25W
Ennis	**14 C5**	52 51N	8 59W
Enniscorthy	**15 D9**	52 30N	6 35W
Enniskillen	**12 C6**	54 20N	7 40W
Ennistimon	**14 C4**	52 56N	9 18W
Eport, L.	**2 G3**	57 33N	7 10W
Epping	**9 C9**	51 42N	0 8 E
Epsom	**9 D8**	51 19N	0 16W
Eriboll, L.	**3 F8**	58 28N	4 41W
Ericht, L.	**3 J9**	56 50N	4 25W
Eriskay, Sd. of	**2 H3**	57 5N	7 20W
Erisort L.	**2 F4**	58 5N	6 30W
Erne →	**12 C5**	54 30N	8 16W
Erne, Lower L.	**12 C6**	54 26N	7 46W
Erne, Upper L.	**12 C7**	54 14N	7 22W
Errigal	**12 A5**	55 2N	8 8W
Erris Hd.	**12 C2**	54 19N	10 0W
Erskine	**4 C7**	55 52N	4 27W
Esha Ness	**2 A14**	60 30N	1 36W
Esher	**9 D8**	51 21N	0 22W
Esk →	**5 E9**	54 58N	3 4W
Eskdale	**5 D9**	55 12N	3 4W
Essex □	**9 C9**	51 55N	0 30 E
Eston	**6 C6**	54 33N	1 6W
Etive, L.	**4 A5**	56 30N	5 12W
Ettrick Water →	**5 C10**	55 31N	2 55W
Evesham	**8 B5**	52 6N	1 57W
Ewe, L.	**2 G6**	57 49N	5 38W
Ewell	**9 D8**	51 20N	0 15W
Exe →	**11 F7**	50 38N	3 27W
Exeter	**11 F6**	50 43N	3 31W
Exmoor	**11 E6**	51 10N	3 59W
Exmouth	**11 F7**	50 37N	3 26W
Eye, *Cambs.*	**7 G8**	52 36N	0 11W
Eye, *Suffolk*	**9 B11**	52 19N	1 9 E
Eye Pen.	**2 F5**	58 13N	6 10W
Eyemouth	**5 C11**	55 53N	2 5W
Eynhallow Sd.	**3 D11**	59 8N	3 7W
Eynort, L.	**2 H3**	57 13N	7 18W

F

Fair Hd.	**13 A9**	55 14N	6 10W
Fair Isle	**2 C14**	59 32N	1 36W
Fairford	**8 C5**	51 42N	1 48W
Fakenham	**9 A10**	52 50N	0 51 E
Faldingworth	**7 F8**	53 21N	0 22W
Falkirk	**5 B8**	56 1N	3 47W
Falkland	**5 B9**	56 15N	3 13W
Falmouth	**11 G3**	50 9N	5 5W
Fanad Hd.	**12 A6**	55 17N	7 40W
Faraid Hd.	**3 E8**	58 35N	4 48W
Fareham	**8 E6**	50 52N	1 11W
Faringdon	**8 C5**	51 39N	1 34W
Farnborough	**9 D7**	51 17N	0 46W
Farne Is.	**6 A5**	55 38N	1 37W
Farnham	**9 D7**	51 13N	0 49W
Farnworth	**7 E4**	53 33N	2 24W
Fauldhouse	**5 C8**	55 50N	3 44W
Faversham	**9 D10**	51 18N	0 54 E
Fawley	**8 E6**	50 49N	1 20W
Feale →	**14 D3**	52 26N	9 40W
Featherbed Moss	**7 E5**	53 31N	1 56W
Felixstowe	**9 C11**	51 58N	1 22 E
Felton	**6 B5**	55 18N	1 42W
Fergus →	**14 C5**	52 45N	9 0W
Fermanagh □	**12 C6**	54 21N	7 40W
Fermoy	**14 D6**	52 4N	8 18W
Ferndown	**8 E5**	50 48N	1 53W
Ferryhill	**6 C5**	54 42N	1 32W
Fethaland, Pt. of	**2 A15**	60 39N	1 20W
Ffestiniog	**10 B6**	52 58N	3 56W
Fife □	**5 B9**	56 13N	3 2W
Fife Ness	**5 B10**	56 17N	2 35W
Filey	**6 D8**	54 13N	0 18W
Filton	**8 C3**	51 30N	2 34W
Findhorn →	**3 G10**	57 38N	3 38W
Findochty	**3 G12**	57 42N	2 53W
Finn →	**12 B6**	54 50N	7 55W
Fionn L.	**2 G7**	57 46N	5 30W
Fishguard	**10 D4**	51 59N	4 59W
Fitful Hd.	**2 C15**	59 54N	1 20W
Five Sisters	**2 H7**	57 11N	5 21W
Flamborough Hd.	**6 D8**	54 8N	0 4W
Fleet	**9 D7**	51 16N	0 50W
Fleet, L.	**3 G9**	57 57N	4 2W
Fleetwood	**7 E2**	53 55N	3 1W
Flint	**10 A7**	53 15N	3 7W
Flitwick	**9 C8**	51 59N	0 30W
Flodden	**6 A4**	55 37N	2 8W
Foinaven	**3 F8**	58 30N	4 53W
Folkestone	**9 D11**	51 5N	1 11 E
Fordingbridge	**8 E5**	50 56N	1 48W
Foreland Pt.	**11 E6**	51 14N	3 47W
Forfar	**5 A10**	56 40N	2 53W
Formartine	**3 H13**	57 20N	2 15W
Formby	**7 E2**	53 33N	3 3W
Forres	**3 G10**	57 37N	3 38W
Fort Augustus	**3 H8**	57 9N	4 40W
Fort William	**2 J7**	56 48N	5 8W
Forth	**5 B8**	56 8N	3 48W
Forth, Firth of	**5 B10**	56 5N	2 55W
Fortrose	**3 G9**	57 35N	4 10W
Fortuneswell	**11 F9**	50 33N	2 26W
Foulness I.	**9 C10**	51 36N	0 55 E
Fowey	**11 G4**	50 20N	4 39W
Fowey →	**11 G4**	50 20N	4 39W
Foyle →	**13 B7**	55 0N	7 13W
Foyle, L.	**13 A7**	55 6N	7 8W
Foynes	**14 C4**	52 37N	9 5W
Framlingham	**9 B11**	52 14N	1 20 E
Fraserburgh	**3 G13**	57 41N	2 3W
Frimley	**9 D7**	51 18N	0 43W
Frinton-on-Sea	**9 C11**	51 50N	1 16 E
Frodsham	**7 F3**	53 17N	2 45W
Frome	**8 D4**	51 16N	2 17W
Frome →	**8 E4**	50 44N	2 5W
Frower Pt.	**14 E6**	51 40N	8 30W
Fulwood	**7 E3**	53 47N	2 41W
Furness	**6 D2**	54 14N	3 8W
Fyne, L.	**4 C5**	56 0N	5 20W

G

Gaillimh = Galway	**14 B4**	53 16N	9 4W
Gainsborough	**7 F7**	53 23N	0 46W
Gairloch	**2 G6**	57 42N	5 40W
Gairloch, L.	**2 G6**	57 43N	5 45W
Galashiels	**5 C10**	55 37N	2 50W
Gallan Hd.	**2 F3**	58 14N	7 2W
Galley Hd.	**14 E5**	51 32N	8 56W
Galloway	**4 D7**	55 1N	4 25W
Galloway, Mull of	**4 E6**	54 38N	4 50W
Galston	**4 C7**	55 36N	4 22W
Galty Mts.	**14 D6**	52 22N	8 10W
Galtymore	**14 D6**	52 22N	8 12W
Galway	**14 B4**	53 16N	9 4W
Galway □	**14 B4**	53 16N	9 3W
Galway B.	**14 B4**	53 10N	9 20W
Gamlingay	**9 B8**	52 9N	0 11W
Gara, L.	**12 D5**	53 57N	8 26W
Garforth	**7 E6**	53 48N	1 22W
Garioch	**3 H12**	57 18N	2 40W
Garron Pt.	**13 A10**	55 3N	6 0W
Garry, L.	**3 H8**	57 5N	4 52W
Garstang	**7 E3**	53 53N	2 47W
Gatehouse of Fleet	**4 E7**	54 53N	4 10W
Gateshead	**6 C5**	54 57N	1 37W
Gatley	**7 F4**	53 25N	2 15W
Gerrans B.	**11 G4**	50 12N	4 57W
Gerrards Cross	**9 C7**	51 35N	0 32W
Giants Causeway	**13 A8**	55 15N	6 30W
Gibraltar Pt.	**7 F9**	53 6N	0 20 E
Gill, L.	**12 C5**	54 15N	8 25W
Gillingham, *Dorset*	**8 D4**	51 2N	2 15W
Gillingham, *Kent*	**9 D10**	51 23N	0 34 E
Girdle Ness	**3 H13**	57 9N	2 2W
Girvan	**4 D6**	55 15N	4 50W
Gisborough Moor	**6 D7**	54 30N	1 2W
Glanaruddery Mts.	**14 D4**	52 20N	9 27W
Glandore Harbour	**14 E4**	51 33N	9 8W
Glas Maol	**3 J11**	56 52N	3 20W
Glasgow	**4 C7**	55 52N	4 14W
Glastonbury	**8 D3**	51 9N	2 42W
Glen Affric	**3 H8**	57 15N	5 0W
Glen B.	**12 B4**	54 43N	8 45W
Glen Garry, *Highl.*	**2 H7**	57 3N	5 7W
Glen Garry, *Tayside*	**3 J9**	56 47N	4 5W
Glen Mor	**3 H8**	57 12N	4 37W
Glen Shiel	**2 H7**	57 8N	5 20W
Glencoe	**4 A5**	56 40N	5 6W
Gleneagles	**5 B8**	56 16N	3 44W
Glengad Hd.	**13 A7**	55 19N	7 11W
Glengarriff	**14 E3**	51 45N	9 33W
Glennamaddy	**12 D4**	53 37N	8 33W
Glenrothes	**5 B9**	56 12N	3 11W
Glenties	**12 B5**	54 48N	8 18W
Glossop	**7 F5**	53 27N	1 56W
Gloucester	**8 C4**	51 52N	2 15W
Gloucestershire □	**8 C4**	51 44N	2 10W
Goat Fell	**4 C5**	55 37N	5 11W
Godalming	**9 D7**	51 12N	0 37W
Goil, L.	**4 B6**	56 8N	4 52W
Golden Vale	**14 C6**	52 33N	8 17W
Golspie	**3 G10**	57 58N	3 58W
Goodwick	**10 C3**	52 1N	5 0W
Goole	**7 E7**	53 42N	0 52W
Gorebridge	**5 C9**	55 51N	3 2W
Gorey	**15 C10**	52 41N	6 18W
Goring-by-Sea	**9 E8**	50 49N	0 26W
Gorleston	**9 A12**	52 35N	1 44 E
Gorseinon	**10 D5**	51 40N	4 2W
Gort	**14 B5**	53 4N	8 50W
Gosport	**8 E6**	50 48N	1 8W
Gourock	**4 C6**	55 58N	4 49W
Gower	**11 D5**	51 35N	4 10W
Grafham Water	**9 B8**	52 18N	0 17W
Gragareth	**6 D4**	54 12N	2 29W
Grampian □	**3 H12**	57 20N	3 0W
Grampian Highlands = Grampian Mts.	**3 J10**	56 50N	4 0W
Grampian Mts.	**3 J10**	56 50N	4 0W
Granard	**12 D6**	53 47N	7 30W
Grand Union Canal	**9 B7**	52 5N	0 52W
Grange-over-Sands	**6 D3**	54 12N	2 55W
Grangemouth	**5 B8**	56 1N	3 43W
Grantham	**7 G7**	52 55N	0 39W
Grantown-on-Spey	**3 H10**	57 19N	3 36W
Grassington	**6 D5**	54 5N	2 0W
Gravesend	**9 D9**	51 25N	0 22 E
Grays	**9 D9**	51 28N	0 23 E
Great Blasket I.	**14 D1**	52 5N	10 30W
Great Driffield = Driffield	**7 D8**	54 1N	0 25W
Great Dunmow	**9 C9**	51 52N	0 22 E
Great Harwood	**7 E4**	53 47N	2 25W
Great I.	**14 E6**	51 52N	8 15W
Great Malvern	**8 B4**	52 7N	2 19W
Great Ormes Hd.	**10 A6**	53 20N	3 52W
Great Ouse →	**9 A9**	52 47N	0 22 E
Great Shunner Fell	**6 D4**	54 22N	2 16W
Great Stour = Stour →	**9 D11**	51 15N	1 20 E
Great Sugar Loaf	**15 B10**	53 10N	6 10W
Great Torrington	**11 F5**	50 57N	4 9W
Great Whernside	**6 D5**	54 9N	1 59W
Great Yarmouth	**9 A12**	52 40N	1 45 E
Greater London □	**9 C8**	51 30N	0 5W
Greater Manchester □	**7 E4**	53 30N	2 15W
Green Lowther	**5 D8**	55 22N	3 44W
Greenholm	**4 C7**	55 40N	4 20W
Greenock	**4 C6**	55 57N	4 46W
Greenore	**13 C9**	54 2N	6 8W
Greenore Pt.	**15 D10**	52 15N	6 20W
Greenstone Pt.	**2 G6**	57 55N	5 38W
Greenwich	**9 D9**	51 28N	0 0 E
Greian Hd.	**2 H2**	57 1N	7 30W
Gretna	**5 E9**	54 59N	3 4W
Gretna Green	**5 E9**	55 0N	3 3W
Greystones	**15 B10**	53 9N	6 4W
Griminish Pt.	**2 G3**	57 40N	7 29W
Grimsby	**7 E8**	53 35N	0 5W
Gruinard B.	**2 G6**	57 56N	5 35W
Gruinart, L.	**4 C3**	55 50N	6 20W
Gruting Voe	**2 B14**	60 12N	1 32W
Guernsey	**11 J8**	49 30N	2 35W
Guildford	**9 D7**	51 14N	0 34W
Guisborough	**6 C6**	54 32N	1 2W
Guiseley	**7 E5**	53 52N	1 43W
Gullane	**5 B10**	56 2N	2 50W
Gurnard's Hd.	**11 G2**	50 12N	5 37W
Gweebarra B.	**12 B5**	54 52N	8 21W
Gweedore	**12 A5**	55 4N	8 15W
Gwent □	**8 D8**	51 45N	2 55W
Gwynedd □	**10 A6**	53 0N	4 0W

H

Hackley Hd.	**3 H14**	57 19N	1 58W
Hackney	**9 C8**	51 33N	0 2W
Haddington	**5 C10**	55 57N	2 48W
Hadleigh, *Essex*	**9 C10**	51 33N	0 37 E
Hadleigh, *Suffolk*	**9 B10**	52 3N	0 58 E
Hags Hd.	**14 C4**	52 57N	9 28W
Hailsham	**9 E9**	50 52N	0 17 E
Halberry Hd.	**3 F11**	58 20N	3 11W
Halesowen	**8 B4**	52 27N	2 2W
Halesworth	**9 B12**	52 21N	1 31 E
Halifax	**7 E5**	53 43N	1 51W
Halkirk	**3 E11**	58 30N	3 30W
Halstead	**9 C10**	51 59N	0 39 E
Haltwhistle	**6 C4**	54 58N	2 27W
Hambleton Hills	**6 D6**	54 17N	1 12W
Hamilton	**4 C7**	55 47N	4 2W
Hammersmith and Fulham	**9 D8**	51 30N	0 15W
Hampshire □	**8 D6**	51 3N	1 20W
Hampshire Downs	**8 D6**	51 10N	1 10W
Handa I.	**2 F7**	58 23N	5 10W
Haringey	**9 C8**	51 35N	0 7W
Harlech	**10 B5**	52 52N	4 7W
Harleston	**9 B11**	52 25N	1 18 E
Harlow	**9 C9**	51 47N	0 9 E
Harpenden	**9 C8**	51 48N	0 20W
Harris	**2 G4**	57 50N	6 55W
Harris, Sd. of	**2 G3**	57 44N	7 6W
Harrogate	**7 E5**	53 59N	1 32W
Harrow	**9 C8**	51 35N	0 15W
Hartland Pt.	**11 E4**	51 2N	4 32W
Hartlepool	**6 C6**	54 42N	1 11W
Harwich	**9 C11**	51 56N	1 18 E
Haslemere	**9 D7**	51 5N	0 41W
Haslingden	**7 E4**	53 43N	2 20W
Hastings	**9 E10**	50 51N	0 36 E
Hatfield, *Herts.*	**9 C8**	51 46N	0 11W
Hatfield, *S. Yorks.*	**7 E7**	53 34N	0 59W
Havant	**9 E7**	50 51N	0 59W
Haverfordwest	**10 D4**	51 48N	4 59W
Haverhill	**9 B9**	52 6N	0 27 E
Havering	**9 C9**	51 33N	0 20 E
Haweswater	**6 C3**	54 32N	2 48W
Hawick	**5 D10**	55 25N	2 48W
Hawkhurst	**9 D10**	51 2N	0 31 E
Hay-on-Wye	**10 C7**	52 4N	3 9W
Hayle	**11 G3**	50 12N	5 25W
Haywards Heath	**9 D8**	51 1N	0 6W
Hazel Grove	**7 F4**	53 23N	2 7W
Healaval Bheag	**2 H4**	57 24N	6 41W
Heanor	**7 F6**	53 1N	1 20W
Heathfield	**9 E9**	50 58N	0 18 E
Heaval	**2 J3**	56 58N	7 30W
Hebburn	**6 C5**	54 59N	1 30W
Hebden Bridge	**7 E5**	53 45N	2 0W
Hecla	**2 H3**	57 18N	7 15W
Hednesford	**7 G5**	52 43N	2 0W
Hedon	**7 E8**	53 44N	0 11W
Helensburgh	**4 B6**	56 1N	4 44W
Helli Ness	**2 B15**	60 3N	1 10W
Helmsdale	**3 F10**	58 8N	3 43W
Helmsley	**6 D6**	54 15N	1 2W
Helston	**11 G3**	50 7N	5 17W
Helvellyn	**6 C2**	54 31N	3 1W
Helvick Hd.	**15 D7**	52 3N	7 33W
Hemel Hempstead	**9 C8**	51 45N	0 28W
Hemsworth	**7 E6**	53 37N	1 21W
Henfield	**9 E8**	50 56N	0 17W
Hengoed	**10 D7**	51 39N	3 14W
Henley-on-Thames	**9 C7**	51 32N	0 53W
Hereford	**8 B3**	52 4N	2 42W
Hereford and Worcester □	**8 B3**	52 10N	2 30W
Herma Ness	**2 A16**	60 50N	0 54W
Herne Bay	**9 D11**	51 22N	1 8 E
Hertford	**9 C8**	51 47N	0 4W
Hertfordshire □	**9 C8**	51 51N	0 5W
Hessle	**7 E8**	53 44N	0 28W
Heswall	**7 F2**	53 19N	3 6W
Hetton-le-Hole	**6 C6**	54 49N	1 26W
Hexham	**6 C4**	54 58N	2 7W
Heysham	**6 D3**	54 5N	2 53W
Heywood	**7 E4**	53 35N	2 13W
High Pike	**6 C2**	54 43N	3 4W
High Willhays	**11 F6**	50 41N	3 59W
High Wycombe	**9 C7**	51 37N	0 45W
Higham Ferrers	**9 B7**	52 18N	0 36W
Highbridge	**8 D3**	51 13N	2 59W
Highland □	**3 H7**	57 30N	5 0W
Highworth	**8 C5**	51 38N	1 42W
Hillingdon	**9 C8**	51 33N	0 29W
Hilpsford Pt.	**6 D2**	54 4N	3 12W
Hinckley	**7 G6**	52 33N	1 21W
Hindley	**7 E3**	53 32N	2 35W
Hinkley Pt.	**8 D2**	51 13N	3 9W
Hitchin	**9 C8**	51 57N	0 16W
Hockley	**9 C10**	51 35N	0 39 E
Hoddesdon	**9 C8**	51 45N	0 1W
Hog's Back	**9 D7**	51 13N	0 40W
Hogs Hd.	**14 E2**	51 46N	10 13W
Holbeach	**7 G9**	52 48N	0 1 E
Holborn Hd.	**3 E10**	58 37N	3 30W
Holderness	**7 E8**	53 45N	0 5W
Holmfirth	**7 E5**	53 34N	1 48W
Holsworthy	**11 F5**	50 48N	4 21W
Holt	**9 A11**	52 55N	1 4 E
Holy I., *Gwynedd*	**10 A4**	53 17N	4 37W
Holy I., *Northumb.*	**6 A5**	55 42N	1 48W
Holyhead	**10 A4**	53 18N	4 38W
Holywell	**10 A7**	53 16N	3 14W
Honiton	**11 F7**	50 48N	3 11W
Hook	**9 D7**	51 17N	0 55W
Hook Hd.	**15 D9**	52 8N	6 57W
Horden	**6 C6**	54 45N	1 17W
Horley	**9 D8**	51 10N	0 10W
Horn Hd.	**12 A6**	55 13N	8 0W
Horncastle	**7 F8**	53 13N	0 8W
Horndean	**9 E6**	50 50N	1 0W
Hornsea	**7 E8**	53 55N	0 10W
Horsforth	**7 E5**	53 50N	1 39W
Horsham	**9 D8**	51 4N	0 20W
Horwich	**7 E3**	53 37N	2 33W
Houghton-le-Spring	**6 C6**	54 51N	1 28W
Houghton Regis	**9 C7**	51 54N	0 32W
Hounslow	**9 D8**	51 29N	0 20W
Hourn, L.	**2 H6**	57 7N	5 35W
Hove	**9 E8**	50 50N	0 10W
Howden	**7 E7**	53 45N	0 52W
Howth Hd.	**15 B10**	53 21N	6 3W
Hoy Sd.	**3 E11**	58 57N	3 20W
Hoylake	**7 F2**	53 24N	3 11W
Hucknall	**7 F6**	53 3N	1 12W
Huddersfield	**7 E5**	53 38N	1 49W
Hull = Kingston upon Hull	**7 E8**	53 45N	0 20W
Humber →	**7 E8**	53 40N	0 10W

37
Naas · Slieve Beagh

N

Naas 15 B9 53 12N 6 40W
Nagles Mts. 14 D5 52 8N 8 30W
Nailsea 8 D3 51 25N 2 44W
Nailsworth 8 C4 51 41N 2 12W
Nairn 3 G10 57 35N 3 54W
Nairn → 3 G10 57 32N 3 58W
Nantwich 7 F3 53 5N 2 31W
Narberth 10 D4 51 48N 4 45W
Narrows 2 H5 57 20N 6 5W
Nash Pt. 8 E6 51 24N 3 34W
Navan = An Uaimh 13 D8 53 39N 6 40W
Naver → 3 E9 58 34N 4 15W
Neagh, L. 13 B9 54 35N 6 25W
Neath 10 D6 51 39N 3 49W
Neath → 10 D6 51 38N 3 35W
Neist Pt. 2 H4 57 24N 6 48W
Nelson 7 E4 53 50N 2 14W
Nenagh 14 C6 52 52N 8 11W
Nenagh → 14 C6 52 56N 8 16W
Nene → 9 A9 52 38N 0 13 E
Nephin 12 C3 54 1N 9 21W
Nephin Beg Range 12 D2 54 0N 9 40W
Ness 2 F5 58 27N 6 20W
Ness, L. 3 H8 57 15N 4 30W
Neston 7 F2 53 17N 3 3W
Nevis, L. 2 J6 57 0N 5 43W
New Alresford 8 D6 51 6N 1 10W
New Bedford R. → 9 A9 52 34N 0 20 E
New Forest 8 E5 50 53N 1 40W
New Galloway 4 D7 55 4N 4 10W
New Holland 7 E8 53 42N 0 22W
New Mills 7 F5 53 22N 2 0W
New Milton 8 E5 50 45N 1 40W
New Quay 10 C5 52 13N 4 21W
New Radnor 10 C7 52 15N 3 10W
New Romney 9 E10 50 59N 0 57 E
New Ross 15 D9 52 24N 6 58W
New Rossington 7 F6 53 30N 1 4W
New Scone 5 B9 56 25N 3 26W
New Tredegar 10 D7 51 43N 3 15W
Newark-on-Trent 7 F7 53 6N 0 48W
Newbiggin-by-the-Sea 6 B5 55 12N 1 31W
Newbridge = Droichead Nua 15 B9 53 11N 6 50W
Newburgh 5 B9 56 21N 3 15W
Newburn 6 C5 54 57N 1 45W
Newbury 8 D6 51 24N 1 19W
Newcastle 13 C10 54 13N 5 54W
Newcastle Emlyn 10 C5 52 2N 4 29W
Newcastle-under-Lyme 7 F4 53 2N 2 15W
Newcastle-upon-Tyne 6 C5 54 59N 1 37W
Newcastle West 14 D4 52 27N 9 3W
Newham 9 C9 51 31N 0 2 E
Newhaven 9 E9 50 47N 0 4 E
Newlyn 11 G2 50 6N 5 33W
Newmarket, *Ireland* 14 D5 52 13N 9 0W
Newmarket, *Suffolk* 9 B9 52 15N 0 23 E
Newmilns 4 C7 55 36N 4 20W
Newport, *Mayo* 12 D2 53 50N 9 31W
Newport, *Gwent* 11 D8 51 35N 3 0W
Newport, *I. of W.* 8 E6 50 42N 1 18W
Newport, *Shrops.* 7 G4 52 47N 2 22W
Newport B. 12 D2 53 52N 9 38W
Newport-on-Tay 5 B10 56 27N 2 56W
Newport Pagnell 9 B7 52 5N 0 42W
Newquay 11 G3 50 24N 5 6W
Newry 13 C9 54 10N 6 20W
Newton Abbot 11 F6 50 32N 3 37W
Newton Aycliffe 6 C5 54 36N 1 33W
Newton le Willows 7 F3 53 28N 2 40W
Newton Stewart 4 E6 54 57N 4 30W
Newtongrange 5 C9 55 52N 3 4W
Newtonmore 3 H9 57 4N 4 7W
Newtown 10 B7 52 31N 3 19W
Newtownabbey 13 B10 54 40N 5 55W
Newtownards 13 B10 54 37N 5 40W
Newtownbarry = Bunclody 15 C9 52 40N 6 40W
Newtownstewart 12 B7 54 43N 7 22W
Neyland 10 D4 51 43N 4 58W
Nidd → 7 E6 53 58N 1 28W
Nidderdale 6 D5 54 5N 1 46W
Nigg B. 3 G9 57 41N 4 5W
Nith → 5 D8 55 20N 3 5W
Nithsdale 5 D8 55 14N 3 50W
Nore → 15 D9 52 24N 6 58W
Norfolk □ 9 A11 52 39N 1 0 E
Norfolk Broads Nat. Park 9 A11 52 45N 1 30 E
Normanton 7 E6 53 41N 1 26W
North Berwick 5 B10 56 4N 2 44W
North Channel 4 D4 55 0N 5 30W
North Dorset Downs 8 E3 50 50N 2 30W
North Downs 9 D9 51 17N 0 30 E
North Esk → 5 A11 56 44N 2 25W
North Foreland 9 D11 51 22N 1 28 E
North Harris 2 G4 58 0N 6 55W
North Minch 2 F6 58 5N 5 55W
North Roe 2 A15 60 40N 1 22W
North Sd. 14 B3 53 10N 9 48W
North Tyne → 6 C4 54 59N 2 7W
North Uist 2 G3 57 40N 7 15W
North Walsham 9 A11 52 49N 1 22 E
North West Highlands 2 G8 57 35N 5 0W
North York Moors 6 D7 54 25N 0 50W
North Yorkshire □ 6 D6 54 15N 1 25W
Northallerton 6 D6 54 20N 1 26W
Northampton 9 B7 52 14N 0 54W
Northamptonshire □ 9 B7 52 16N 0 55W
Northern Ireland □ 13 B8 54 45N 7 0W
Northfleet 9 D9 51 26N 0 20 E
Northumberland □ 6 B5 55 12N 2 0W
Northwich 7 F3 53 16N 2 31W
Norton 6 D7 54 9N 0 48W
Norwich 9 A11 52 38N 1 17 E
Noss Hd. 3 F11 58 29N 3 4W
Nottingham 7 G6 52 57N 1 10W
Nottinghamshire □ 7 F7 53 10N 1 0W
Noup Hd. 3 D11 59 20N 3 2W
Nowen Hill 14 E4 51 42N 9 15W
Nuneaton 8 A6 52 32N 1 29W

O

Oa, Mull of 4 C3 55 35N 6 20W
Oadby 7 G6 52 37N 1 7W
Oakengates 7 G4 52 42N 2 29W
Oakham 7 G7 52 40N 0 43W
Oban 4 B5 56 25N 5 30W
Ochil Hills 5 B8 56 14N 3 40W
Offaly □ 15 B7 53 15N 7 30W
Okehampton 11 F5 50 44N 4 1W
Old Bedford R. → 9 A9 52 36N 0 20 E
Old Fletton 7 G8 52 34N 0 13W
Old Man of Hoy 3 E11 58 53N 3 25W
Oldbury 8 C3 51 38N 2 30W
Oldcastle 13 D7 53 46N 7 10W
Oldham 7 E4 53 33N 2 8W
Oldmeldrum 3 H13 57 20N 2 19W
Olney 9 B7 52 9N 0 42W
Omagh 12 B7 54 36N 7 20W
Orford Ness 9 B12 52 6N 1 31 E
Orkney □ 3 D11 59 0N 3 0W
Ormskirk 7 E3 53 35N 2 53W
Oronsay, Passage of 4 C3 56 0N 6 10W
Orwell → 9 B11 52 2N 1 12 E
Ossett 7 E5 53 40N 1 35W
Oswaldtwistle 7 E4 53 44N 2 27W
Oswestry 7 G2 52 52N 3 3W
Otley 7 E5 53 54N 1 41W
Ottery St. Mary 11 F7 50 45N 3 16W
Oughter, L. 12 C7 54 2N 7 30W
Oughterard 14 B4 53 26N 9 20W
Oundle 9 B8 52 28N 0 28W
Ouse → 7 E7 53 33N 0 44W
Outer Hebrides 2 J2 57 30N 7 40W
Owel, L. 12 D7 53 34N 7 24W
Oxford 8 C6 51 45N 1 15W
Oxfordshire □ 8 C6 51 45N 1 15W
Oxted 9 D9 51 14N 0 0 E
Oxwich Pt. 11 D5 51 33N 4 8W
Oykel → 3 G9 57 55N 4 26W

P

Pabbay, Sd. of 2 G3 57 45N 7 4W
Paddock Wood 9 D9 51 13N 0 24 E
Padiham 7 E4 53 48N 2 20W
Padstow 11 F4 50 33N 4 57W
Paignton 11 G6 50 26N 3 33W
Painshawfield 6 C5 54 56N 1 54W
Paisley 4 C7 55 51N 4 27W
Papa, Sd. of 2 B14 60 19N 1 40W
Papa Sd. 3 D12 59 20N 2 56W
Parrett → 8 D3 51 7N 3 0W
Partry Mts. 12 D3 53 40N 9 28W
Parys Mt. 10 A5 53 23N 4 18W
Passage West 14 E6 51 52N 8 20W
Patna 4 D6 55 21N 4 30W
Peak District Nat. Park 7 F5 58 21N 1 6W
Peebles 5 C9 55 40N 3 12W
Peel 13 C12 54 13N 4 41W
Peel Fell 6 B3 55 17N 2 35W
Pegwell B. 9 D11 51 18N 1 22 E
Pembroke 10 D4 51 41N 4 57W
Pen-y-Ghent 6 D4 54 10N 2 15W
Penarth 8 E7 51 26N 3 11W
Pendle Hill 7 E4 53 53N 2 18W
Penicuik 5 C9 55 50N 3 14W
Penistone 7 E5 53 31N 1 38W
Penkridge 7 G4 52 44N 2 8W
Penmaenmawr 10 A6 53 16N 3 55W
Pennines 6 C4 54 50N 2 20W
Penrith 6 C3 54 40N 2 45W
Penryn 11 G3 50 10N 5 7W
Pentire Pt. 11 F4 50 35N 4 57W
Pentland Firth 3 E11 58 43N 3 10W
Pentland Hills 5 C9 55 48N 3 25W
Penzance 11 G2 50 7N 5 32W
Perranporth 11 G3 50 21N 5 9W
Pershore 8 B4 52 7N 2 4W
Perth 5 B9 56 24N 3 27W
Peterborough 7 G8 52 35N 0 14W
Peterculter 3 H13 57 5N 2 18W
Peterhead 3 G14 57 30N 1 49W
Peterlee 6 C6 54 45N 1 18W
Petersfield 9 D7 51 0N 0 56W
Petworth 9 E7 50 59N 0 37W
Pewsey, Vale of 8 D5 51 20N 1 46W
Pickering 6 D7 54 15N 0 46W
Pickering, Vale of 6 D7 54 14N 0 45W
Pilsdon Pen 8 E3 50 49N 2 51W
Pitlochry 5 A8 56 43N 3 43W
Pittenweem 5 B10 56 13N 2 43W
Plymouth 11 G5 50 23N 4 9W
Plympton 11 G5 50 24N 4 2W
Plymstock 11 G5 50 22N 4 6W
Plynlimon = Pumlumon Fawr 10 C6 52 29N 3 47W
Pocklington 7 E7 53 56N 0 48W
Polegate 9 E9 50 49N 0 15 E
Polperro 11 G4 50 19N 4 31W
Pontardawe 10 D6 51 43N 3 51W
Pontardulais 10 D5 51 42N 4 3W
Pontefract 7 E6 53 42N 1 19W
Ponteland 6 B5 55 7N 1 45W
Pontypool 10 D7 51 42N 3 1W
Pontypridd 11 D7 51 36N 3 21W
Poole 8 E5 50 42N 1 58W
Poole Harbour 8 E5 50 41N 2 0W
Port Bannatyne 4 C5 55 51N 5 4W
Port Ellen 4 C3 55 38N 6 10W
Port Erin 13 C12 54 5N 4 45W
Port Eynon Pt. 11 D5 51 32N 4 12W
Port Glasgow 4 C6 55 57N 4 40W
Port Isaac B. 11 F4 50 36N 4 50W
Port Lairge = Waterford 15 D8 52 16N 7 8W
Port Laoise 15 B8 53 2N 7 20W
Port Talbot 11 D6 51 35N 3 48W
Portadown 13 C9 54 27N 6 26W
Portaferry 13 C10 54 23N 5 32W
Portarlington 15 B8 53 10N 7 10W
Porth Neigwl 10 B4 52 48N 4 33W
Porthcawl 11 E6 51 28N 3 42W
Porthleven 11 G3 50 5N 5 19W
Porthmadog 10 B5 52 55N 4 13W
Portishead 8 D3 51 29N 2 46W
Portknockie 3 G12 57 40N 2 52W
Portland, I. of 11 F9 50 32N 2 25W
Portland Bill 11 F9 50 31N 2 27W
Portmadoc = Porthmadog 10 B5 52 55N 4 13W
Portpatrick 4 E5 54 50N 5 7W
Portree 2 H5 57 25N 6 11W
Portrush 13 A8 55 13N 6 40W
Portslade 9 E8 50 50N 0 11W
Portsmouth 8 E6 50 48N 1 6W
Portsoy 3 G12 57 41N 2 41W
Portstewart 13 A8 55 12N 6 43W
Portumna 14 B6 53 5N 8 12W
Potters Bar 9 C8 51 42N 0 11W
Poulaphouca Res. 15 B10 53 8N 6 30W
Poulton le Fylde 7 E3 53 51N 2 59W
Powys □ 8 C7 52 20N 3 20W
Prawle Pt. 11 G6 50 13N 3 41W
Prestatyn 10 A7 53 20N 3 24W
Prestbury 8 C4 51 54N 2 2W
Presteigne 10 C7 52 17N 3 0W
Preston 7 E3 53 46N 2 42W
Prestonpans 5 C10 55 58N 2 58W
Prestwich 7 E4 53 32N 2 18W
Prestwick 4 D6 55 30N 4 38W
Princes Risborough 9 C7 51 43N 0 50W
Prudhoe 6 C5 54 57N 1 52W
Pudsey 7 E5 53 47N 1 40W
Pulborough 9 E8 50 58N 0 30W
Pumlumon Fawr 10 C6 52 29N 3 47W
Purbeck, I. of 8 E4 50 40N 2 5W
Purfleet 9 D9 51 29N 0 15 E
Pwllheli 10 B5 52 54N 4 26W

Q

Quantock Hills 8 D2 51 8N 3 10W
Queenborough 9 D10 51 24N 0 46 E
Queensbury 7 E5 53 46N 1 50W
Quendale, B. of 2 C15 59 53N 1 20W
Quinag 2 F7 58 13N 5 5W
Quoich, L. 2 H7 57 4N 5 20W

R

Raasay 2 H5 57 25N 6 4W
Radcliffe 7 E4 53 35N 2 19W
Radcliffe-on-Trent 7 G6 52 57N 1 3W
Radlett 9 C8 51 41N 0 19W
Radnor Forest 10 C7 52 17N 3 10W
Radstock 8 D4 51 17N 2 25W
Rainham 9 D10 51 22N 0 36 E
Rame Hd. 11 G5 50 19N 4 14W
Ramsbottom 7 E4 53 36N 2 20W
Ramsey, *Cambs.* 9 B8 52 27N 0 6W
Ramsey, *I. of M.* 13 C13 54 20N 4 21W
Ramsgate 9 D11 51 20N 1 25 E
Randalstown 13 B9 54 45N 6 20W
Rannoch 4 A7 56 40N 4 20W
Rannoch, L. 4 A7 56 41N 4 20W
Rannoch Moor 4 A6 56 38N 4 48W
Rath Luirc 14 D5 52 21N 8 40W
Rathdrum 15 C10 52 57N 6 13W
Rathkeale 14 C5 52 32N 8 57W
Rathlin I. 13 A9 55 18N 6 14W
Rathmelton 12 A6 55 0N 7 35W
Rattray 5 A9 56 36N 3 20W
Rattray Hd. 3 G14 57 38N 1 50W
Raunds 9 B7 52 20N 0 32W
Ravenshead 7 F6 53 5N 1 10W
Rawmarsh 7 F6 53 27N 1 20W
Rawtenstall 7 E4 53 42N 2 18W
Rayleigh 9 C10 51 36N 0 38 E
Reading 9 D7 51 27N 0 57W
Red B. 13 A9 55 4N 6 2W
Red Wharf B. 10 A5 53 18N 4 10W
Redbridge 9 C9 51 35N 0 7 E
Redcar 6 C6 54 37N 1 4W
Redditch 8 B5 52 18N 1 57W
Redhill 9 D8 51 14N 0 10W
Redruth 11 G3 50 14N 5 14W
Ree, L. 12 D6 53 35N 8 0W
Reigate 9 D8 51 14N 0 11W
Renfrew 4 C7 55 52N 4 24W
Renish Pt. 2 G4 57 44N 6 59W
Retford 7 F7 53 19N 0 55W
Rhayader 10 C7 52 19N 3 30W
Rhinns Pt. 4 C3 55 42N 6 29W
Rhois-Bheinn 2 J6 56 50N 5 40W
Rhondda 10 D6 51 39N 3 30W
Rhosllanerchrugog 10 A7 53 3N 3 4W
Rhossili B. 11 D5 51 33N 4 15W
Rhum 2 J5 57 0N 6 20W
Rhum, Sd. of 2 J5 56 54N 6 14W
Rhyl 10 A7 53 19N 3 29W
Rhymney 10 D7 51 45N 3 17W
Ribble → 6 E3 53 46N 2 42W
Richmond 6 D5 54 24N 1 43W
Richmond-upon-Thames 9 D8 51 28N 0 18W
Rickmansworth 9 C8 51 38N 0 28W
Ringwood 8 E5 50 50N 1 48W
Ripley 7 F6 53 3N 1 24W
Ripon 6 D5 54 8N 1 31W
Risca 11 D7 51 36N 3 6W
Rishton 7 E4 53 46N 2 26W
Roag, L. 2 F4 58 10N 6 55W
Roaringwater B. 14 F3 51 30N 9 30W
Robin Hood's Bay 6 D7 54 26N 0 31W
Rochdale 7 E4 53 36N 2 10W
Rochester 9 D10 51 22N 0 30 E
Rochford 9 C10 51 36N 0 42 E
Rockingham Forest 9 B7 52 28N 0 42W
Roe → 13 A8 55 10N 6 59W
Rogans Seat 6 D4 54 25N 2 10W
Romney Marsh 9 D10 51 4N 0 58 E
Romsey 8 E6 51 0N 1 29W
Ronas Hill 2 A15 60 33N 1 25W
Rora Hd. 3 E11 58 51N 3 21W
Roscommon 12 D5 53 38N 8 11W
Roscommon □ 12 D5 53 40N 8 15W
Roscrea 14 C7 52 58N 7 50W
Rose Ness 3 E12 58 52N 2 50W
Ross-on-Wye 8 C3 51 55N 2 34W
Rossall Pt. 7 E2 53 55N 3 2W
Rossan Pt. 12 B4 54 42N 8 47W
Rosscarbery B. 14 E5 51 32N 9 0W
Rosses B. 12 A5 55 2N 8 30W
Rosslare 15 D10 52 17N 6 23W
Rosyth 5 B9 56 2N 3 26W
Rotherham 7 F6 53 26N 1 21W
Rothes 3 G11 57 31N 3 12W
Rothesay 4 C5 55 50N 5 3W
Rothwell, *Northants.* 9 B7 52 25N 0 48W
Rothwell, *W. Yorks.* 7 E6 53 46N 1 29W
Rottingdean 9 E8 50 48N 0 3W
Rough Pt. 14 D2 52 19N 10 2W
Royal Leamington Spa 8 B5 52 18N 1 32W
Royal Tunbridge Wells 9 D9 51 7N 0 16 E
Royston, *Herts.* 9 B8 52 3N 0 1W
Royston, *S. Yorks.* 7 E6 53 36N 1 27W
Royton 7 E4 53 34N 2 7W
Rubh a' Mhail 4 C3 55 55N 6 10W
Rubha Ardvule 2 H3 57 17N 7 29W
Rubha Coigeach 2 F7 58 6N 5 27W
Rubha Hunish 2 G5 57 42N 6 20W
Rubha Robhanais = Lewis, Butt of 2 E5 58 30N 6 12W
Rubh'an Dunain 2 H5 57 10N 6 20W
Rugby 8 B6 52 23N 1 16W
Rugeley 7 G5 52 47N 1 56W
Runabay Hd. 13 A9 55 10N 6 2W
Runcorn 7 F3 53 20N 2 44W
Rush 13 D9 53 31N 6 7W
Rushden 9 B7 52 17N 0 37W
Rutherglen 4 C7 55 50N 4 11W
Ruthin 10 A7 53 7N 3 20W
Rutland Water 7 G7 52 38N 0 38W
Ryan, L. 4 E5 55 0N 5 2W
Ryde 8 E6 50 44N 1 9W
Rye 9 E10 50 57N 0 46 E

S

Sacquoy Hd. 3 D11 59 12N 3 5W
Saddle Hd. 12 C1 54 1N 10 10W
Saffron Walden 9 B9 52 2N 0 15 E
St. Abb's Hd. 5 C11 55 55N 2 10W
St. Agnes Hd. 11 G3 50 19N 5 14W
St. Albans 9 C8 51 44N 0 19W
St. Alban's Hd. 8 E4 50 34N 2 3W
St. Andrews 5 B10 56 20N 2 48W
St. Ann's Hd. 10 D3 51 41N 5 11W
St. Asaph 10 A7 53 15N 3 27W
St. Austell 11 G4 50 20N 4 48W
St. Bee's Hd. 6 C1 54 30N 3 38W
St. Brides B. 10 D3 51 48N 5 15W
St. Catherine's Hd. 8 E6 50 36N 1 18W
St. Catherine's Pt. 8 E6 50 34N 1 18W
St. David's 10 D3 51 54N 5 16W
St. David's Hd. 10 D3 51 55N 5 16W
St. Finan's B. 14 E2 51 50N 10 22W
St. George's Channel 15 D11 52 0N 6 0W
St. Govan's Hd. 11 D4 51 35N 4 56W
St. Helens 7 F3 53 28N 2 44W
St. Helier 11 J9 49 11N 2 6W
St. Ives, *Cambs.* 9 B8 52 20N 0 5W
St. Ives, *Corn.* 11 G3 50 13N 5 29W
St. Ives B. 11 G3 50 15N 5 27W
St. John's Pt., *Ireland* 12 B5 54 35N 8 26W
St. John's Pt., *Down* 13 C10 54 14N 5 40W
St. Just 11 G2 50 7N 5 41W
St. Leonards 9 E10 50 51N 0 33 E
St. Magnus B. 2 B14 60 25N 1 35W
St. Mary's Sd. 11 H1 49 53N 6 19W
St. Mawes 11 G3 50 10N 5 1W
St. Michael's Mount 11 G3 50 7N 5 30W
St. Monance 5 B10 56 13N 2 46W
St. Neots 9 B8 52 14N 0 16W
St. Ouens B. 11 J9 49 13N 2 14W
St. Peter Port 11 J8 49 27N 2 31W
Saintfield 13 C10 54 28N 5 50W
Salcombe 11 G6 50 14N 3 47W
Sale 7 F4 53 26N 2 19W
Salford 7 F4 53 30N 2 17W
Salisbury 8 D5 51 4N 1 48W
Salisbury Plain 8 D5 51 13N 1 50W
Saltash 11 G5 50 25N 4 13W
Saltburn by the Sea 6 C7 54 35N 0 58W
Saltcoats 4 C6 55 38N 4 47W
Sanday Sd. 3 D12 59 11N 2 31W
Sandbach 7 F4 53 9N 2 22W
Sandgate 9 D11 51 5N 1 9 E
Sandness 2 B14 60 18N 1 38W
Sandown 8 E6 50 39N 1 9W
Sandringham 9 A10 52 50N 0 30 E
Sandwich 9 D11 51 16N 1 21 E
Sandy 9 B8 52 8N 0 18W
Sanquhar 5 D8 55 21N 3 56W
Sawbridgeworth 9 C9 51 49N 0 10 E
Sawel 13 B7 54 48N 7 5W
Saxmundham 9 B12 52 13N 1 31 E
Scafell Pike 6 D2 54 26N 3 14W
Scalby 6 D8 54 18N 0 26W
Scalloway 2 B15 60 9N 1 16W
Scalpay 2 H6 57 18N 6 0W
Scapa Flow 3 E11 58 52N 3 6W
Scarborough 6 D8 54 17N 0 24W
Scavaig, L. 2 H5 57 8N 6 10W
Schiehallion 4 A7 56 40N 4 6W
Scilly, Isles of 11 H1 49 55N 6 15W
Score Hd. 2 B15 60 12N 1 5W
Scotch Corner 6 D5 54 27N 1 40W
Scridain, L. 4 B3 56 23N 6 7W
Scunthorpe 7 E7 53 35N 0 38W
Seaford 9 E9 50 46N 0 8 E
Seaforth, L. 2 G4 57 52N 6 36W
Seaham 6 C6 54 51N 1 20W
Seahouses 6 A5 55 35N 1 39W
Seascale 6 D2 54 24N 3 29W
Seaton 11 F7 50 42N 3 3W
Sedbergh 6 D3 54 20N 2 31W
Selby 7 E6 53 47N 1 5W
Selkirk 5 C10 55 33N 2 50W
Selsey 9 E7 50 44N 0 47W
Selsey Bill 9 E7 50 44N 0 47W
Settle 6 D4 54 5N 2 18W
Seven Heads 14 E5 51 35N 8 43W
Sevenoaks 9 D9 51 16N 0 11 E
Severn → 8 C3 51 35N 2 38W
Sgurr a' Choire Ghlais 3 H8 57 30N 4 56W
Sgurr Mor 3 G7 57 42N 5 0W
Sgurr na Ciche 2 H7 57 0N 5 29W
Sgurr na Lapaich 2 H7 57 23N 5 5W
Shaftesbury 8 E4 51 0N 2 12W
Shanklin 8 E6 50 39N 1 9W
Shannon → 14 C3 52 35N 9 38W
Shannon Airport 14 C5 52 42N 8 57W
Shapinsay Sd. 3 D12 59 0N 2 51W
Sheelin, L. 12 D7 53 48N 7 20W
Sheep Haven 12 A6 55 12N 7 55W
Sheeps Hd. 14 E3 51 32N 9 50W
Sheerness 9 D10 51 26N 0 47 E
Sheffield 7 F6 53 23N 1 28W
Shehy Mts. 14 E4 51 47N 9 15W
Shell, L. 2 F5 58 0N 6 28W
Shenfield 9 C9 51 39N 0 21 E
Sheppey, I. of 9 D10 51 23N 0 50 E
Shepshed 7 G6 52 47N 1 18W
Shepton Mallet 8 D3 51 11N 2 31W
Sherborne 8 E3 50 56N 2 31W
Sheringham 9 A11 52 56N 1 11 E
Sherwood Forest 7 F6 53 5N 1 5W
Shetland □ 2 B15 60 30N 1 30W
Shiant, Sd. of 2 G5 57 54N 6 30W
Shiel, L. 2 J6 56 48N 5 32W
Shildon 6 C5 54 37N 1 39W
Shillelagh 15 C9 52 46N 6 32W
Shin → 3 G9 57 58N 4 26W
Shin, L. 3 F8 58 7N 4 30W
Shining Tor 7 F4 53 15N 2 0W
Shipley 7 E5 53 50N 1 47W
Shipston-on-Stour 8 B5 52 4N 1 38W
Shirebrook 7 F6 53 13N 1 11W
Shoeburyness 9 C10 51 31N 0 49 E
Shoreham by Sea 9 E8 50 50N 0 17W
Shotts 5 C8 55 49N 3 47W
Shrewsbury 7 G3 52 42N 2 45W
Shropshire □ 7 G3 52 36N 2 45W
Sidlaw Hills 5 A9 56 32N 3 10W
Sidmouth 11 F7 50 40N 3 13W
Sighty Crag 6 B3 55 8N 2 37W
Silloth 5 E9 54 53N 3 25W
Silsden 7 E5 53 55N 1 55W
Silvermine Mts. 14 C6 52 47N 8 15W
Simonside 6 B5 55 17N 1 58W
Sinclair's B. 3 E11 58 30N 3 0W
Sion Mills 12 B7 54 47N 7 29W
Sittingbourne 9 D10 51 20N 0 43 E
Sixmilebridge 14 C5 52 45N 8 46W
Sizewell 9 B12 52 13N 1 38 E
Skaw Taing 2 B16 60 23N 0 57W
Skegness 7 F9 53 9N 0 20 E
Skelmersdale 7 E3 53 34N 2 49W
Skelmorlie 4 C6 55 52N 4 53W
Skelton 6 C7 54 33N 0 59W
Skibbereen 14 E4 51 33N 9 16W
Skiddaw 6 C2 54 39N 3 9W
Skipton 7 E4 53 57N 2 1W
Skokholm I. 10 D3 51 42N 5 16W
Skomer I. 10 D3 51 44N 5 19W
Skull 14 E3 51 32N 9 40W
Skye 2 H5 57 15N 6 10W
Slaney → 15 D10 52 20N 6 30W
Slea Hd. 14 D2 52 7N 10 30W
Sleaford 7 F8 53 1N 0 22W
Sleat, Pt. of 2 H5 57 1N 6 0W
Sleat, Sd. of 2 H6 57 5N 5 47W
Slieve Anierin 12 C6 54 5N 7 58W
Slieve Aughty 14 B5 53 4N 8 30W
Slieve Beagh 13 C7 54 20N 7 12W

Slieve Bernagh · **Youghal**

WORLD MAPS

EUROPE 4-15, ASIA 16-25, AFRICA 26-33, AUSTRALIA AND OCEANIA 34-37,
NORTH AMERICA 38-45, SOUTH AMERICA 46-47

SETTLEMENTS

◌ PARIS   ◼ Berne   ◉ Livorno   ◉ Brugge   ◉ Algeciras   ⊙ *Frejus*   ○ *Oberammergau*   ○ *Thira*

Settlement symbols and type styles vary according to the scale of each map and indicate the importance
of towns on the map rather than specific population figures

∴   Ruins or Archæological Sites   ᵕ   Wells in Desert

ADMINISTRATION

International Boundaries

International Boundaries
(Undefined or Disputed)

Internal Boundaries

National Parks

Country Names

NICARAGUA

Administrative
Area Names

KENT

CALABRIA

International boundaries show the *de facto* situation where there are rival claims to territory

COMMUNICATIONS

——— Principal Roads   ✧ Airfields   ⌒ Other Railways

⌒ Other Roads   ⌒ Principal Railways   ⧢---⧢ Railway Tunnels

-⌒- Trails and Seasonal Roads   -⌒- Railways
Under Construction   ·········· Principal Canals

≍ Passes

PHYSICAL FEATURES

⌒ Perennial Streams   ⬡ Intermittent Lakes   ▲ 8848 Elevations in metres

-⌒- Intermittent Streams   Swamps and Marshes   ▼ 8050 Sea Depths in metres

⬭ Perennial Lakes   Permanent Ice
and Glaciers   *1134* Height of Lake Surface
Above Sea Level
in metres

ELEVATION AND DEPTH TINTS

Height of Land Above Sea Level   Land Below Sea Level   Depth of Sea

in metres	6000	4000	3000	2000	1500	1000	400	200	0							
										6000	12 000	15 000	18 000	24 000	in feet
in feet	18 000	12 000	9000	6000	4500	3000	1200	600								
								0	200	2000	4000	5000	6000	8000	in metres

Some of the maps have different contours to highlight and clarify the principal relief features

A

1 2 3 4 5 6 7 8 9
180 160 140 120 100 80 60 40 20

Queen Elizabeth Is.

GREENLAND

60

Victoria I.

Baffin I.

ICELAND

Anchorage

Churchill

Hudson Bay

UNITED KINGDOM
Glasgo
IRELAND

B

Edmonton

Newfoundland

Lo

Vancouver

C A N A D A

FR

Calgary

Winnipeg

Seattle

Quebec
Montreal

40

Chicago

Toronto

San Francisco

Denver

St. Louis

Detroit

Boston

New York

Washington

Azores

PORTUGAL

Ma

UNITED STATES

PORTUGAL

Lisbon

S

C

Los Angeles

Dallas

Bermuda

Casablanca

MOROCCO

Tropic of Cancer

Canary Is.

Houston

Gulf of Mexico

Miami

ATLANTIC

W. SAHARA

Hawaiian Islands
(U.S.)

20

MEXICO

BAHAMAS

Havana

CUBA

West Indies

MAURITANIA

Mexico

JAMAICA

HAITI

DOMINICAN REP.

PUERTO RICO

C. Verde Is.

SENEGAL

GUATEMALA

BELIZE

HONDURAS

Caribbean Sea

GAMBIA

GUINEA-BISSAU

EL SALVADOR

NICARAGUA

GUINEA

D

Caracas

SIERRA LEONE

IVOR
COAS

COSTA RICA

PANAMA

VENEZUELA

GUYANA

SURINAM

LIBERIA

P A C I F I C

Palmyra Is.
(U.S.)

Bogota

FR. GUIANA

O C E A N

Tabuaeran

COLOMBIA

Kiritimati

Quito

Belém

0

Equator

Galapagos Is.
(Ecuador)

ECUADOR

Manaus

Phoenix Is.

B R A Z I L

Recife

Ascension
(Br.)

Tokelau Is.
(N.Z.)

PERU

Lima

E

Samoan Is.

O C E A N

Brasilia

Salvador

St. Helena
(Br.)

La Paz

Society Is.
(Fr.)

Tuamotu Archipelago
(Fr.)

BOLIVIA

Tonga

Rio de Janeiro

20

PARAGUA

Tubuai Is.
(Fr.)

Easter I.

Asunción

São Paulo

Tropic of Capricorn

C

URUGUAY

Kermadec Is.
(N.Z.)

A R G E N T I N A

Montevideo

Tristan d
Cunha
(Br.)

F

Santiago

Buenos Aires

40

Chatham Is.
(N.Z.)

Falkland Is.

S. Georgia

Tierra del Fuego

G

FALKLAND IS. DEPENDENCIES(Br.)

60

West from Greer

H

80 140 100 80 60 40 20
180 160

1 2 3 4 5 6 7 8 9

1 2 3 4 5 6 7 8 9

Projection: Hammer Equal Area

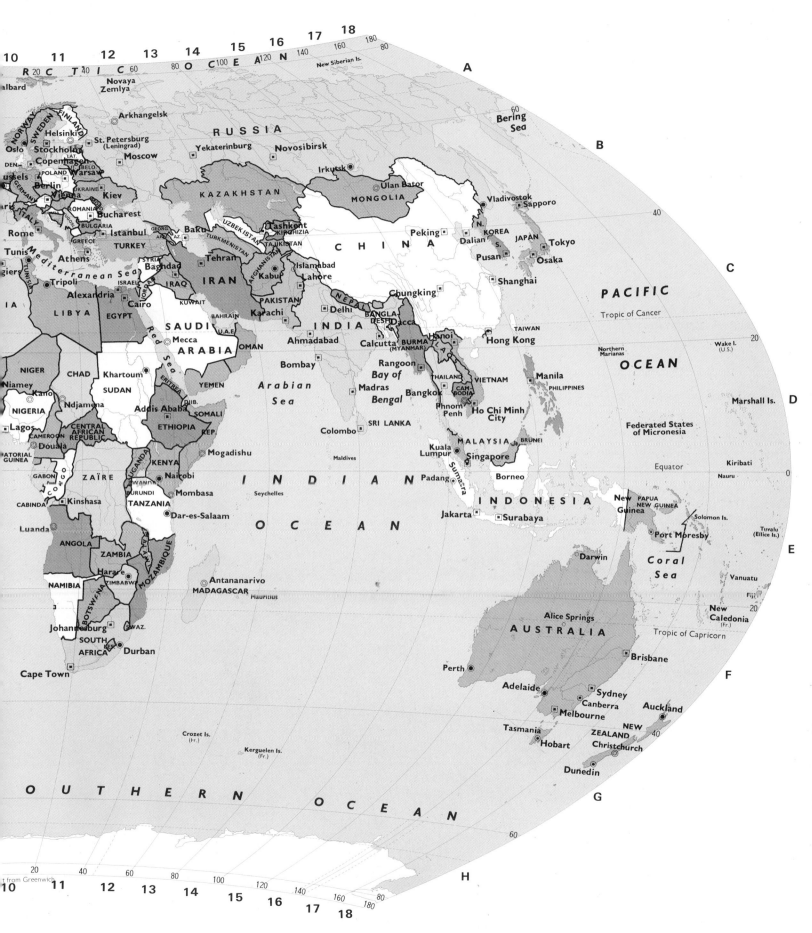

1:80 000 000

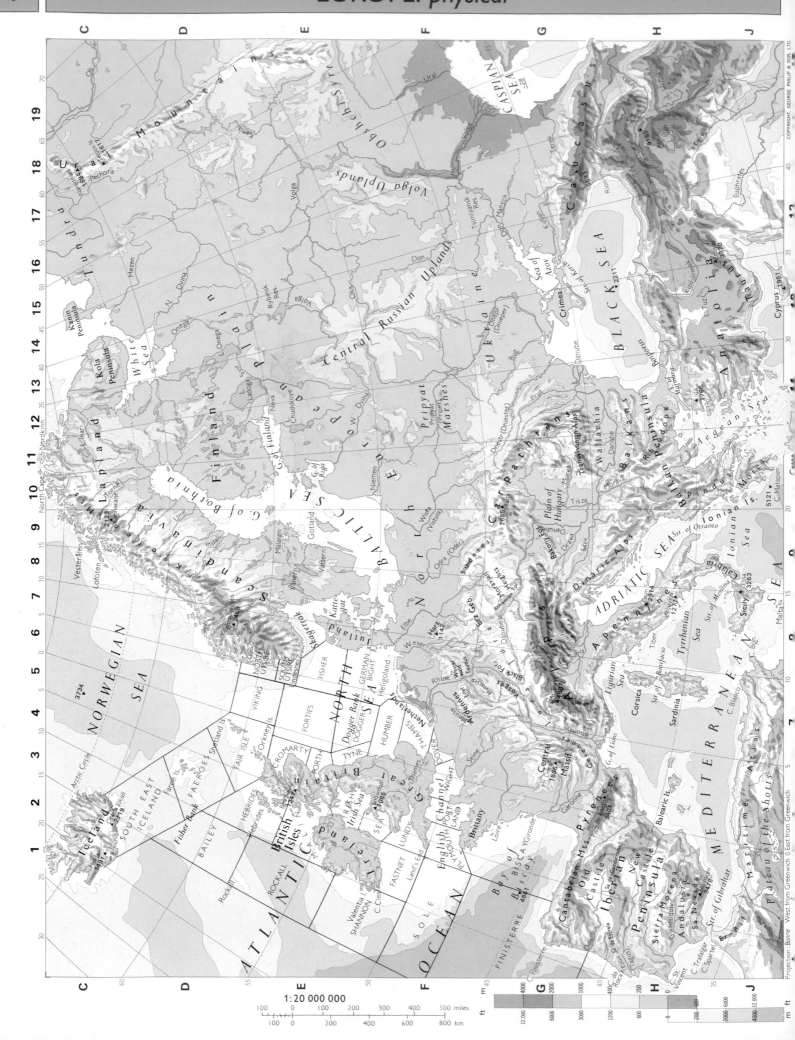

1:20 000 000

Projection Bonne   West from Greenwich 0 East from Greenwich

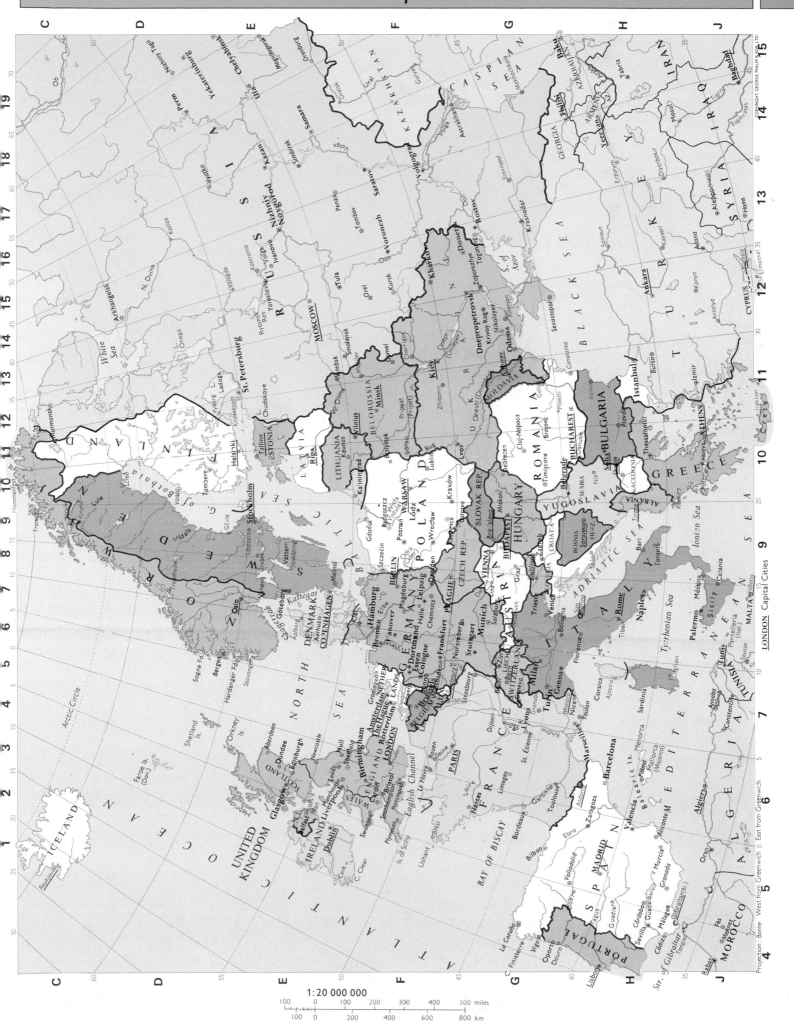

1:20 000 000

ICELAND
On the same scale
West from Greenwich

Projection: Conical with two standard parallels

East from Greenwich

1:10 000 000

COPYRIGHT. GEORGE PHILIP & SON. LTD.

Projection: *Conical with two standard parallels*

1 : 4 000 000

COPYRIGHT. GEORGE PHILIP & SON. LTD.

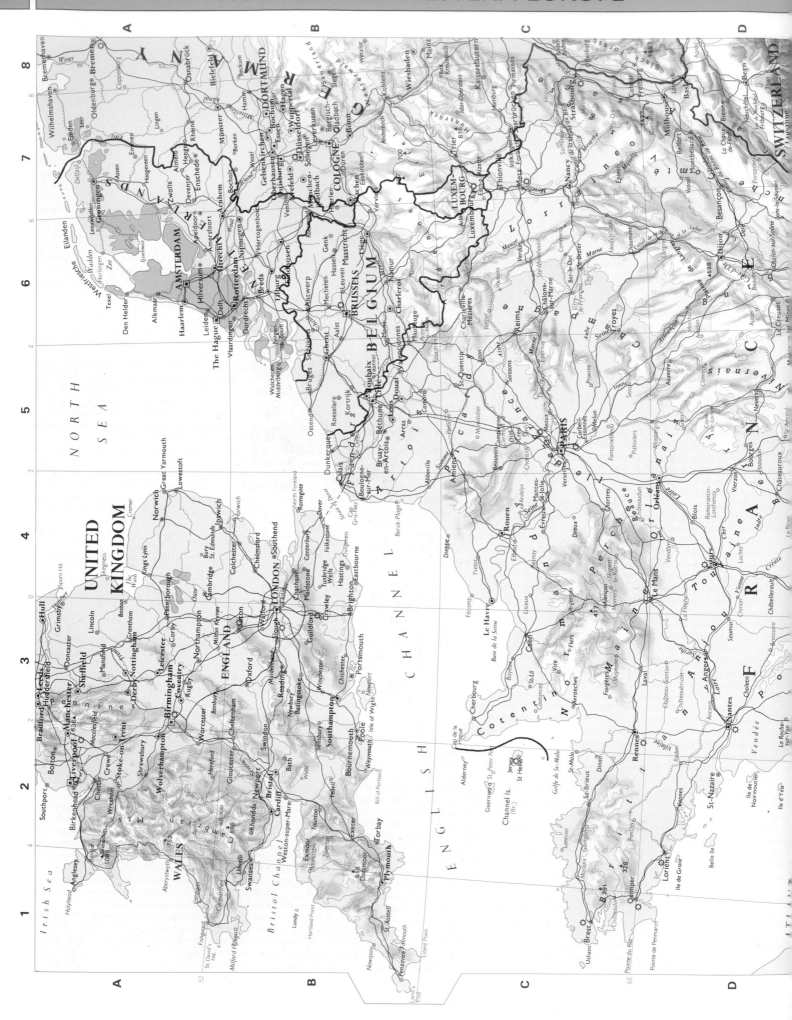

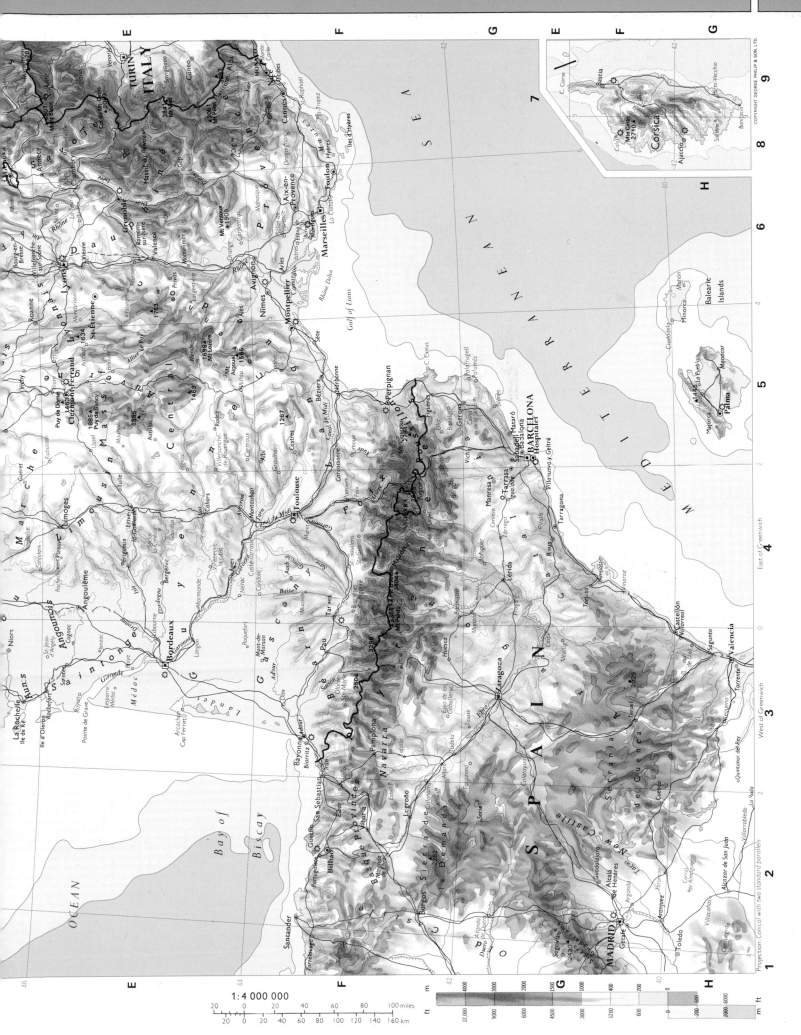

ITALY

TURIN

Corsica

MEDITERRANEAN SEA

Bay of Biscay

OCEAN

ATLANTIC

SPAIN

MADRID

BARCELONA

Valencia

Bordeaux

Lyons

Marseilles

Toulouse

Montpellier

Zaragoza

Bilbao

Pyrenees

Balearic Islands

Palma

1 : 4 000 000

COPYRIGHT GEORGE PHILIP & SON. LTD.

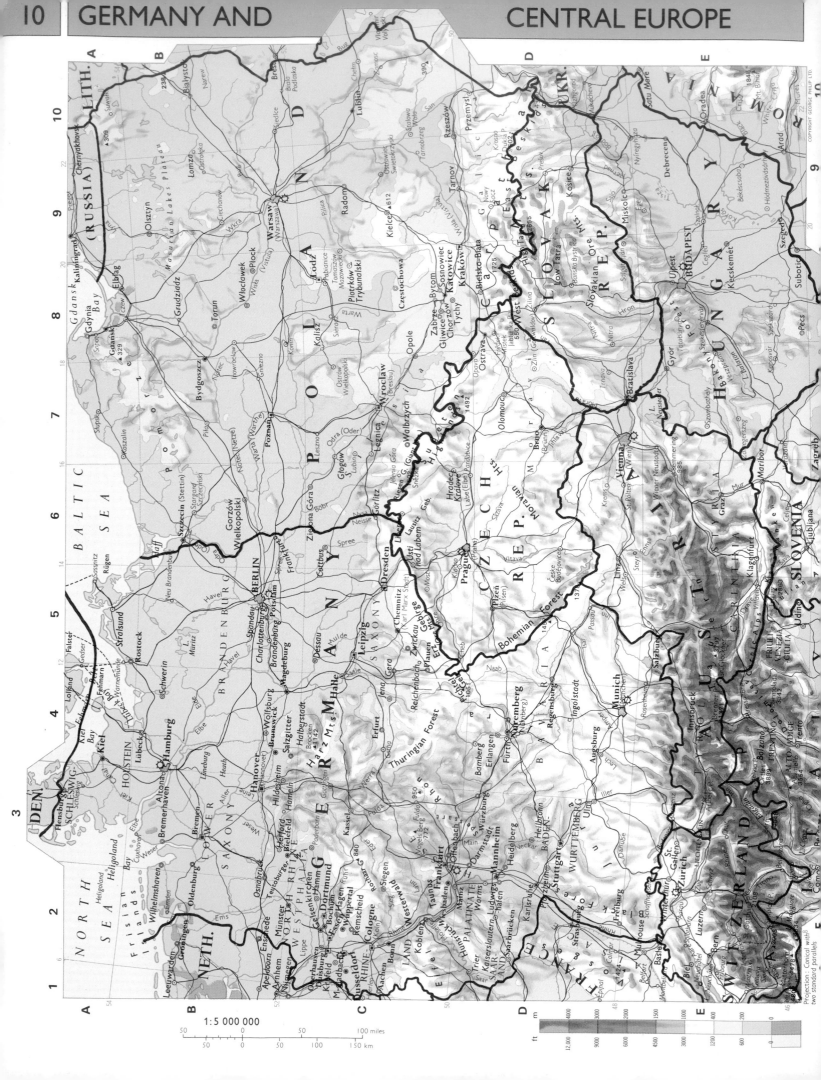

1:5 000 000

Projection: Conical with two standard parallels

COPYRIGHT GEORGE PHILIP LTD.

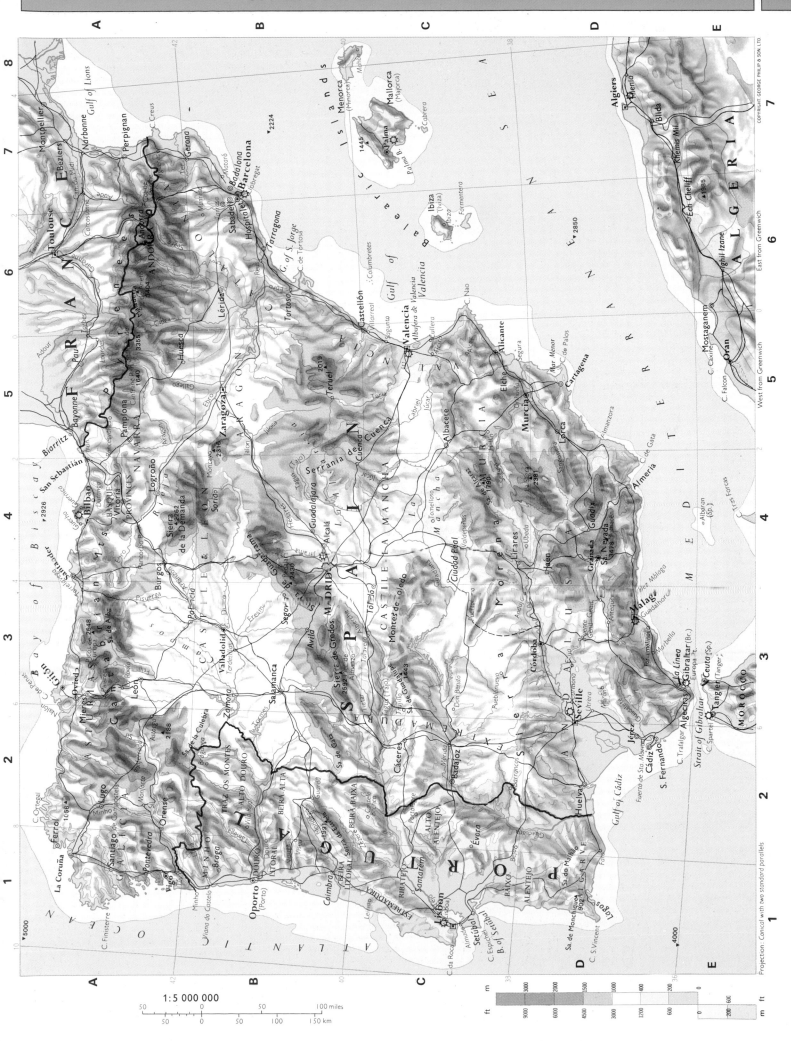

1:5 000 000

East from Greenwich

West from Greenwich

COPYRIGHT GEORGE PHILIP & SON LTD.

Projection: Conical with two standard parallels

Projection: Conical with two standard parallels

1:5 000 000

E F G H

9

8

7

6

5

4

1 Kabardino-Balkar Rep.
2 North Ossetian Rep. (Azer)
3 Nakhichevan Rep.
4 Checheno-Ingush Rep.
    Karagiye Depression

KAZAKHSTAN

K i r g i z   S t e p p e

Aktyubinsk

Oktabrsk

Emba

Makat

Kulsary

Guryev

Aleksandrov Gai

Kalmykovo

Ural

-28m below
sea-level

Fort
Shevchenko

Aktau 132

Karagiye
Gol.

Kara
Bogaz
Gol.

C A S P I A N   S E A

995

Bandar Torkeman

Demavend 5604

TEHRAN

Qom

Ardq

E L B U R Z

I R A N

Hamadan

Rasht

Lenkoran

Ardabil
4824

Tabriz

L. Urmia

Bakhtiaran

Kazvin

Ardq

Saratov

Reservo

Lit.

Volzhskiy

VOLGOGRAD
(Stalingrad)

Tsimlyansk
Res.

Volga

Verkhniy Baskunchak

Astrakhan

KALMYK

REP.

Ergeni Heights

Elista

L. Manych-
Gudilo

Budennovsk

Kizlyar

Makhachkala

Derbent

DAGESTAN

Grozny

Vladikavkaz
5047

Nalchik

Elbrus
5633

Kislovodsk

Pyatigorsk

Stavropol

Kropotkin

Maykop

Armavir

Sukhumi

Sochi

ABKHAZ REP.

Kutaisi

TBILISI

Batumi

ADZHAR REP.

GEORGIA

AZERBAIJAN

Kuba

Khatkerdze

Gyandzha

Mingechaur Res.

Kura

BAKU

Sevan

Kura

YEREVAN

ARMENIA

Aragats
4165

Nakhichevan

Khalkendi

Urmia
4168

Ararat
5165

Kars

Van

L. Van

Ani

MOSUL

Erbil

Kirkuk

Little Zab

Tigris

BAGHDAD

Diyala

I R A Q

Dokan

Great Zab

SYRIA

ALEPPO
(Halab)

Hama

HOMS

DAMASCUS
(Esh Sham)

2814

LEBANON

Beirut

Tripoli
(Tarabulus)

Latakia
(El Ladhiqiya)

Iskenderun

Antioch
(Antak)

G. of Iskenderun

S y r i a n   D e s e r t

Euphrates

Tigris

Sanliurfa
(Urfa)

Gaziantep

Diyarbakir

Mardin

Cizre

K u r d i s t a n

Urfa

Mus

Bitlis

Zab

Siirt

Van

T U R K E Y

Erzurum

Erzincan

Kelkit

Kars Su

Sivas

Trabzon

Giresun

Ordu

Samsun

C a n i k   (P o n t i n e)   M t s.
3937

Malatya

Elazig

Kayseri

Corum

Yozgat

Sinop

C. Ince

ANKARA

Kizilirmak

Tuz Golu

Kirsehir

Kirikkale

Konya

Eregli

Nigde

Adana

Tarsus

Mersin

Silifke

Kirikkale

Antalya

G. of Antalya

CYPRUS

Nicosia

Limassol

Larnaca

Famagusta

M E D I T E R R A N E A N   S E A

L e v a n t

Rhodes
Rodhos
4486

Karpathos

Dodecanese

Kos

Samos

Izmir

Aydin

Mendere

Denizli

Kutahya

Bursa

Balikesir

Canakkale

Edirne

ISTANBUL

Uskudar

Izmit

Adapazari

Eskisehir

Bolu

Zonguldak

Bartin

Kastamonu
2565

Taurus Mountains
3086

Anti-Taurus Mts.

Sea of
Marmara

Gallipoli

Maritza

BULGARIA

Burgas

Varna

ROMANIA

BUCHAREST
(Bucuresti)

Danube

Ruse

Ploesti

Brasov
2535

Pitesti

Sibiu

MOLDAVIA

Iasi

Kishinev
(Chisinau)

Galati

Braila

Izmail

Siret

Prut

Dnestr

Bolgrad

Belgorod

KHARKOV
(Kharkiv)

Sumy

Poltava

Kremenchug

Kirovograd

Cherkassy

KIEV
(Kyyiv)

U K R A I N E

Zhitomir

Vinnitsa

Berdichev

Khmelnitskiy

Chernovtsy

Ternopol

Lvov

Ivano-Frankovsk

Nezhin

Belaya Tserkov

Dnepr

Chernigov

S. Bug

Balta

Tiraspol

ODESSA

Nikolayev

Kherson

Kakhovka Res.

Krivoy Rog

DNEPROPETROVSK

Dneprodzerzhinsk

Zaporozhye

DONETSK

Makeyevka

Gorlovka

Kramatorsk

LUGANSK

Kadiyevka
(Stakharov)

N. Donets

Yenakiyevo

Shakhty

Novoshakhtinsk

Rostov

Novocherkassk

Taganrog

Zhdanov
(Zhdanov)

Mariupol

Berdyansk

Melitopol

Yeysk

Krasnodar

Kuban

Novorossiysk

Sea of Azov

Kerch Str.

Crimea

Simferopol

Yevpatoriya

Sevastopol

Balaklava

Yalta

G. of Karkinitsk

C. Tarkhankut

Kherson

B L A C K   S E A

2211

C A U C A S U S

V O L G A

Volga

Don

Tsimlyansk
Res.

Buturlinovka

Don

Kamyshin

45

50

45

40

35

50

45

40

35

30

COPYRIGHT. GEORGE PHILIP & SON, LTD.

East from Greenwich

Projection: Conical with two standard parallels

Division between Greeks and Turks
in Cyprus. Turks to the North

1:10 000 000

50 0 50 100 150 200 250 miles

50 0 50 100 150 200 250 300 350 400 km

m   ft
12,000 4000
6000   2000
3000   1000
1200   600
600   200
0   0

m
4000 12,000
2000 6000
1000 3000
600   2000
200   1000
0   400
      200
      0

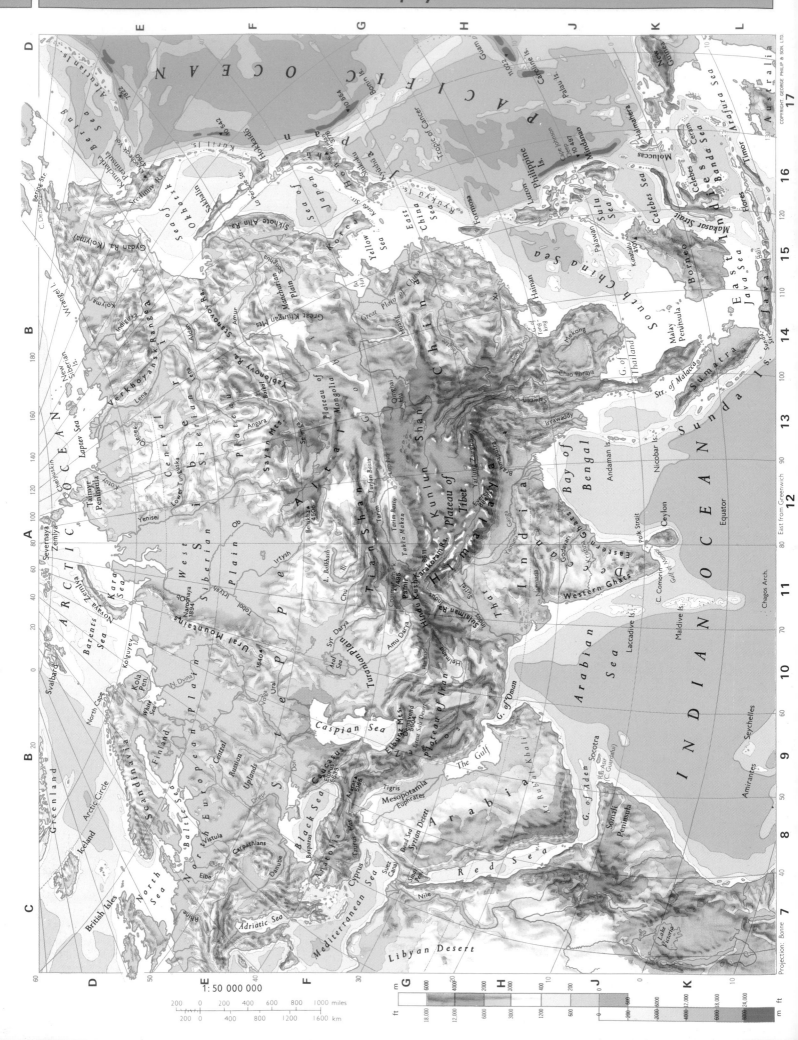

1 : 50 000 000

Projection: Bonne

East from Greenwich

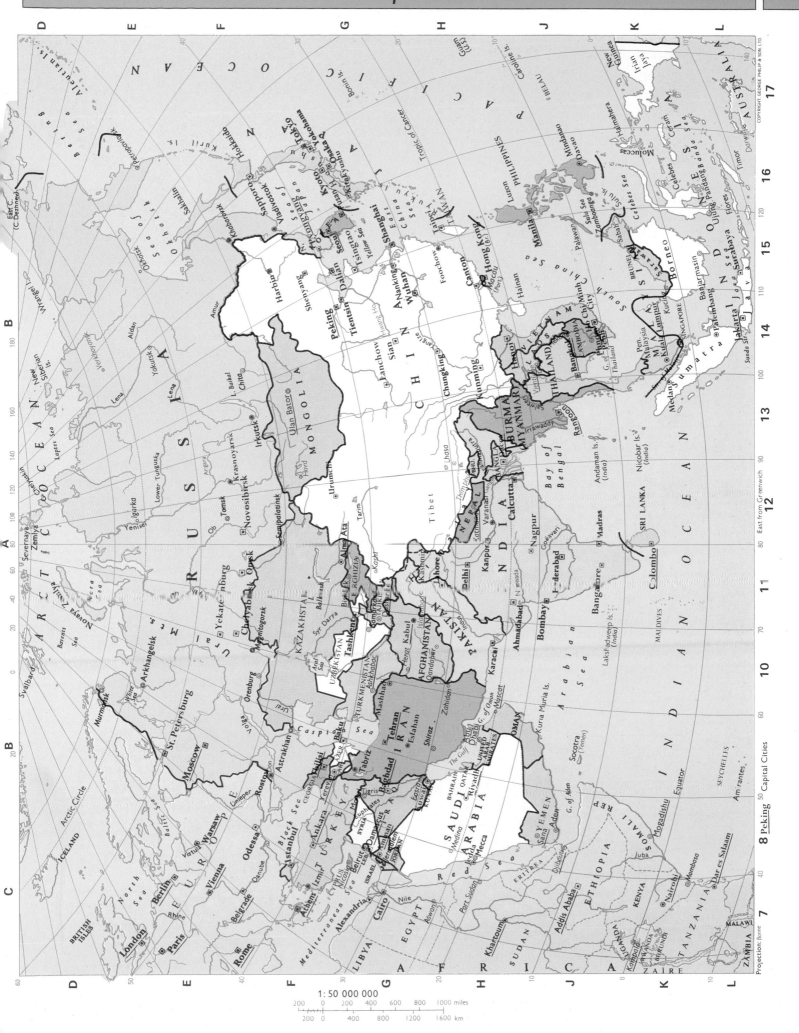

Projection: Bonne

1 : 50 000 000

200   0   200   400   600   800   1000 miles

200   0   400   800   1200   1600 km

8 Peking   50 Capital Cities

East from Greenwich

18

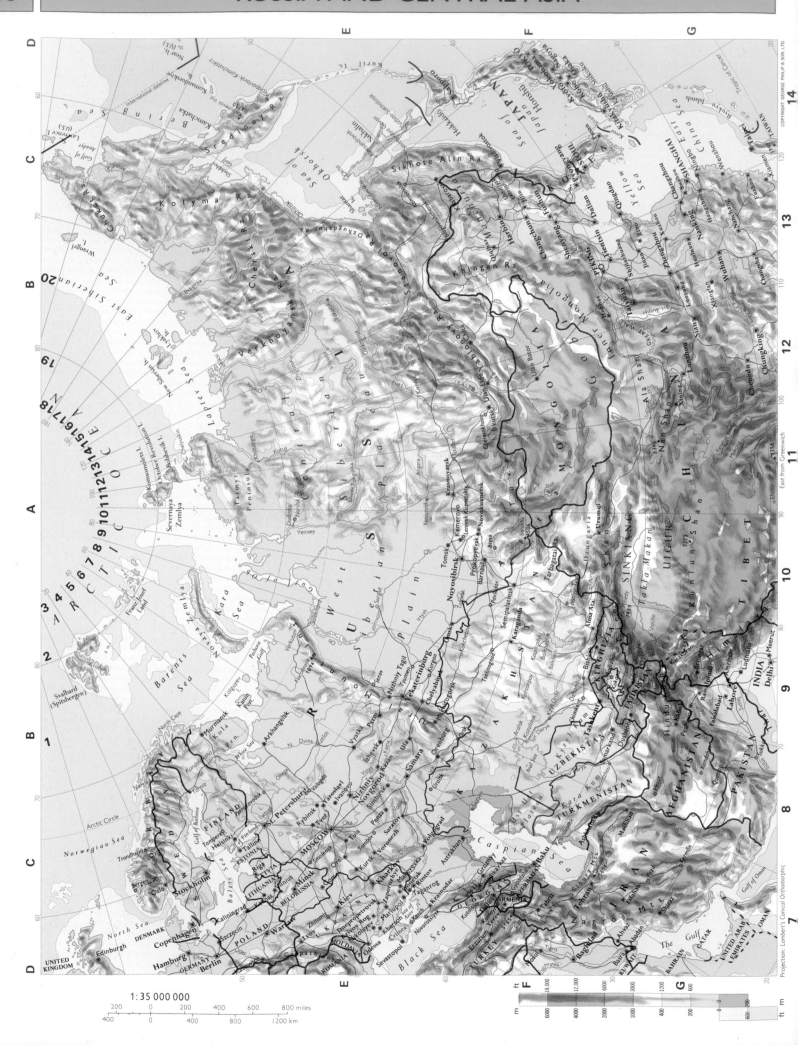

1:35 000 000

Projection: Lambert's Conical Orthomorphic

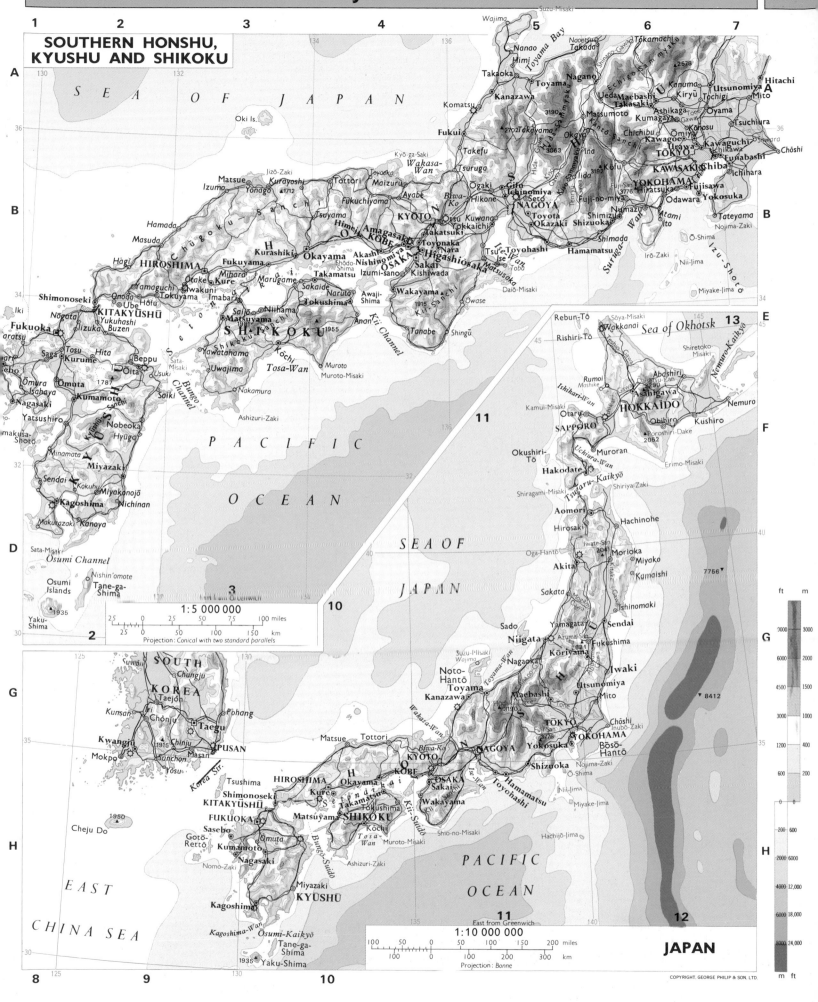

SOUTHERN HONSHU, KYUSHU AND SHIKOKU

SEA OF JAPAN

PACIFIC OCEAN

1:5 000 000

Projection: Conical with two standard parallels

SEA OF OKHOTSK

HOKKAIDŌ

SAPPORO

SEA OF JAPAN

SOUTH KOREA

EAST CHINA SEA

PACIFIC OCEAN

1:10 000 000

East from Greenwich

Projection: Bonne

JAPAN

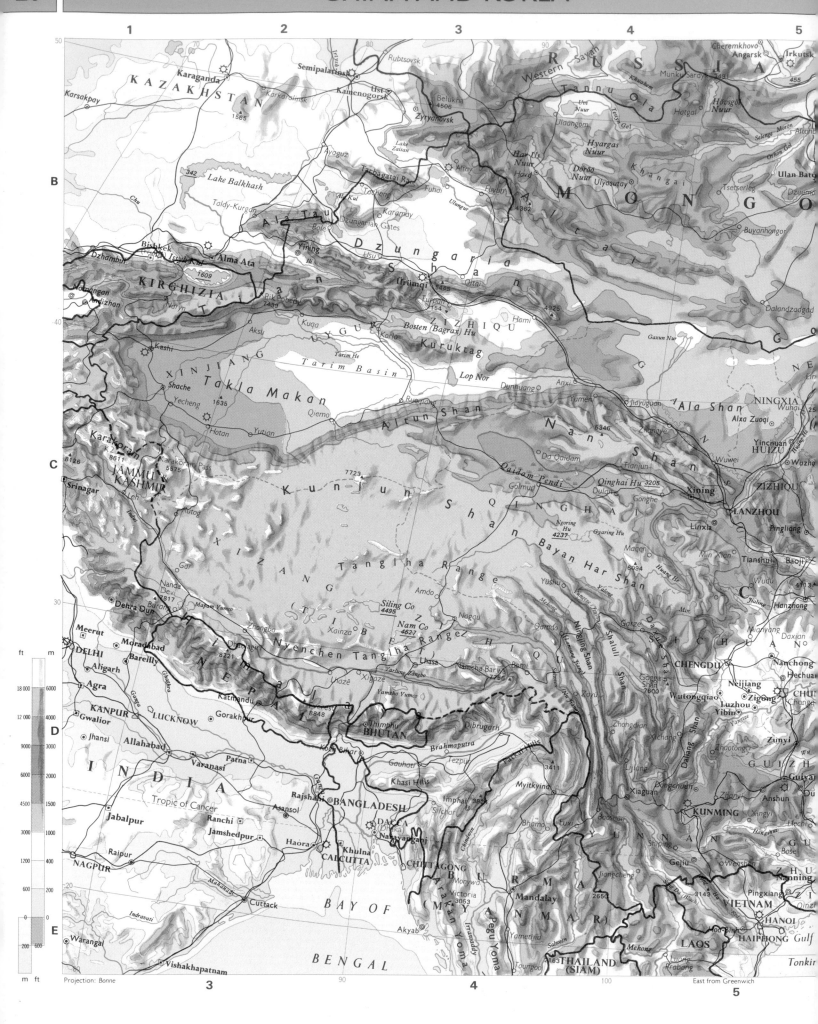

50

1   2   3   4   5

Rubtsovsk

Karaganda

Semipalatinsk

K A Z A K H S T A N

Karsakpay

1565

Karkaralinsk

Ust Kamenogorsk

Zyryanovsk

Belukha 4506

R U S S I A

Western Sayan

Tannu Ola

Cheremkhovo

Angarsk

Irkutsk

455

3491 Munku Sardy

B

Karkaralinsk

Ayaguz

Lake Zaisan

Tarbagatai Ra.

Fuhai

Ulungur

Uvs Nuur

Ulaangom

Har-Us Nuur

Hovd

Doröö Nuur

Ulyasutay

Hyargas Nuur

Khangai

Hatgal

Hövsgöl Nuur

Tsetserleg

Selenge Mörön

Orhon Gol

M O N G O L

Ulan Bator

Dzuuno

Chu

Lake Balkhash

342

Taldy-Kurgan

Alma Ata

Taldy-Kurgan

Alakol

Tasheng

Dzungarian Gates

Bole

Karamay

4362

Buyanhongor

Dalandzadgad

Bishkek

Issyk Kul

1609

Yining

Ili

Usu

Urümqi

5445

Turpan

154

ZIZHIQU

Hami

4925

Gaxun Nur

K I R G H I Z I A

Namangan

Andizhan

Pik Pobedy 7439

Naryn

Aksu

Kuqa

Korla

Bosten (Bagrax) Hu

Kuruktag

Da Qaidam

6346

N a n   S h a n

Zhangye

Wuhai

NINGXIA

Alxa Zuoqi

40

Kashi

U Y G U R

Tarim He

Tarim Basin

Lop Nor

Dunhuang

Anxi

Yumen

Jiayuguan

Yinchuan

HUIZU

Wuzho

X I N J I A N G

Shache

Yecheng

1635

Takla Makan

Hotan

Qiemo

Ruoqiang

Altun Shan

Tianjun

Wuwei

ZIZHIQU

Karakoram

K2 8611

5575

8126

JAMMU KASHMIR

Karakoram Pass

Srinagar

Leh

Rutog

K u n l u n   S h a n

7723

Qaidam Pendi

Golmud

Qinghai Hu 3205

Dulan

Gonghe

Xining

Linxia

LANZHOU

Pingliang

C

X i z a n g

Nanda Devi 7817

Burang

Mapam Yumco

Gar

Tanglha Range

Amdo

Ngoring Hu 4237

Gyaring Hu

Magen

6094

Min Xian

Tianshui

Baoji

30

Dehra Dun

Zhongba

Siling Co 4495

Xainza

Nam Co 4627

Naqqu

Bayan Har Shan

Yushu

Yalong

Huang He

Wudu

4113

Meerut

Moradabad

8221

Dhaulagiri

N E P A L

Nyenchen Tanglha Range

Lhasa

Namcha Barwa 7756

Bomi

Ningjing Shan

Qamdo

Shaluli Shan

Gonga Shan 7600

Gyaze

Zayu

Mianyang

Daxian

Hanzhong

SICHUAN

CHENGDU

Nanchong

Hechuan

DELHI

Aligarh

Bareilly

Agra

KANPUR

LUCKNOW

Ghaghra

Gorakhpur

8848

Everest

Xigaze

Yarlung Zangbo

Yamdok Yumco

THIMPHU

BHUTAN

Dibrugarh

Brahmaputra

Patkai Hills

Neijiang

Zigong

Yibin

Luzhou

Wutongqiao

CHU

Chongq

D

Jhansi

Allahabad

Varanasi

Patna

Kosi

Bihar

Gauhati

Tezpur

Khasi Hills

3411

Myitkyina

Zhangdian

Xichang

Lijiang

Daliang Shan

Zhaotong

Zunyi

GUIZH

I N D I A

Jabalpur

Ranchi

Jamshedpur

Rajshahi

Asansol

BANGLADESH

DACCA (Dhaka)

Narayanganj

Haora

Silchar

Imphal

Bhamo

Luxi

Baoshan

KUNMING

Xiguan

Dongchuan

Zhanyi

Anshun

Xingyi

Guiyang

Guyang

Du

Tropic of Cancer

Haora

CALCUTTA

CHITTAGONG

B U R M A

Monywa

Mandalay

2650

Shiping

Gejiu

Jiangcheng

Y U N N A N

Hongshui

Weishan

Pingxiang

ZHU

Nanning

GU

Bose

Hechi

NAGPUR

Raipur

Mahanadi

Khulna

Arakan Yoma

Victoria 3053

Pegu Yoma

Irrawaddy

Chindwin

M Y A N M A R

3143

Da (Black)

VIETNAM

HAIPHONG Gulf

E

Warangal

Indravati

Cuttack

B A Y   O F

Akyab

Arakan Yoma

Salween

Yamethin

Toungoo

Mekong

3163 THAILAND (SIAM)

Luang Prabang

LAOS

HANOI

Tonkir

Vishakhapatnam

B E N G A L

Projection: Bonne

90

100

East from Greenwich

ft   m

18 000   6000

12 000   4000

9000   3000

6000   2000

4500   1500

3000   1000

1200   400

600   200

0   0

200   600

m   ft

3   4   5

Lake Baykal

'Ulan Ude
Chita
Yablonovyy Range
ta Yablonovyy Range

Nerchinsk

Svobodny
Blagoveshchensk
Aihui
Komsomolsk
L. Bolon
Khabarovsk
Aleksandrovsk
Poronaysk
C. Terpeniya

Sakhalin

Yuzhno-Sakhalinsk

Manzhouli
Borzya
Oroqen Zizhiqi
HEILONGJIANG
Little Khingan Mts.
Birobidzhan

entyn
ürüü
Hailar
Hulun
Nur
Nenjiang
Bei'an
Yichun
Hegang
Hamusi
Shuangyashan
Sikhote Alin Ra.

La Perouse Str.
Wakkanai

B

L I A
Buir
Nur
Butha Qi
Qiqihar
Anda
Suihua

Jixi
Mishan
Lake
Khanka

Asahigawa
2290
Hokkaido
Otaru
SAPPORO
Kushiro

Choybalsan
Kerulen
Horqin Youyi
Qiangqi
Tao'an
Manchuria
HARBIN
Mudanjiang
Ussuriysk

Saynshand
JILIN
CHANGCHUN
Jilin
Vladivostok
Yanji
Nakhodka
Hakodate
C. Erimo

Abagnar Qi
1949
Shuangliao
Tongliao
Siping
Liaoyuan Lake
Songhua

Dzamin Uud
Erenhot
INNER MONGOLIA
Chifeng
Fuxin
27
Chongjin
Tsugaru Strait
Aomori
Hachinohe
Morioka

b
i
Great Khingan Mts.
Chaoyang
FUSHUN
Yongjup
NORTH
SEA OF
Akita

Hohhot
Jining
Zhangjiakou
Chengde
Liaoyang
SHENYANG
Benxi
ANSHAN
Dandong
Yalu
Hungnam
Sado
Sendai

Baotou
Datong
Xuanhua
Qinghuangdao
Jinzhou
Yingkou
G. of
Liaodong
Wŏnsan
JAPAN
Niigata
Koriyama

rdos
GREAT WALL
PEKING
(Beijing)
Tangshan
Liaodong
Pen.
Korea Bay
YONGYANG
Kanazawa
Toyama
Utsunomiya

s
(no)
Baoding
3058
HEBEI
TIENTSIN (Tianjin)
DALIAN
(Lüda)
Haeju
Kaesong
SEOUL
Okayama
TOKYO
KAWASAKI

TAIYUAN
Yangquan
Shijiazhuang
Cangzhou
G. of Chihli
(Bo Hai)
Yantai
Weihai
INCHON
SOUTH
NAGOYA
YOKOHAMA

Fenyang
Yuci
Dezhou
Huang He (Yellow)
Weifang
YELLOW
Taejon
TAEGU
Hiroshima
Fuji 3776
Yokosuka
Shizuoka

Tongchuan
JINAN
Zibo
Tai'an
SEA
PUSAN
Masan
1915
KOBE
KYOTO
OSAKA
Hamamatsu

an
Handan
Anyang
Jining
SHANDONG
QINGDAO
Kwangju
Shimonoseki
Sakai
Wakayama

SIAN
(Xi'an)
ZHENGZHOU
Kaifeng
Xinxiang
Grand Canal
Lianyungang
KITAKYUSHU
FUKUOKA
SHIKOKU
Kochi
Matsuyama

Luoyang
HENAN
Shangqiu
Xuzhou
Qingjiang
Cheju Do
Sasebo
Kumamoto

Pingdingshan
Shangshui
Hongze
Hu
JIANGSU
1950
Nagasaki
Kyushu

Nanyang
Zhumadian
Huainan
Zhenjiang
Nantong
Kagoshima

ba Shan
Xiangfan
Dabie Shan
NANKING
(Nanjing)
ANHUI
Changzhou
Wuxi
Suzhou
Tanega

Xichuan
Yichang
WUHAN
HUBEI
Hefei
Wuhu
Tongling
SHANGHAI
Hangzhou Wan

Shashi
Anqing
Huangshi
Hangzhou
Shaoxing
Ningbo

Changde
Dongting
L.
Yunyang
Tunxi
ZHEJIANG
Jingdezhen
Jinhua
Wenzhou

EAST CHINA
SEA
Amami-ō-Shima

Yiyang
Nanchang
Shangrao

HUNAN
Changsha
JIANGXI
Wu Shan 2120

Shaoyang
Xiangtan
Zhuzhou
Jian
Nanping

Hengyang
Sanming
Fuzhou

Guilin
Ganzhou
FUJIAN
Quanzhou
Chilung
TAIPEI
Taichung
Ryukyu Islands
Naha
Okinawa
D

zhou
GUANGDONG
Shaoguan
Zhangzhou
Xiamen
(Amoy)
Chiai
Yu Shan
3997
TAIWAN
Sakashima Gunto

GXI
Wuzhou
Mei Xian
Chao'an
Nan
CANTON
(Guangzhou)
Foshan
Shantou
Tropic of Cancer

hai
Jiangmen
HONG KONG (Br.)
Macau
(Port.)
KAOHSIUNG
Tainan

Maoming
Zhanjiang
SOUTH CHINA
PACIFIC

zhou
enin
Haikou
HAINAN
1879
Hainan Str.
SEA
Babuyan Is.
Batan Is.
OCEAN

COPYRIGHT GEORGE PHILIP & SON LTD

1:15 000 000

100   0   100   200   300   400 miles
100   0   100   200   300   400   500   600 km

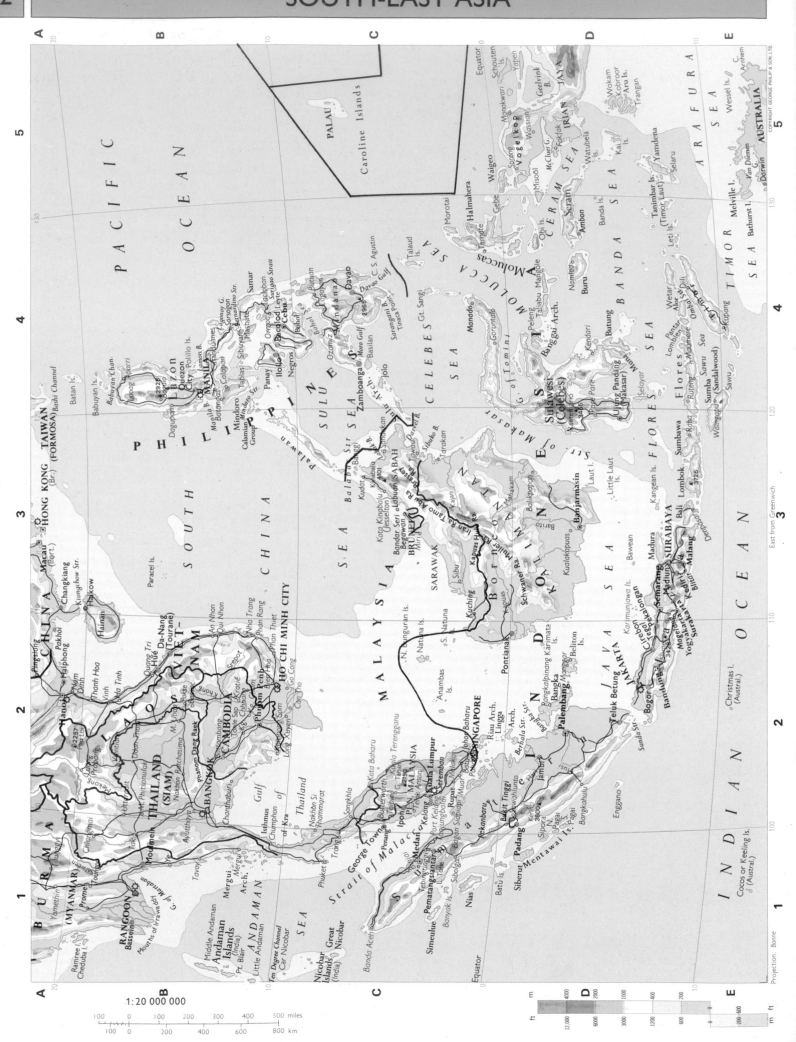

1:20 000 000

100   0   100   200   300   400   500 miles

100   0   200   400   600   800 km

East from Greenwich

Projection: Bonne

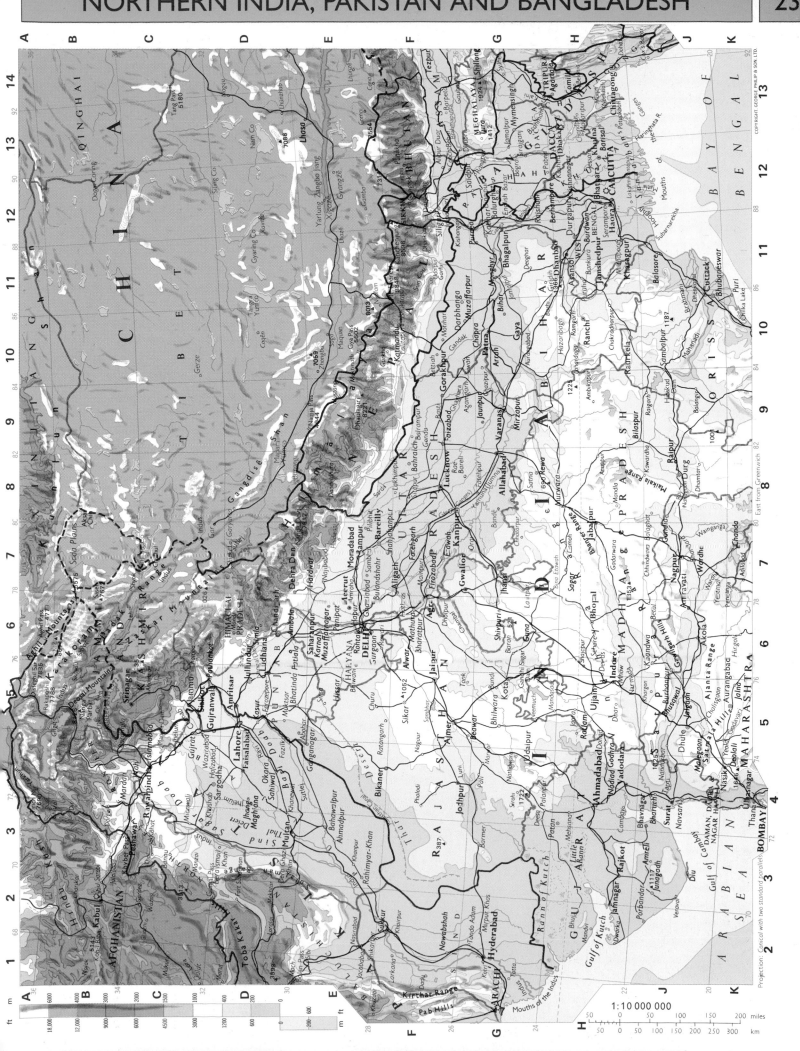

Projection: Conical with two standard parallels

1:10 000 000

Projection : Alber's Equal Area with two standard parallels

East from Greenwich

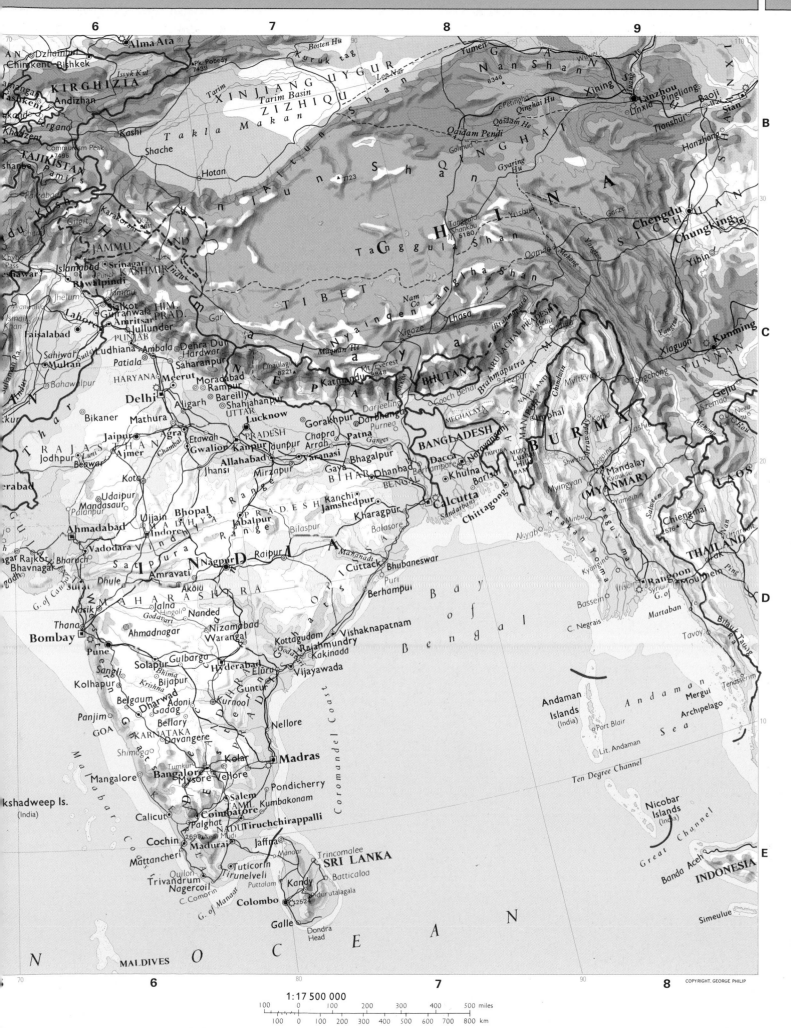

1:17 500 000

COPYRIGHT. GEORGE PHILIP

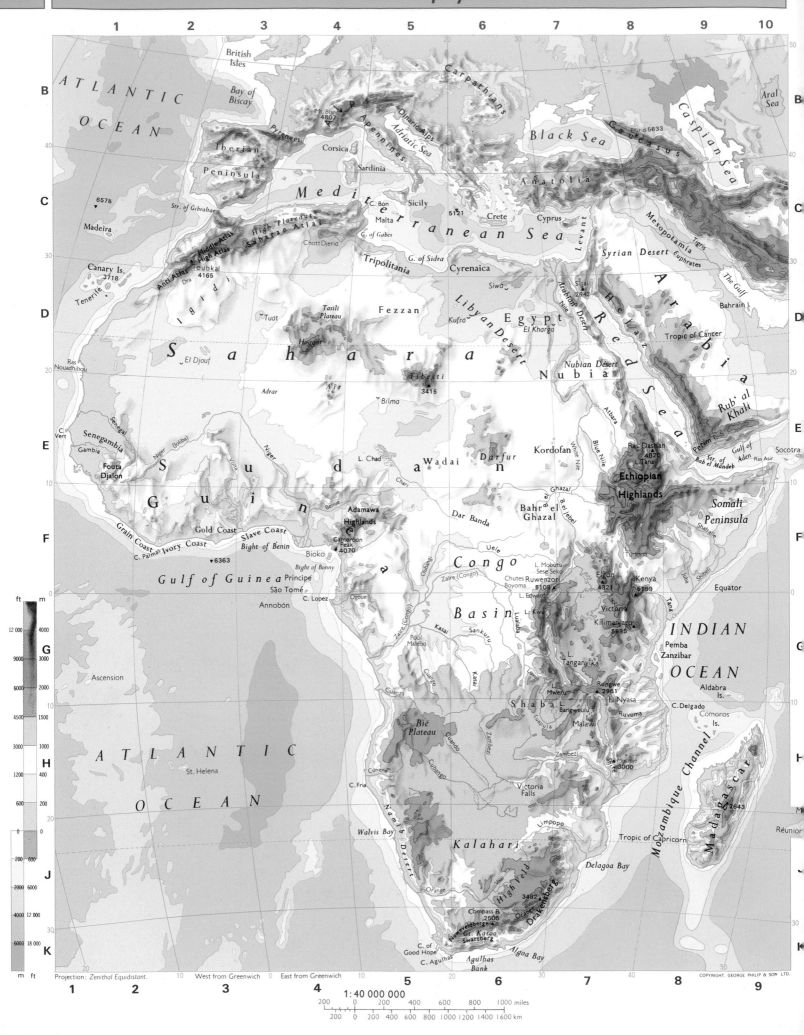

AFRICA: physical

ATLANTIC OCEAN

British Isles

Bay of Biscay

Carpathians

Black Sea

Caucasus

Elbrus 5633

Caspian Sea

Aral Sea

Iberian Peninsula

Pyrenees

Alps

Mt. Blanc 4807

Apennines

Dinaric Alps

Adriatic Sea

Anatolia

Corsica

Sardinia

6576

Madeira

Str. of Gibraltar

Middle Atlas

High Atlas

High Plateaus

Saharan Atlas

Mediterranean Sea

C. Bon

Sicily

Malta

5121

Crete

Cyprus

Levant

Mesopotamia

Tigris

Euphrates

Syrian Desert

The Gulf

Canary Is. 3718

Tenerife

Anti Atlas

Toubkal 4165

Dra

Igidi

Chott Djerid

Tripolitania

G. of Gabes

G. of Sidra

Cyrenaica

Siwa

Libyan Desert

Egypt

Arabian Desert

Sinai 2642

Hejaz

Red Sea

Arabia

Bahrain I.

Tropic of Cancer

Ras Nouadhibou

S a h a r a

Tasili Plateau

Fezzan

Kufra

El Kharga

Nile

Nubian Desert

Rub' al Khali

Tuat

Hoggar

Tibesti 3415

Nubia

Adrar

Air

Bilma

El Djouf

C. Vert

Senegambia

Gambia

Senegal

Niger (Joliba)

Niger

Volta

L. Chad

Wadai

Darfur

Kordofan

White Nile

Blue Nile

Atbara

Ras Dashan 4620

L. Tana

Penim I.

Str. of Bab el Mandeb

Gulf of Aden

Socotra

Ras Asir

Fouta Djalon

S u d a n

Chari

Ethiopian Highlands

Somali Peninsula

G u i n e a

Benue

Adamawa Highlands

Dar Banda

Bahr el Ghazal

Bahr el Ghazal

Bahr el Jebel

Shabelle

Grain Coast

Gold Coast

Ivory Coast

Slave Coast

Bight of Benin

Bioko

Cameroon Peak 4070

Uele

Congo

L. Mobutu Sese Seko

Ruwenzori

Chutes Boyoma 5109

Turkana

Elgon 4321

Kenya 5199

Juba

Shibeli

C. Palmas

6363

Bight of Bonny

Príncipe

São Tomé

C. Lopez

Ogoue

Zaire (Congo)

L. Edward

L. Kivu

Kilimanjaro 5895

Tana

Equator

Gulf of Guinea

Annobón

Kasai

Sankuru

Lualaba

Basin

L. Victoria

INDIAN OCEAN

Pemba

Zanzibar

Ascension

Zaire (Congo)

Pool Malebo

Kasai

Cuango

Cuanza

Lomami

L. Tanganyika

Luvua

Rungwe 2961

L. Mweru

L. Nyasa

Ruvuma

C. Delgado

Comoros Is.

Aldabra Is.

St. Helena

ATLANTIC

Cuanza

Bié Plateau

Cuando

Cubango

Luapula

L. Bangweulu

Shabal.

Malawi

Zambezi

Mlanje 3000

Madagascar 2643

OCEAN

Cunene

C. Fria

Namib Desert

Victoria Falls

Limpopo

Mozambique Channel

Réunion

Walvis Bay

Kalahari

Delagoa Bay

Tropic of Capricorn

Orange

High Veld

Drakensberg 3482

Compass B. 2505

Nieuweveldberge

Gt. Karoo

Swartberg

Orange

C. of Good Hope

C. Agulhas

Agulhas Bank

Algoa Bay

Projection: Zenithal Equidistant.

West from Greenwich   East from Greenwich

1 : 40 000 000

200   0   200   400   600   800   1000 miles

200   0   200   400   600   800   1000   1200   1400   1600 km

COPYRIGHT. GEORGE PHILIP & SON LTD.

ft   m
12 000   4000
9000   3000
6000   2000
4500   1500
3000   1000
1200   400
600   200
0   0
0   0
600   200
2000   6000
4000   12 000
6000   18 000
m   ft

Projection: *Zenithal Equidistant.*

West from Greenwich | East from Greenwich

1:40 000 000

Nairobi Capital Cities

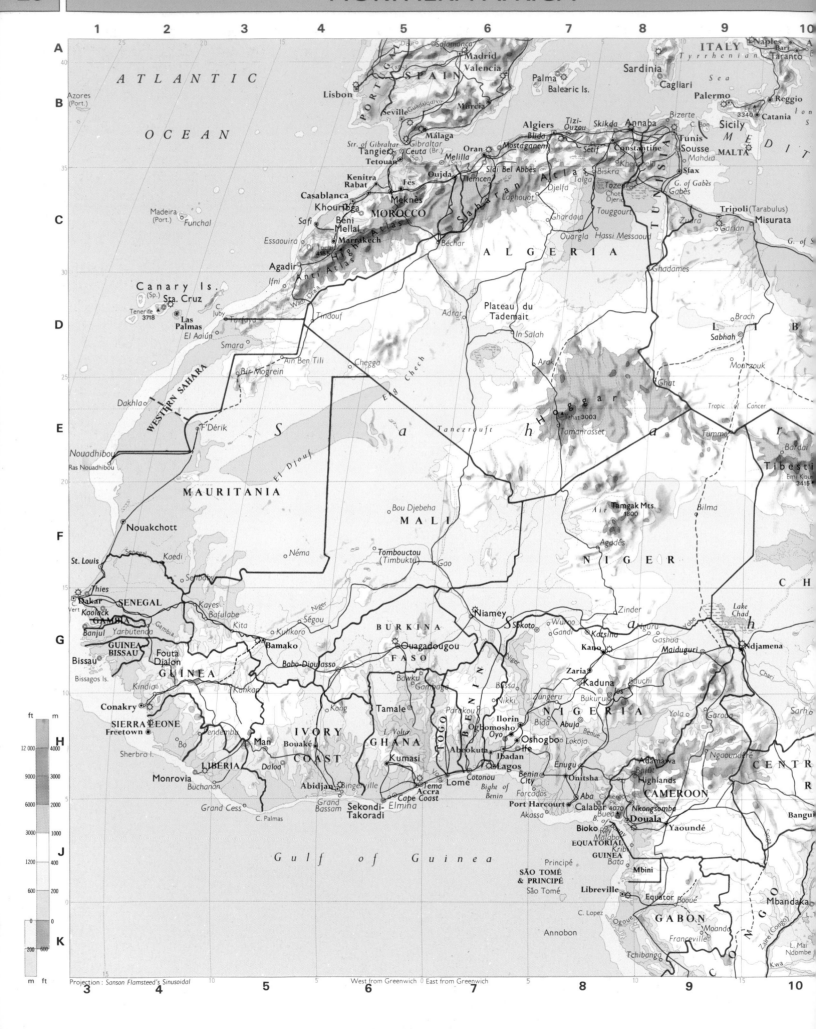

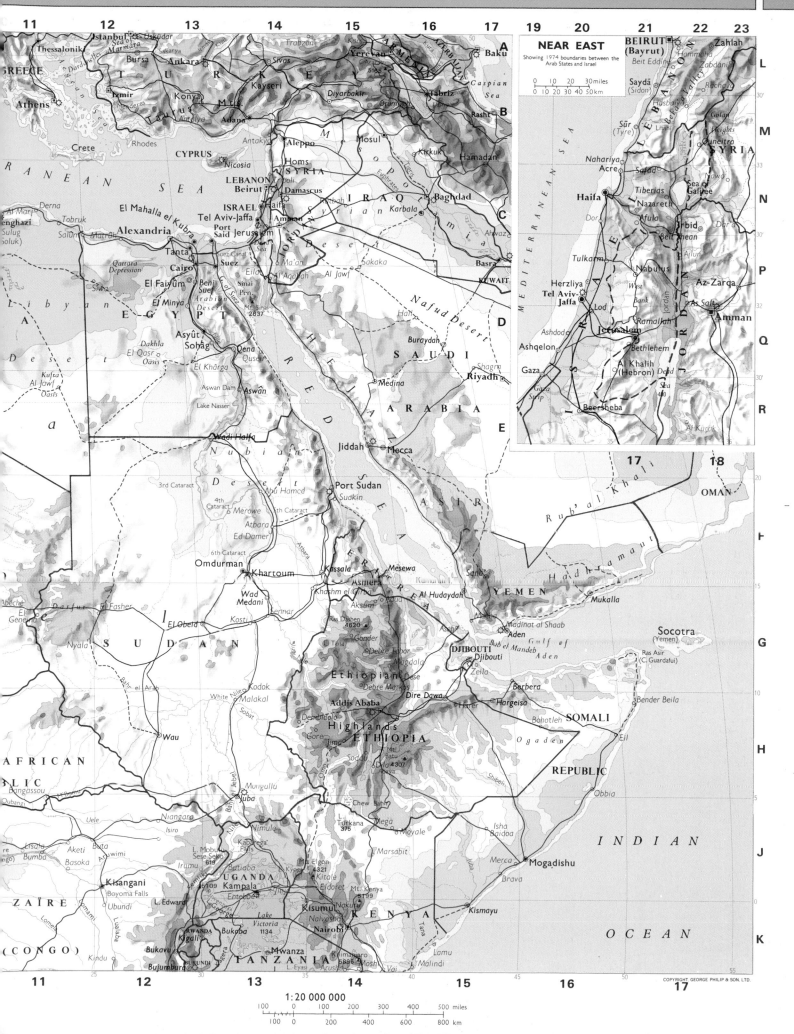

NEAR EAST

Showing 1974 boundaries between the Arab States and Israel

0 10 20 30 miles
0 10 20 30 40 50 km

1:20 000 000

100   0   100   200   300   400   500 miles

100 0   200   400   600   800 km

COPYRIGHT. GEORGE. PHILIP & SON. LTD.

1:8 000 000

Projection: Lambert's Equivalent Azimuthal

East from Greenwich

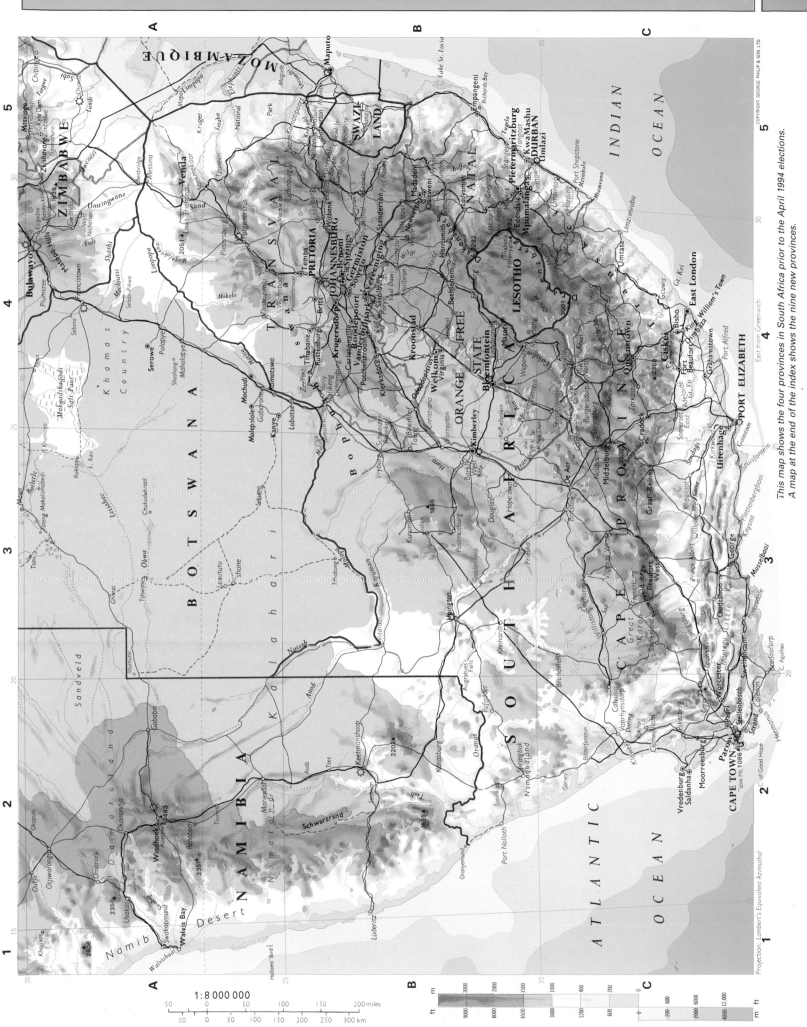

This map shows the four provinces in South Africa prior to the April 1994 elections. A map at the end of the index shows the nine new provinces.

COPYRIGHT GEORGE PHILIP & SON LTD.

Projection: Lambert's Equivalent Azimuthal

1 : 8 000 000

50   0   50   100   150   200 miles

50   0   50   100   150   200   250   300 km

East from Greenwich

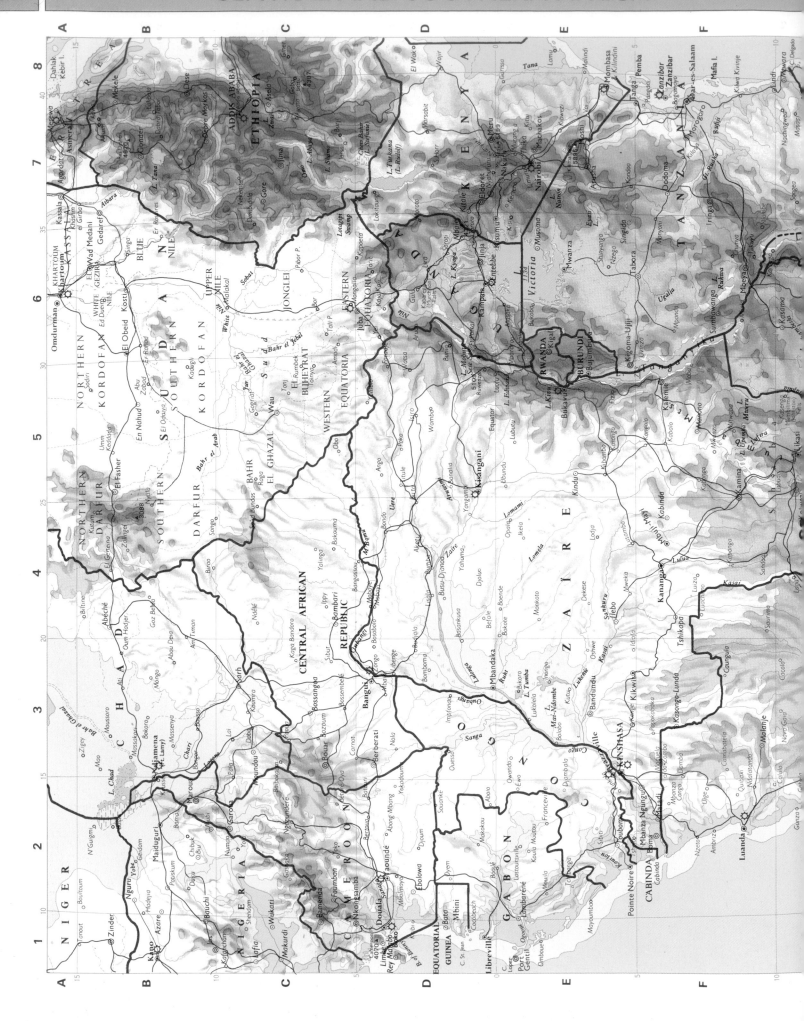

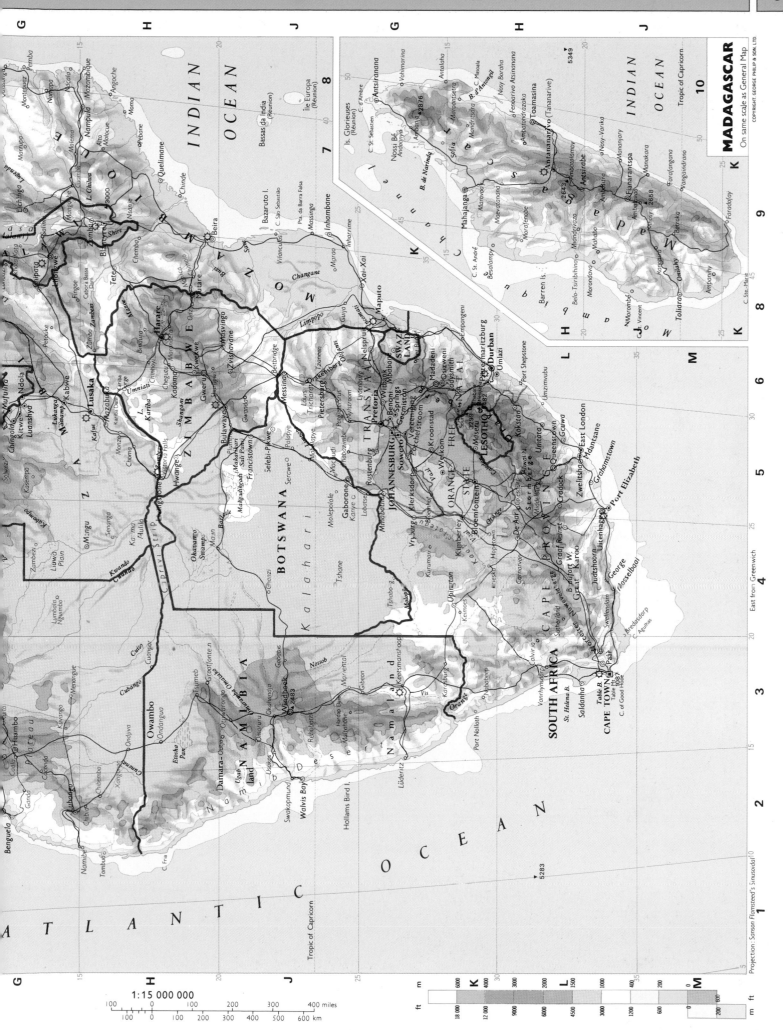

COPYRIGHT. GEORGE PHILIP & SON, LTD.

MADAGASCAR
On same scale as General Map

ATLANTIC OCEAN

INDIAN OCEAN

Tropic of Capricorn

1:15 000 000

Projection: Sanson Flamsteed's Sinusoidal

East from Greenwich

| 100 | 0 | 100 | 200 | 300 | 400 miles |
| 100 | 0 | 100 | 200 | 300 | 400 | 500 | 600 km |

South Africa
Cape Town
Johannesburg
Pretoria
Durban
Port Elizabeth
Bloemfontein
East London
Lesotho
Swaziland
Orange Free State
Transvaal
Cape Province
Natal
Botswana
Namibia
Zimbabwe
Harare
Bulawayo
Lusaka
Beira
Maputo
Antananarivo (Tananarive)
Toamasina
Antsiranana
Mahajanga
Toliara

1:20 000 000

100   0   100   200   300   400   500 miles

100   0   200   400   600   800 km

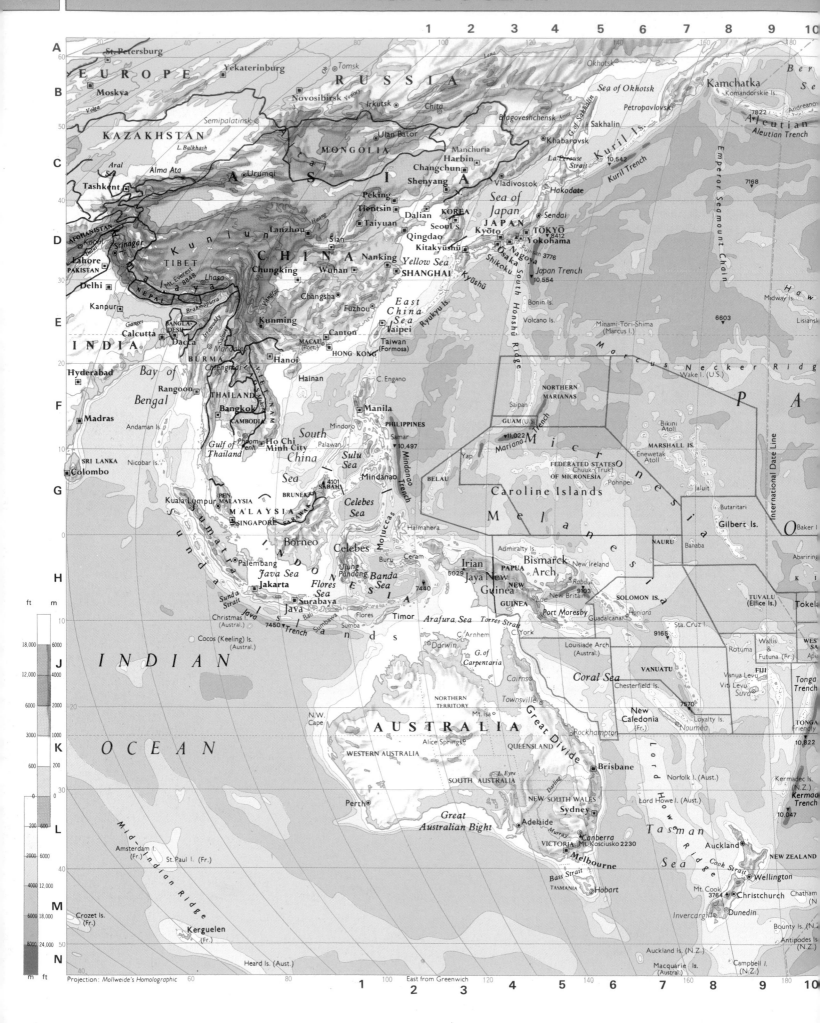

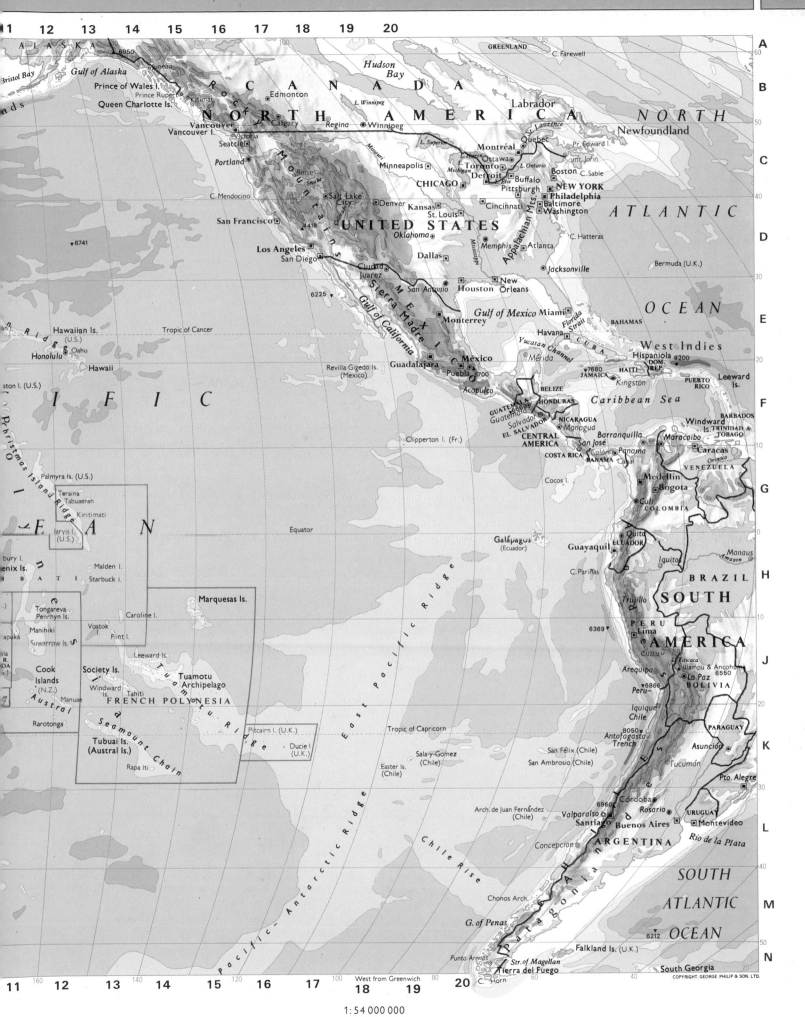

1:54 000 000

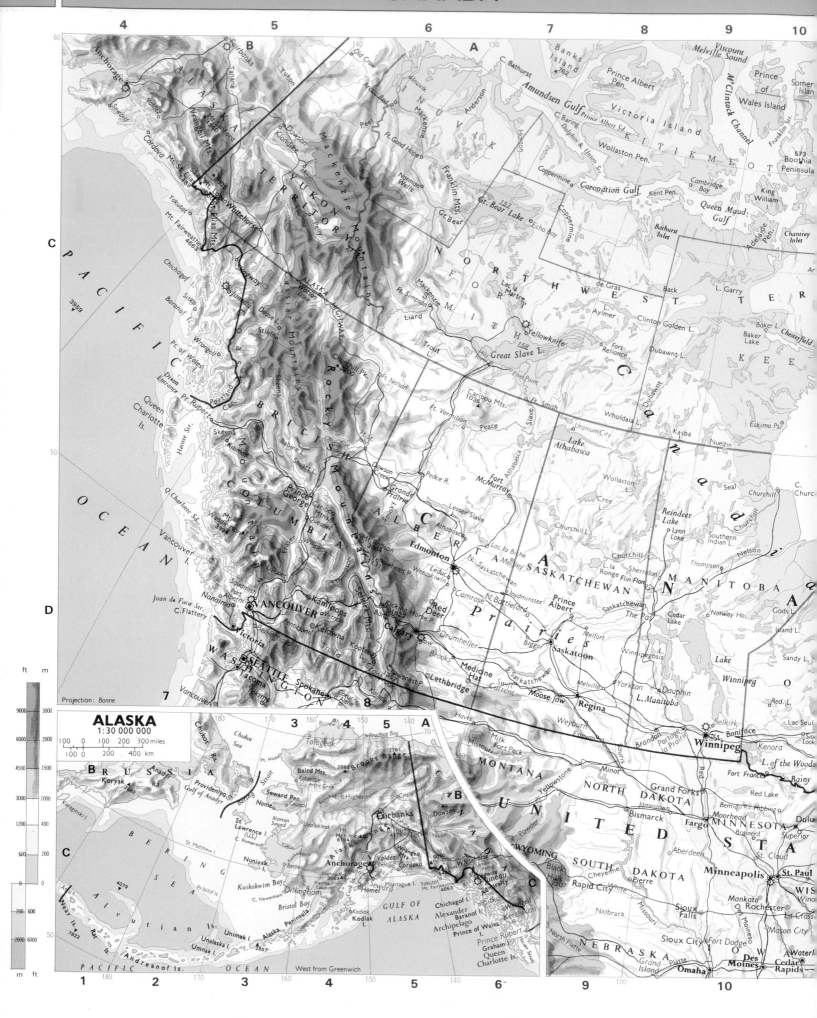

CANADA

PACIFIC OCEAN

ALASKA

YUKON TERRITORY

NORTHWEST TERRITORIES

BRITISH COLUMBIA

ALBERTA

SASKATCHEWAN

MANITOBA

Prairies

Rocky Mountains

Coast Mountains

Cassiar Mountains

Columbia Mountains

Mackenzie Mountains

Anchorage
Seward
Cordova
Mt. St. Elias 5489
Yakutat
Mt. Fairweather 4663
Whitehorse
Skagway
Juneau
Sitka
Chichagof I.
Baranof I.
Pr. of Wales
Queen Charlotte Is.
Pr. Rupert
Skeena
Kitimat
Vancouver I.
Nanaimo
Port Alberni
Victoria
VANCOUVER
Kamloops
Kelowna
Penticton
Prince George
Quesnel
Williams L.
Squamish
Red Deer
Calgary
Edmonton
Leduc
Wetaskiwin
Camrose
Grande Prairie
Lethbridge
Medicine Hat
Brooks
Drumheller
Saskatoon
Biggar
Melfort
Moose Jaw
Regina
Weyburn
Estevan
Swift Current
Yorkton
Dauphin
Brandon
Portage la Prairie
WINNIPEG
St. Boniface
Selkirk
Kenora
L. of the Woods
Fort Frances
Rainy

Whitehorse
Dawson
Old Crow
Inuvik
Arctic Red R.
Ft. Good Hope
Normans Wells
Ft. Simpson
Ft. Liard
Ft. Nelson
Yellowknife
Great Slave L.
Ft. Smith
Ft. Vermilion
Hay River
Fort McMurray
Peace River
Lake Athabasca
Uranium City
Great Bear Lake
Coppermine
Coronation Gulf
Amundsen Gulf
Victoria Island
Banks Island
Prince Albert Pen.
C. Bathurst
Melville Sound
Viscount
Prince of Wales Island
Somerset Island
Boothia Peninsula
King William
Queen Maud Gulf
Bathurst Inlet
Chantrey Inlet
Baker Lake
Chesterfield
Dubawnt L.
Wholdaia L.
Kasba L.
Nueltin
Reindeer Lake
Lynn Lake
Southern Indian L.
Flin Flon
Thompson
Churchill
Seal
Nelson
Prince Albert
N. Battleford
Lloydminster
Wadena
The Pas
Cedar Lake
Norway Ho.
Gods L.
Island L.
Lake Winnipeg
L. Manitoba
Winnipegosis
Sandy L.
Red L.

MONTANA
NORTH DAKOTA
SOUTH DAKOTA
WYOMING
NEBRASKA
MINNESOTA
WISCONSIN
IOWA
UNITED STATES
Seattle
Tacoma
Spokane
WASHINGTON
Vancouver
Havre
Great Falls
Yellowstone
Milk
Missouri
Minot
Grand Forks
Fargo
Bismarck
Jamestown
Aberdeen
Pierre
Rapid City
Cheyenne
Black Hills
Sioux Falls
Sioux City
Minneapolis
St. Paul
St. Cloud
Rochester
Mankato
Des Moines
Omaha
Grand Island
North Platte
Niobrara
Duluth
Superior
La Crosse
Waterloo
Cedar Rapids
Bemidji
Hibbing
Red Lake
Moorhead

Scale/Legend

Projection: Bonne

ft m
9000 3000
6000 2000
4500 1500
3000 1000
1200 400
600 200
0 0
200 600
2000 6000
m ft

ALASKA
1:30 000 000

100 0 100 200 300 miles
100 0 200 400 km

RUSSIA
Koryak Ra.
Anadyr
Provideniya
Gulf of Anadyr
Chukot Pen.
Chukot Sea
Pt. Hope
Barrow
Prudhoe Bay
Brooks Range
Baird Mts.
Kotzebue
Seward Pen.
Nome
Council
Hughes
Circle
Fairbanks
Mt. McKinley 6194
Dawson
Whitehorse
Valdez
Cordova
Anchorage
Homer
Kodiak
Seldovia
Dillingham
Bristol Bay
Kuskokwim Bay
Bethel
Nunivak
St. Matthew I.
St. Lawrence I. (U.S.)
Pribilof Is.
BERING SEA
Unalaska I.
Unimak I.
Umnak I.
Andreanof Is.
Rat Is.
Attu Is.
Aleutian Is.
PACIFIC OCEAN
Juneau
Sitka
Admiralty
Chichagof I.
Baranof I.
Prince of Wales
Ketchikan
Wrangell
Alexander Archipelago
Prince Rupert
Graham
Queen Charlotte Is.
Mt. Fairweather 4663
Yakutat

West from Greenwich

West from Greenwich

COPYRIGHT. GEORGE PHILIP & SON. LTD.

1:15 000 000

100   0   100   200   300   400 miles

100   0   100   200   300   400   500   600 km

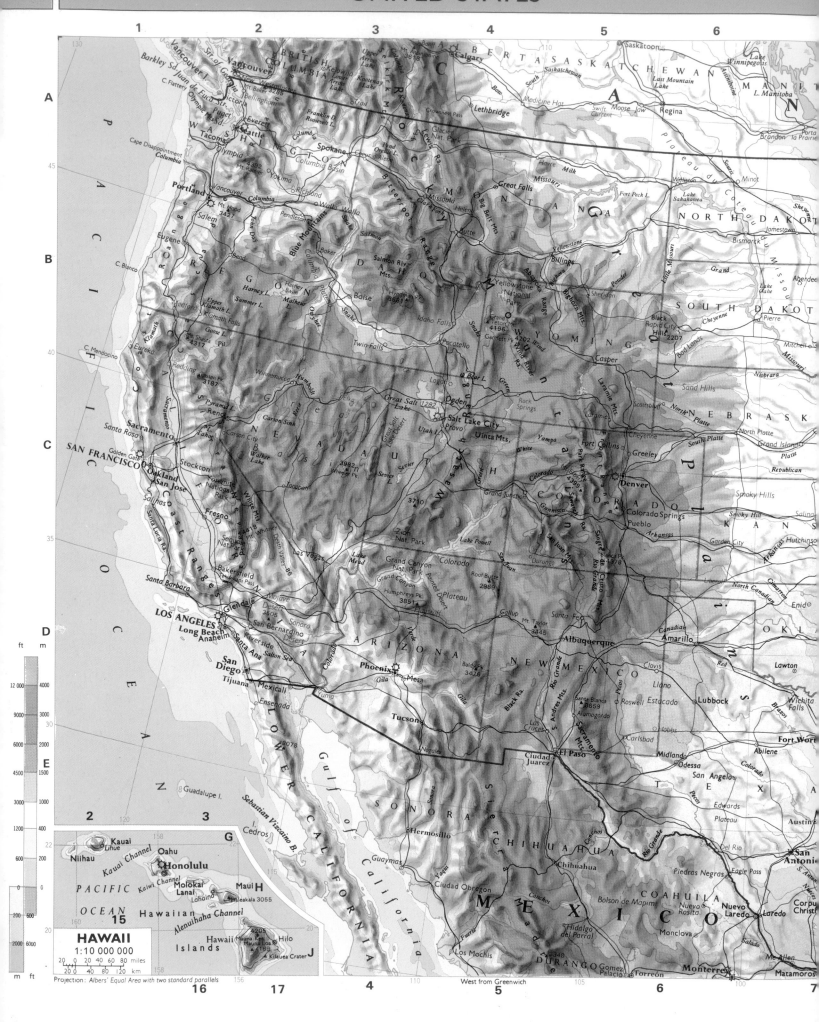

1:12 000 000

50   0   50   100   150   200   250   300 miles

50   0   50 100 150 200 250 300 350 400 450 500 km

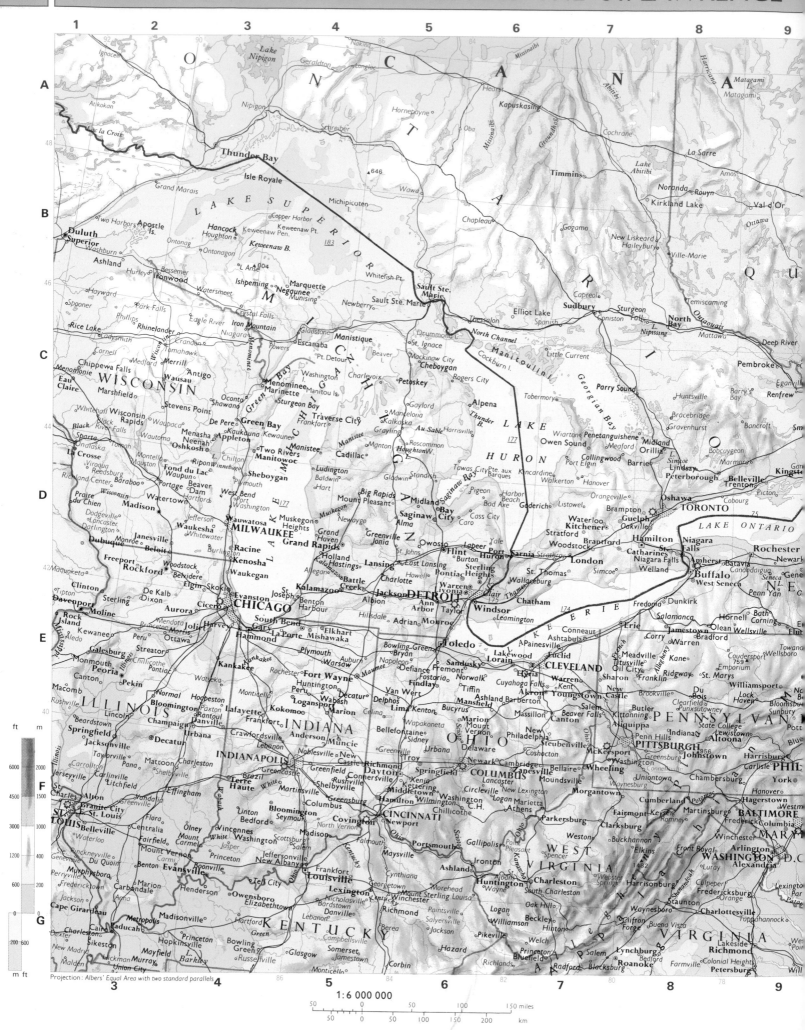

1 : 6 000 000

50   0   50   100   150 miles

50   0   50   100   150   200 km

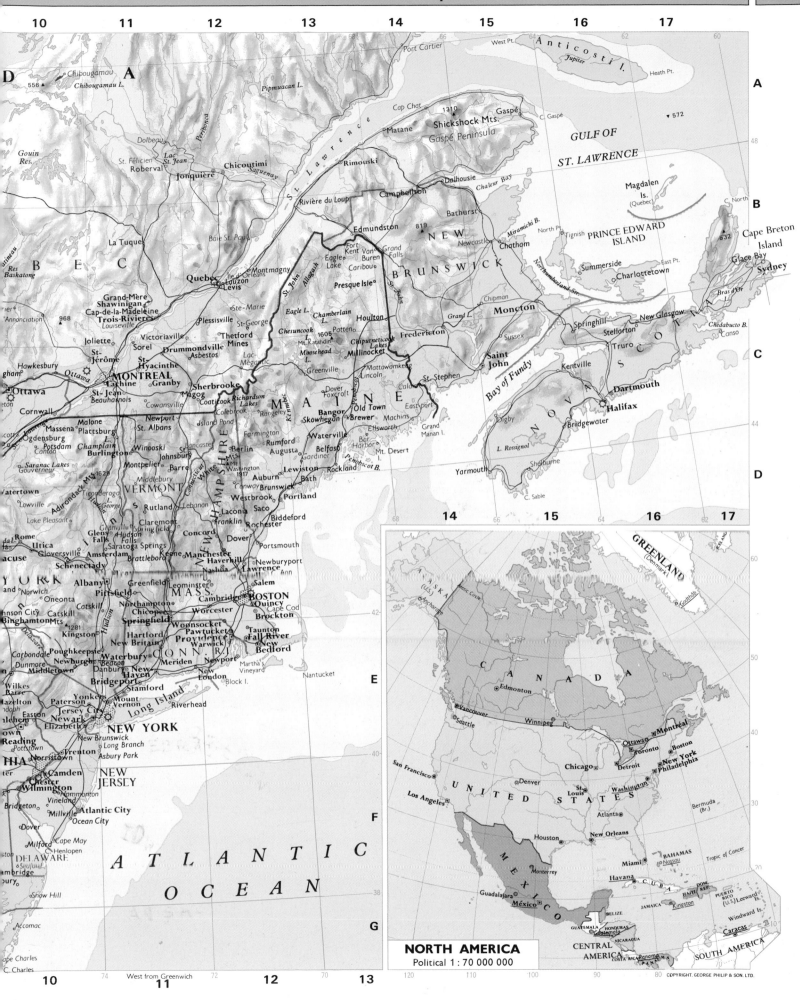

NORTH AMERICA
Political 1 : 70 000 000

PANAMA CANAL
1 : 1 000 000

JAMAICA
1 : 5 000 000

**TRINIDAD
AND TOBAGO**
1 : 5 000 000

**LEEWARD
ISLANDS**
1 : 5 000 000

**WINDWARD
ISLANDS**
1 : 5 000 000

Projection : Bonne

8   **9**   **10**   **11**   **12**   **13**

A

B

C

D

E

F

G

30

25

20

15

10

Colombus
C. Fear
Atlanta
Augusta
Macon
ombus
Charleston
Savannah
Albany
lahassee
Jacksonville
Daytona Beach
Orlando
C. Canaveral
Tampa
tersburg
West Palm Beach
Grand Bahama I.
L. Okeechobee
Miami
Fort Lauderdale
Freeport
Gt. Abaco I.
New Providence I.
C. Sable
Eleuthera I.
Key West
Nassau
Cat I.
S. Salvador
Havana
Matanzas
Cárdenas
Sagua la Grande
Sta. Clara
BAHAMAS
Long I.
Mayaguana
Río
Cienfuegos
Sancti Spiritus
Ciego de Avila
Morón
Camagüey
Acklins I.
Turks & Caicos Is. (Br.)
I. de Juventud
C U B A
Holguín
Gt. Inagua I.
Manzanillo
Bayamo
Guantánamo
Grand Cayman (Br.)
Santiago de Cuba
Windward Passage
Cap Haitien
Gonaives
Santiago
San Francisco de Macorís
DOMINICAN REP.
La Romana
PUERTO RICO (U.S.A.)
San Juan
St. Thomas (U.S.A.)
Charlotte Amalie
Virgin Is. (Br.)
Anguilla
St. Martin (Fr. & Neth.)
ST. CHRISTOPHER-NEVIS (St. Kitts)
ANTIGUA & BARBUDA
St. John's
Montserrat
Guadeloupe (Fr.)
Pointe à Pitre
DOMINICA
Montego Bay
JAMAICA
Kingston
Port au Prince
Hispaniola
Santo Domingo
Ponce
Mayagüez
Caguas
St. Croix (U.S.A.)
Les Cayes
Barahona
Baní
Mona Passage
Leeward Islands
LESSER
ANTILLES
Martinique (Fr.)
Fort de France
St. LUCIA
BARBADOS
Bridgetown
GRENADA
Windward
ST. VINCENT
&
THE GRENADINES Islands
GREATER   ANTILLES
ATLANTIC OCEAN
Bermuda
Hamilton
Tropic of Cancer
Andros I.
Caratásca Lagoon
C. Gracias á Dios
CARIBBEAN SEA
Providencia (Col.)
San Andrés (Col.)
Bluefields
Mosquito Coast
Limón
Colón
PANAMA
Panama
David
Azuero Pen.
Coiba
Vol. Barú
G. of Panama
G. of Darién
Cartagena
Barranquilla
Santa Marta
Pen. de la Guajira
Pta. Gallinas
Gulf of Venezuela
Aruba (Neth.)
Curacao
Willemstad
Bonaire
Pen. de Paraguaná
NETH. ANTILLES
Punto Fijo
Coro
La Tortuga (Ven.)
La Blanquilla (Ven.)
Margarita
Carúpano
Cumaná
San Fernando
Port of Spain
TRINIDAD & TOBAGO
Tobago
Maracaibo
Cabimas
L. de Maracaibo
Sierra Nevada de Santa Marta
Maracay
Caracas
Valencia
Barquisimeto
Barcelona
El Tigre
Maturín
G. of Paria
Delta of the Orinoco
Sincelejo
Medellín
Quibdó
Manizales
Pereira
COLOMBIA
Bogotá
Armenia
Girardot
Buenaventura
Cali
Popayán
Valera
Mérida
Cord. de Mérida
San Cristóbal
Cúcuta
Bucaramanga
Barrancabermeja
Barinas
Apure
San Fernando de Apure
Arauca
VENEZUELA
Meta
Pto. Ayacucho
Ciudad Bolívar
Ciudad Guayana
Orinoco
Angel Falls
Roraima
Sierra Pacaraima
Caura
GUYANA
Georgetown
New Amsterdam
Cuyuni
Essequibo
Corentyne
SURINAM
BRAZIL
Casiquiare
Guaviare
Atrato
Cauca
Magdalena
Tunja

West from Greenwich

80   75   70   65   60   55

8   **9**   **10**   **11**   **12**   **13**

COPYRIGHT. GEORGE PHILIP & SON. LTD.

1:15 000 000

100 0 100 200 300 400 miles
100 0 100 200 300 400 500 600 km

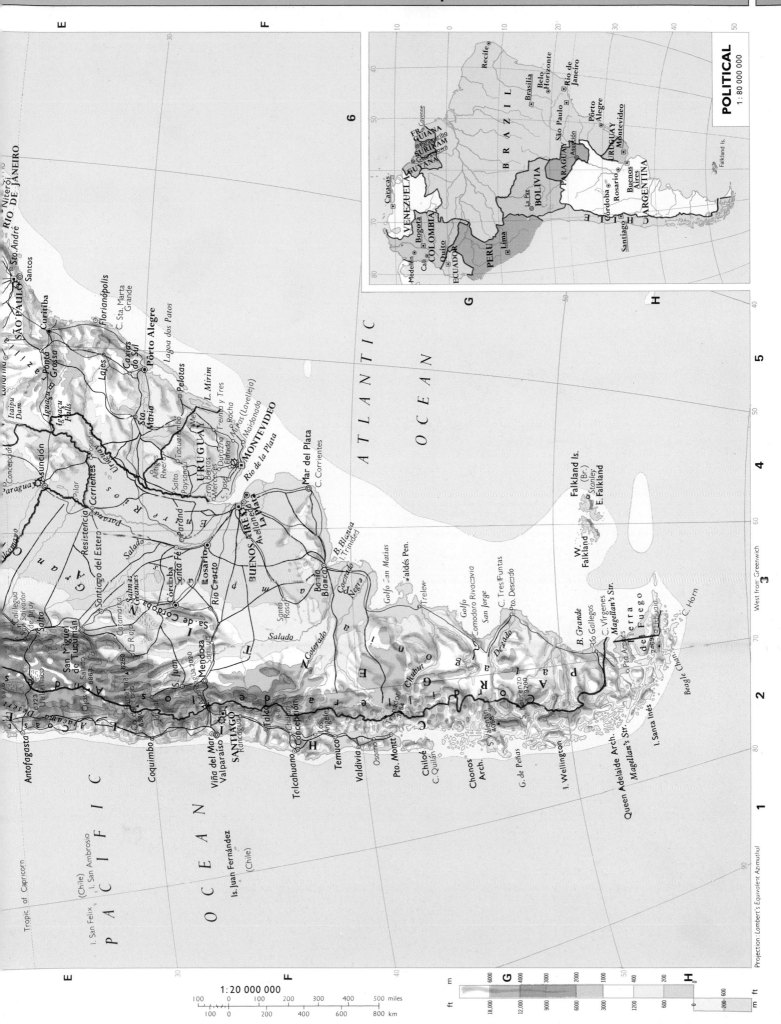

POLITICAL
1 : 80 000 000

1 : 20 000 000

100   0   100   200   300   400   500 miles

100   0   200   400   600   800 km

Projection : Lambert's Equivalent Azimuthal

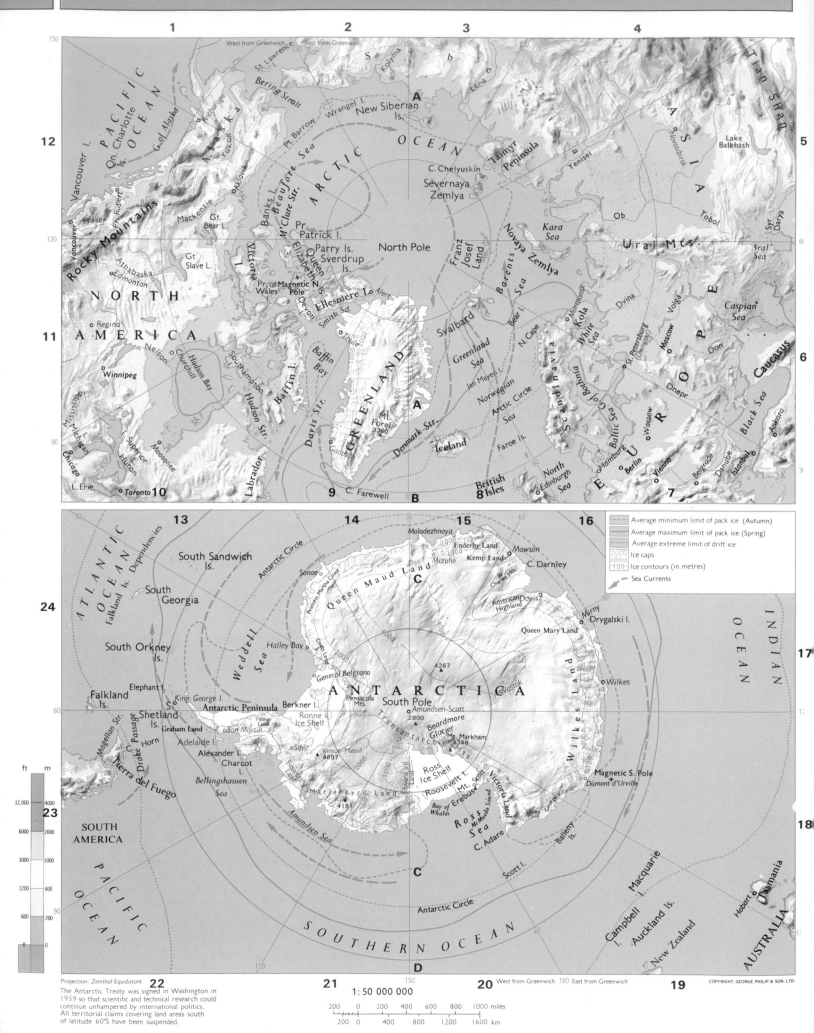

Projection: Zenithal Equidistant

The Antarctic Treaty was signed in Washington in 1959 so that scientific and technical research could continue unhampered by international politics. All territorial claims covering land areas south of latitude 60°S have been suspended.

1 : 50 000 000

Average minimum limit of pack ice (Autumn)
Average maximum limit of pack ice (Spring)
Average extreme limit of drift ice
Ice caps
100 Ice contours (in metres)
Sea Currents

WORLD THEMATIC MAPS

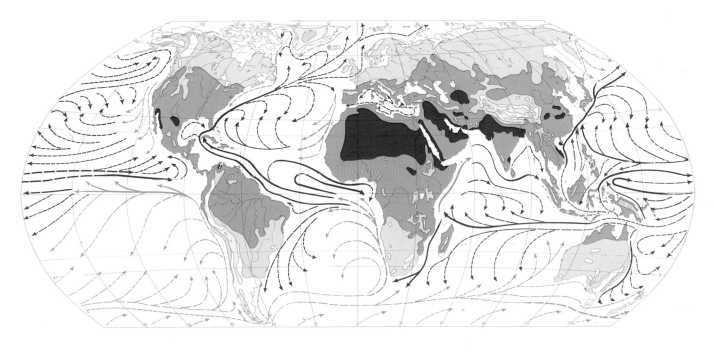

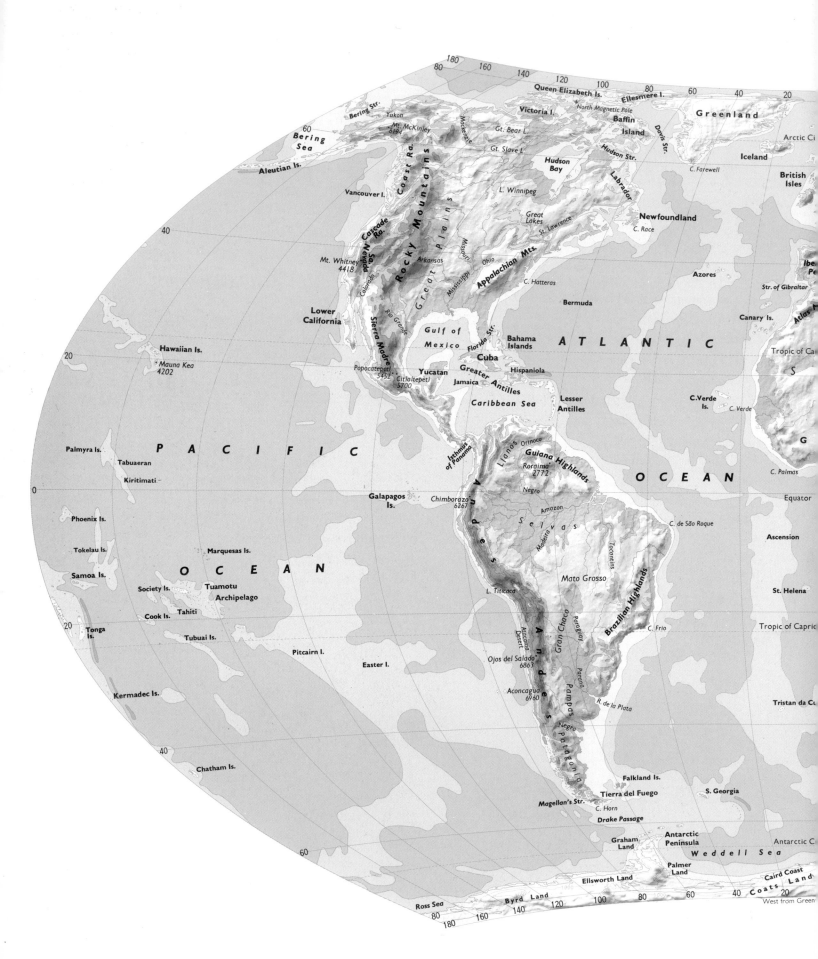

180   80   160   140   120   100   80   60   40   20

Queen Elizabeth Is.
Ellesmere I.
Victoria I.
+ North Magnetic Pole
Greenland
Bering Str.
Yukon
Mt. McKinley 6194
Gt. Bear L.
Baffin Island
Davis Str.
Arctic Ci
60
Bering Sea
Mackenzie
Gt. Slave L.
Hudson Str.
Iceland
Aleutian Is.
Hudson Bay
C. Farewell
Vancouver I.
L. Winnipeg
Labrador
British Isles
40
Coast Ra.
Rocky Mountains
Great Lakes
St. Lawrence
Newfoundland
C. Race
Cascade Ra.
Great Plains
Missouri
Ohio
Appalachian Mts.
Azores
Ibe Pe
Mt. Whitney 4418
Arkansas
Mississippi
C. Hatteras
Str. of Gibraltar
Colorado
Rio Grande
Bermuda
Canary Is.
Atlas M
Lower California
Sierra Madre
Gulf of Mexico
Florida Str.
Bahama Islands
ATLANTIC
Tropic of Ca
20
Hawaiian Is.
Cuba
Hispaniola
C. Verde Is.
S
Mauna Kea 4202
Popocatepetl 5452
Yucatan
Greater Antilles
C. Verde
Citlaltepetl 5700
Jamaica
Caribbean Sea
Lesser Antilles
OCEAN
G
PACIFIC
Isthmus of Panama
Llanos
Orinoco
Guiana Highlands
Roraima 2772
C. Palmas
Palmyra Is.
Tabuaeran
Negro
Ascension
0
Kiritimati
Galapagos Is.
Chimborazo 6267
Andes
Amazon
Equator
Phoenix Is.
Madeira
Selvas
C. de São Roque
Tokelau Is.
Marquesas Is.
St. Helena
Samoa Is.
OCEAN
Mato Grosso
Society Is.
Tuamotu Archipelago
L. Titicaca
Brazilian Highlands
Cook Is.
Tahiti
Gran Chaco
Paraguay
C. Frio
20
Tonga Is.
Tubuai Is.
Pampas
Tropic of Capric
Pitcairn I.
Atacama Desert
Paraná
Easter I.
Ojos del Salado 6863
Negro
Kermadec Is.
Aconcagua 6960
Andes
R. de la Plata
Tristan da Cu
Patagonia
Chatham Is.
40
Falkland Is.
S. Georgia
Tierra del Fuego
Magellan's Str.
C. Horn
Drake Passage
Antarctic Peninsula
Antarctic C
Graham Land
Weddell Sea
60
Palmer Land
Ellsworth Land
Caird Coast
Ross Sea
Byrd Land
Coats Land
20
West from Green
80   160   140   120   100   80   60   40
180

Projection: Hammer Equal Area

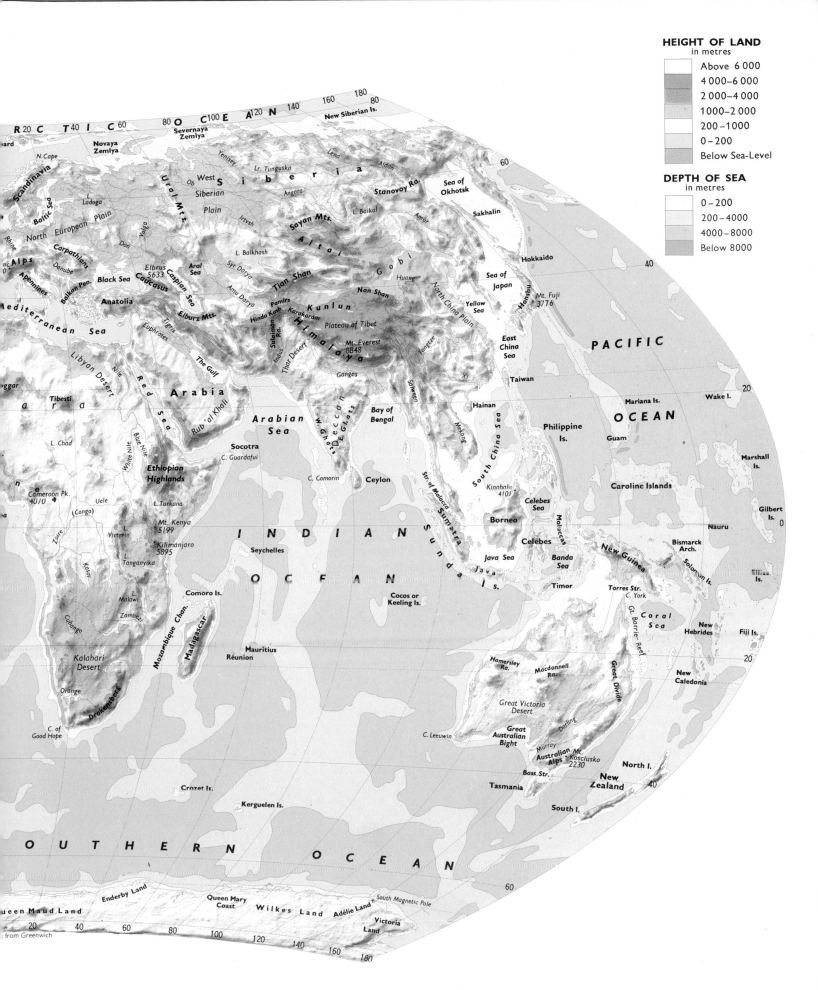

HEIGHT OF LAND
in metres

Above 6 000
4 000–6 000
2 000–4 000
1 000–2 000
200–1 000
0–200
Below Sea-Level

DEPTH OF SEA
in metres

0–200
200–4 000
4 000–8 000
Below 8000

A R C T I C O C E A N

New Siberian Is.
Severnaya Zemlya
Novaya Zemlya
N. Cape
Scandinavia
Baltic Sea
North European Plain
Rhine
Carpathians
Alps
Apennines
Danube
Balkan Pen.
Black Sea
Anatolia
Mediterranean Sea
L. Ladoga
Ob
West Siberian Plain
Volga
Don
Ural Mts.
Aral Sea
Elbrus 5633
Caucasus
Caspian Sea
Elburz Mts.
Amu Darya
Syr Darya
L. Balkhash
Yenisey
Irtysh
Lr. Tunguska
Lena
Angara
Sayan Mts.
L. Baikal
Altai
Stanovoy Ra.
Aldan
Amur
Sea of Okhotsk
Sakhalin
Hokkaido
Gobi
Nan Shan
Tian Shan
Kunlun
Pamirs
Hindu Kush
Karakoram
Sulaiman Ra.
Plateau of Tibet
Himalaya
Mt. Everest 8848
Thar Desert
Indus
Ganges
Deccan
W. Ghats
E. Ghats
Bay of Bengal
Tigris
Euphrates
Nile
Libyan Desert
Red Sea
Arabia
Rub 'al Khali
Socotra
C. Guardafui
Arabian Sea
Tibesti
Sahara
Ahaggar
L. Chad
White Nile
Blue Nile
Ethiopian Highlands
Cameroon Pk. 4070
Uele
(Congo)
Zaire
Kasai
L. Turkana
Mt. Kenya 5199
Kilimanjaro 5895
L. Victoria
L. Tanganyika
Malawi
Zambezi
Cubango
Comoro Is.
Madagascar
Mozambique Chan.
Kalahari Desert
Orange
Drakensberg
C. of Good Hope
Seychelles
Comoro Is.
C. Comorin
Ceylon
I N D I A N O C E A N
Cocos or Keeling Is.
Mauritius
Réunion
Crozet Is.
Kerguelen Is.
Huang
Yellow Sea
North China Plain
East China Sea
Yangtze
Xi
Taiwan
Hainan
Mekong
Salween
Str. of Malacca
Sumatra
South China Sea
Kinabalu 4101
Borneo
Celebes Sea
Celebes
Java Sea
Java
Sunda Is.
Timor
Banda Sea
Molucca Sea
Sea of Japan
Honshu
Mt. Fuji 3776
P A C I F I C O C E A N
Mariana Is.
Wake I.
Guam
Caroline Islands
Marshall Is.
Nauru
Gilbert Is.
Bismarck Arch.
New Guinea
Solomon Is.
Ellice Is.
Torres Str.
C. York
Gt. Barrier Reef
Coral Sea
New Hebrides
New Caledonia
Fiji Is.
Hamersley Ra.
Macdonnell Ra.
Great Victoria Desert
Great Australian Bight
C. Leeuwin
Murray
Darling
Australian Alps
Mt. Kosciusko 2230
Great Divide
Bass Str.
Tasmania
North I.
New Zealand
South I.
Philippine Is.
S O U T H E R N O C E A N
Queen Maud Land
Enderby Land
Queen Mary Coast
Wilkes Land
Adélie Land
South Magnetic Pole
Victoria Land
from Greenwich

1:80 000 000

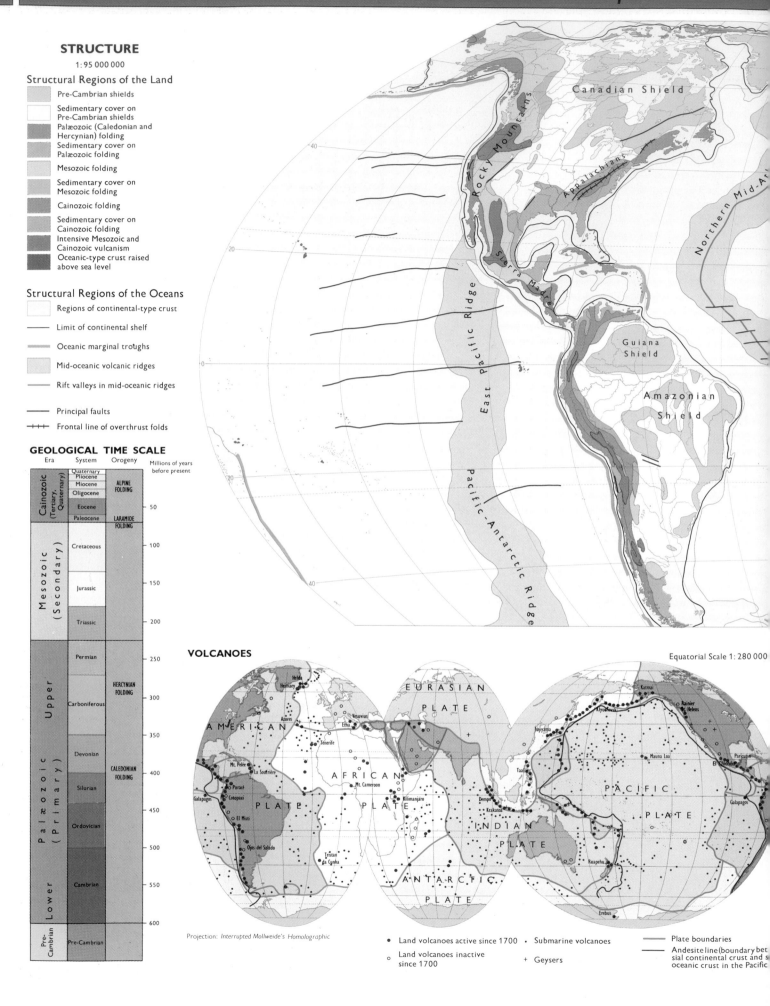

STRUCTURE

1:95 000 000

Structural Regions of the Land

- Pre-Cambrian shields
- Sedimentary cover on Pre-Cambrian shields
- Palæozoic (Caledonian and Hercynian) folding
- Sedimentary cover on Palæozoic folding
- Mesozoic folding
- Sedimentary cover on Mesozoic folding
- Cainozoic folding
- Sedimentary cover on Cainozoic folding
- Intensive Mesozoic and Cainozoic vulcanism
- Oceanic-type crust raised above sea level

Structural Regions of the Oceans

- Regions of continental-type crust
- Limit of continental shelf
- Oceanic marginal troughs
- Mid-oceanic volcanic ridges
- Rift valleys in mid-oceanic ridges
- Principal faults
- ++++ Frontal line of overthrust folds

GEOLOGICAL TIME SCALE

Era	System	Orogeny	Millions of years before present
Cainozoic (Tertiary, Quaternary)	Quaternary		
	Pliocene	ALPINE FOLDING	
	Miocene		
	Oligocene		
	Eocene		— 50
	Paleocene	LARAMIDE FOLDING	
Mesozoic (Secondary)	Cretaceous		— 100
	Jurassic		— 150
	Triassic		— 200
Palæozoic (Primary) Upper	Permian		— 250
	Carboniferous	HERCYNIAN FOLDING	— 300
	Devonian		— 350
		CALEDONIAN FOLDING	— 400
Lower	Silurian		
	Ordovician		— 450
			— 500
	Cambrian		— 550
Pre-Cambrian	Pre-Cambrian		— 600

VOLCANOES

Equatorial Scale 1: 280 000

Projection: *Interrupted Mollweide's Homolographic*

- ● Land volcanoes active since 1700
- ○ Land volcanoes inactive since 1700
- • Submarine volcanoes
- + Geysers
- —— Plate boundaries
- —— Andesite line (boundary between sial continental crust and s... oceanic crust in the Pacific

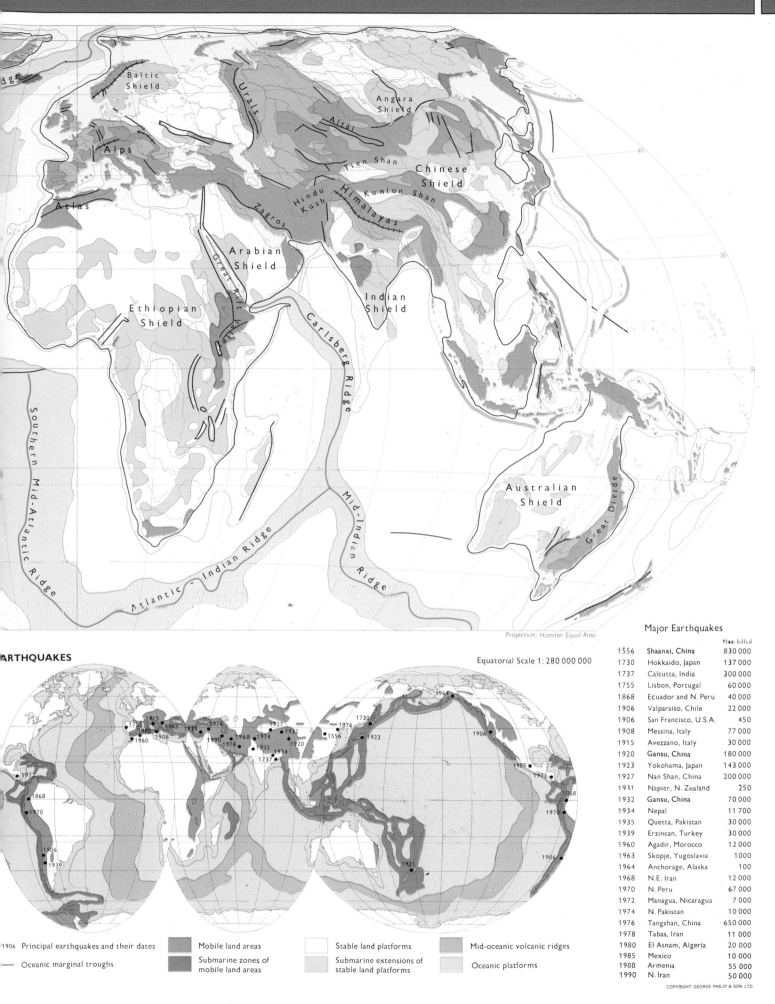

Baltic Shield

Urals

Angara Shield

Altai

Alps

Tien Shan

Chinese Shield

Atlas

Hindu Kush

Himalayas

Kunlun Shan

Zagros

Arabian Shield

Great Rift

Indian Shield

Ethiopian Shield

Carlsberg Ridge

Southern Mid-Atlantic Ridge

Australian Shield

Atlantic – Indian Ridge

Mid-Indian Ridge

Great Divide

Projection: Hammer Equal Area

EARTHQUAKES

Equatorial Scale 1 : 280 000 000

1906 Principal earthquakes and their dates

Oceanic marginal troughs

Mobile land areas

Submarine zones of mobile land areas

Stable land platforms

Submarine extensions of stable land platforms

Mid-oceanic volcanic ridges

Oceanic platforms

Major Earthquakes

Year	Location	Nos. killed
1556	**Shaanxi, China**	830 000
1730	Hokkaido, Japan	137 000
1737	Calcutta, India	300 000
1755	Lisbon, Portugal	60 000
1868	Ecuador and N. Peru	40 000
1906	Valparaiso, Chile	22 000
1906	San Francisco, U.S.A.	450
1908	Messina, Italy	77 000
1915	Avezzano, Italy	30 000
1920	**Gansu, China**	180 000
1923	Yokohama, Japan	143 000
1927	Nan Shan, China	200 000
1931	Napier, N. Zealand	250
1932	**Gansu, China**	70 000
1934	Nepal	11 700
1935	Quetta, Pakistan	30 000
1939	Erzincan, Turkey	30 000
1960	Agadir, Morocco	12 000
1963	Skopje, Yugoslavia	1 000
1964	Anchorage, Alaska	100
1968	N.E. Iran	12 000
1970	N. Peru	67 000
1972	Managua, Nicaragua	7 000
1974	N. Pakistan	10 000
1976	Tangshan, China	650 000
1978	Tabas, Iran	11 000
1980	El Asnam, Algeria	20 000
1985	Mexico	10 000
1988	Armenia	55 000
1990	N. Iran	50 000

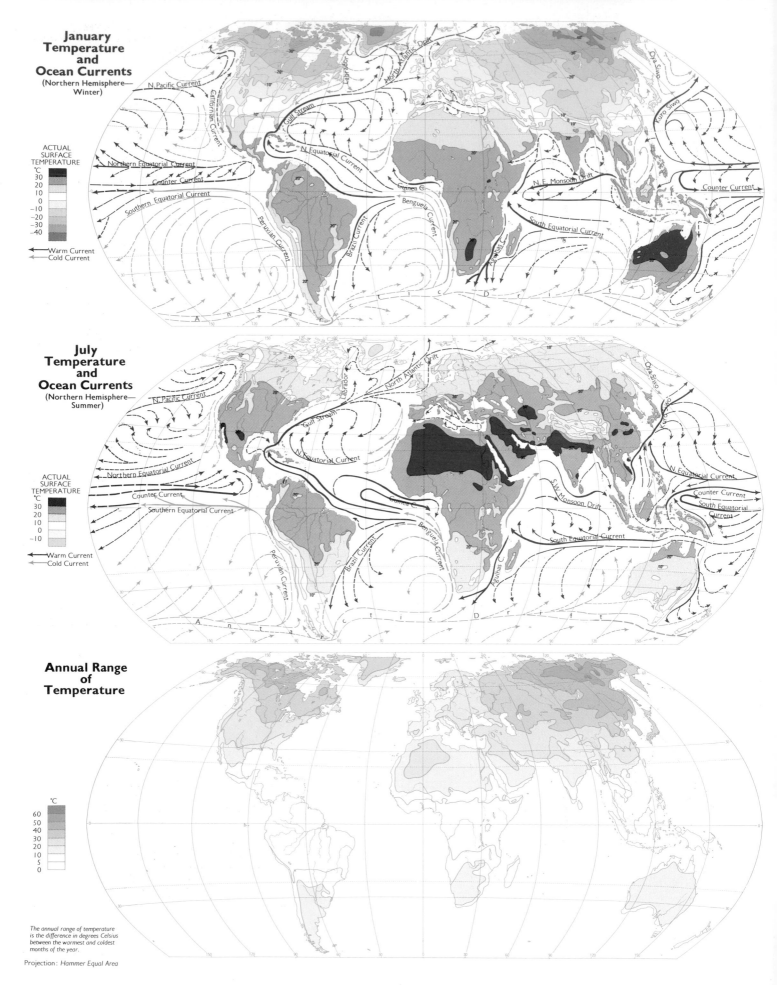

January Temperature and Ocean Currents
(Northern Hemisphere— Winter)

ACTUAL SURFACE TEMPERATURE
°C
30
20
10
0
-10
-20
-30
-40

→ Warm Current
→ Cold Current

N. Pacific Current
Californian Current
Northern Equatorial Current
Counter Current
Southern Equatorial Current
Peruvian Current
Labrador
North Atlantic Drift
Gulf Stream
N. Equatorial Current
Guinea C.
Benguela Current
Brazil Current
Agulhas C.
South Equatorial Current
N.E. Monsoon Drift
Counter Current
Kuro Siwo
Oya Siwo
A n t a r c t i c   D r i f t

July Temperature and Ocean Currents
(Northern Hemisphere— Summer)

ACTUAL SURFACE TEMPERATURE
°C
30
20
10
0
-10

→ Warm Current
→ Cold Current

N. Pacific Current
Northern Equatorial Current
Counter Current
Southern Equatorial Current
Peruvian Current
Labrador
North Atlantic Drift
Gulf Stream
N. Equatorial Current
Guinea C.
Benguela Current
Brazil Current
Agulhas C.
South Equatorial Current
S.W. Monsoon Drift
N. Equatorial Current
Counter Current
South Equatorial Current
Kuro Siwo
Oya Siwo
A n t a r c t i c   D r i f t

Annual Range of Temperature

°C
60
50
40
30
20
10
5
0

The annual range of temperature is the difference in degrees Celsius between the warmest and coldest months of the year.

Projection: *Hammer Equal Area*

1:190 000 000

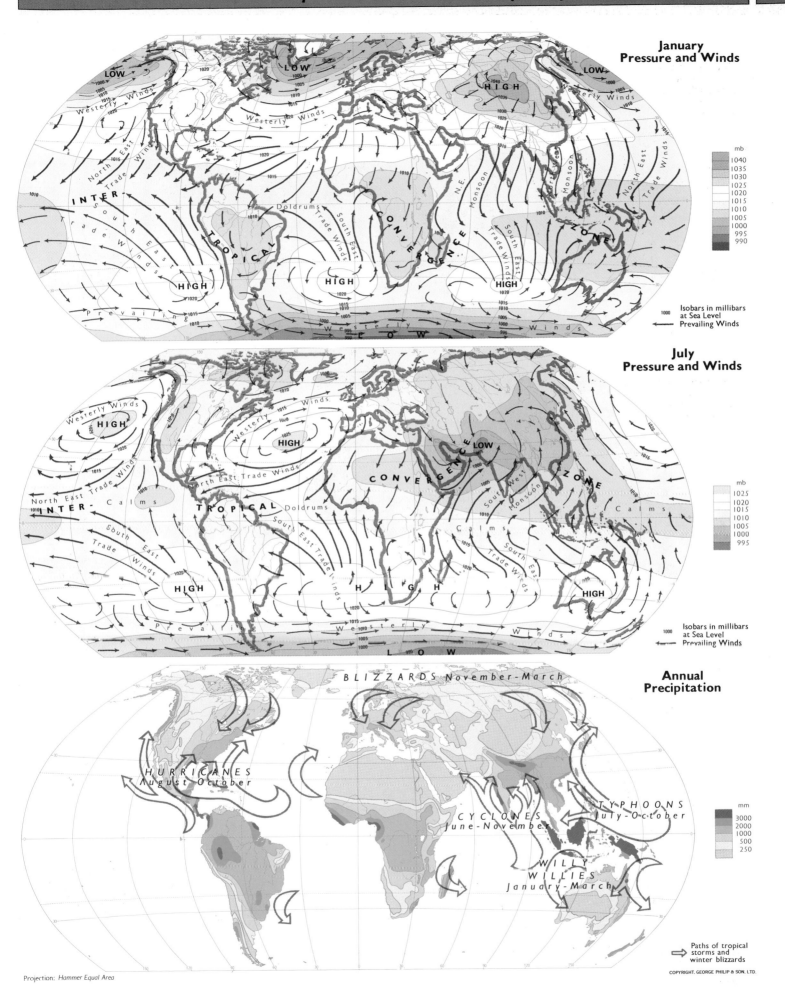

January Pressure and Winds

mb
1040
1035
1030
1025
1020
1015
1010
1005
1000
995
990

1000 ——— Isobars in millibars at Sea Level
⟵ Prevailing Winds

July Pressure and Winds

mb
1025
1020
1015
1010
1005
1000
995

1000 ——— Isobars in millibars at Sea Level
⟵ Prevailing Winds

Annual Precipitation

BLIZZARDS November–March

HURRICANES August–October

CYCLONES June–November

TYPHOONS July–October

WILLY WILLIES January–March

mm
3000
2000
1000
500
250

⟹ Paths of tropical storms and winter blizzards

COPYRIGHT. GEORGE PHILIP & SON. LTD.

Projection: Hammer Equal Area

1:190 000 000

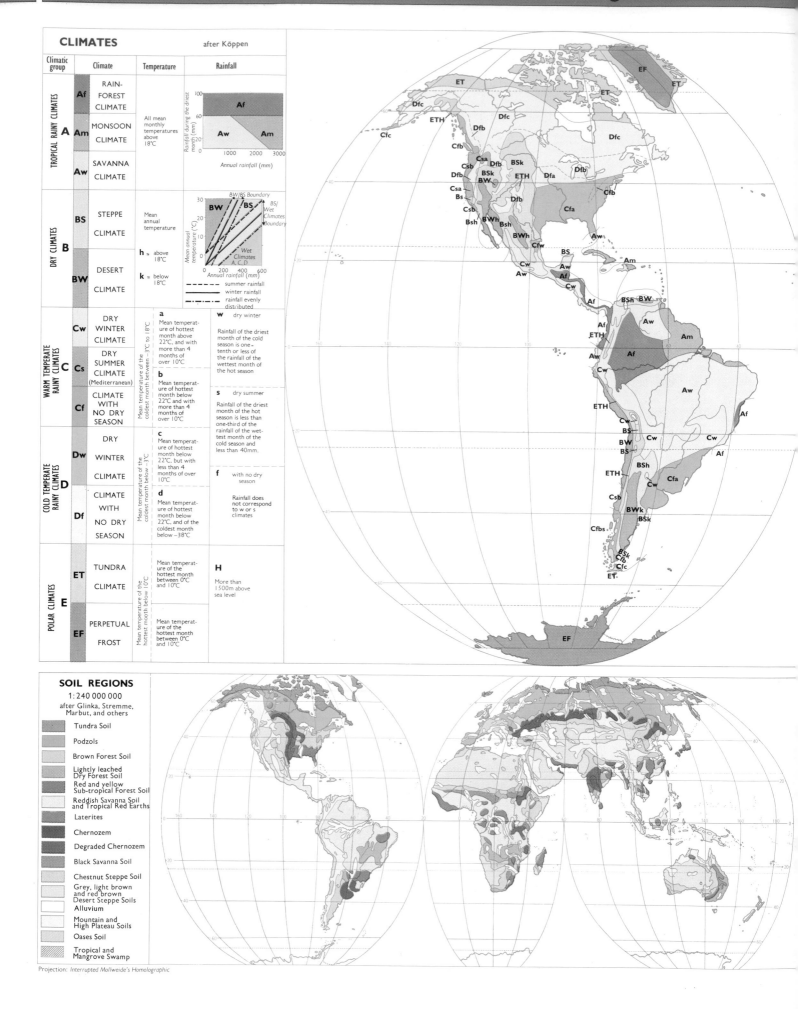

CLIMATES
after Köppen

Climatic group		Climate	Temperature	Rainfall
A TROPICAL RAINY CLIMATES	**Af**	RAIN-FOREST CLIMATE	All mean monthly temperatures above 18°C	
	Am	MONSOON CLIMATE		
	Aw	SAVANNA CLIMATE		
B DRY CLIMATES	**BS**	STEPPE CLIMATE	Mean annual temperature	
	BW	DESERT CLIMATE	**h** = above 18°C **k** = below 18°C	
C WARM TEMPERATE RAINY CLIMATES	**Cw**	DRY WINTER CLIMATE	Mean temperature of the coldest month between -3°C to 18°C	
	Cs	DRY SUMMER CLIMATE (Mediterranean)		
	Cf	CLIMATE WITH NO DRY SEASON		
D COLD TEMPERATE RAINY CLIMATES	**Dw**	DRY WINTER CLIMATE	Mean temperature of the coldest month below -3°C	
	Df	CLIMATE WITH NO DRY SEASON		
E POLAR CLIMATES	**ET**	TUNDRA CLIMATE	Mean temperature of the hottest month between 0°C and 10°C	**H** More than 1500m above sea level
	EF	PERPETUAL FROST	Mean temperature of the hottest month below 10°C	

Rainfall (Af/Aw/Am diagram): Rainfall during the driest month (mm) 100, 60, 20 — Annual rainfall (mm) 1000, 2000, 3000

BW/BS Boundary / BS/Wet Climates Boundary diagram: Mean annual temperature (°C) 30, 20, 10, 0 — Annual rainfall (mm) 0 200 400 600 — Wet Climates A, C, D
— summer rainfall
— winter rainfall
— rainfall evenly distributed

a Mean temperature of hottest month above 22°C, and with more than 4 months of over 10°C

b Mean temperature of hottest month below 22°C and with more than 4 months of over 10°C

c Mean temperature of hottest month below 22°C, but with less than 4 months of over 10°C

d Mean temperature of hottest month below 22°C, and of the coldest month below -38°C

w dry winter
Rainfall of the driest month of the cold season is one-tenth or less of the rainfall of the wettest month of the hot season

s dry summer
Rainfall of the driest month of the hot season is less than one-third of the rainfall of the wettest month of the cold season and less than 40mm.

f with no dry season
Rainfall does not correspond to w or s climates

SOIL REGIONS
1:240 000 000
after Glinka, Stremme, Marbut, and others

- Tundra Soil
- Podzols
- Brown Forest Soil
- Lightly leached Dry Forest Soil
- Red and yellow Sub-tropical Forest Soil
- Reddish Savanna Soil and Tropical Red Earths
- Laterites
- Chernozem
- Degraded Chernozem
- Black Savanna Soil
- Chestnut Steppe Soil
- Grey, light brown and red brown Desert Steppe Soils
- Alluvium
- Mountain and High Plateau Soils
- Oases Soil
- Tropical and Mangrove Swamp

Projection: Interrupted Mollweide's Homolographic

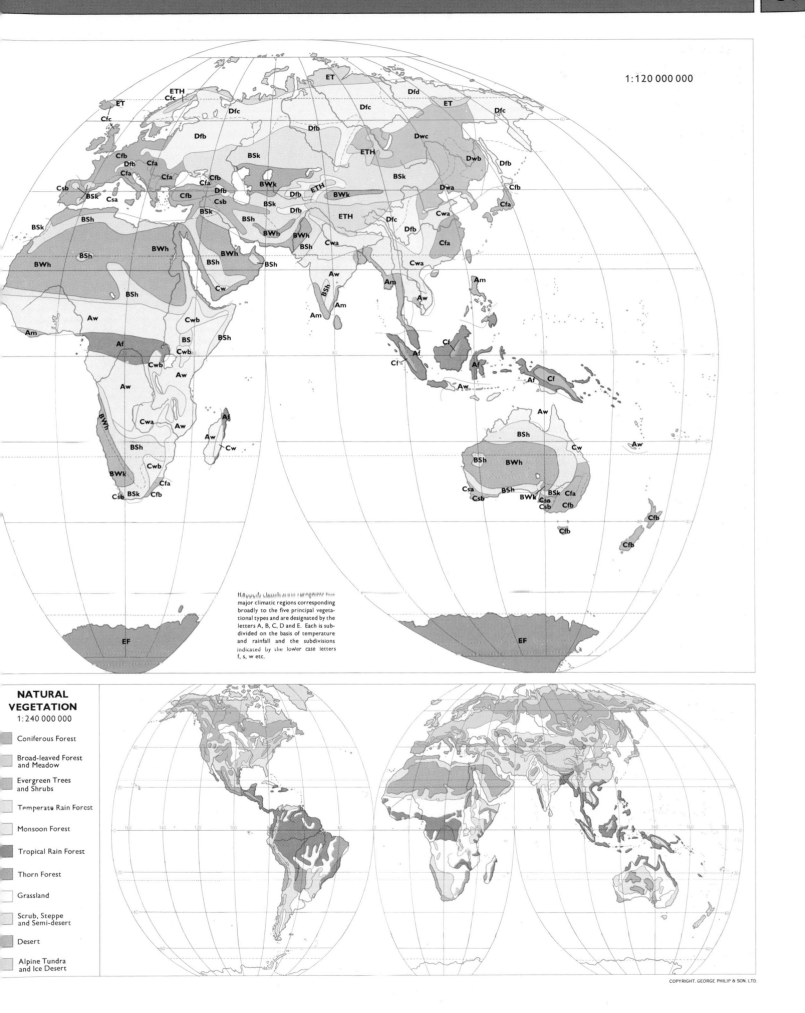

1:120 000 000

Köppen's classification recognises five major climatic regions corresponding broadly to the five principal vegetational types and are designated by the letters A, B, C, D and E. Each is subdivided on the basis of temperature and rainfall and the subdivisions indicated by the lower case letters f, s, w etc.

NATURAL VEGETATION

1:240 000 000

- Coniferous Forest
- Broad-leaved Forest and Meadow
- Evergreen Trees and Shrubs
- Temperate Rain Forest
- Monsoon Forest
- Tropical Rain Forest
- Thorn Forest
- Grassland
- Scrub, Steppe and Semi-desert
- Desert
- Alpine Tundra and Ice Desert

COPYRIGHT. GEORGE PHILIP & SON. LTD.

Addis Ababa Ethiopia 2410m — Height of meteorological station above sea level in metres
Temperature Daily Max.°C 23 24 — Average monthly maximum temperature in degrees Celsius
Daily Min.°C 6 7 — Average monthly minimum temperature in degrees Celsius
Average Monthly °C 14 15 — Average monthly temperature in degrees Celsius
Rainfall Monthly Total mm 13 35 — Average monthly precipitation in millimetres
No. of Days 3 5 — Number of days per month with over 0.1 mm precipitation
Sunshine Hours per Day 8.7 8.2 — Average daily duration of bright sunshine per month in hours

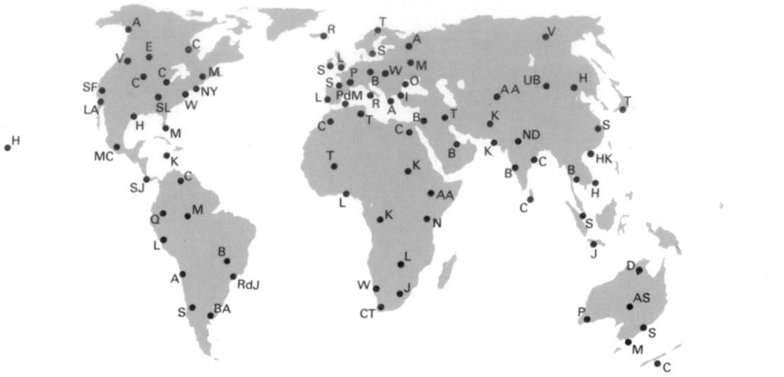

Addis Ababa Ethiopia 2410m

	Jan	Feb	Mar	Apr	May	June	July	Aug	Sep	Oct	Nov	Dec	Year
Temperature Daily Max.°C	23	24	25	24	25	23	20	20	21	22	23	22	23
Daily Min.°C	6	7	9	10	9	10	11	11	10	7	5	5	8
Average Monthly °C	14	15	17	17	17	16	16	15	15	15	14	14	15
Rainfall Monthly Total mm	13	35	67	91	81	117	247	255	167	29	8	5	1115
No. of Days	3	5	10	12	10	20	27	28	21	7	2	1	146
Sunshine Hours per Day	8.7	8.2	7.6	8.1	6.5	4.8	2.8	3.2	5.2	7.6	6.7	7	6.4

Alice Springs Australia 580m

	Jan	Feb	Mar	Apr	May	June	July	Aug	Sep	Oct	Nov	Dec	Year
Temperature Daily Max.°C	35	35	32	27	23	19	19	23	27	31	33	35	28
Daily Min.°C	21	20	17	12	8	5	4	6	10	15	18	20	13
Average Monthly °C	28	27	25	20	15	12	12	14	18	23	25	27	21
Rainfall Monthly Total mm	44	33	27	10	15	13	7	8	7	18	29	38	249
No. of Days	4	3	3	2	2	2	1	2	1	3	4	4	31
Sunshine Hours per Day	10.3	10.4	9.3	9.2	8	8	8.9	9.8	10	9.7	10.1	10	9.5

Alma Ata Kazakhstan 848m

	Jan	Feb	Mar	Apr	May	June	July	Aug	Sep	Oct	Nov	Dec	Year
Temperature Daily Max.°C	-3	-2	6	17	22	27	29	28	19	14	5	-1	13
Daily Min.°C	-14	-13	-6	3	9	13	16	14	5	1	-7	-12	1
Average Monthly °C	-9	-7	0	10	15	20	22	21	12	8	-1	-6	7
Rainfall Monthly Total mm	26	32	64	89	99	59	35	23	25	46	48	35	581
No. of Days	8	8	11	12	11	10	9	6	5	7	9	9	105
Sunshine Hours per Day	3.7	3.8	4.5	6.3	7.8	9.1	10.2	9.6	8	6.4	4.2	3.6	6.6

Anchorage USA 183m

	Jan	Feb	Mar	Apr	May	June	July	Aug	Sep	Oct	Nov	Dec	Year
Temperature Daily Max.°C	-7	-3	0	7	13	18	19	17	13	6	-2	-6	-6
Daily Min.°C	-15	-12	-9	-2	4	8	10	9	5	-2	-9	-14	-2
Average Monthly °C	-11	-7	-4	3	9	13	15	13	9	2	-5	-10	-4
Rainfall Monthly Total mm	20	18	13	11	13	25	47	64	64	47	28	24	374
No. of Days	5	10	7	7	7	9	13	13	13	11	10	11	116
Sunshine Hours per Day	2.4	4.1	6.6	8.3	8.3	9.2	8.5	6	4.4	3.1	2.6	1.6	5.4

Antofagasta Chile 95m

	Jan	Feb	Mar	Apr	May	June	July	Aug	Sep	Oct	Nov	Dec	Year
Temperature Daily Max.°C	25	25	24	21	20	19	17	17	18	19	21	22	21
Daily Min.°C	17	17	16	15	13	11	11	11	12	13	15	16	14
Average Monthly °C	21	21	20	18	16	15	5	14	15	16	18	19	17
Rainfall Monthly Total mm	0	0	0	1	1	3	5	3	1	3	1	0	18
No. of Days	0	0	0	0.1	0.1	0.2	0.5	0.4	0.5	0.2	0.3	0	2.3
Sunshine Hours per Day	10.5	10.3	8	7.3	6.3	6.1	6	5.5	6	5.5	6.5	8.9	7.2

Archangel Russia 4m

	Jan	Feb	Mar	Apr	May	June	July	Aug	Sep	Oct	Nov	Dec	Year
Temperature Daily Max.°C	-9	-8	-2	5	11	18	22	17	13	6	-2	-7	6
Daily Min.°C	-17	-17	-14	-7	0	6	9	10	3	-3	-8	-14	-4
Average Monthly °C	-13	-12	-8	-1	6	12	16	13	8	1	-5	-10	1
Rainfall Monthly Total mm	33	28	28	28	39	59	63	57	66	55	44	39	539
No. of Days	22	19	19	15	14	14	12	14	19	21	21	23	213
Sunshine Hours per Day	0.2	1.3	3.9	6	7.2	9.2	9.8	7.4	3.3	1.9	0.6	0.1	4.3

Athens Greece 107m

	Jan	Feb	Mar	Apr	May	June	July	Aug	Sep	Oct	Nov	Dec	Year
Temperature Daily Max.°C	13	14	16	20	25	30	33	33	29	24	19	15	23
Daily Min.°C	6	7	8	11	16	20	23	23	19	15	12	8	14
Average Monthly °C	10	10	12	16	20	25	28	28	24	20	15	11	18
Rainfall Monthly Total mm	62	37	37	23	23	14	6	7	15	51	56	71	402
No. of Days	6	11	11	9	8	4	2	3	4	8	12	15	103
Sunshine Hours per Day	3.9	5.2	5.8	7.7	8.9	10.7	11.9	11.5	9.4	6.8	4.8	3.8	7.3

Bahrain City Bahrain 2m

	Jan	Feb	Mar	Apr	May	June	July	Aug	Sep	Oct	Nov	Dec	Year
Temperature Daily Max.°C	20	21	25	29	33	36	37	38	36	32	27	22	30
Daily Min.°C	14	15	18	22	25	29	31	32	29	25	22	16	23
Average Monthly °C	17	18	21	25	29	32	34	35	32	29	25	19	26
Rainfall Monthly Total mm	18	12	10	9	2	0	0	0	0	0.4	3	16	70
No. of Days	3	3	3	2	1	0	0	0	0	0	0.1	3	15
Sunshine Hours per Day	5.9	6.9	7.9	8.8	10.6	13.2	12.1	12	12	10.3	7.7	6.4	9.5

Bangkok Thailand 10m

	Jan	Feb	Mar	Apr	May	June	July	Aug	Sep	Oct	Nov	Dec	Year
Temperature Daily Max.°C	32	33	34	35	34	33	32	32	32	31	31	31	33
Daily Min.°C	20	23	24	26	25	25	25	24	24	24	23	20	24
Average Monthly °C	26	28	29	30	30	29	28	28	28	28	27	26	28
Rainfall Monthly Total mm	9	30	36	82	165	153	168	183	310	239	55	8	1438
No. of Days	2	2	4	5	14	16	19	21	23	17	7	1	131
Sunshine Hours per Day	8.2	8	8	10	7.5	6.1	4.7	5.2	5.2	6.1	7.3	7.8	7

Beirut Lebanon 35m

	Jan	Feb	Mar	Apr	May	June	July	Aug	Sep	Oct	Nov	Dec	Year
Temperature Daily Max.°C	16	17	19	22	26	29	31	32	30	27	23	19	24
Daily Min.°C	11	11	12	15	18	21	23	24	23	20	16	13	17
Average Monthly °C	13	14	16	19	22	25	27	28	26	24	20	16	21
Rainfall Monthly Total mm	195	156	94	51	17	3	0.5	0.5	7	48	130	185	887
No. of Days	16	14	11	6	3	1	0.1	0.2	1	4	9	14	79
Sunshine Hours per Day	4.8	5.4	6.3	7.5	9.9	12.1	11.9	11.3	9.2	8.2	6.6	4.7	8.2

Berlin Germany 55m

	Jan	Feb	Mar	Apr	May	June	July	Aug	Sep	Oct	Nov	Dec	Year
Temperature Daily Max.°C	2	3	8	14	19	22	24	23	20	13	7	3	13
Daily Min.°C	-4	-3	0	4	8	11	13	13	9	5	2	-1	5
Average Monthly °C	-1	0	4	9	14	17	19	18	14	9	4	1	9
Rainfall Monthly Total mm	43	40	31	41	46	62	70	68	46	47	46	41	581
No. of Days	11	9	8	9	9	9	11	9	8	9	10	9	111
Sunshine Hours per Day	1.6	2.5	4.3	5.3	6.9	7.8	7.1	6.6	5.7	3.4	1.6	1.1	4.5

Bombay India 10m

	Jan	Feb	Mar	Apr	May	June	July	Aug	Sep	Oct	Nov	Dec	Year
Temperature Daily Max.°C	28	28	30	32	33	31	30	29	30	32	32	30	31
Daily Min.°C	19	20	22	24	27	26	25	24	24	24	23	21	23
Average Monthly °C	24	24	26	28	30	29	27	27	27	28	27	25	27
Rainfall Monthly Total mm	2	1	0	3	16	520	709	419	297	88	21	2	2078
No. of Days	0	0	0	0	1	16	26	20	14	3	1	0	81
Sunshine Hours per Day	9	9.3	9	9.1	9.3	5	3.1	2.5	5.4	7.7	9.7	9.6	7.4

Brasilia Brazil 910m

	Jan	Feb	Mar	Apr	May	June	July	Aug	Sep	Oct	Nov	Dec	Year
Temperature Daily Max.°C	28	28	28	28	27	27	27	29	30	29	28	27	28
Daily Min.°C	18	18	18	17	15	13	13	14	16	18	18	18	16
Average Monthly °C	23	23	23	22	21	20	20	21	23	24	23	22	22
Rainfall Monthly Total mm	252	204	227	93	17	3	6	3	30	127	255	343	1560
No. of Days	21	16	18	13	5	2	1	3	7	12	19	23	140
Sunshine Av. Monthly Dur.	5.8	5.7	6	7.4	8.7	9.3	9.6	9.8	7.9	6.5	4.8	4.4	7.2

Buenos Aires Argentina 25m

	Jan	Feb	Mar	Apr	May	June	July	Aug	Sep	Oct	Nov	Dec	Year
Temperature Daily Max.°C	30	29	26	22	18	14	14	16	18	21	25	28	22
Daily Min.°C	17	17	16	12	9	5	6	6	8	10	14	16	11
Average Monthly °C	23	23	21	17	13	10	10	11	13	15	19	22	16
Rainfall Monthly Total mm	79	71	109	89	76	61	56	61	79	86	84	99	950
No. of Days	7	6	7	8	7	7	8	9	8	9	9	8	93
Sunshine Hours per Day	9.2	8.5	7.5	6.8	4.9	3.5	3.8	5.2	6	6.8	8.1	8.5	6.6

Cairo Egypt 75m

	Jan	Feb	Mar	Apr	May	June	July	Aug	Sep	Oct	Nov	Dec	Year
Temperature Daily Max.°C	19	21	24	28	32	35	35	35	33	30	26	21	28
Daily Min.°C	9	9	12	14	18	20	22	22	20	18	14	10	16
Average Monthly °C	14	15	18	21	25	28	29	28	26	24	20	16	22
Rainfall Monthly Total mm	4	4	3	1	2	1	0	0	1	1	3	7	25
No. of Days	3	2	1	1	1	0	0	0	1	1	1	2	12
Sunshine Hours per Day	6.9	8.4	8.7	9.7	10.5	11.9	11.7	11.3	10.4	9.4	8.3	6.4	9.5

Calcutta India 5m

	Jan	Feb	Mar	Apr	May	June	July	Aug	Sep	Oct	Nov	Dec	Year
Temperature Daily Max.°C	27	29	34	36	35	34	32	32	32	32	29	26	31
Daily Min.°C	13	15	21	24	25	26	26	26	26	23	18	13	21
Average Monthly °C	20	22	27	30	30	30	29	29	29	28	23	20	26
Rainfall Monthly Total mm	10	30	34	44	140	297	325	332	253	114	20	5	1604
No. of Days	3	4	3	5	9	17	23	23	18	9	1	1	116
Sunshine Hours per Day	8.6	8.7	8.9	9	8.7	5.4	4.1	4.1	5.1	6.5	8.3	8.4	7.1

Cape Town South Africa 44m

	Jan	Feb	Mar	Apr	May	June	July	Aug	Sep	Oct	Nov	Dec	Year
Temperature Daily Max.°C	26	26	25	23	20	18	17	18	19	21	24	25	22
Daily Min.°C	15	15	14	11	9	7	7	7	8	10	13	15	11
Average Monthly °C	21	20	20	17	14	13	12	12	14	16	18	20	16
Rainfall Monthly Total mm	12	19	17	42	67	98	68	76	36	45	12	13	505
No. of Days	5	5	5	9	13	12	12	13	10	9	5	5	103
Sunshine Hours per Day	11.4	10.2	9.4	7.7	6.1	5.7	6.4	6.6	7.6	8.6	10.2	10.9	8.4

Caracas Venezuela 1040m

	Jan	Feb	Mar	Apr	May	June	July	Aug	Sep	Oct	Nov	Dec	Year
Temperature Daily Max.°C	24	25	26	27	27	26	26	26	27	26	25	26	26
Daily Min.°C	14	14	15	16	17	17	16	16	16	16	16	15	16
Average Monthly °C	19	19	20	21	22	21	21	21	21	21	20	20	21
Rainfall Monthly Total mm	23	10	15	33	79	102	109	109	107	109	94	46	836
No. of Days	6	2	3	4	9	14	15	15	13	12	13	10	116
Sunshine Hours per Day	7.6	7.8	7.5	6.4	6.4	6.4	7.3	7.4	7.2	6.8	6.9	6.7	7

Casablanca Morocco 59m

	Jan	Feb	Mar	Apr	May	June	July	Aug	Sep	Oct	Nov	Dec	Year
Temperature Daily Max.°C	17	18	20	21	22	24	26	26	26	24	21	18	22
Daily Min.°C	8	9	11	12	15	18	19	20	18	15	12	10	14
Average Monthly °C	13	13	15	16	18	21	23	23	22	20	17	14	18
Rainfall Monthly Total mm	78	61	54	37	20	3	0	1	6	28	58	94	440
No. of Days	11	8	9	5	4	2	0	1	2	6	9	10	67
Sunshine Hours per Day	5.2	6.3	7.3	9	9.4	9.7	10.2	9.7	9.1	7.4	5.9	5.3	7.9

Cheyenne USA 1869m

	Jan	Feb	Mar	Apr	May	June	July	Aug	Sep	Oct	Nov	Dec	Year
Temperature Daily Max.°C	3	4	6	12	18	24	29	28	23	16	8	5	15
Daily Min.°C	-9	-9	-7	-2	4	9	12	12	7	1	-5	-7	1
Average Monthly °C	-3	-2	0	5	11	16	21	20	15	9	2	-1	8
Rainfall Monthly Total mm	13	14	31	48	64	55	46	37	28	21	16	11	384
No. of Days	6	7	10	10	13	11	11	10	7	5	6	5	101
Sunshine Hours per Day	6	6.9	7.8	8	8.4	10.3	10.1	9.2	9.1	8	6	5.5	7.9

Chicago USA 186m

	Jan	Feb	Mar	Apr	May	June	July	Aug	Sep	Oct	Nov	Dec	Year
Temperature Daily Max.°C	0.6	1.5	6.4	14.1	20.6	26.4	28.9	28	23.8	17.4	8.4	2.1	14.9
Daily Min.°C	-7	-6	-2	5	11	16	20	19	14	8	0	-5	-6
Average Monthly °C	-3	-2	2	9	16	21	24	23	19	13	4	-2	4
Rainfall Monthly Total mm	47	41	70	77	96	103	86	80	69	71	56	48	843
No. of Days	10	10	12	12	13	11	9	9	8	8	10	10	122
Sunshine Hours per Day	4	5	6.6	6.9	8.9	10.2	10	9.2	8.2	6.9	4.5	3.7	7

Christchurch New Zealand 5m

	Jan	Feb	Mar	Apr	May	June	July	Aug	Sep	Oct	Nov	Dec	Year
Temperature Daily Max.°C	21	21	19	17	13	11	10	11	14	17	19	21	16
Daily Min.°C	12	12	10	7	4	2	1	3	5	7	8	11	7
Average Monthly °C	16	16	15	12	9	6	6	7	9	12	13	16	11
Rainfall Monthly Total mm	56	46	43	46	76	69	61	58	51	51	51	61	669
No. of Days	10	8	9	10	12	13	14	11	10	11	10	11	129
Sunshine Hours per Day	7	6.5	5.6	4.7	4.3	3.9	4.1	4.7	5.6	6.1	6.9	6.3	5.5

Churchill Canada 35m

	Jan	Feb	Mar	Apr	May	June	July	Aug	Sep	Oct	Nov	Dec	Year
Temperature Daily Max.°C	-24	-22	-15	-7	1	10	17	16	9	2	-7	-18	-3
Daily Min.°C	-32	-31	-24	-15	-5	2	7	8	3	-4	-15	-26	-11
Average Monthly °C	-28	-27	-19	-11	-2	6	12	12	6	-1	-11	-22	-7
Rainfall Monthly Total mm	14	16	18	30	34	44	30	62	53	42	42	25	410
No. of Days	9	9	10	13	11	10	12	13	15	16	17	14	149
Sunshine Hours per Day	2.6	6.6	6.1	6.2	5.6	7.1	9.2	7.5	3.4	2.2	1.6	1.9	4.8

Colombo Sri Lanka 10m

	Jan	Feb	Mar	Apr	May	June	July	Aug	Sep	Oct	Nov	Dec	Year
Temperature Daily Max.°C	30	31	31	31	30	30	29	29	30	29	29	30	30
Daily Min.°C	22	22	23	24	25	25	25	25	25	24	23	22	24
Average Monthly °C	26	26	27	28	28	27	27	27	27	27	26	26	27
Rainfall Monthly Total mm	101	66	118	230	394	220	140	102	174	348	333	142	2368
No. of Days	10	6	11	17	23	22	16	14	17	22	20	12	190
Sunshine Hours per Day	7.9	9	8.1	7.2	6.4	5.4	6.1	6.3	6.2	6.5	6.4	7.8	6.9

Darwin Australia 30m

	Jan	Feb	Mar	Apr	May	June	July	Aug	Sep	Oct	Nov	Dec	Year
Temperature Daily Max.°C	32	32	33	33	33	31	31	32	33	34	34	33	33
Daily Min.°C	25	25	25	24	23	21	19	21	23	25	26	26	24
Average Monthly °C	29	29	29	29	28	26	25	26	28	29	30	29	28
Rainfall Monthly Total mm	405	309	279	77	8	2	0	1	15	48	108	214	1466
No. of Days	20	18	17	6	1	1	0.1	0.1	2	5	10	15	95
Sunshine Hours per Day	5.8	5.8	6.6	9.8	9.3	10	9.9	10.4	10.1	9.4	9.6	6.8	8.6

Edmonton Canada 676m

	Jan	Feb	Mar	Apr	May	June	July	Aug	Sep	Oct	Nov	Dec	Year
Temperature Daily Max.°C	-9	-7	0	10	17	20	24	22	17	11	0	-5	8
Daily Min.°C	-19	-17	-10	-2	4	8	11	9	5	-1	-9	-14	-3
Average Monthly °C	-14	-12	-5	4	11	14	17	15	11	5	-4	-10	3
Rainfall Monthly Total mm	24	22	20	26	42	77	82	70	34	21	20	22	460
No. of Days	11	11	10	8	9	13	13	12	9	7	8	11	122
Sunshine Hours per Day	2.9	4.1	5.3	7.3	8.5	8.4	9.8	8.5	6.3	5.1	3.5	2.6	6

Harbin China 175m

	Jan	Feb	Mar	Apr	May	June	July	Aug	Sep	Oct	Nov	Dec	Year
Temperature Daily Max.°C	-14	-9	0	12	21	26	29	27	20	12	-1	-11	9
Daily Min.°C	-26	-23	-12	-1	7	14	18	16	8	0	-12	-22	-3
Average Monthly °C	-20	-16	-6	6	14	20	23	22	14	6	-7	-17	3
Rainfall Monthly Total mm	4	6	17	23	44	92	167	119	52	36	12	5	577
No. of Days	5	5	6	7	11	15	16	13	12	7	6	6	109
Sunshine Hours per Day	6.4	7.8	8	7.8	8.3	8.6	8.6	8.2	7.2	6.9	6.1	5.7	7.5

Ho Chi Minh Vietnam 10m

	Jan	Feb	Mar	Apr	May	June	July	Aug	Sep	Oct	Nov	Dec	Year
Temperature Daily Max.°C	32	33	34	35	33	32	31	31	31	31	31	31	32
Daily Min.°C	21	22	23	24	24	24	24	24	23	23	23	22	23
Average Monthly °C	26	27	29	30	29	28	28	28	27	27	27	26	28
Rainfall Monthly Total mm	16	3	13	42	220	331	314	269	336	269	115	56	1984
No. of Days	2	1	2	5	17	22	23	21	22	20	11	7	153
Sunshine Hours per Day	6.3	7.1	6.8	6.7	5.1	5	3.9	5	4	4.5	5.2	5.7	5.4

Hong Kong Hong Kong 35m

	Jan	Feb	Mar	Apr	May	June	July	Aug	Sep	Oct	Nov	Dec	Year
Temperature Daily Max.°C	18	18	20	24	28	30	31	31	30	27	24	20	25
Daily Min.°C	13	13	16	19	23	26	26	26	25	23	19	15	20
Average Monthly °C	16	15	18	22	25	28	28	28	27	25	21	17	23
Rainfall Monthly Total mm	30	60	70	133	332	479	286	415	364	33	46	17	2265
No. of Days	6	8	11	11	16	21	19	17	15	8	5	5	142
Sunshine Hours per Day	4.7	3.5	3.1	3.8	5	5.4	6.8	6.5	6.6	7	6.2	5.5	5.3

Honolulu Hawaii 5m

	Jan	Feb	Mar	Apr	May	June	July	Aug	Sep	Oct	Nov	Dec	Year
Temperature Daily Max.°C	26	26	26	27	28	29	29	29	30	29	28	26	28
Daily Min.°C	19	19	19	20	21	22	23	23	23	22	21	20	21
Average Monthly °C	23	22	23	23	24	26	26	26	26	26	24	23	24
Rainfall Monthly Total mm	96	84	73	33	25	8	11	23	25	47	55	76	556
No. of Days	10	10	9	9	6	6	8	7	7	10	10	11	103
Sunshine Hours per Day	7.3	7.7	8.3	8.6	8.8	9.1	9.4	9.3	9.2	8.3	7.5	6.2	8.3

Houston USA 12m

	Jan	Feb	Mar	Apr	May	June	July	Aug	Sep	Oct	Nov	Dec	Year
Temperature Daily Max.°C	17	18	22	25	29	32	34	34	31	28	21	18	26
Daily Min.°C	8	9	12	16	20	23	24	24	22	17	12	9	16
Average Monthly °C	12	14	17	21	25	28	29	29	27	22	16	14	21
Rainfall Monthly Total mm	94	82	61	87	113	97	131	90	97	91	103	104	1150
No. of Days	11	10	9	8	7	8	10	9	9	6	8	10	105
Sunshine Hours per Day	5.1	5.6	6.6	7.3	9.3	10.9	10.4	9.7	8.7	8.3	6.6	5.5	7.8

Istanbul Turkey 40m

	Jan	Feb	Mar	Apr	May	June	July	Aug	Sep	Oct	Nov	Dec	Year
Temperature Daily Max.°C	9	9	11	16	21	26	29	29	25	21	15	11	18
Daily Min.°C	3	2	3	7	12	16	18	20	15	12	8	5	10
Average Monthly °C	6	6	7	12	16	21	23	24	20	16	12	8	14
Rainfall Monthly Total mm	88	80	61	37	32	27	27	22	49	61	87	96	667
No. of Days	18	15	14	9	8	5	4	3	6	10	13	17	122
Sunshine Hours per Day	2.6	3.8	4.5	6.3	8.6	10.6	11.6	10.9	8.2	5.3	3.7	2.8	6.6

Jakarta Indonesia 10m

	Jan	Feb	Mar	Apr	May	June	July	Aug	Sep	Oct	Nov	Dec	Year
Temperature Daily Max.°C	29	29	30	31	31	31	31	31	31	31	30	29	30
Daily Min.°C	23	23	23	24	24	23	23	23	23	23	23	23	23
Average Monthly °C	26	26	27	27	27	27	27	27	27	27	27	26	27
Rainfall Monthly Total mm	300	300	211	147	114	97	64	43	66	112	142	203	1799
No. of Days	18	17	15	11	9	7	5	4	5	8	12	14	125
Sunshine Av. Monthly Dur.	6.1	6.5	7.7	8.5	8.4	8.5	9.1	9.5	9.6	9	7.7	7.1	8.1

Johannesburg South Africa 1692m

	Jan	Feb	Mar	Apr	May	June	July	Aug	Sep	Oct	Nov	Dec	Year
Temperature Daily Max.°C	25	25	24	21	19	16	17	19	23	24	24	25	22
Daily Min.°C	14	14	13	10	7	4	4	6	9	11	13	14	10
Average Monthly °C	20	20	18	16	13	10	10	13	16	18	18	19	16
Rainfall Monthly Total mm	112	97	75	61	22	9	8	5	25	69	116	111	710
No. of Days	15	11	10	10	5	2	1	2	3	10	15	15	99
Sunshine Av. Monthly Dur.	8.4	8.3	7.9	9.1	8.8	8.8	9.2	9.7	9.5	8.9	8.3	8.4	

Kabul Afghanistan 1791 m

	Jan	Feb	Mar	Apr	May	June	July	Aug	Sep	Oct	Nov	Dec	Year
Temperature Daily Max.°C	2	4	12	19	26	31	33	33	30	22	17	8	20
Daily Min.°C	-8	-6	1	6	11	13	16	15	11	6	1	-3	5
Average Monthly °C	-3	-1	6	13	18	22	25	24	20	14	9	3	12
Rainfall Monthly Total mm	28	61	72	117	33	1	7	1		1	37	14	372
No. of Days	6	7	9	11	8	3	2	1	1	3	2	5	58
Sunshine Av. Monthly Dur.	5.9	6	5.7	6.8	10.1	11.5	11.4	11.2	9.8	9.4	7.8	6.1	8.5

Karachi Pakistan 5m

	Jan	Feb	Mar	Apr	May	June	July	Aug	Sep	Oct	Nov	Dec	Year
Temperature Daily Max.°C	24	25	28	30	31	32	31	30	30	31	30	26	29
Daily Min.°C	14	16	20	23	26	28	27	26	25	23	19	16	22
Average Monthly °C	19	21	24	27	29	30	29	28	27	27	25	21	26
Rainfall Monthly Total mm	13	10	8	3	3	18	81	41	13	0.5	3	5	198
No. of Days	2	3	1	1	0.1	1	6	3	1	0.2	0.4	1.3	20
Sunshine Av. Monthly Dur.	8.8	9.3	9	9.9	10.1	7.8	4.4	4.8	7.1	9.3	9.3	8.7	8.2

Khartoum Sudan 380m

	Jan	Feb	Mar	Apr	May	June	July	Aug	Sep	Oct	Nov	Dec	Year
Temperature Daily Max.°C	32	33	37	40	42	41	38	36	38	39	35	32	37
Daily Min.°C	16	17	20	23	26	27	26	25	25	25	21	17	22
Average Monthly °C	24	25	28	32	34	34	32	30	32	32	28	25	30
Rainfall Monthly Total mm	0	0	0	1	7	5	56	80	28	2	0	0	179
No. of Days	0	0	0	0	1	1	6	8	3	1	0	0	20
Sunshine Av. Monthly Dur.	10.6	11.2	10.4	10.8	10.4	10.1	8.6	8.6	9.6	10.3	10.8	10.6	10.2

Kingston Jamaica 35m

	Jan	Feb	Mar	Apr	May	June	July	Aug	Sep	Oct	Nov	Dec	Year
Temperature Daily Max.°C	30	30	30	31	31	32	32	32	32	31	31	31	31
Daily Min.°C	20	20	20	21	22	24	23	23	23	23	22	21	22
Average Monthly °C	25	25	25	26	26	28	28	28	27	27	26	26	26
Rainfall Monthly Total mm	23	15	23	31	102	89	38	91	99	180	74	36	801
No. of Days	3	3	2	3	4	5	4	7	6	9	5	4	55
Sunshine Av. Monthly Dur.	8.3	8.8	8.7	8.7	8.3	7.8	8.5	8.5	7.6	7.3	8.3	7.7	8.2

Kinshasa Zaire 311m

	Jan	Feb	Mar	Apr	May	June	July	Aug	Sep	Oct	Nov	Dec	Year
Temperature Daily Max.°C	31	31	32	32	31	28	27	29	30	31	31	30	30
Daily Min.°C	22	22	22	22	22	19	17	18	20	21	21	22	21
Average Monthly °C	26	26	27	27	26	24	22	23	25	26	26	26	25
Rainfall Monthly Total mm	128	142	173	222	129	4	3	3	46	145	246	161	1402
No. of Days	9	10	13	15	10	1	0	1	5	10	16	13	103
Sunshine Av. Monthly Dur.	4.3	4.8	4.8	5.5	4.5	4.6	4	4.7	4.3	4.7	4.4	4.6	4.6

Lagos Nigeria 40m

	Jan	Feb	Mar	Apr	May	June	July	Aug	Sep	Oct	Nov	Dec	Year
Temperature Daily Max.°C	32	33	33	32	31	29	28	28	29	30	31	32	31
Daily Min.°C	22	23	23	23	23	22	22	21	22	22	23	22	22
Average Monthly °C	27	28	28	28	27	26	25	24	25	26	27	27	26
Rainfall Monthly Total mm	28	41	99	99	203	300	180	56	180	190	63	25	1464
No. of Days	1	4	7	8	14	18	14	9	16	16	7	2	116
Sunshine Av. Monthly Dur.	5.9	6.8	6.3	6.1	5.6	3.8	2.8	3.3	3	5.1	6.6	6.5	5.2

Lima Peru 120m

	Jan	Feb	Mar	Apr	May	June	July	Aug	Sep	Oct	Nov	Dec	Year
Temperature Daily Max.°C	28	29	29	27	24	20	20	19	20	22	24	26	24
Daily Min.°C	19	20	19	17	16	15	14	14	14	15	16	17	16
Average Monthly °C	24	24	24	22	20	17	17	16	17	18	20	21	20
Rainfall Monthly Total mm	1	1	1	1	5	5	8	8	8	3	3	1	45
No. of Days	1	0	0	0	1	1	1	2	1	0	0	0	7
Sunshine Av. Monthly Dur.	6.3	6.8	6.9	6.7	4	1.4	1.1	1	1.1	2.5	4.1	5	3.9

Lisbon Portugal 77m

	Jan	Feb	Mar	Apr	May	June	July	Aug	Sep	Oct	Nov	Dec	Year
Temperature Daily Max.°C	14	15	17	20	21	25	27	28	26	22	17	15	21
Daily Min.°C	8	8	10	12	13	15	17	17	17	14	11	9	13
Average Monthly °C	11	12	14	16	17	20	22	23	21	18	14	12	17
Rainfall Monthly Total mm	111	76	109	54	44	16	3	4	33	62	93	103	708
No. of Days	15	12	14	10	10	5	2	2	6	9	13	15	113
Sunshine Av. Monthly Dur.	4.7	5.9	6	8.3	9.1	10.6	11.4	10.7	8.4	6.7	5.2	4.6	7.7

London (Kew) United Kingdom 5m

	Jan	Feb	Mar	Apr	May	June	July	Aug	Sep	Oct	Nov	Dec	Year
Temperature Daily Max.°C	6	7	10	13	17	20	22	21	19	14	10	7	14
Daily Min.°C	2	2	3	6	8	12	14	13	11	8	5	4	7
Average Monthly °C	4	5	7	9	12	16	18	17	15	11	8	5	11
Rainfall Monthly Total mm	54	40	37	37	46	45	57	59	49	57	64	48	593
No. of Days	15	13	11	12	12	11	12	11	13	13	15	15	153
Sunshine Av. Monthly Dur.	1.7	2.3	3.5	5.7	6.7	7	6.6	6	5	3.3	1.9	1.4	4.3

Los Angeles USA 30m

	Jan	Feb	Mar	Apr	May	June	July	Aug	Sep	Oct	Nov	Dec	Year
Temperature Daily Max.°C	18	18	18	19	20	22	24	24	24	23	22	19	21
Daily Min.°C	7	8	9	11	13	15	17	17	16	14	11	9	12
Average Monthly °C	12	13	14	15	17	18	21	21	20	18	16	14	17
Rainfall Monthly Total mm	69	74	46	28	3	3	0	0	5	10	28	61	327
No. of Days	7	6	5	4	1	1	0	1	1	2	3	6	37
Sunshine Av. Monthly Dur.	6.9	8.2	8.9	8.8	9.5	10.3	11.7	11	10.1	8.6	8.2	7.6	9.2

Lusaka Zambia 1154m

	Jan	Feb	Mar	Apr	May	June	July	Aug	Sep	Oct	Nov	Dec	Year
Temperature Daily Max.°C	26	26	26	27	25	23	23	26	29	31	29	27	27
Daily Min.°C	17	17	16	15	12	10	9	11	15	18	18	17	15
Average Monthly °C	22	22	21	21	18	17	16	19	22	25	23	22	21
Rainfall Monthly Total mm	224	173	90	19	3	1	0	1	1	17	85	196	810
No. of Days	19	18	12	3	1	0	0	0	0	3	10	18	84
Sunshine Av. Monthly Dur.	5.1	5.4	6.9	8.9	9	9	9.1	9.6	9.5	9	7	5.5	7.8

Manaus Brazil 45m

	Jan	Feb	Mar	Apr	May	June	July	Aug	Sep	Oct	Nov	Dec	Year
Temperature Daily Max.°C	31	31	31	31	31	31	32	33	34	34	33	32	32
Daily Min.°C	24	24	24	24	24	24	24	24	24	25	25	24	24
Average Monthly °C	28	28	28	27	28	28	28	29	29	29	29	28	28
Rainfall Monthly Total mm	278	278	300	287	193	99	61	41	62	112	165	220	2096
No. of Days	20	19	20	19	18	11	8	6	7	11	12	16	167
Sunshine Av. Monthly Dur.	3.9	4	3.6	3.9	5.4	6.9	7.9	8.2	7.5	6.6	5.9	4.9	5.7

Melbourne Australia 35m

	Jan	Feb	Mar	Apr	May	June	July	Aug	Sep	Oct	Nov	Dec	Year
Temperature Daily Max.°C	26	26	24	20	17	14	13	15	17	19	22	24	20
Daily Min.°C	14	14	13	11	8	7	6	6	8	9	11	12	10
Average Monthly °C	20	20	18	15	13	10	9	11	13	14	16	18	15
Rainfall Monthly Total mm	47	50	56	57	48	52	48	51	55	66	58	60	648
No. of Days	9	8	9	13	14	16	17	17	15	14	13	11	156
Sunshine Av. Monthly Dur.	8.3	8.4	6.7	5.3	4.4	3.6	4.1	4.9	5.7	6.4	7.6	7.9	6.1

Mexico City Mexico 2309m

	Jan	Feb	Mar	Apr	May	June	July	Aug	Sep	Oct	Nov	Dec	Year
Temperature Daily Max.°C	21	23	26	27	26	25	23	24	23	22	21	21	24
Daily Min.°C	5	6	7	9	10	11	11	11	11	9	6	5	8
Average Monthly °C	13	15	16	18	18	18	17	17	17	16	14	13	16
Rainfall Monthly Total mm	8	4	9	23	57	111	160	149	119	46	16	7	709
No. of Days	2	3	4	6	14	17	22	22	20	11	3	3	127
Sunshine Av. Monthly Dur.	7.3	8.1	8.5	8.1	7.8	7	6.2	6.4	5.6	6.3	7	7.3	7.1

Miami USA 2m

	Jan	Feb	Mar	Apr	May	June	July	Aug	Sep	Oct	Nov	Dec	Year
Temperature Daily Max.°C	24	25	27	28	30	31	32	32	31	29	27	25	28
Daily Min.°C	14	15	16	19	21	23	24	24	24	22	18	15	20
Average Monthly °C	19	20	21	23	25	27	28	28	27	25	22	20	24
Rainfall Monthly Total mm	51	48	58	99	163	188	170	178	241	208	71	43	1518
No. of Days	6	6	6	8	10	13	17	16	19	15	9	7	132
Sunshine Av. Monthly Dur.	7.7	8.3	8.7	9.4	8.9	8.5	8.7	8.4	7.1	6.5	7.5	7.1	8.1

Montreal Canada 57m

	Jan	Feb	Mar	Apr	May	June	July	Aug	Sep	Oct	Nov	Dec	Year
Temperature Daily Max.°C	-6	-4	2	11	18	23	26	25	20	14	5	-3	11
Daily Min.°C	-13	-11	-5	2	9	14	17	16	11	6	0	-9	3
Average Monthly °C	-9	-8	-2	6	13	19	22	20	16	10	3	-6	7
Rainfall Monthly Total mm	87	76	86	83	81	91	98	87	96	84	89	89	1047
No. of Days	17	15	15	14	13	12	13	10	13	12	15	17	166
Sunshine Av. Monthly Dur.	2.8	3.4	4.5	5.2	6.7	7.7	8.2	7.7	5.6	4.3	2.4	2.2	5.1

Moscow Russia 156m

	Jan	Feb	Mar	Apr	May	June	July	Aug	Sep	Oct	Nov	Dec	Year
Temperature Daily Max.°C	-6	-4	1	9	18	22	24	22	17	10	1	-5	9
Daily Min.°C	-14	-16	-11	-1	5	9	12	9	4	-2	-6	-12	-2
Average Monthly °C	-10	-10	-5	4	12	15	18	16	10	4	-2	-8	4
Rainfall Monthly Total mm	31	28	33	35	52	67	74	74	58	51	36	36	575
No. of Days	17	15	14	13	12	15	16	16	17	16	17	19	187
Sunshine Av. Monthly Dur.	1	1.9	3.7	5.2	7.8	8.3	8.4	7.1	4.4	2.4	1	0.6	4.4

Nairobi Kenya 1616m

	Jan	Feb	Mar	Apr	May	June	July	Aug	Sep	Oct	Nov	Dec	Year
Temperature Daily Max.°C	27	28	28	26	25	24	23	23	26	27	25	25	25
Daily Min.°C	13	13	14	15	14	12	11	12	12	13	14	14	13
Average Monthly °C	20	21	21	20	19	18	17	17	19	20	19	19	19
Rainfall Monthly Total mm	49	36	85	153	126	32	13	18	21	48	132	75	788
No. of Days	5	4	8	16	14	5	4	5	4	7	16	11	99
Sunshine Av. Monthly Dur.	8.8	9.4	8.7	7.3	5.9	5.9	4.3	4.2	5.8	7.1	7	8.1	6.9

New Delhi India 220m

	Jan	Feb	Mar	Apr	May	June	July	Aug	Sep	Oct	Nov	Dec	Year
Temperature Daily Max.°C	21	24	29	36	41	39	35	34	34	34	28	23	32
Daily Min.°C	6	10	14	20	26	28	27	26	24	17	11	7	18
Average Monthly °C	14	17	22	28	33	34	31	30	29	26	20	15	25
Rainfall Monthly Total mm	25	21	13	8	13	77	178	184	123	10	2	11	665
No. of Days	3	4	2	2	2	6	14	11	7	0.4	0.3	2	54
Sunshine Av. Monthly Dur.	7.7	8.2	8.2	8.7	9.2	7.9	6	6.3	6.9	9.4	8.7	8.3	8

New York USA 3m

	Jan	Feb	Mar	Apr	May	June	July	Aug	Sep	Oct	Nov	Dec	Year
Temperature Daily Max.°C	4	4	9	15	21	26	28	27	24	18	12	6	16
Daily Min.°C	-3	-2	1	6	12	17	20	19	16	10	4	-1	8
Average Monthly °C	1	1	5	11	16	21	24	23	20	14	8	2	12
Rainfall Monthly Total mm	89	74	104	89	91	86	102	119	89	84	89	84	1100
No. of Days	11	10	12	11	12	10	10	10	8	8	9	10	121
Sunshine Av. Monthly Dur.	4.9	5.9	6.7	7.1	8.1	10	9.9	8.9	7.9	7	5.7	5.1	7.3

Odessa Ukraine 64m

	Jan	Feb	Mar	Apr	May	June	July	Aug	Sep	Oct	Nov	Dec	Year
Temperature Daily Max.°C	1	2	6	12	19	24	27	26	21	15	8	4	14
Daily Min.°C	-6	-7	-2	4	11	15	18	17	12	8	1	-4	6
Average Monthly °C	-3	-2	2	8	15	19	22	21	17	11	5	0	10
Rainfall Monthly Total mm	28	26	20	27	34	45	34	37	29	35	43	31	389
No. of Days	11	10	10	9	9	9	7	6	6	8	10	11	106
Sunshine Av. Monthly Dur.	2.3	2.6	4.6	6.7	9	9.9	11.3	10.4	8.2	5.7	2.2	1.9	6.3

Palma Spain 93m

	Jan	Feb	Mar	Apr	May	June	July	Aug	Sep	Oct	Nov	Dec	Year
Temperature Daily Max.°C	13	14	16	18	21	25	28	28	25	21	16	13	20
Daily Min.°C	6	7	9	11	14	18	21	21	19	15	11	8	13
Average Monthly °C	10	10	12	15	18	22	24	24	22	18	13	10	17
Rainfall Monthly Total mm	31	39	48	43	54	37	27	49	76	86	52	45	587
No. of Days	5	5	8	9	8	6	4	6	7	9	6	6	79
Sunshine Av. Monthly Dur.	4.8	5.9	5.7	7.1	8.1	9.3	10.1	8.8	6.7	5.7	5	4.3	6.8

Paris France 75m

	Jan	Feb	Mar	Apr	May	June	July	Aug	Sep	Oct	Nov	Dec	Year
Temperature Daily Max.°C	6	7	12	16	20	23	25	24	21	16	10	7	16
Daily Min.°C	1	1	4	6	10	13	15	14	12	8	5	2	8
Average Monthly °C	3	4	8	11	15	18	20	19	17	12	7	4	12
Rainfall Monthly Total mm	56	46	35	42	57	54	59	64	55	50	51	50	619
No. of Days	17	14	12	13	12	12	12	13	13	13	15	16	162
Sunshine Av. Monthly Dur.	2	2.9	4.9	6.6	7.3	7.2	7.3	6.6	6	4	2.1	1.5	4.9

Perth Australia 60m

	Jan	Feb	Mar	Apr	May	June	July	Aug	Sep	Oct	Nov	Dec	Year
Temperature Daily Max.°C	29	30	27	25	21	18	17	18	19	21	25	27	23
Daily Min.°C	17	18	16	14	12	10	9	9	10	11	14	16	13
Average Monthly °C	23	24	22	19	16	14	13	13	15	16	19	22	18
Rainfall Monthly Total mm	8	13	22	44	128	189	177	145	84	58	19	13	900
No. of Days	3	3	5	8	15	17	19	19	15	12	7	5	128
Sunshine Av. Monthly Dur.	10.4	9.8	8.8	7.5	5.7	4.8	5.4	6	7.2	8.1	9.6	10.4	7.8

Quito Ecuador 2875m

	Jan	Feb	Mar	Apr	May	June	July	Aug	Sep	Oct	Nov	Dec	Year
Temperature Daily Max.°C	22	22	22	21	21	22	22	23	23	22	22	22	22
Daily Min.°C	8	9	9	9	9	7	7	7	7	8	7	8	8
Average Monthly °C	15	15	15	15	15	14	14	15	15	15	15	15	15
Rainfall Monthly Total mm	119	131	154	185	130	54	20	25	81	134	96	104	1233
No. of Days	16	17	20	22	21	12	7	9	14	18	14	16	186
Sunshine Av. Monthly Dur.	5.4	5	4.2	4.5	5.2	6.3	7.2	7.1	6.1	5.4	5.6	5.6	5.6

Reykjavik Iceland 18m

	Jan	Feb	Mar	Apr	May	June	July	Aug	Sep	Oct	Nov	Dec	Year
Temperature Daily Max.°C	2	3	5	6	10	13	15	14	12	8	5	4	8
Daily Min.°C	-3	-3	-1	1	4	7	9	8	6	3	0	-2	3
Average Monthly °C	0	0	2	4	7	10	12	11	9	5	3	1	5
Rainfall Monthly Total mm	89	64	62	56	42	42	50	56	67	94	78	79	779
No. of Days	20	17	18	18	16	15	15	16	19	21	18	20	213
Sunshine Av. Monthly Dur.	0.8	2	3.6	4.5	5.9	6.1	5.8	5.4	3.5	2.3	1.1	0.3	3.7

Rio de Janeiro Brazil 60m

	Jan	Feb	Mar	Apr	May	June	July	Aug	Sep	Oct	Nov	Dec	Year
Temperature Daily Max.°C	29	30	29	27	25	25	24	25	24	25	26	28	26
Daily Min.°C	23	23	22	21	19	18	17	18	19	19	20	22	20
Average Monthly °C	26	26	25	24	22	21	21	21	21	22	23	25	23
Rainfall Monthly Total mm	125	122	130	107	79	53	41	43	66	79	104	137	1086
No. of Days	13	11	12	10	10	7	7	7	11	13	13	14	128
Sunshine Av. Monthly Dur.	6.9	6.9	6.8	6.3	6.2	6.3	6.5	6.6	5.1	5.1	5.7	5.6	6.2

Rome Italy 46m

	Jan	Feb	Mar	Apr	May	June	July	Aug	Sep	Oct	Nov	Dec	Year
Temperature Daily Max.°C	11	12	15	19	23	27	30	30	26	21	16	12	20
Daily Min.°C	4	4	7	9	13	17	19	19	16	13	8	6	11
Average Monthly °C	7	8	11	14	18	22	25	25	21	17	12	9	16
Rainfall Monthly Total mm	76	89	77	73	63	48	14	22	70	128	117	107	882
No. of Days	7	6	8	9	6	4	2	2	5	6	8	8	68
Sunshine Av. Monthly Dur.	4.3	4.7	6.6	7	8.6	9.4	10.8	9.9	8.1	6.4	4.1	3.3	6.9

St Denis Réunion 10m

	Jan	Feb	Mar	Apr	May	June	July	Aug	Sep	Oct	Nov	Dec	Year
Temperature Av. Daily Max.	30	30	29	28	27	26	25	25	25	26	27	29	27
Av. Daily Min.	23	23	23	21	20	18	17	17	17	19	20	22	20
Av. Monthly	26	26	26	25	23	22	21	21	21	22	24	25	24
Rainfall Monthly Total mm	263	216	290	160	81	75	70	49	47	44	95	151	1541
No. of Days	19	17	18	13	14	14	17	16	14	12	13	16	183
Sunshine Av. Monthly Dur.	7.7	7.7	6.7	7.4	7.6	7.3	7.2	7.1	7.2	7.1	7.1	7	7.3

St Louis USA 172m

	Jan	Feb	Mar	Apr	May	June	July	Aug	Sep	Oct	Nov	Dec	Year
Temperature Daily Max.°C	5	7	12	19	24	30	32	31	27	21	12	6	19
Daily Min.°C	-5	-4	0	7	12	17	19	19	14	8	1	-3	7
Average Monthly °C	0	2	6	13	18	23	26	25	21	15	7	2	13
Rainfall Monthly Total mm	50	52	78	94	95	109	84	77	70	73	65	50	897
No. of Days	7	8	10	11	10	9	9	7	9	8	8	9	105
Sunshine Av. Monthly Dur.	4.4	5.3	6.8	7.7	9.2	9.9	10.6	9.4	8.8	7.9	5.7	4.3	7.6

San Francisco USA 5m

	Jan	Feb	Mar	Apr	May	June	July	Aug	Sep	Oct	Nov	Dec	Year
Temperature Daily Max.°C	13	15	16	17	17	18	18	18	21	20	18	14	17
Daily Min.°C	8	9	9	10	11	12	12	12	13	12	11	9	11
Average Monthly °C	10	12	13	13	14	15	15	15	17	16	14	0	14
Rainfall Monthly Total mm	116	93	74	37	16	4	0.3	1	6	23	51	108	528
No. of Days	11	10	10	6	3	1	1	1	1	4	8	11	67
Sunshine Av. Monthly Dur.	4.9	6.9	7.9	9.1	9.6	11	9.3	8.3	8.8	7.5	6.3	4.6	7.9

San Jose Costa Rica 1145m

	Jan	Feb	Mar	Apr	May	June	July	Aug	Sep	Oct	Nov	Dec	Year
Temperature Daily Max.°C	24	25	26	26	27	26	25	26	26	25	25	24	25
Daily Min.°C	15	15	15	17	17	17	17	16	16	16	16	15	16
Average Monthly °C	19	20	21	21	22	21	21	21	21	20	20	19	20
Rainfall Monthly Total mm	8	5	10	37	244	284	230	233	342	333	172	46	1944
No. of Days	3	1	2	7	19	22	23	24	24	25	14	6	170
Sunshine Av. Monthly Dur.	7	7.8	8	7	5.2	4	4	4.4	5	4.4	4.5	5.9	5.6

Santander Spain 66m

	Jan	Feb	Mar	Apr	May	June	July	Aug	Sep	Oct	Nov	Dec	Year
Temperature Daily Max.°C	12	12	14	15	17	20	22	22	21	18	15	13	17
Daily Min.°C	7	7	8	10	11	14	16	16	15	12	10	8	11
Average Monthly °C	9	9	11	12	14	17	19	19	18	15	12	10	14
Rainfall Monthly Total mm	119	88	78	83	89	63	54	84	114	133	125	159	1189
No. of Days	16	14	13	13	14	13	11	14	14	14	15	18	169
Sunshine Av. Monthly Dur.	2.7	3.5	4.5	5.5	6	6.7	6.8	6.4	5.2	4.3	3.2	2.4	4.8

Santiago Chile 520m

	Jan	Feb	Mar	Apr	May	June	July	Aug	Sep	Oct	Nov	Dec	Year
Temperature Daily Max.°C	30	29	27	24	19	15	15	17	19	22	26	29	23
Daily Min.°C	12	11	10	7	5	3	3	4	6	7	9	11	7
Average Monthly °C	21	20	18	15	12	9	9	10	12	15	17	20	15
Rainfall Monthly Total mm	3	3	5	13	64	84	76	56	31	15	8	5	363
No. of Days	0	0	1	1	5	6	6	5	3	3	1	0	31
Sunshine Av. Monthly Dur.	10.8	8.9	8.5	5.5	3.6	3.3	3.3	3.6	4.8	6.1	8.7	10.1	6.4

Shanghai China 5m

	Jan	Feb	Mar	Apr	May	June	July	Aug	Sep	Oct	Nov	Dec	Year
Temperature Daily Max.°C	8	8	13	19	24	28	32	32	27	23	17	10	20
Daily Min.°C	-1	0	4	9	14	19	23	23	19	13	7	2	11
Average Monthly °C	3	4	8	14	19	23	27	27	23	18	12	6	15
Rainfall Monthly Total mm	48	59	84	94	94	180	147	142	130	71	51	36	1136
No. of Days	10	10	12	13	12	14	11	11	12	9	8	8	130
Sunshine Av. Monthly Dur.	4	3.7	4.4	4.8	5.4	4.7	6.9	7.5	5.3	5.6	4.7	4.5	5.1

Shannon Ireland 2m

	Jan	Feb	Mar	Apr	May	June	July	Aug	Sep	Oct	Nov	Dec	Year
Temperature Daily Max.°C	8	9	11	13	16	10	10	20	17	14	11	9	14
Daily Min.°C	2	2	4	5	7	10	12	12	10	7	5	3	7
Average Monthly °C	5	5	7	9	12	14	16	16	14	11	8	6	10
Rainfall Monthly Total mm	94	67	56	53	61	57	77	79	86	86	96	117	929
No. of Days	15	11	11	11	11	11	14	14	14	14	15	18	159
Sunshine Av. Monthly Dur.	1.8	2.6	3.4	5.1	6.8	5.8	4.9	5.1	3.7	2.8	2.1	1.4	3.8

Singapore Singapore 10m

	Jan	Feb	Mar	Apr	May	June	July	Aug	Sep	Oct	Nov	Dec	Year
Temperature Daily Max.°C	31	31	31	31	31	31	31	31	30	31	30	30	31
Daily Min.°C	23	23	24	24	24	25	25	24	24	24	24	23	24
Average Monthly °C	27	27	27	27	28	28	28	27	27	27	27	27	27
Rainfall Monthly Total mm	252	175	200	196	173	171	165	191	178	206	251	265	2423
No. of Days	17	12	14	15	15	13	13	15	14	16	19	19	182
Sunshine Av. Monthly Dur.	5.1	5.7	6	5.8	5.7	5.7	5.9	5.7	5.6	5	4.6	4.3	5.4

Stockholm Sweden 44m

	Jan	Feb	Mar	Apr	May	June	July	Aug	Sep	Oct	Nov	Dec	Year
Temperature Daily Max.°C	-1	-1	2	8	15	19	22	20	15	9	5	2	10
Daily Min.°C	-5	-6	-4	1	6	10	14	13	9	5	1	-2	4
Average Monthly °C	-3	-3	-1	5	10	15	18	17	12	7	3	0	7
Rainfall Monthly Total mm	46	32	27	33	36	45	61	77	59	50	56	50	572
No. of Days	10	7	6	7	7	8	9	10	9	9	10	11	103
Sunshine Av. Monthly Dur.	1.3	2.4	5	6.8	8.7	9.6	9.1	7.3	5.6	2.8	1.3	0.7	5.1

Sydney Australia 40m

	Jan	Feb	Mar	Apr	May	June	July	Aug	Sep	Oct	Nov	Dec	Year
Temperature Daily Max.°C	26	26	25	22	19	17	17	18	20	22	24	25	22
Daily Min.°C	18	19	17	14	11	9	8	9	11	13	16	17	14
Average Monthly °C	22	22	21	18	15	13	12	13	16	18	20	21	18
Rainfall Monthly Total mm	89	101	127	135	127	117	117	76	74	71	74	74	1182
No. of Days	13	13	14	13	13	12	12	11	12	12	12	13	150
Sunshine Av. Monthly Dur.	7.5	7	6.4	6.1	5.7	5.3	6.1	7	7.3	7.5	7.5	7.5	6.8

Tehran Iran 1191m

	Jan	Feb	Mar	Apr	May	June	July	Aug	Sep	Oct	Nov	Dec	Year
Temperature Daily Max.°C	9	11	16	21	29	30	37	36	29	24	16	11	22
Daily Min.°C	-1	1	4	10	16	20	23	23	18	12	6	1	11
Average Monthly °C	4	6	10	15	22	25	30	29	23	18	11	6	17
Rainfall Monthly Total mm	37	23	36	31	14	2	1	1	1	5	29	27	207
No. of Days	4	4	3	6	3	0.6	0.2	0.3	0.4	2	4	5	32
Sunshine Av. Monthly Dur.	5.9	6.7	7.5	7.4	8.6	11.6	11.2	11	10.1	7.6	6.9	6.3	8.4

Timbuktu Mali 269m

	Jan	Feb	Mar	Apr	May	June	July	Aug	Sep	Oct	Nov	Dec	Year
Temperature Daily Max.°C	31	35	38	41	43	42	38	35	38	40	37	31	37
Daily Min.°C	13	16	18	22	26	27	25	24	24	23	18	14	21
Average Monthly °C	22	25	28	31	34	34	32	30	31	31	28	23	29
Rainfall Monthly Total mm	0	0	0	1	4	20	54	93	31	3	0	0	206
No. of Days	0	0	0	0	1	4	8	10	5	1	0	0	29
Sunshine Av. Monthly Dur.	9.1	9.6	9.6	9.7	9.8	9.4	9.6	9	9.3	9.5	9.5	8.9	9.4

Tokyo Japan 5m

	Jan	Feb	Mar	Apr	May	June	July	Aug	Sep	Oct	Nov	Dec	Year
Temperature Daily Max.°C	9	9	12	18	22	25	29	30	27	20	16	11	19
Daily Min.°C	-1	-1	3	4	13	17	22	23	19	13	7	1	10
Average Monthly °C	4	4	8	11	18	21	25	26	23	17	11	6	14
Rainfall Monthly Total mm	48	73	101	135	131	182	146	147	217	220	101	61	1562
No. of Days	6	7	10	11	12	12	11	10	13	12	8	5	117
Sunshine Av. Monthly Dur.	6	5.9	5.7	6	6.2	5	5.8	6.6	4.5	4.4	4.8	5.4	5.5

Tromsø Norway 100m

	Jan	Feb	Mar	Apr	May	June	July	Aug	Sep	Oct	Nov	Dec	Year
Temperature Daily Max.°C	-2	-2	0	3	7	12	16	14	10	5	2	0	5
Daily Min.°C	-6	-6	-5	-2	1	6	9	8	5	1	-2	-4	0
Average Monthly °C	-4	-4	-3	0	4	9	13	11	7	3	0	-2	3
Rainfall Monthly Total mm	96	79	91	65	61	59	56	80	109	115	88	95	994
No. of Days	14	12	15	12	11	11	10	14	15	16	13	13	156
Sunshine Av. Monthly Dur.	0.1	1.6	2.9	6.1	5.7	6.9	7.9	4.8	3.5	1.7	0.3	0	3.5

Tunis Tunisia 65m

	Jan	Feb	Mar	Apr	May	June	July	Aug	Sep	Oct	Nov	Dec	Year
Temperature Daily Max.°C	15	16	18	21	25	29	32	33	30	25	20	16	23
Daily Min.°C	7	7	9	11	14	18	20	21	19	15	11	7	13
Average Monthly °C	11	12	13	16	19	23	26	27	25	20	15	12	18
Rainfall Monthly Total mm	65	49	43	40	22	10	2	7	34	56	54	62	444
No. of Days	13	12	11	9	6	5	2	3	7	9	11	14	102
Sunshine Av. Monthly Dur.	5.6	6.7	7.2	7.8	9.9	10.6	12.1	11.3	8.6	7	6.1	5.3	8.2

Ulan Bator Mongolia 1305m

	Jan	Feb	Mar	Apr	May	June	July	Aug	Sep	Oct	Nov	Dec	Year
Temperature Daily Max.°C	-19	-13	-4	7	13	21	22	21	14	6	-6	-16	104
Daily Min.°C	-32	-29	-22	-8	-2	7	11	8	2	-8	-20	-28	-10
Average Monthly °C	-26	-21	-13	-1	6	14	16	14	8	-1	-13	-22	47
Rainfall Monthly Total mm	1	1	2	5	10	28	76	51	23	5	5	2	209
No. of Days	1	1	2	2	4	5	10	8	3	2	2	1	41
Sunshine Av. Monthly Dur.	6.4	7.8	8	7.8	8.3	8.6	8.6	8.2	7.2	6.9	6.1	5.7	7.5

Vancouver Canada 5m

	Jan	Feb	Mar	Apr	May	June	July	Aug	Sep	Oct	Nov	Dec	Year
Temperature Daily Max.°C	6	7	10	14	17	20	23	22	19	14	9	7	14
Daily Min.°C	0	1	3	5	8	11	13	12	10	7	3	2	6
Average Monthly °C	3	4	6	9	13	16	18	17	14	10	6	4	10
Rainfall Monthly Total mm	214	161	151	90	69	65	39	44	83	172	198	243	1529
No. of Days	20	16	17	13	10	10	7	7	10	15	18	21	164
Sunshine Av. Monthly Dur.	1.6	3	3.8	5.9	7.5	7.4	9.5	8.2	6	3.7	2	1.4	5

Verkhoyansk Russia 137m

	Jan	Feb	Mar	Apr	May	June	July	Aug	Sep	Oct	Nov	Dec	Year
Temperature Daily Max.°C	-47	-40	-20	-1	11	21	24	21	12	-8	-33	-42	-8
Daily Min.°C	-51	-48	-40	-25	-7	4	6	1	-6	-20	-39	-50	-23
Average Monthly °C	-49	-44	-30	-13	2	12	15	11	3	-14	-36	-46	-16
Rainfall Monthly Total mm	7	5	5	4	5	25	33	30	13	11	10	7	155
No. of Days	9	8	7	5	6	10	9	9	8	10	12	11	104
Sunshine Av. Monthly Dur.	0	2.6	6.9	9.6	9.7	10	9.7	7.5	4.1	2.4	0.6	0	5.4

Warsaw Poland 110m

	Jan	Feb	Mar	Apr	May	June	July	Aug	Sep	Oct	Nov	Dec	Year
Temperature Daily Max.°C	0	0	6	12	20	23	24	23	19	13	6	2	12
Daily Min.°C	-6	-6	-2	3	9	12	15	14	10	5	1	-3	4
Average Monthly °C	-3	-3	2	7	14	17	19	18	14	9	3	0	8
Rainfall Monthly Total mm	27	32	27	37	46	69	96	65	43	38	31	44	555
No. of Days	15	14	11	13	11	13	16	13	12	12	12	16	158
Sunshine Av. Monthly Dur.	1.7	2	3.7	5.3	8.1	8.1	7.1	6.9	5.3	3.8	1.6	1.3	4.6

Washington USA 22m

	Jan	Feb	Mar	Apr	May	June	July	Aug	Sep	Oct	Nov	Dec	Year
Temperature Daily Max.°C	7	8	12	19	25	29	31	30	26	20	14	8	19
Daily Min.°C	-1	-1	2	8	13	18	21	20	16	10	4	-1	9
Average Monthly °C	3	3	7	13	19	24	26	25	21	15	9	4	14
Rainfall Monthly Total mm	84	68	96	85	103	88	108	120	100	78	75	75	1080
No. of Days	11	9	12	10	12	10	11	10	9	8	9	10	121
Sunshine Av. Monthly Dur.	4.4	5.7	6.7	7.4	8.2	8.8	8.6	8.2	7.5	6.5	5.3	4.5	6.8

Windhoek Namibia 1728m

	Jan	Feb	Mar	Apr	May	June	July	Aug	Sep	Oct	Nov	Dec	Year
Temperature Daily Max.°C	30	29	27	26	23	20	21	24	27	29	30	30	26
Daily Min.°C	17	17	15	13	9	7	7	9	12	15	16	17	13
Average Monthly °C	24	23	21	19	16	13	14	16	20	22	23	24	20
Rainfall Monthly Total mm	71	76	77	41	5	2	1	1	3	13	35	39	364
No. of Days	12	11	10	5	2	0	0	0	1	3	7	7	58
Sunshine Av. Monthly Dur.	8.9	8.6	8.3	9.5	10	10	10	10.5	10.4	10.2	9.7	9.8	9.7

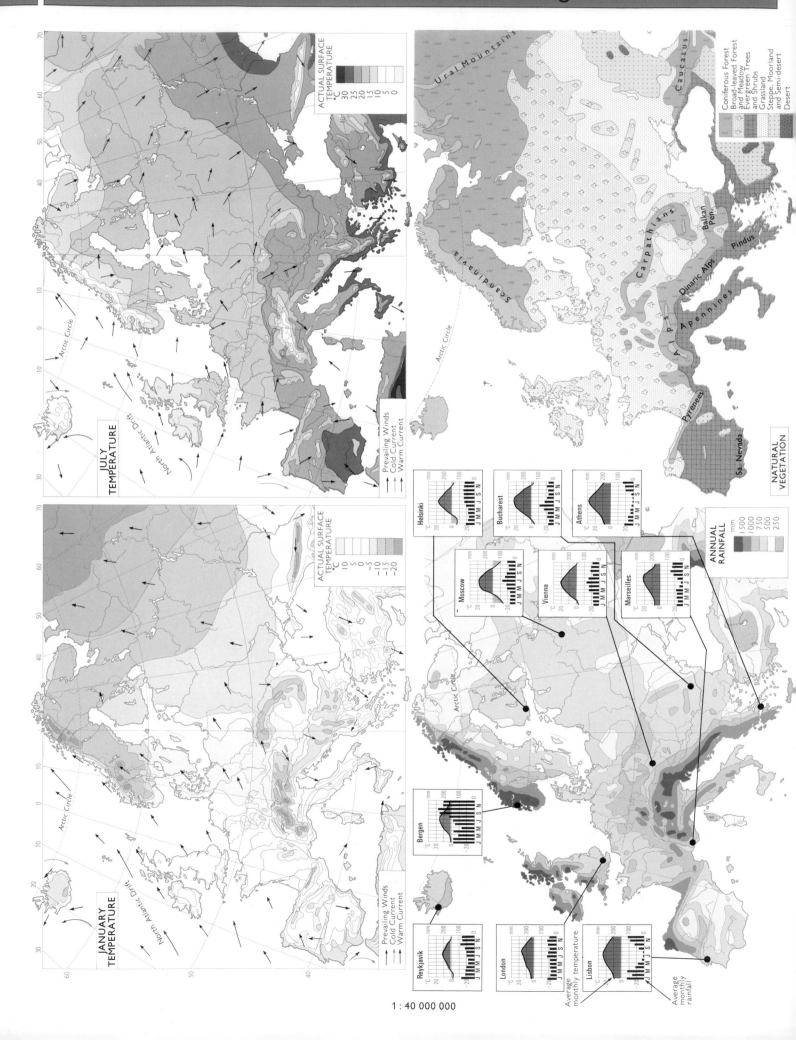

ACTUAL SURFACE TEMPERATURE
°C
30
25
20
15
10
5
0

JULY TEMPERATURE

Prevailing Winds
Cold Current
Warm Current

North Atlantic Drift

Arctic Circle

ACTUAL SURFACE TEMPERATURE
°C
10
5
-5
-10
-15
-20

JANUARY TEMPERATURE

Prevailing Winds
Cold Current
Warm Current

North Atlantic Drift

Arctic Circle

Ural Mountains
Caucasus
Scandinavia
Carpathians
Balkan Pen.
Pindus
Dinaric Alps
Alps
Apennines
Pyrenees
Sa. Nevada

Coniferous Forest
Broad-leaved Forest
Meadow
Evergreen Trees and Shrubs
Grassland
Steppe, Moorland and Semi-desert
Desert

NATURAL VEGETATION

ANNUAL RAINFALL
mm
1500
1000
750
500
250

Helsinki
Bucharest
Athens
Moscow
Vienna
Marseilles
Bergen
Reykjavik
London
Lisbon

Average monthly temperature
Average monthly rainfall

1 : 40 000 000

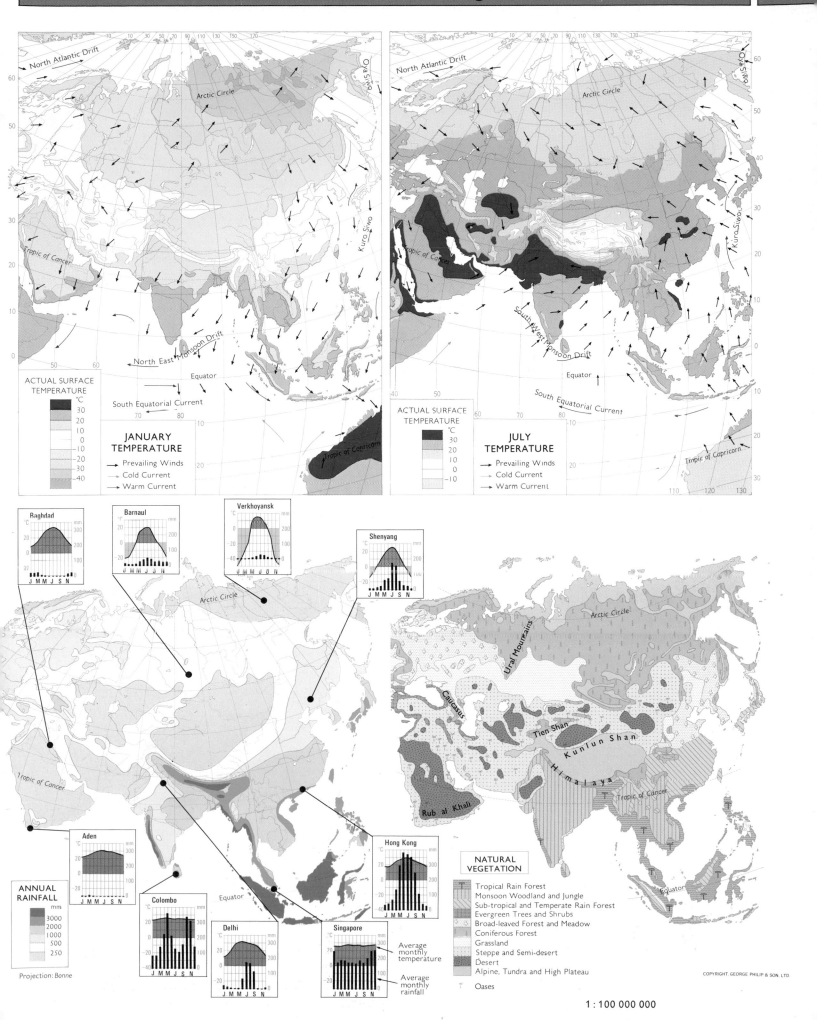

ACTUAL SURFACE TEMPERATURE

°C
30
20
10
0
-10
-20
-30
-40

JANUARY TEMPERATURE

→ Prevailing Winds
→ Cold Current
→ Warm Current

ACTUAL SURFACE TEMPERATURE

°C
30
20
10
0
-10

JULY TEMPERATURE

→ Prevailing Winds
→ Cold Current
→ Warm Current

North Atlantic Drift
Arctic Circle
Oya Siwo
Tropic of Cancer
Kuro Siwo
North East Monsoon Drift
Equator
South Equatorial Current
Tropic of Capricorn

South West Monsoon Drift

Baghdad
Barnaul
Verkhoyansk
Shenyang

Aden
Colombo
Delhi
Singapore
Hong Kong

ANNUAL RAINFALL

mm
3000
2000
1000
500
250

Projection: Bonne

Average monthly temperature
Average monthly rainfall

NATURAL VEGETATION

- Tropical Rain Forest
- Monsoon Woodland and Jungle
- Sub-tropical and Temperate Rain Forest
- Evergreen Trees and Shrubs
- Broad-leaved Forest and Meadow
- Coniferous Forest
- Grassland
- Steppe and Semi-desert
- Desert
- Alpine, Tundra and High Plateau
- T Oases

Ural Mountains
Arctic Circle
Caucasus
Tien Shan
Kun Lun Shan
Himalaya
Rub al Khali
Tropic of Cancer
Equator

COPYRIGHT. GEORGE PHILIP & SON. LTD.

1 : 100 000 000

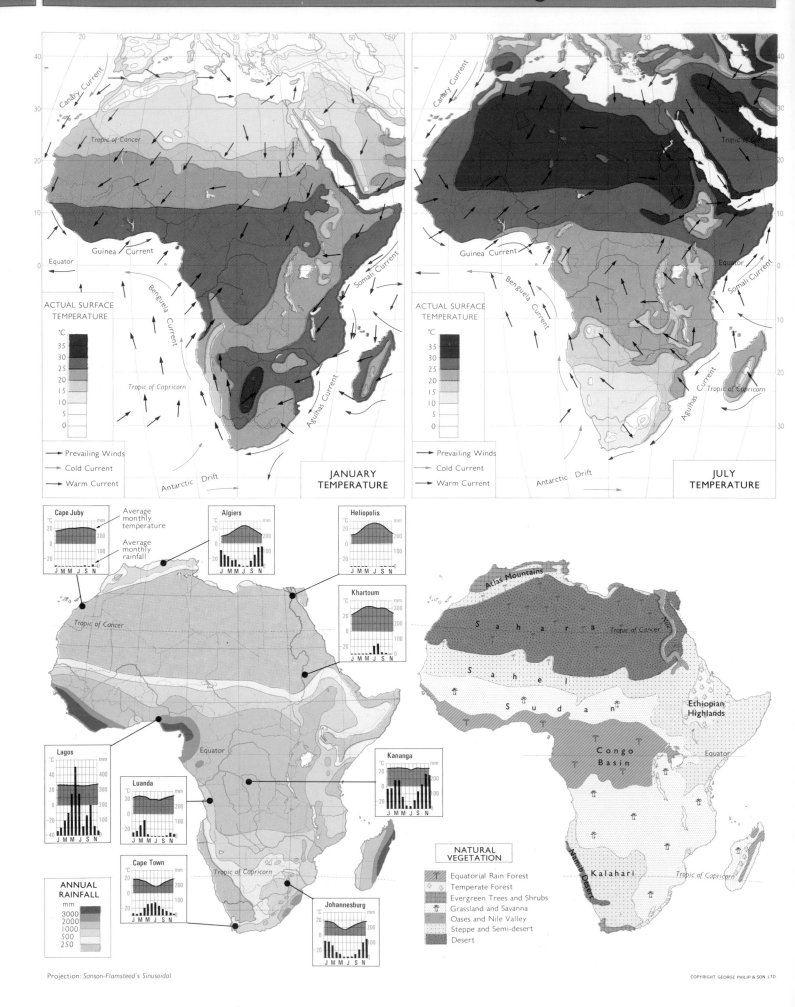

ACTUAL SURFACE TEMPERATURE

°C
35
30
25
20
15
10
5
0

→ Prevailing Winds
→ Cold Current
→ Warm Current

JANUARY TEMPERATURE

Canary Current
Tropic of Cancer
Guinea Current
Equator
Benguela Current
Somali Current
Tropic of Capricorn
Agulhas Current
Antarctic Drift

ACTUAL SURFACE TEMPERATURE

°C
35
30
25
20
15
10
5
0

→ Prevailing Winds
→ Cold Current
→ Warm Current

JULY TEMPERATURE

Canary Current
Tropic of Cancer
Guinea Current
Equator
Benguela Current
Somali Current
Tropic of Capricorn
Agulhas Current
Antarctic Drift

Cape Juby — Average monthly temperature
Algiers
Heliopolis — Average monthly rainfall
Khartoum
Tropic of Cancer
Lagos
Equator
Luanda
Kananga
Cape Town
Tropic of Capricorn
Johannesburg

ANNUAL RAINFALL

mm
3000
2000
1000
500
250

Atlas Mountains
Sahara
Tropic of Cancer
Sahel
Sudan
Ethiopian Highlands
Congo Basin
Equator
Namib Desert
Kalahari
Tropic of Capricorn

NATURAL VEGETATION

Equatorial Rain Forest
Temperate Forest
Evergreen Trees and Shrubs
Grassland and Savanna
Oases and Nile Valley
Steppe and Semi-desert
Desert

Projection: *Sanson-Flamsteed's Sinusoidal*

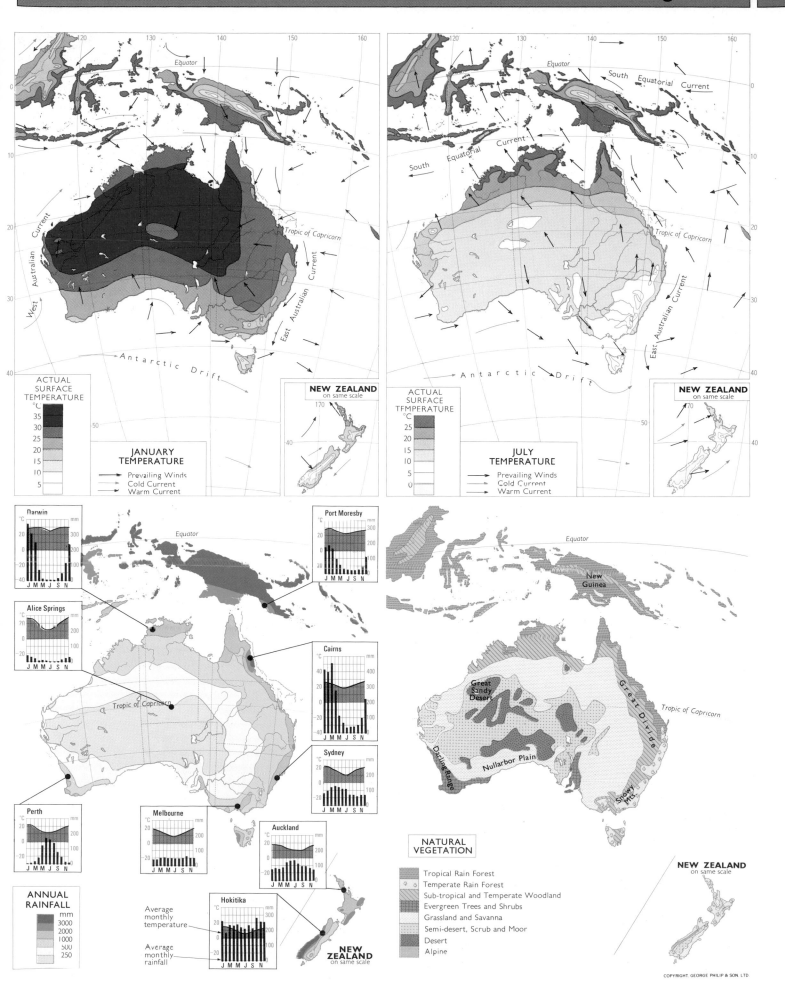

ACTUAL SURFACE TEMPERATURE
°C
35
30
25
20
15
10
5

JANUARY TEMPERATURE
→ Prevailing Winds
→ Cold Current
→ Warm Current

NEW ZEALAND on same scale

ACTUAL SURFACE TEMPERATURE
°C
25
20
15
10
5
0

JULY TEMPERATURE
→ Prevailing Winds
→ Cold Current
→ Warm Current

NEW ZEALAND on same scale

Darwin
Alice Springs
Port Moresby
Cairns
Sydney
Perth
Melbourne
Auckland
Hokitika

Average monthly temperature
Average monthly rainfall

NEW ZEALAND on same scale

ANNUAL RAINFALL
mm
3000
2000
1000
500
250

Great Sandy Desert
Nullarbor Plain
Darling Range
Great Divide
Snowy Mts.
New Guinea
Tropic of Capricorn
Equator

NATURAL VEGETATION
Tropical Rain Forest
Temperate Rain Forest
Sub-tropical and Temperate Woodland
Evergreen Trees and Shrubs
Grassland and Savanna
Semi-desert, Scrub and Moor
Desert
Alpine

NEW ZEALAND on same scale

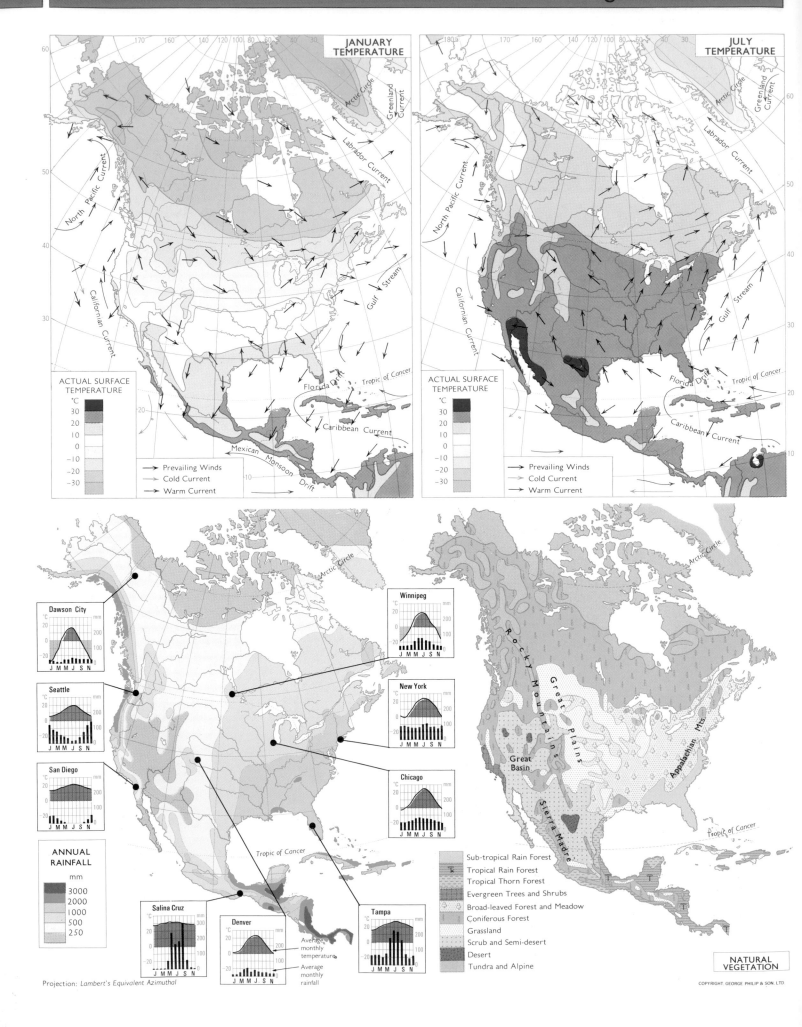

JANUARY
TEMPERATURE

ACTUAL SURFACE
TEMPERATURE
°C
30
20
10
0
-10
-20
-30

→ Prevailing Winds
→ Cold Current
→ Warm Current

JULY
TEMPERATURE

ACTUAL SURFACE
TEMPERATURE
°C
30
20
10
0
-10
-20
-30

→ Prevailing Winds
→ Cold Current
→ Warm Current

Dawson City
Seattle
San Diego

Winnipeg
New York
Chicago

Salina Cruz
Denver
Tampa

Average
monthly
temperature
Average
monthly
rainfall

ANNUAL
RAINFALL

mm
3000
2000
1000
500
250

Projection: *Lambert's Equivalent Azimuthal*

Rocky Mountains
Great Plains
Great Basin
Sierra Madre
Appalachian Mts

Sub-tropical Rain Forest
Tropical Rain Forest
Tropical Thorn Forest
Evergreen Trees and Shrubs
Broad-leaved Forest and Meadow
Coniferous Forest
Grassland
Scrub and Semi-desert
Desert
Tundra and Alpine

NATURAL
VEGETATION

COPYRIGHT GEORGE PHILIP & SON. LTD.

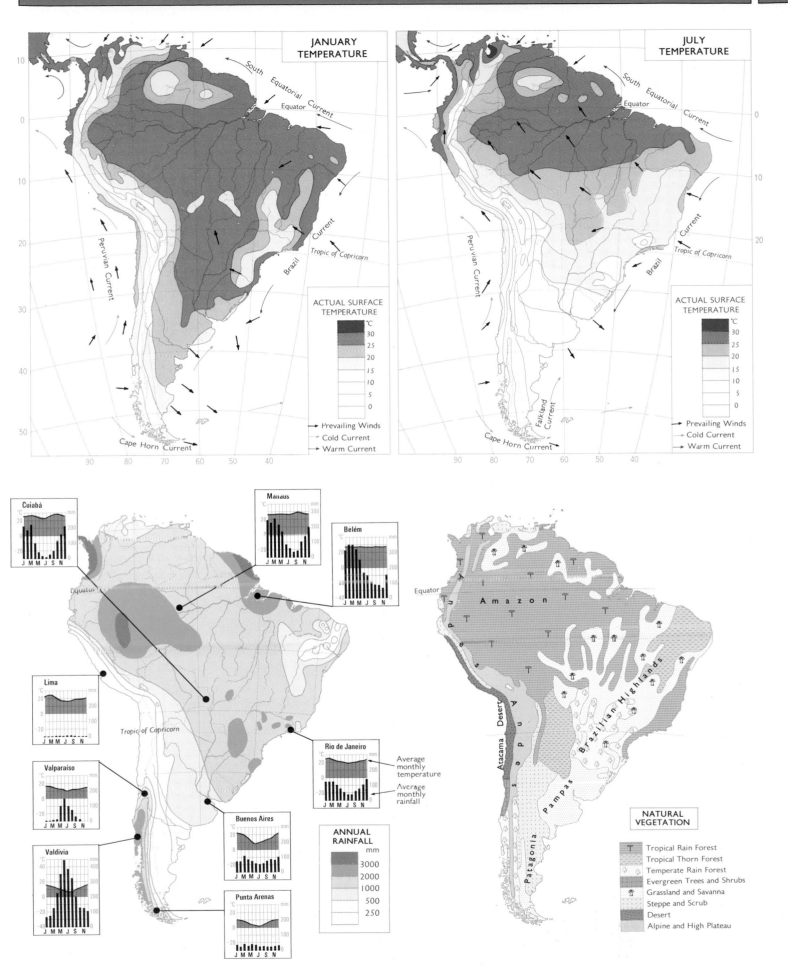

JANUARY TEMPERATURE

JULY TEMPERATURE

ACTUAL SURFACE TEMPERATURE
°C
30
25
20
15
10
5
0

→ Prevailing Winds
→ Cold Current
→ Warm Current

South Equatorial Current
Equator
Peruvian Current
Brazil Current
Tropic of Capricorn
Falkland Current
Cape Horn Current

Cuiabá
Manaus
Belém
Lima
Valparaíso
Buenos Aires
Valdivia
Punta Arenas
Rio de Janeiro

Average monthly temperature
Average monthly rainfall

ANNUAL RAINFALL
mm
3000
2000
1000
500
250

Equator
Tropic of Capricorn

Amazon
Andes
Atacama Desert
Pampas
Brazilian Highlands
Patagonia

NATURAL VEGETATION

Tropical Rain Forest
Tropical Thorn Forest
Temperate Rain Forest
Evergreen Trees and Shrubs
Grassland and Savanna
Steppe and Scrub
Desert
Alpine and High Plateau

Projection: *Lambert's Equivalent Azimuthal*

COPYRIGHT. GEORGE PHILIP & SON. LTD

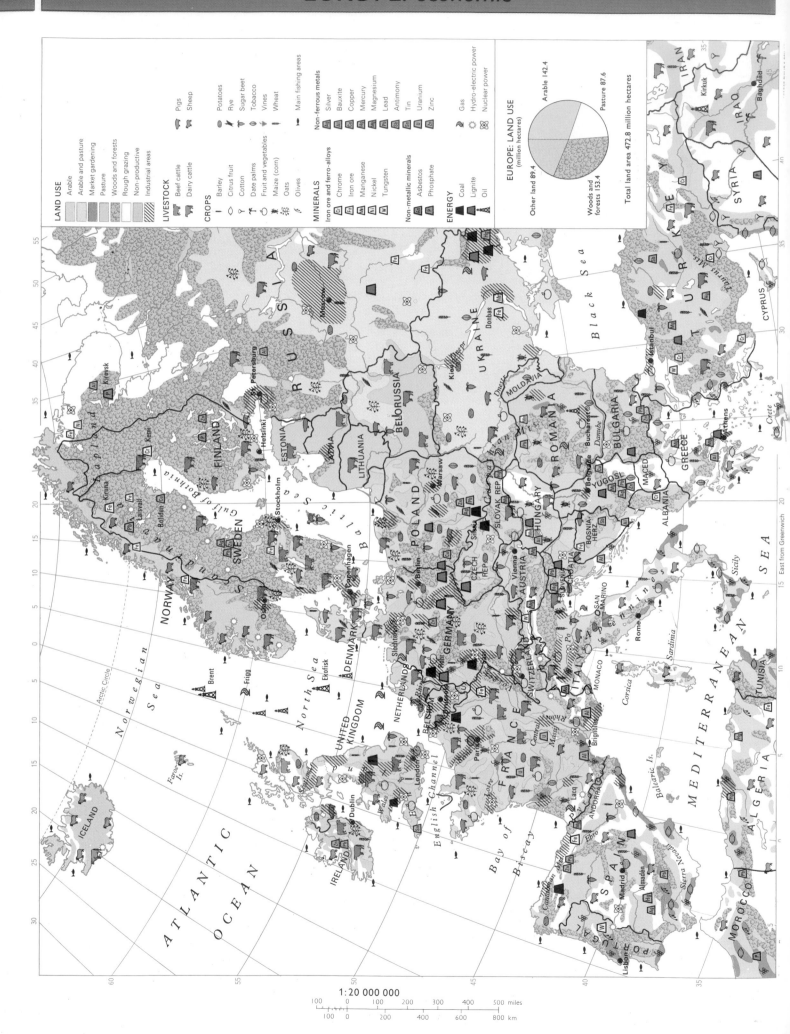

LAND USE
- Arable
- Arable and pasture
- Market gardening
- Pasture
- Woods and forests
- Rough grazing
- Non-productive
- Industrial areas

LIVESTOCK
- Beef cattle
- Dairy cattle
- Pigs
- Sheep

CROPS
- Barley
- Citrus fruit
- Cotton
- Date palms
- Fruit and vegetables
- Maize (corn)
- Oats
- Olives
- Potatoes
- Rye
- Sugar beet
- Tobacco
- Vines
- Wheat
- Main fishing areas

MINERALS

Iron ore and ferro-alloys
- Chrome
- Iron ore
- Manganese
- Nickel
- Tungsten

Non-ferrous metals
- Silver
- Bauxite
- Copper
- Mercury
- Magnesium
- Lead
- Antimony
- Tin
- Uranium
- Zinc

Non-metallic minerals
- Asbestos
- Phosphate

ENERGY
- Coal
- Lignite
- Oil
- Gas
- Hydro-electric power
- Nuclear power

EUROPE: LAND USE
(million hectares)

Arable 142.4
Pasture 87.6
Woods and forests 153.4
Other land 89.4

Total land area 472.8 million hectares

1:20 000 000

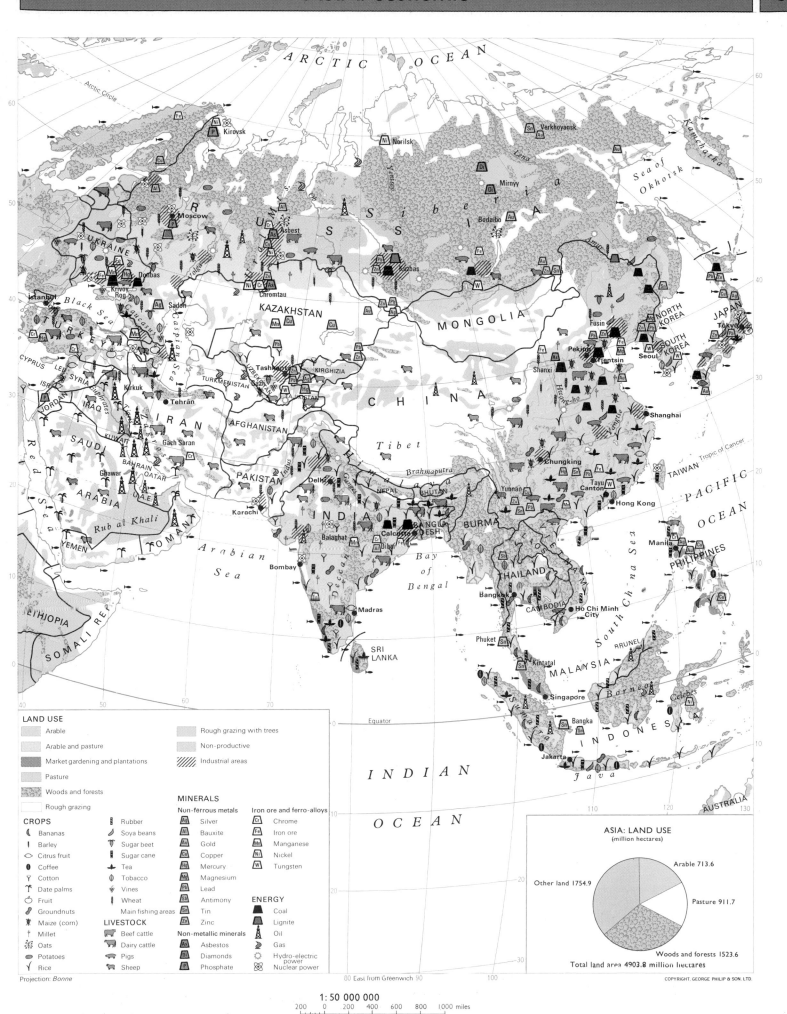

LAND USE

Arable

Arable and pasture

Market gardening and plantations

Pasture

Woods and forests

Rough grazing

Rough grazing with trees

Non-productive

Industrial areas

CROPS

- Bananas
- Barley
- Citrus fruit
- Coffee
- Cotton
- Date palms
- Fruit
- Groundnuts
- Maize (corn)
- Millet
- Oats
- Potatoes
- Rice

- Rubber
- Soya beans
- Sugar beet
- Sugar cane
- Tea
- Tobacco
- Vines
- Wheat
- Main fishing areas

LIVESTOCK

- Beef cattle
- Dairy cattle
- Pigs
- Sheep

MINERALS

Non-ferrous metals

- Ag Silver
- Al Bauxite
- Au Gold
- Cu Copper
- Hg Mercury
- Mg Magnesium
- Pb Lead
- Sb Antimony
- Sn Tin
- Zn Zinc

Non-metallic minerals

- As Asbestos
- Di Diamonds
- P Phosphate

Iron ore and ferro-alloys

- Cr Chrome
- Fe Iron ore
- Mn Manganese
- Ni Nickel
- W Tungsten

ENERGY

- Coal
- Lignite
- Oil
- Gas
- Hydro-electric power
- Nuclear power

ASIA: LAND USE
(million hectares)

Arable 713.6

Pasture 911.7

Woods and forests 1523.6

Other land 1754.9

Total land area 4903.8 million hectares

Projection: *Bonne*

00 East from Greenwich 90   100

COPYRIGHT. GEORGE PHILIP & SON, LTD.

1: 50 000 000

200 0   200   400   600   800   1000 miles

200 0   400   800   1200   1600 km

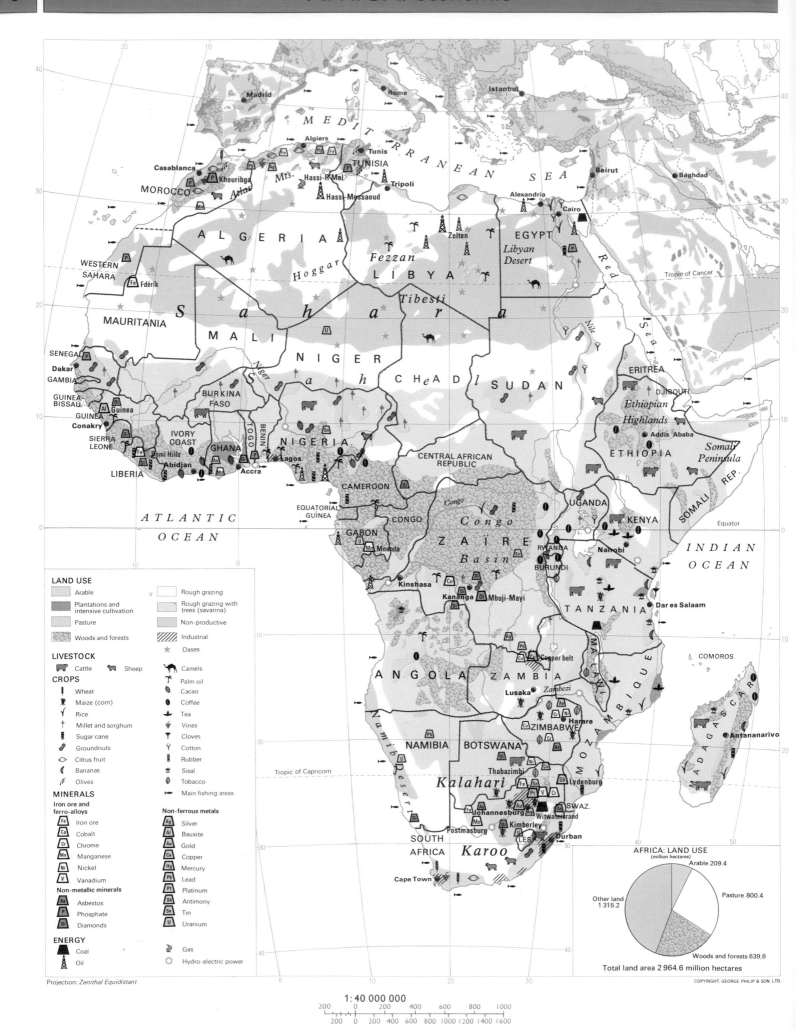

LAND USE
- Arable
- Plantations and intensive cultivation
- Pasture
- Woods and forests
- Rough grazing
- Rough grazing with trees (savanna)
- Non-productive
- Industrial
- Oases

LIVESTOCK
- Cattle
- Sheep
- Camels

CROPS
- Wheat
- Maize (corn)
- Rice
- Millet and sorghum
- Sugar cane
- Groundnuts
- Citrus fruit
- Bananas
- Olives
- Palm oil
- Cacao
- Coffee
- Tea
- Vines
- Cloves
- Cotton
- Rubber
- Sisal
- Tobacco
- Main fishing areas

MINERALS

Iron ore and ferro-alloys
- Fe Iron ore
- Co Cobalt
- Cr Chrome
- Mn Manganese
- Ni Nickel
- V Vanadium

Non-ferrous metals
- Ag Silver
- Al Bauxite
- Au Gold
- Cu Copper
- Hg Mercury
- Pb Lead
- Pt Platinum
- Sb Antimony
- Sn Tin
- U Uranium

Non-metallic minerals
- As Asbestos
- Phosphate
- Di Diamonds

ENERGY
- Coal
- Oil
- Gas
- Hydro-electric power

AFRICA: LAND USE
(million hectares)

Arable 209.4
Pasture 800.4
Woods and forests 639.6
Other land 1 315.2

Total land area 2 964.6 million hectares

Projection: *Zenithal Equidistant*

COPYRIGHT. GEORGE PHILIP & SON. LTD.

1:40 000 000

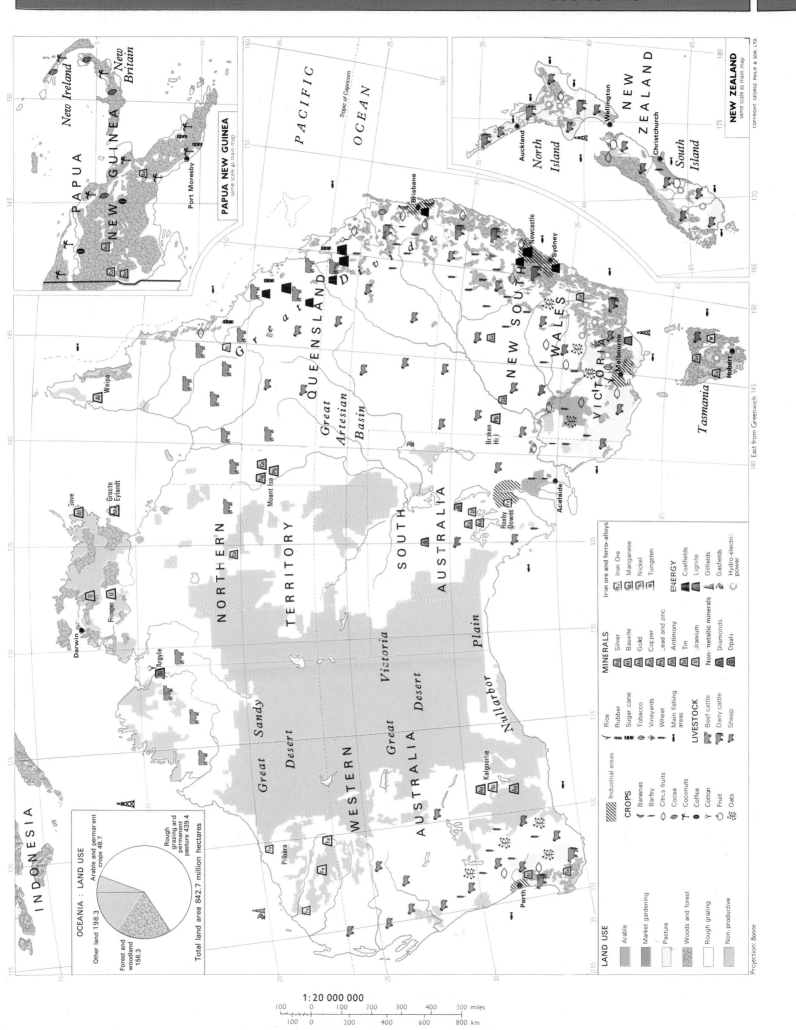

PAPUA NEW GUINEA
same scale as main map

PACIFIC

OCEAN

Tropic of Capricorn

NEW ZEALAND
same scale as main map

COPYRIGHT GEORGE PHILIP & SON, LTD

NEW
ZEALAND

North
Island

South
Island

Auckland

Wellington

Christchurch

PAPUA

NEW GUINEA

New Ireland

New
Britain

Port Moresby

Brisbane

Newcastle

Sydney

NEW SOUTH

WALES

VICTORIA

Melbourne

Hobart

Tasmania

Weipa

QUEENSLAND

Great

Artesian

Basin

Broken
Hill

Adelaide

Roxby Downs

SOUTH

AUSTRALIA

Mount Isa

Gove

Groote
Eylandt

NORTHERN

TERRITORY

Finniss

Darwin

Argyle

Great Sandy

Desert

WESTERN

AUSTRALIA

Great Victoria

Desert

Nullarbor

Plain

Kalgoorlie

Pilbara

Perth

INDONESIA

East from Greenwich 145

Projection: Bonne

LAND USE

Arable

Market gardening

Pasture

Woods and forest

Rough grazing

Non-productive

OCEANIA : LAND USE

Other land 198.3

Arable and permanent
crops 48.7

Forest and
woodland 156.3

Rough grazing and
permanent
pasture 439.4

Total land area 842.7 million hectares

Industrial areas

CROPS
Rice
Bananas
Barley
Citrus fruits
Cocoa
Coconuts
Coffee
Cotton
Fruit
Oats

Rubber
Sugar cane
Tobacco
Vineyards
Wheat
Main fishing
areas

LIVESTOCK
Beef cattle
Dairy cattle
Sheep

MINERALS
Silver
Bauxite
Gold
Copper
Lead and zinc
Antimony
Tin
Uranium
Non-metallic minerals
Diamonds
Opals

Iron ore and ferro-alloys
Iron Ore
Manganese
Nickel
Tungsten

ENERGY
Coalfields
Lignite
Oilfields
Gasfields
Hydro-electric
power

1:20 000 000

100   0   100   200   300   400   500 miles

100 0   200   400   600   800 km

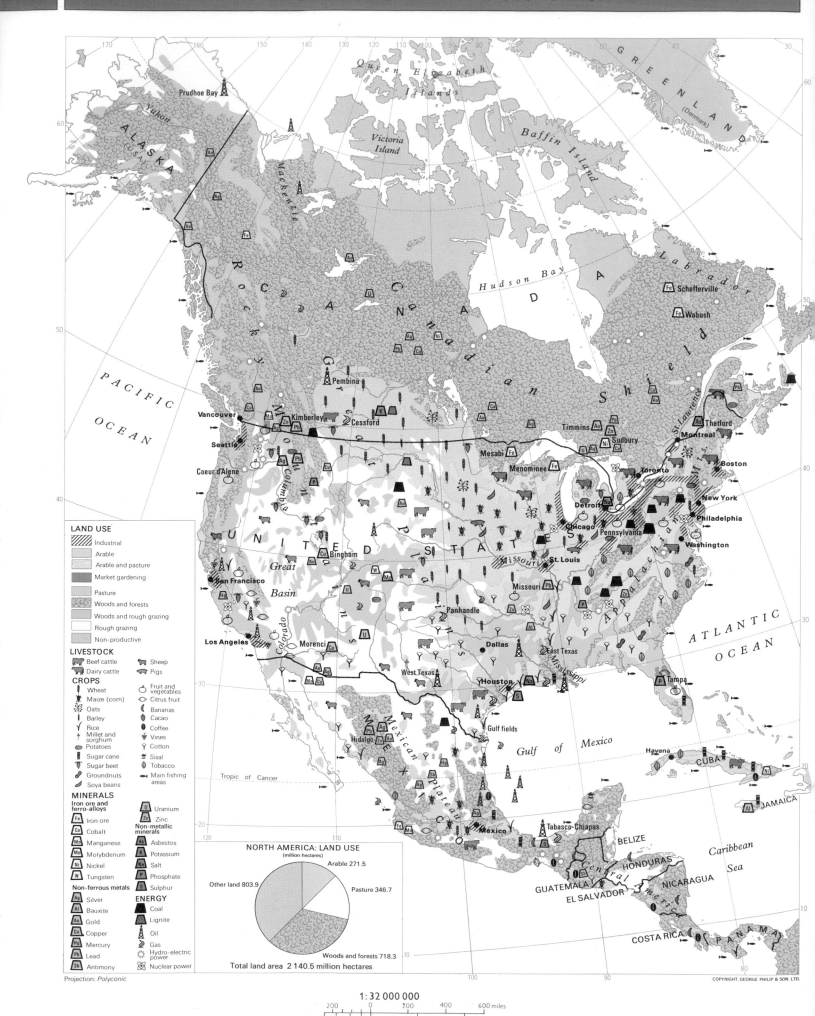

LAND USE
- ⬚ Industrial
- ⬚ Arable
- ⬚ Arable and pasture
- ⬚ Market gardening
- ⬚ Pasture
- ⬚ Woods and forests
- ⬚ Woods and rough grazing
- ⬚ Rough grazing
- ⬚ Non-productive

LIVESTOCK
- Beef cattle
- Dairy cattle
- Sheep
- Pigs

CROPS
- Wheat
- Maize (corn)
- Oats
- Barley
- Rice
- Millet and sorghum
- Potatoes
- Sugar cane
- Sugar beet
- Groundnuts
- Soya beans
- Fruit and vegetables
- Citrus fruit
- Bananas
- Cacao
- Coffee
- Vines
- Cotton
- Sisal
- Tobacco
- Main fishing areas

MINERALS
Iron ore and ferro-alloys
- Fe Iron ore
- Co Cobalt
- Mn Manganese
- Mo Molybdenum
- Ni Nickel
- W Tungsten

Non-ferrous metals
- Ag Silver
- Al Bauxite
- Au Gold
- Cu Copper
- Hg Mercury
- Pb Lead
- Sb Antimony

- U Uranium
- Zn Zinc

Non-metallic minerals
- As Asbestos
- K Potassium
- Na Salt
- P Phosphate
- S Sulphur

ENERGY
- Coal
- Lignite
- Oil
- Gas
- Hydro-electric power
- Nuclear power

NORTH AMERICA: LAND USE
(million hectares)

Arable 271.5
Pasture 346.7
Woods and forests 718.3
Other land 803.9

Total land area 2 140.5 million hectares

Projection: Polyconic

1:32 000 000

200 0 200 400 600 miles
400 0 400 800 km

COPYRIGHT. GEORGE PHILIP & SON. LTD.

SOUTH AMERICA: LAND USE
(million hectares)

Other land 283.5 — Arable 104.1

Pasture 441.8

Woods and forests 924.3

Total land area 1 753.7 million hectares

LAND USE

- Industrial
- Arable
- Market gardening and plantations
- Pasture
- Woods and forests
- Rough grazing
- Non-productive

LIVESTOCK

- Beef cattle
- Sheep
- Dairy cattle
- Pigs

CROPS

- Wheat
- Coconut palms
- Maize (corn)
- Cacao
- Rice
- Coffee
- Millet and sorghum
- Tea
- Potatoes
- Vines
- Sugar cane
- Cotton
- Groundnuts
- Rubber
- Fruit and vegetables
- Tobacco
- Citrus fruit
- Main fishing areas
- Bananas

MINERALS

Iron ore and ferro-alloys

- Fe Iron ore
- Cr Chrome
- Mn Manganese
- Mo Molybdenum
- W   Tungsten

Non-metallic minerals

- N   Saltpetre

Non-ferrous metals

- Ag Silver
- Al Bauxite
- Au Gold
- Cu Copper
- Pb Lead
- Sb Antimony
- Sn Tin
- Zn Zinc

ENERGY

- Coal
- Oil
- Nuclear power
- Gas
- Hydro-electric power

Projection: *Lambert's Equivalent Azimuthal*

COPYRIGHT GEORGE PHILIP & SON LTD

1:30 000 000

200   0   200   400   600 miles

200 0 200 400 600 800 km

Wheat

The most important grain crop in the temperate regions though it is also grown in a variety of climates e.g. in Monsoon lands as a winter crop.

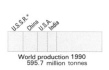

World production 1990
595.7 million tonnes

Oats

Widely grown in temperate regions with the limit fixed by early autumn frosts. Mainly fed to cattle. The best quality oats are used for oatmeal, porridge and breakfast foods.

World production 1990
43.8 million tonnes

- Wheat
- Oats

1 dot represents
2 million tonnes

Rye

The hardiest of cereals and more resistant to cold, pests and disease than wheat. An important foodstuff in Central and E. Europe.

World production 1990
36.6 million tonnes

Maize (or Corn)

Needs plenty of sunshine, summer rain or irrigation and frost free for 6 months. Important as animal feed and for human food in Africa, Latin America and as a vegetable and breakfast cereal.

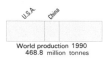

World production 1990
468.8 million tonnes

- Rye
- Maize

1 dot represents
2 million tonnes

Barley

Has the widest range of cultivation requiring only 8 weeks between seed time and harvest. Used mainly as animal-feed and by the malting industry.

World production 1990
181.2 million tonnes

Rice

The staple food of half the human race. The main producing areas are the flood plains and hill terraces of S. and E. Asia where water is abundant in the growing season.

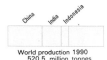

World production 1990
520.5 million tonnes

- Barley
- Rice

1 dot represents
2 million tonnes

Millets

The name given to a number of related members of the grass family, of which sorghum is one of the most important. They provide nutritious grain.

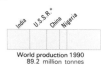

World production 1990
89.2 million tonnes

Potatoes

An important food crop though less nutritious weight for weight than grain crops. Requires a temperate climate with a regular and plentiful supply of rain.

World production 1990
268.4 million tonnes

- Millets
- Potatoes

1 dot represents
2 million tonnes

Vegetable oilseeds and oils

Despite the increasing use of synthetic chemical products and animal and marine fats, vegetable oils extracted from these crops grow in quantity, value and importance. Food is the major use- in margarine and cooking fats.

Groundnuts are also a valuable subsistence crop and the meal is used as animal feed. Soya-bean meal is a growing source of protein for humans and animals, The Mediterranean lands are the prime source of olive oil.

 Groundnut

 Soya bean

 Sunflower

- Groundnuts

Soya beans

- Sunflower seed

1 dot represents
1 million tonnes

Statistics for each of the new republics of the former U.S.S.R., Czechoslovakia and Yugoslavia are not yet available.

Tea and cacao

Tea requires plentiful rainfall and well-drained, sloping ground, whereas cacao prefers a moist heavy soil. Both are grown mainly for export.

Coffee

Prefers a hot climate, wet and dry seasons and an elevated location. It is very susceptible to frost, drought and market fluctuations.

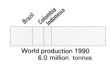

World production 1990
6.0 million tonnes

- Tea
- Cacao
- Coffee

1 dot represents
100 000 tonnes

Sugar beet

Requires a deep, rich soil and a temperate climate. Europe produces over 90% of the world's beets mainly for domestic consumption.

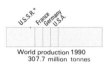

World production 1990
307.7 million tonnes

Sugar cane

Also requires deep and rich soil but a tropical climate. It produces a much higher yield per hectare than beet and is grown primarily for export.

World production 1990
1044.3 million tonnes

- Sugar beet
- Sugar cane

1 dot represents
10 million tonnes

Fruit

With the improvements in canning, drying and freezing, and in transport and marketing, the international trade and consumption of deciduous and soft fruits, citrus fruits and tropical fruits has greatly increased. Recent developments in the use of the peel will give added value to some of the fruit crops.

Fish

Commercial fishing requires large shoals of fish of one species within reach of markets. Freshwater fishing is also important. A rich source of protein, fish will become an increasingly valuable food source.

World catch 1988
98.0 million tonnes

- Temperate fruit
- Citrus fruit
- Principal fishing grounds

Beef cattle

Australia, New Zealand and Argentina provide the major part of international beef exports. Western U.S.A. and Europe have considerable production of beef for their local high demand.

World production 1989
49.4 million tonnes of meat

Dairy cattle

The need of herds for a rich diet and for nearby markets result in dairying being characteristic of densely-populated areas of the temperate zones - U.S.A., N.W. Europe, and S.E. Australia.

World production 1989
474.0 million tonnes of milk

- Cattle

1 dot represents
10 million head

- Dairy produce

Sheep

Raised mostly for wool and meat, their skins and the cheese from their milk are important products in some countries. The merino yields a fine wool and crossbreeds are best for meat.

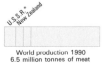

World production 1990
6.5 million tonnes of meat

Pigs

Can be reared in most climates from monsoon to cool temperate. They are abundant in China, the Corn Belt of the U.S.A. N.W. and C. Europe, Brazil and Russia.

World production 1990
67.1 million tonnes of meat

- Sheep
- Pigs

1 dot represents
10 million head

Statistics for each of the new republics of the former U.S.S.R., Czechoslovakia and Yugoslavia are not yet available.

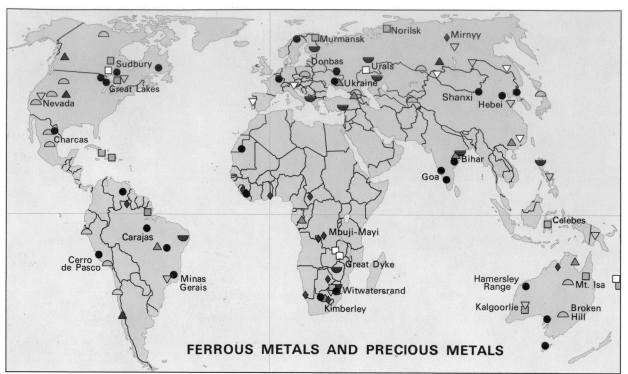

FERROUS METALS AND PRECIOUS METALS

Precious Metals

▽ Gold
World total (1990)
1,750 tonnes

South Africa	34.9%
U.S.A.	16.9%
U.S.S.R.	16.0%
Australia	13.8%
Canada	9.4%

⌒ Silver
World total (1990)
14,654 tonnes

Mexico	15.7%
U.S.A.	13.7%
Peru	12.6%
U.S.S.R.	10.2%
Canada	8.9%

♦ Diamonds
World total (1990)
108,000,000 carats

Australia	33.3%
Zaire	22.2%
Botswana	16.0%
U.S.S.R.	13.9%
South Africa	7.9%

● **Iron Ore** World total (1990) 962,000,000 tonnes	☐ **Nickel** World total (1990) 865,000 tonnes	◗ **Chrome** World total (1990) 12,000 tonnes	▲ **Manganese** World total (1990) 24,000 tonnes	☐ **Cobalt** World total (1988) 43,900 tonnes	▲ **Molybdenum** World total (1988) 94,700 tonnes	▽ **Tungsten** World total (1990) 45,000 tonnes
U.S.S.R. 14.8%	U.S.S.R. 24.3%	South Africa 35.0%	U.S.S.R. 37.5%	Zaire 57.9%	U.S.A. 45.4%	China 44.4%
Brazil 10.9%	Canada 23.5%	U.S.S.R. 31.7%	South Africa 15.8%	Zambia 15.3%	Chile 18.0%	U.S.S.R. 15.6%
China 8.8%	New Caledonia 11.1%	India 6.3%	China 11.3%	U.S.S.R. 6.6%	Canada 13.1%	Mongolia 3.3%
Australia 7.3%	Australia 7.5%	Albania 5.8%	Australia 9.6%	Canada 5.7%	U.S.S.R. 12.1%	Austria 3.1%
U.S.A. 3.6%	Indonesia 6.9%	Turkey 5.0%	Gabon 9.2%	New Caledonia 4.8%	Mexico 4.5%	Portugal 3.1%

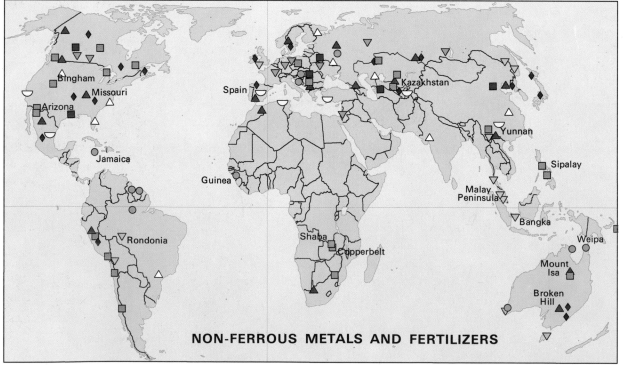

NON-FERROUS METALS AND FERTILIZERS

Fertilizers

■ Nitrates
World total (1989)
85,151,000 tonnes

U.S.S.R.	18.3%
China	16.4%
U.S.A.	14.9%
Hungary	7.9%
Canada	3.2%

△ Phosphates
World total (1989)
41,532,000 tonnes

U.S.A.	22.9%
U.S.S.R.	22.0%
China	9.1%
India	5.5%
Brazil	3.4%

▽ Potash
World total (1989)
31,151,000 tonnes

U.S.S.R.	36.3%
Canada	26.0%
Germany	18.5%
France	4.5%
Israel	3.9%

■ **Copper** World total (1989) 9,129,000 tonnes	▲ **Lead** World total (1989) 3,341,000 tonnes	● **Bauxite** World total (1989) 106,560,000 tonnes	▽ **Tin** World total (1989) 223,000 tonnes	♦ **Zinc** World total (1989) 7,138,000 tonnes	▽ **Mercury** World total (1990) 5,541 tonnes
Chile 17.6%	U.S.S.R. 15.0%	Australia 36.2%	Brazil 22.5%	Canada 17.0%	U.S.S.R. 45.1%
U.S.A. 17.3%	Australia 14.8%	Guinea 16.4%	China 14.8%	U.S.S.R. 13.2%	China 18.8%
U.S.S.R. 10.4%	U.S.A. 12.5%	Jamaica 8.8%	Malaysia 14.3%	Australia 11.2%	Spain 12.9%
Canada 8.0%	China 10.2%	Brazil 7.4%	Indonesia 14.0%	China 8.7%	Algeria 12.6%
Zambia 5.5%	Canada 8.2%	U.S.S.R. 5.4%	Bolivia 7.1%	Peru 8.4%	Mexico 3.5%

Some countries are highly dependent upon minerals. The following are dependent on metals and minerals for over 50% of the value of their exports:
Zambia 93%,
New Caledonia 81%,
Zaire 55%.

Statistics for each of the new republics of the former U.S.S.R., Czechoslovakia and Yugoslavia are not yet available.

Projection : *Modified Hammer Equal Area*

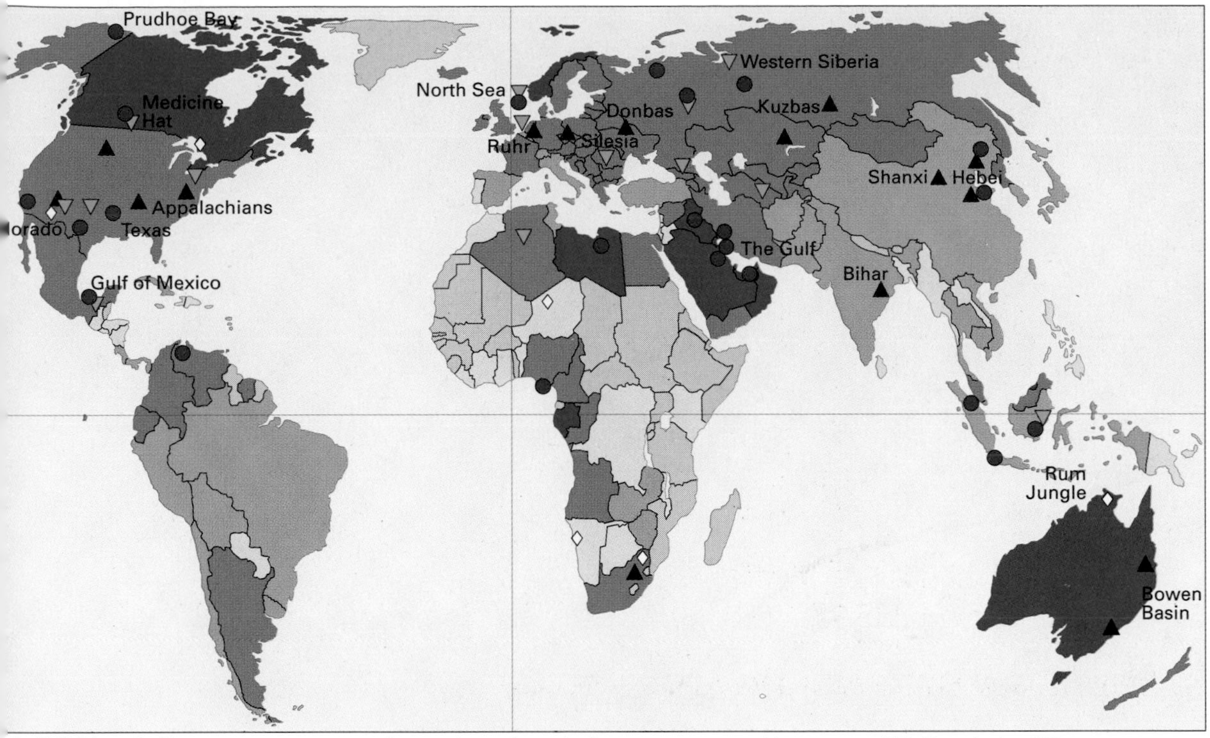

ENERGY PRODUCTION

Primary energy production expressed in kilograms of coal equivalent per person 1989

- Over 10 000 kg per person
- 1 000-10 000 kg per person
- 100-1 000 kg per person
- 10-100 kg per person
- Under 10 kg per person

● Oil

▽ Natural gas

▲ Coal and lignite

◇ Uranium (the fuel used to generate nuclear power)

In developing countries traditional fuels are still very important. Sometimes called biomass fuels, they include wood, charcoal and dried dung. The pie graph for Nigeria at the foot of the page shows their importance.

Map labels: Prudhoe Bay, Medicine Hat, Appalachians, Colorado, Texas, Gulf of Mexico, North Sea, Ruhr, Donbas, Silesia, Western Siberia, Kuzbas, Shanxi, Hebei, The Gulf, Bihar, Rum Jungle, Bowen Basin

Projection: Modified Hammer Equal Area

Top 5 producers for each primary energy source with percentage of World production 1990

Oil		Natural Gas		Coal (bituminous)		Brown Coal (lignite)		Uranium		Nuclear Power		Hydro-Electric Power	
World total (1990) 0 000 000 tonnes		World total (1990) 3 007 075 tonnes		World total (1990) 3 562 000 000 tonnes		World total (1990) 1 176 000 000 tonnes		World total (1990) 37 000 tonnes		World total (1990) 461 100 000 tonnes of oil equivalent		World total (1990) 540 600 000 tonnes of oil equivalent	
..S.R.	18,1%	U.S.S.R.	37,2%	China	29,5%	Germany	30,4%	Canada	23,0%	U.S.A.	33,8%	U.S.A.	13,3%
..A.	13,2%	U.S.A.	25,2%	U.S.A.	24,2%	U.S.S.R.	13,4%	U.S.S.R.	12,5%	France	13,3%	Canada	11,8%
di Arabia	10,4%	Canada	5,0%	U.S.S.R.	13,3%	Czechoslovakia	7,3%	Germany	11,8%	Japan	10,6%	U.S.S.R.	10,3%
	4,9%	Netherlands	3,1%	India	5,6%	U.S.A.	7,0%	U.S.A.	10,4%	U.S.S.R.	9,4%	Brazil	8,8%
na	4,4%	U.K.	2,3%	South Africa	5,1%	China	9,6%	Australia	7,4%	Germany	7,2%	China	5,0%

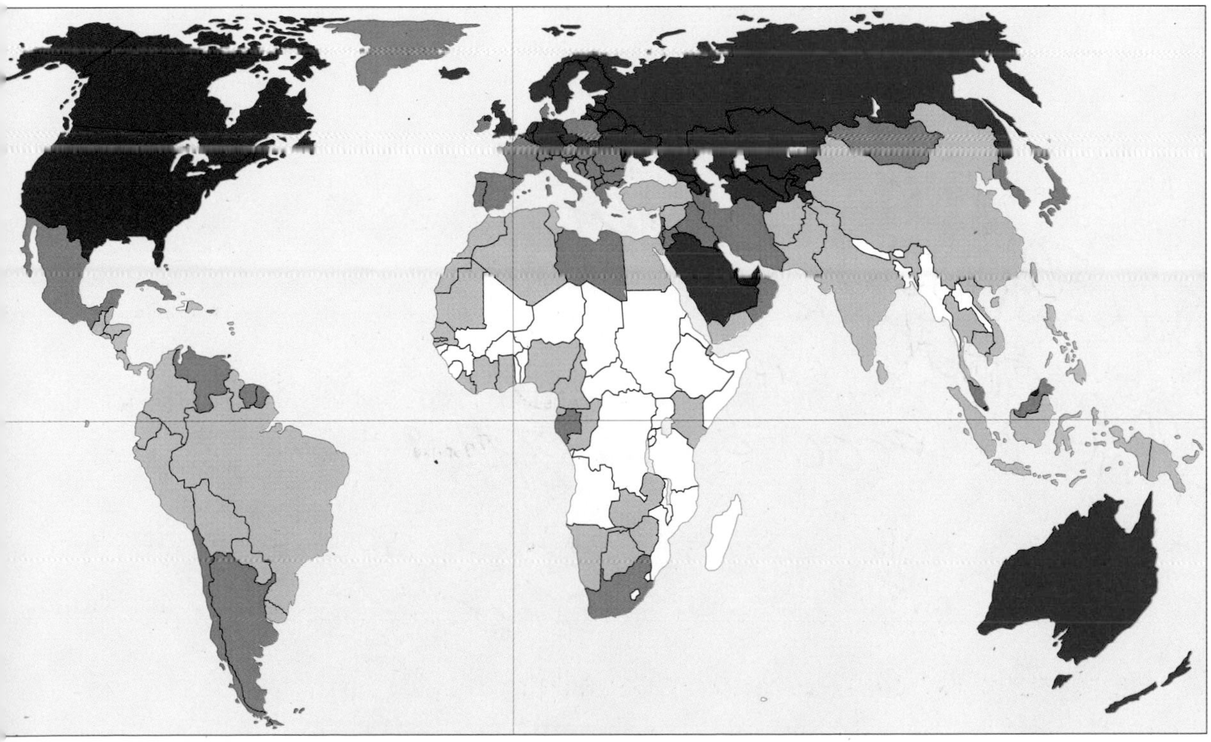

ENERGY CONSUMPTION

Primary energy consumption expressed in kilograms of coal equivalent per person 1989

- Over 10 000 kg per person
- 5 000-10 000 kg per person
- 1 000-5 000 kg per person
- 100-1 000 kg per person
- Under 100 kg per person

Energy Consumption by Continent 1990

		Change 1989-90
Europe*	38,5%	(-2,6%)
North America	27,6%	(-0,2%)
Asia	23,9%	(+4,9%)
South America	5,9%	(+3,7%)
Africa	2,8%	(+2,6%)
Australasia	1,3%	(+2,7%)
*includes U.S.S.R.		

TYPE OF ENERGY CONSUMED BY SELECTED COUNTRIES

Legend:
- Coal and Lignite
- Oil
- Natural Gas
- Hydro-electricity
- Nuclear electricity
- Traditional Fuels

NIGERIA CHINA JAPAN FRANCE

U.S.A.

NORWAY

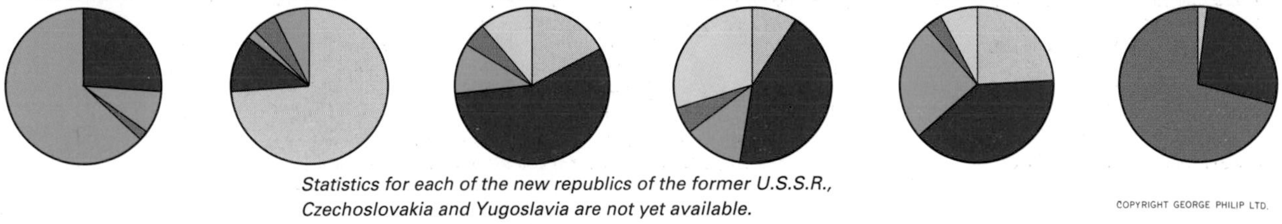

Statistics for each of the new republics of the former U.S.S.R., Czechoslovakia and Yugoslavia are not yet available.

AGE DISTRIBUTION PYRAMIDS

The bars represent the percentage of the total population (males plus females) in the age group shown.

Developed countries such as the U.K. have populations evenly spread across age groups and usually a growing percentage of elderly people. Developing countries such as Kenya have the great majority of their people in the younger age groups, about to enter their most fertile years.

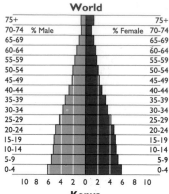

World

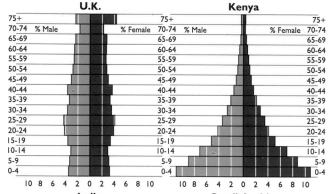

U.K.   **Kenya**

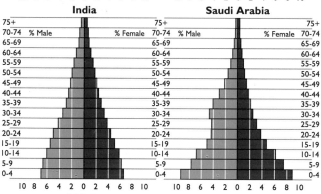

India   **Saudi Arabia**

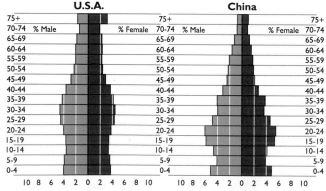

U.S.A.   **China**

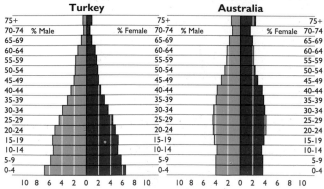

Turkey   **Australia**

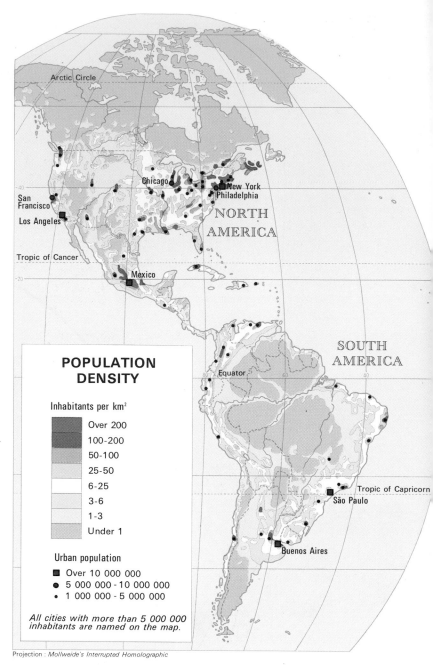

POPULATION DENSITY

Inhabitants per km²

- Over 200
- 100-200
- 50-100
- 25-50
- 6-25
- 3-6
- 1-3
- Under 1

Urban population

- ■ Over 10 000 000
- ● 5 000 000 - 10 000 000
- • 1 000 000 - 5 000 000

All cities with more than 5 000 000 inhabitants are named on the map.

Projection : *Mollweide's Interrupted Homolographic*

POPULATION CHANGE 1930-2020   Population totals are in millions

Figures in italics represent the percentage average annual increase for the period show

	1930	1930-1960	1960	1960-1990	1990	1990-2020	2020
World	2013	*1.4%*	3019	*1.9%*	5292	*1.4%*	8062
Africa	155	*2.0%*	281	*2.8%*	648	*2.7%*	1441
North America	135	*1.3%*	199	*1.1%*	276	*0.6%*	327
Latin America*	129	*1.8%*	218	*2.4%*	448	*1.6%*	719
Asia	1073	*1.5%*	1669	*2.1%*	3108	*1.4%*	4680
Europe	355	*0.6%*	425	*0.5%*	498	*0.1%*	514
Oceania	10	*1.4%*	16	*1.7%*	27	*1.1%*	37
C.I.S. †	176	*0.7%*	214	*1.0%*	288	*0.6%*	343

* *South America plus Central America, Mexico and the West Indies*
† *Commonwealth of Independent States, formerly the U.S.S.R.*

1 : 105 000 000

Arctic Circle

EUROPE

London
Paris

Moscow

Istanbul

Tehran

Cairo

ASIA

Beijing
Tianjin
Seoul
Tokyo
Shanghai

Tropic of Cancer

Karachi

Delhi

Calcotta

Bombay

Bangkok

AFRICA

Equator

Jakarta

AUSTRALIA

Tropic of Capricorn

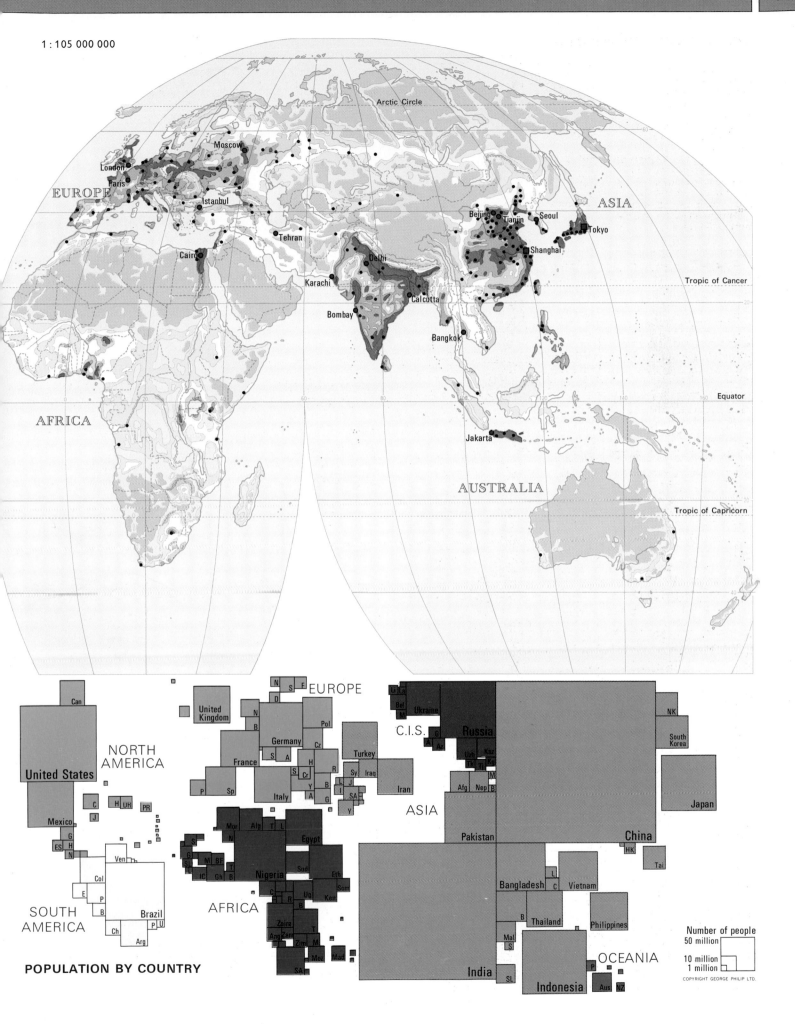

POPULATION BY COUNTRY

Can

United Kingdom

EUROPE

N
S
F

D

N

Pol

NORTH AMERICA

B

Germany

Cz

Turkey

C.I.S.

Ukraine

Russia

NK

South Korea

United States

France

S A

H

R

Syr
Iraq

G

A

Uzb
Kaz

Kir
T

IM

Japan

C

H UK

PR

S Cr

L

J

SA

Iran

Afg
Nep
B

Mexico

P Sp

Italy

A

G

Y

G

ES H

N

Ven

Mor
Alg
T
L

Egypt

Pakistan

China

HK

Col

S

N

Sud

Tai

E

P

G M BF

Eth

Bangladesh

L

C

Vietnam

SOUTH AMERICA

B

Brazil

P U

JC
Gh
T
B

Nigeria

Ug
Ken

Som

B

Thailand

Philippines

Ch

Arg

C

R

AFRICA

Zaire

Ang Zam

Zim

Mal

S

OCEANIA

 Mo

Mad

SA

India

SL

Indonesia

Aus
NZ

ASIA

Number of people
50 million

10 million
1 million

COPYRIGHT GEORGE PHILIP LTD.

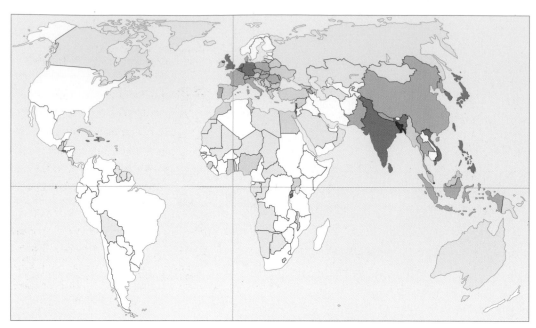

POPULATION DENSITY BY COUNTRY

Density of people per square kilometre 1991

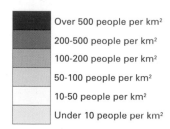

Over 500 people per km²	
200-500 people per km²	
100-200 people per km²	
50-100 people per km²	
10-50 people per km²	
Under 10 people per km²	

Top 5 countries		Bottom 5 countries	
Macau	24 850 per km²	Mauritania	2.0 per km²
Hong Kong	5 960 per km²	Mongolia	1.5 per km²
Singapore	4 667 per km²	French Guiana	1.1 per km²
Gibraltar	3 000 per km²	Congo	0.7 per km²
Malta	1 333 per km²	Greenland	0.2 per km²

U.K. 238 per km²

POPULATION CHANGE 1990-2000

Expected percentage population change between 1990 and 2000*

Over 40% population gain	
30-40% population gain	
20-30% population gain	
10-20% population gain	
0-10% population gain	
No change or population loss	

Top 5 countries		Bottom 5 countries	
Afghanistan	+60%	Hungary	-0.2%
Mali	+56%	Singapore	-0.2%
Tanzania	+55%	Grenada	-2.4%
Ivory Coast	+47%	Tonga	-3.2%
Saudi Arabia	+46%	Germany	-3.2%

U.K. +2.0%

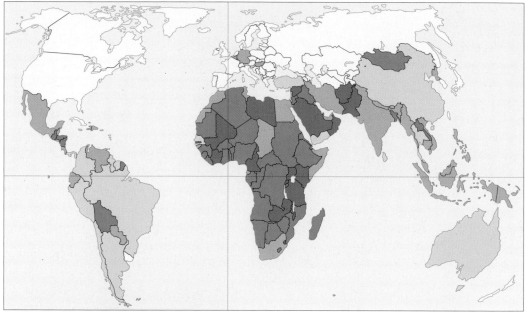

URBAN POPULATION

Percentage of total population living in towns and cities 1990

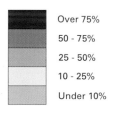

Over 75%	
50-75%	
25-50%	
10-25%	
Under 10%	

Most urbanized		Least urbanized	
Singapore	100%	Bhutan	5%
Belgium	97%	Burundi	7%
Kuwait	96%	Rwanda	8%
Hong Kong	93%	Burkina Faso	9%
U.K.	93%	Nepal	10%

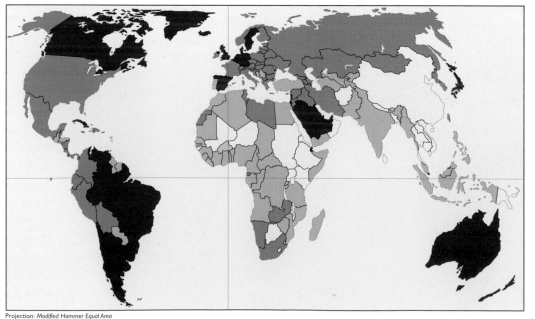

Projection: *Modified Hammer Equal Area*

Statistics for the new republics of the former U.S.S.R., Czechoslovakia and Yugoslavia are not yet available. The map shows the statistics for the entire U.S.S.R., Czechoslovakia and Yugoslavia.

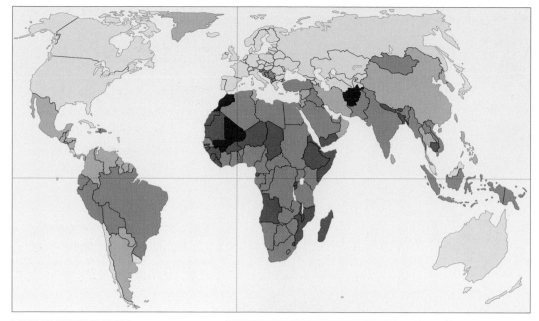

CHILD MORTALITY

The number of babies who will die under the age of one, per 1 000 births (average 1990-95)*

- Over 150 deaths per 1 000 births
- 100-150 deaths per 1 000 births
- 50-100 deaths per 1 000 births
- 20-50 deaths per 1 000 births
- 10-20 deaths per 1 000 births
- Under 10 deaths per 1 000 births

Highest child mortality		Lowest child mortality	
Afghanistan	162 deaths	Hong Kong	6 deaths
Mali	159 deaths	Denmark	6 deaths
Sierra Leone	143 deaths	Japan	5 deaths
Guinea-Bissau	140 deaths	Iceland	5 deaths
Malawi	138 deaths	Finland	5 deaths
		U.K.	8 deaths

LIFE EXPECTANCY

Average expected lifespan in years of babies born in the period 1990-95*

- Over 75 years
- 70-75 years
- 65-70 years
- 60-65 years
- 55-60 years
- 50-55 years
- Under 50 years

Highest life expectancy		Lowest life expectancy	
Japan	79 years	Gambia	45 years
Iceland	78 years	Guinea	45 years
Sweden	78 years	Afghanistan	44 years
Hong Kong	78 years	Guinea-Bissau	44 years
Switzerland	78 years	Sierra Leone	43 years
		U.K.	76 years

FAMILY SIZE

The average number of children a woman can expect to bear during her lifetime 1991

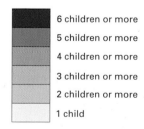

- 6 children or more
- 5 children or more
- 4 children or more
- 3 children or more
- 2 children or more
- 1 child

In the U.K. the average family size is 1.8 children per family, whilst in Kenya the average size is 6.8 children.

Projection: Modified Hammer Equal Area

Statistics for the new republics of the former U.S.S.R., Czechoslovakia and Yugoslavia are not yet available. The map shows the statistics for the entire U.S.S.R., Czechoslovakia and Yugoslavia.

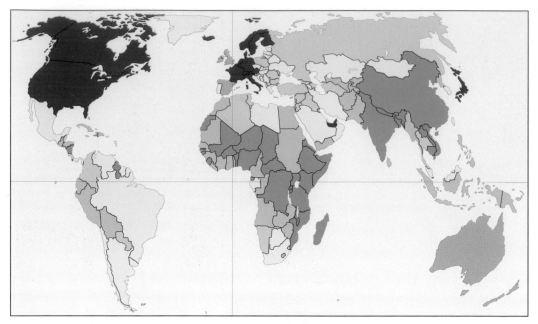

WEALTH

The value of total production in 1991 divided by the population. (The Gross National Product per capita)

- Over 400% of world average
- 200 - 400% of world average
- 100 - 200% of world average

World average wealth per person $4 210

- 50 - 100% of world average
- 25 - 50% of world average
- 10 - 25% of world average
- Under 10% of world average

Top 5 countries		Bottom 5 countries	
Switzerland	$33 510	Mozambique	$70
Luxembourg	$31 080	Tanzania	$100
Japan	$26 920	Ethiopia	$120
Sweden	$25 490	Somalia	$150
Bermuda	$25 000	Uganda	$160
		U.K.	$16 750

AID

Aid provided or received, divided by the total population 1990*

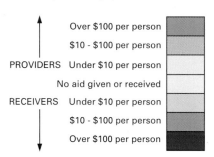

PROVIDERS	Over $100 per person	
	$10 - $100 per person	
	Under $10 per person	
	No aid given or received	
RECEIVERS	Under $10 per person	
	$10 - $100 per person	
	Over $100 per person	

Top 5 providers		Top 5 receivers	
Kuwait	$793	Israel	$295
U.A.E.	$555	Djibouti	$293
Norway	$287	Jordan	$221
Saudi Arabia	$248	Dominica	$185
Sweden	$234	Surinam	$135
U.K.	$46		

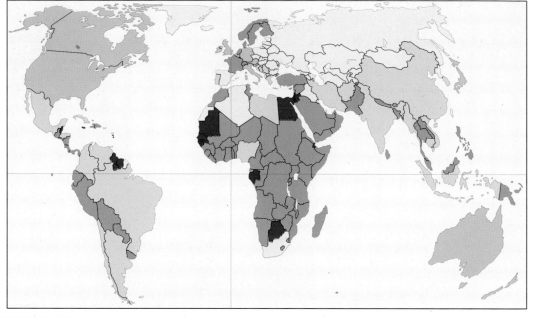

ILLITERACY

Percentage of the total population unable to read or write (latest available year)*

- Over 75% of population illiterate
- 50 - 75% of population illiterate
- 25 - 50% of population illiterate
- 10 - 25% of population illiterate
- Under 10% of population illiterate

Educational expenditure per person (latest available year)

Top 5 countries		Bottom 5 countries	
Sweden	$997	Chad	$2
Qatar	$989	Bangladesh	$3
Canada	$983	Ethiopia	$3
Norway	$971	Nepal	$4
Switzerland	$796	Somalia	$4
		U.K.	$447

Projection: *Modified Hammer Equal Area*

Statistics for the new republics of the former U.S.S.R., Czechoslovakia and Yugoslavia are not yet available. The map shows the statistics for the entire U.S.S.R., Czechoslovakia and Yugoslavia.

THE IMPORTANCE OF AGRICULTURE

The percentage of the total population who depend on agriculture 1991

Over 75% dependent

50 - 75% dependent

25 - 50% dependent

10 - 25% dependent

Under 10% dependent

Top 5 countries		Bottom 5 countries	
Nepal	92%	Singapore	0.9%
Rwanda	91%	Hong Kong	1.2%
Burundi	91%	Bahrain	1.7%
Bhutan	91%	Belgium	1.7%
Niger	87%	U.K.	1.9%

DAILY FOOD CONSUMPTION

Average daily food intake in calories per person 1989*

Over 3 500 cals. per person

3 000 - 3 500 cals. per person

2 500 - 3 000 cals. per person

2 000 - 2 500 cals. per person

Under 2 000 cals. per person

No available data

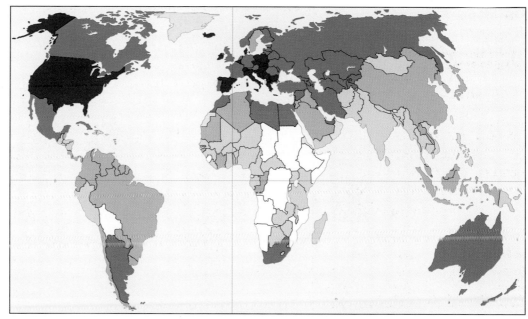

Top 5 countries		Bottom 5 countries	
Belgium	3 902	Ethiopia	1 666
Greece	3 825	Mozambique	1 679
Ireland	3 778	Chad	1 742
Bulgaria	3 707	Sierra Leone	1 799
U.S.A.	3 670	Angola	1 806
		U.K.	3 148

HEALTH CARE

Number of people per doctor (latest available year)*

Over 25 000 people per doctor

10 000 - 25 000 people per doctor

5 000 - 10 000 people per doctor

1 000 - 5 000 people per doctor

500 - 1 000 people per doctor

Under 500 people per doctor

Most people per doctor		Least people per doctor	
Ethiopia	78 740	Russia	235
Equatorial Guinea	62 000	Austria	256
Mozambique	50 817	Hungary	304
Chad	47 640	Spain	316
Burkina Faso	42 128	Belgium	342
		U.K.	668

Projection: *Modified Hammer Equal Area*

Statistics for the new republics of the former U.S.S.R., Czechoslovakia and Yugoslavia are not yet available. The map shows the statistics for the entire U.S.S.R., Czechoslovakia and Yugoslavia.

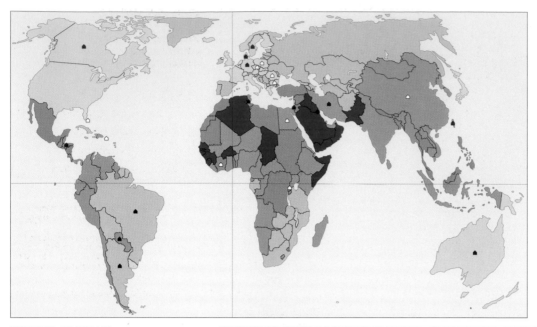

HOUSING

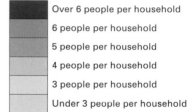

Number of people per household
(latest available year)*

■	Over 6 people per household
	6 people per household
	5 people per household
	4 people per household
	3 people per household
	Under 3 people per household

Expenditure on housing and energy as a
percentage of total consumer spending

▲	Over 20% spent
△	Under 5% spent

WATER SUPPLY

Percentage of total population
with access to safe drinking water
(latest available year)*

	Over 90% with safe water
	75 - 90% with safe water
	60 - 75% with safe water
	45 - 60% with safe water
	30 - 45% with safe water
	Under 30% with safe water

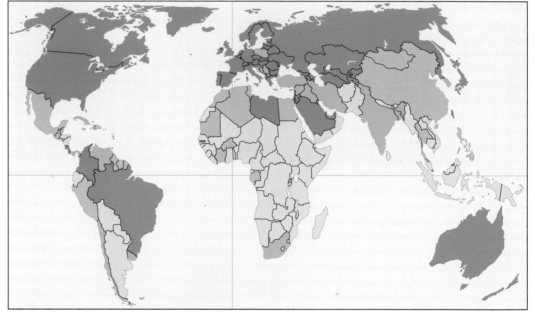

Least well provided countries

Cambodia	3%	Afghanistan	21%
Central Africa	12%	Congo	21%
Ethiopia	19%	Guinea Bissau	21%
Uganda	20%	Sudan	21%

CAR OWNERSHIP

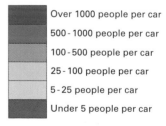

Number of people per car
(latest available year)*

	Over 1000 people per car
	500 - 1000 people per car
	100 - 500 people per car
	25 - 100 people per car
	5 - 25 people per car
	Under 5 people per car

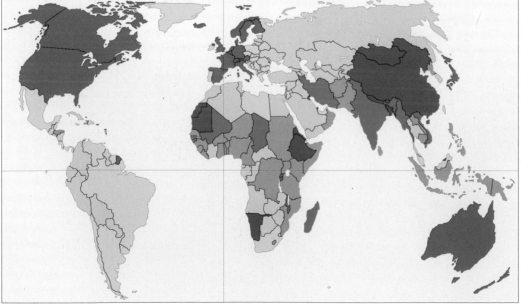

Most people per car		Most cars (millions)	
China	4300	U.S.A.	140.7
Mauritania	3400	Japan	30.8
Bangladesh	2053	Germany	29.2
Nepal	2000	France	27.0
Togo	1237	Italy	23.5

Projection: *Modified Hammer Equal Area*

*Statistics for the new republics of the former U.S.S.R., Czechoslovakia and Yugoslavia are not yet available.
The map shows the statistics for the entire U.S.S.R., Czechoslovakia and Yugoslavia.

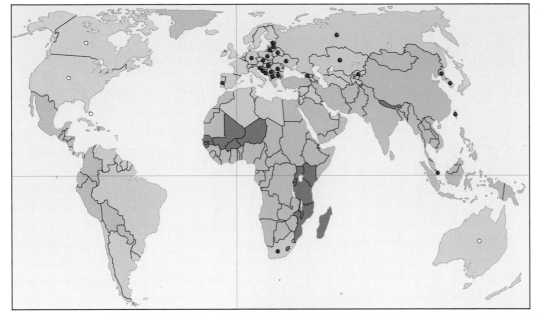

TYPE OF WORK

Percentage of total workforce employed in agriculture†, (latest available year)*

- Over 75% in agriculture
- 50 - 75% in agriculture
- 25 - 50% in agriculture
- 10 - 25% in agriculture
- Under 10% in agriculture

● Over 25% of total workforce employed in manufacturing

○ Over 75% of total workforce employed in service industries (work in offices, shops, tourism, transport, construction and government)

† Includes forestry and fishing

WOMEN IN THE WORKFORCE

Working women as a percentage of the total workforce (latest available year)

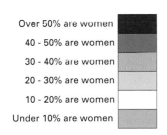

- Over 50% are women
- 40 - 50% are women
- 30 - 40% are women
- 20 - 30% are women
- 10 - 20% are women
- Under 10% are women

Most women in the workforce		Fewest women in the workforce	
Kazakhstan	54%	Guinea Bissau	3%
Rwanda	54%	Oman	6%
Botswana	53%	Afghanistan	8%
Burundi	53%	Libya	8%
Mozambique	52%	Algeria	9%
U.K.	43%		

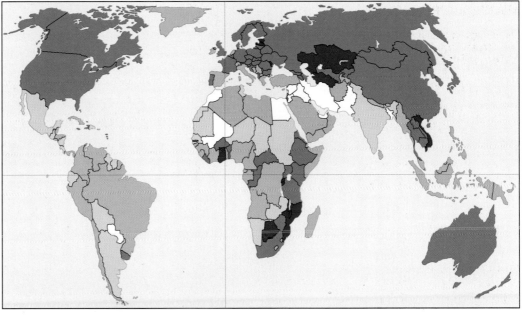

SELF SUFFICIENCY IN FOOD

Balance of trade in food products as a percentage of total trade in food products 1988*

- Over 50% surplus
- 10 - 50% surplus
- 10% either side
- 10 - 50% deficit
- Over 50% deficit

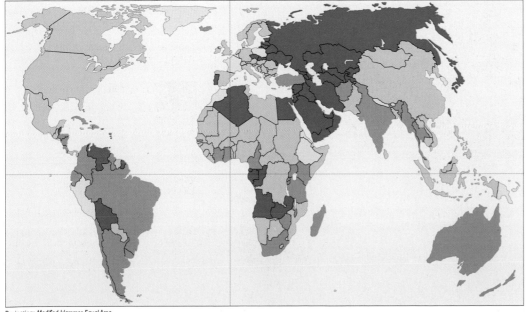

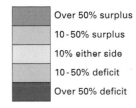

Projection: Modified Hammer Equal Area

CARTOGRAPHY BY PHILIP'S. COPYRIGHT REED INTERNATIONAL BOOKS LTD

*Statistics for the new republics of the former U.S.S.R., Czechoslovakia and Yugoslavia are not yet available. The map shows the statistics for the entire U.S.S.R., Czechoslovakia and Yugoslavia.

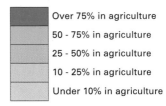

ACID RAIN

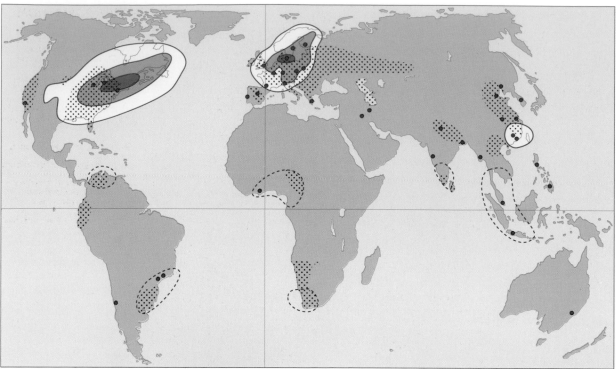

Acid rain is caused by high levels of sulphur and nitro[gen] in the atmosphere. They combine with water vapou[r] and oxygen to form acids (H_2SO_4 and HNO_3) which fall as precipitation.

 Main areas of sulph[ur] and nitrogen emiss[ion] (from the burning o[f] fossil fuels)

• Major cities with hi[gh] levels of air polluti[on] (including sulphur [and] nitrogen emissions)

Areas of acid deposition

(pH numbers measure acidit[y] normal rain is pH 5.6)

pH less than 4.0 (most acidic)

pH 4.0 - 4.5

pH 4.5 - 5.0

Potential problem areas

GLOBAL WARMING

Global warming is caused by high levels of carbon dioxide and other gases in the atmosphere (the Greenhouse Effect). It is estimated that by 2020 the world could be approximately 1.3°C warmer than now.

Carbon dioxide (CO_2) emissions in tonnes per person per year*

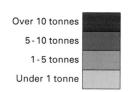

Over 10 tonnes

5 - 10 tonnes

1 - 5 tonnes

Under 1 tonne

Coastal areas vulnerable to rising sea levels caused by global warming

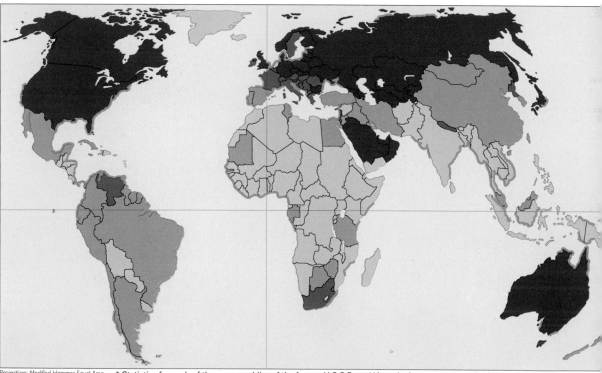

Projection: Modified Hammer Equal Area

*Statistics for each of the new republics of the former U.S.S.R. and Yugoslavia are not yet available. The map shows the statistics for the entire U.S.S.R. and Yugoslavia.

THE GREENHOUSE EFFECT

Carbon dioxide is increased by burning fossil fuels and cutting forests

Rising temperatures would melt snow and ice.

Melting glacial ice could cause oceans to rise.

Carbon Dioxide

The carbon dioxide traps the heat being reflected from the Earth, although some heat is lost.

The warming increases water-vapour in the air, leading to even greater absorption of heat.

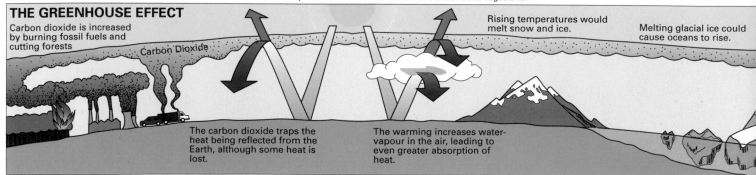

WATER POLLUTION

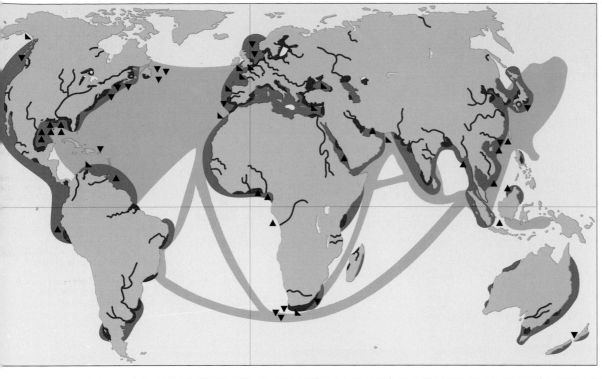

Severely polluted
sea areas and lakes

Other polluted sea
areas and lakes

Sea areas of frequent oil
pollution from shipping

◣ Major oil tanker spills

▲ Major oil rig blow-outs

▼ Offshore dumpsites
for industrial and
municipal waste

── Severely polluted rivers

...SERTIFICATION

Existing deserts

...as with a high risk
of desertification

...as with a moderate
...k of desertification

...FORESTATION
...THE TROPICS

Former areas of
rainforest

Existing rainforest

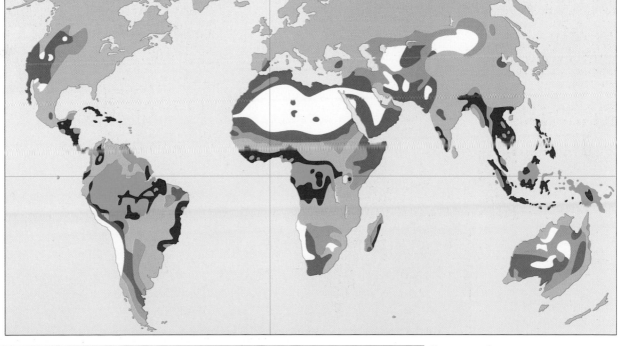

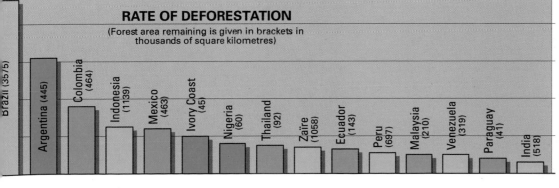

RATE OF DEFORESTATION

(Forest area remaining is given in brackets in
thousands of square kilometres)

Brazil (3575)
Argentina (445)
Colombia (464)
Indonesia (1139)
Mexico (463)
Ivory Coast (45)
Nigeria (60)
Thailand (92)
Zaïre (1058)
Ecuador (143)
Peru (697)
Malaysia (210)
Venezuela (319)
Paraguay (41)
India (518)

Forest area lost
each year in the 1980s
20 000km²

15 000km²

Rate of deforestation
(% each year)

Over 2.5%

1.0 - 2.5%

0 - 1.0%

10 000km²

5 000km²

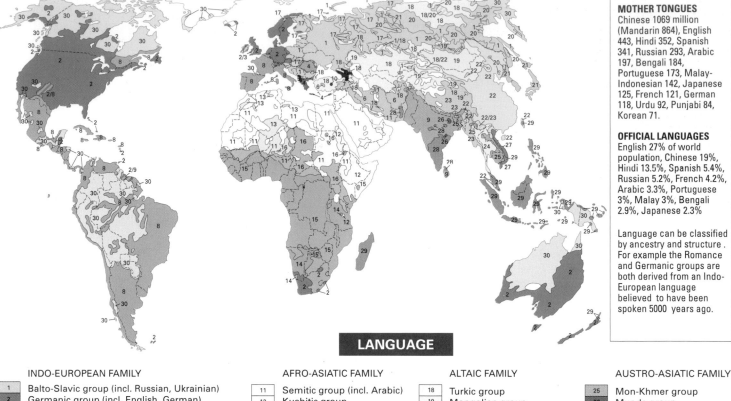

MOTHER TONGUES
Chinese 1069 million (Mandarin 864), English 443, Hindi 352, Spanish 341, Russian 293, Arabic 197, Bengali 184, Portuguese 173, Malay-Indonesian 142, Japanese 125, French 121, German 118, Urdu 92, Punjabi 84, Korean 71.

OFFICIAL LANGUAGES
English 27% of world population, Chinese 19%, Hindi 13.5%, Spanish 5.4%, Russian 5.2%, French 4.2%, Arabic 3.3%, Portuguese 3%, Malay 3%, Bengali 2.9%, Japanese 2.3%

Language can be classified by ancestry and structure. For example the Romance and Germanic groups are both derived from an Indo-European language believed to have been spoken 5000 years ago.

LANGUAGE

INDO-EUROPEAN FAMILY
- 1 Balto-Slavic group (incl. Russian, Ukrainian)
- 2 Germanic group (incl. English, German)
- 3 Celtic group
- 4 Greek
- 5 Albanian
- 6 Iranian group
- 7 Armenian
- 8 Romance group (incl. Spanish, Portuguese, French, Italian)
- 9 Indo-Aryan group (incl. Hindi, Bengali, Urdu, Punjabi, Marathi)
- 10 CAUCASIAN FAMILY

AFRO-ASIATIC FAMILY
- 11 Semitic group (incl. Arabic)
- 12 Kushitic group
- 13 Berber group
- 14 KHOISAN FAMILY
- 15 NIGER-CONGO FAMILY
- 16 NILO-SAHARAN FAMILY
- 17 URALIC FAMILY

ALTAIC FAMILY
- 18 Turkic group
- 19 Mongolian group
- 20 Tungus-Manchu group
- 21 Japanese and Korean

SINO-TIBETAN FAMILY
- 22 Sinitic (Chinese) languages
- 23 Tibetic-Burmic languages
- 24 TAI FAMILY

AUSTRO-ASIATIC FAMILY
- 25 Mon-Khmer group
- 26 Munda group
- 27 Vietnamese
- 28 DRAVIDIAN FAMILY (incl. Telugu, Tamil)
- 29 AUSTRONESIAN FAMILY (incl. Malay-Indonesian)
- 30 OTHER LANGUAGES

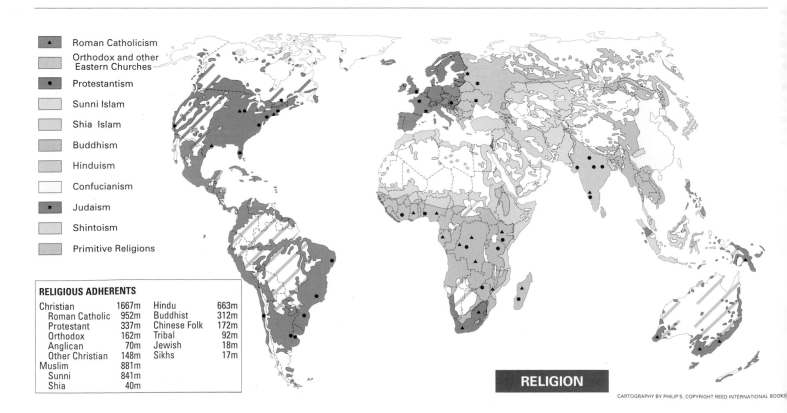

- ▲ Roman Catholicism
- Orthodox and other Eastern Churches
- ● Protestantism
- Sunni Islam
- Shia Islam
- Buddhism
- Hinduism
- Confucianism
- ✶ Judaism
- Shintoism
- Primitive Religions

RELIGIOUS ADHERENTS

Christian		Hindu	663m
Roman Catholic	952m	Buddhist	312m
Protestant	337m	Chinese Folk	172m
Orthodox	162m	Tribal	92m
Anglican	70m	Jewish	18m
Other Christian	148m	Sikhs	17m
Muslim	881m		
Sunni	841m		
Shia	40m		

Christian 1667m

RELIGION

UNITED NATIONS

Created in 1945 to promote peace and co-operation and based in New York, the United Nations is the world's largest international organization, with 184 members and an annual budget of US $2.6 billion (1994–95). Each member of the General Assembly has one vote, while the permanent members of the 15-nation Security Council – USA, Russia, China, UK and France – hold a veto. The 54 members of the Economic and Social Council are responsible for economic, social, cultural, educational, health and related matters. The Secretariat is the UN's principal administrative arm; the only territory now administered by the Trusteeship Council is Belau (by the USA). The UN has 16 specialized agencies – based in Canada, France, Switzerland and Italy as well as the USA – which help members in fields such as education (UNESCO), agriculture (FAO), medicine (WHO) and finance (IFC).

[The International Court of Justice is based in The Hague]

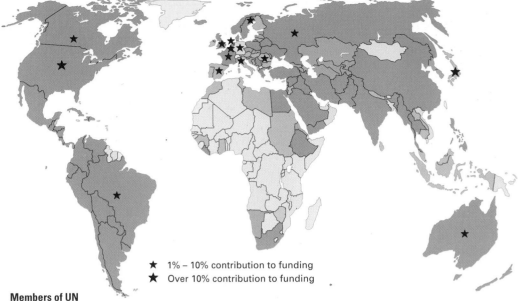

★ 1% – 10% contribution to funding
★ Over 10% contribution to funding

Members of UN
Year of joining
- 1940s
- 1950s
- 1960s
- 1970s
- 1980s
- 1990s
- Non members

MEMBERSHIP There are 7 independent states who are not members of the UN – Kiribati, Nauru, Switzerland, Taiwan, Tonga, Tuvalu and Vatican City. By the end of 1992, all the successor states of the former USSR had joined. There were 51 members in 1945. Official languages are Chinese, English, French, Russian, Spanish and Arabic.
FUNDING The UN budget for 1994–95 is US $ 2.6 billion. Contributions are assessed by the members' ability to pay, with the maximum 25% of the total, the minimum 0.01%. Contributions for 1992–94 were: USA 25%, Japan 12.45%, Germany 8.93%, Russia 6.71%, France 6%, UK 5.02%, Italy 4.29%, Canada 3.11% (others 28.49%).
PEACEKEEPING The UN has been involved in 33 peacekeeping operations worldwide since 1948 and there are currently 17 areas of UN patrol. In July 1993 there were 80,146 'blue berets' from 74 countries.

EC As from December 1993 the European Union (EU) refers to matters of foreign policy, security and justice. The European Community (EC) refers to all other matters. The 12 members – Belgium, Denmark, France, Germany, Greece, Ireland, Italy, Luxembourg, Netherlands, Portugal, Spain and the UK – aim to integrate economies, co-ordinate social developments and bring about political union. These members of what is now the world's biggest market share agricultural and industrial policies and tariffs on trade.
EFTA European Free Trade Association (formed in 1960). Portugal left the 'Seven' in 1989 to join the EC.
ACP African-Caribbean-Pacific (1963).
NATO North Atlantic Treaty Organization (formed in 1949). It continues after 1991 despite the winding up of the Warsaw Pact.
OAS Organization of American States (1949). It aims to promote social and economic co-operation between developed countries of North America and developing nations of Latin America.
ASEAN Association of South-east Asian Nations (1967).
OAU Organization of African Unity (1963). Its 52 members represent over 90% of Africa's population.
LAIA Latin American Integration Association (1980).
OECD Organization for Economic Co-operation and Development (1961). The 24 major western free-market economies. 'G7' is its 'inner group' of USA, Canada, Japan, UK, Germany, Italy and France.
COMMONWEALTH The Commonwealth of Nations evolved from the British Empire; it comprises 18 nations recognizing the British monarch as head of state and 32 with their own heads of state.

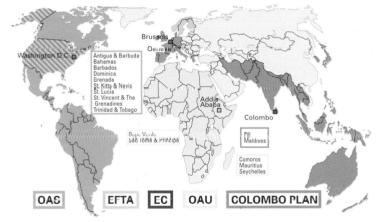

| OAS | EFTA | EC | OAU | COLOMBO PLAN |

OPEC Organization of Petroleum Exporting Countries (1960). It controls about three-quarters of the world's oil supply.
ARAB LEAGUE (1945) The League's aim is to promote economic, social, political and military co-operation.
COLOMBO PLAN (1951) Its 26 members aim to promote economic and social development in Asia and the Pacific.

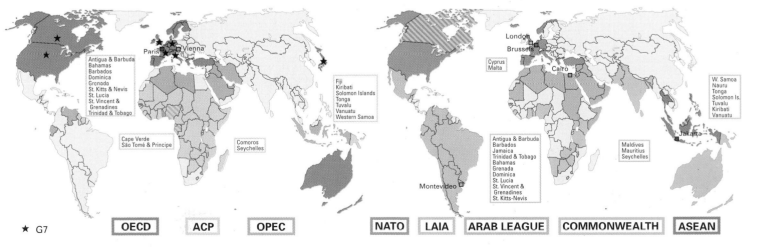

★ G7

| OECD | ACP | OPEC |

| NATO | LAIA | ARAB LEAGUE | COMMONWEALTH | ASEAN |

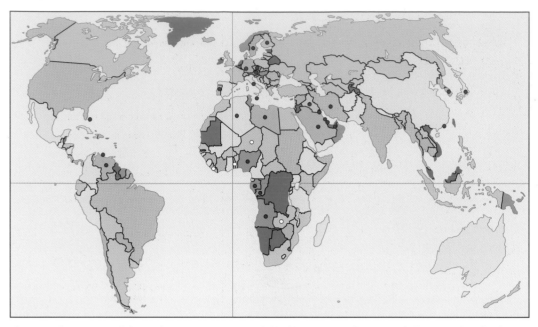

DEPENDENCE ON TRADE

Value of exports as a percentage of G.D.P. (Gross Domestic Product) 1989

- Over 50% G.D.P.
- 40-50% G.D.P.
- 30-40% G.D.P.
- 20-30% G.D.P.
- 10-20% G.D.P.
- Under 10% G.D.P.

- ● Most dependent on industrial exports (over 75% of total exports)
- ● Most dependent on fuel exports (over 75% of total exports)
- ○ Most dependent on metal and mineral exports (over 75% of total exports)

BALANCE OF TRADE

Value of exports in proportion to the value of imports (latest available year)

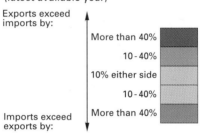

Exports exceed imports by:

- More than 40%
- 10-40%
- 10% either side
- 10-40%
- More than 40%

Imports exceed exports by:

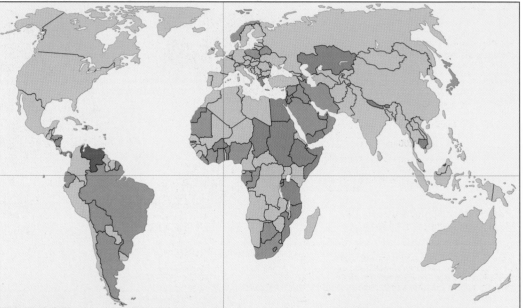

SHARE OF WORLD TRADE

Percentage share of total world exports by value 1990*

- Over 10% of world trade
- 5-10% of world trade
- 1-5% of world trade
- 0.5-1% of world trade
- 0.25-0.5% of world trade
- Under 0.25% of world trade

Projection: *Modified Hammer Equal Area*

*Statistics for the new republics of the former U.S.S.R., Czechoslovakia and Yugoslavia are not yet available. The map shows the statistics for the entire U.S.S.R., Czechoslovakia and Yugoslavia.

SHIPPING

Freight unloaded in
millions of tonnes
(latest available year)*

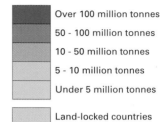

Over 100 million tonnes

50 - 100 million tonnes

10 - 50 million tonnes

5 - 10 million tonnes

Under 5 million tonnes

Land-locked countries

Major Seaports

● Handling over 100 million
tonnes p.a.

○ Handling 50 - 100 million
tonnes p.a.

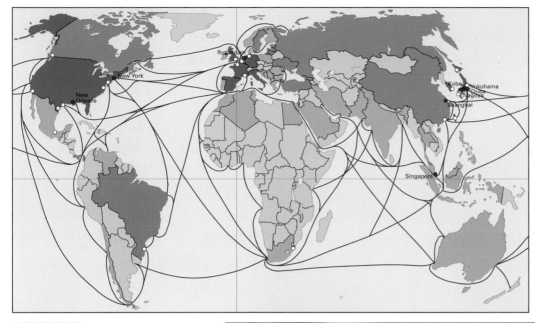

AIR TRAVEL

Passenger kilometres flown
(latest available year)

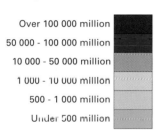

Over 100 000 million

50 000 - 100 000 million

10 000 - 50 000 million

1 000 - 10 000 million

500 - 1 000 million

Under 500 million

Major airports (handling over
20 million passengers in 1991) ○

Passenger kilometres are the number of
passengers (international and domestic)
multiplied by the distance flown by each
passenger from the airport of origin.

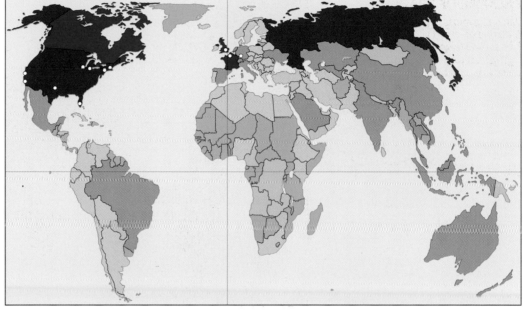

TOURISM

Tourism receipts as a percentage of
G.N.P. (Gross National Product) 1990*

Over 10% of G.N.P. from tourism

5 - 10% of G.N.P. from tourism

2.5 - 5% of G.N.P. from tourism

1 - 2.5% of G.N.P. from tourism

0.5 - 1% of G.N.P. from tourism

Under 0.5% of G.N.P. from tourism

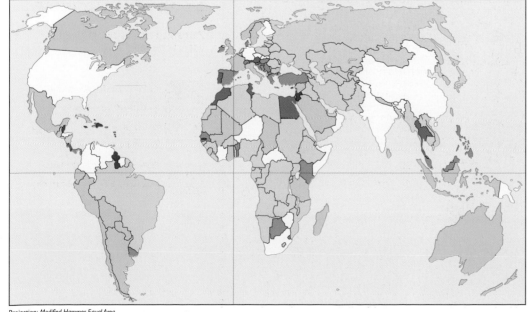

Largest percentage share of total world spending on tourism 1991		Largest percentage share of total world receipts from tourism 1991	
U.S.A.	16%	U.S.A.	16%
Germany	13%	France	8%
Japan	10%	Italy	8%
U.K.	7%	Spain	7%
Italy	6%	U.K.	6%

Projection: *Modified Hammer Equal Area*

*Statistics for the new republics of the former U.S.S.R., Czechoslovakia and Yugoslavia are not yet available.
The map shows the statistics for the entire U.S.S.R., Czechoslovakia and Yugoslavia.*

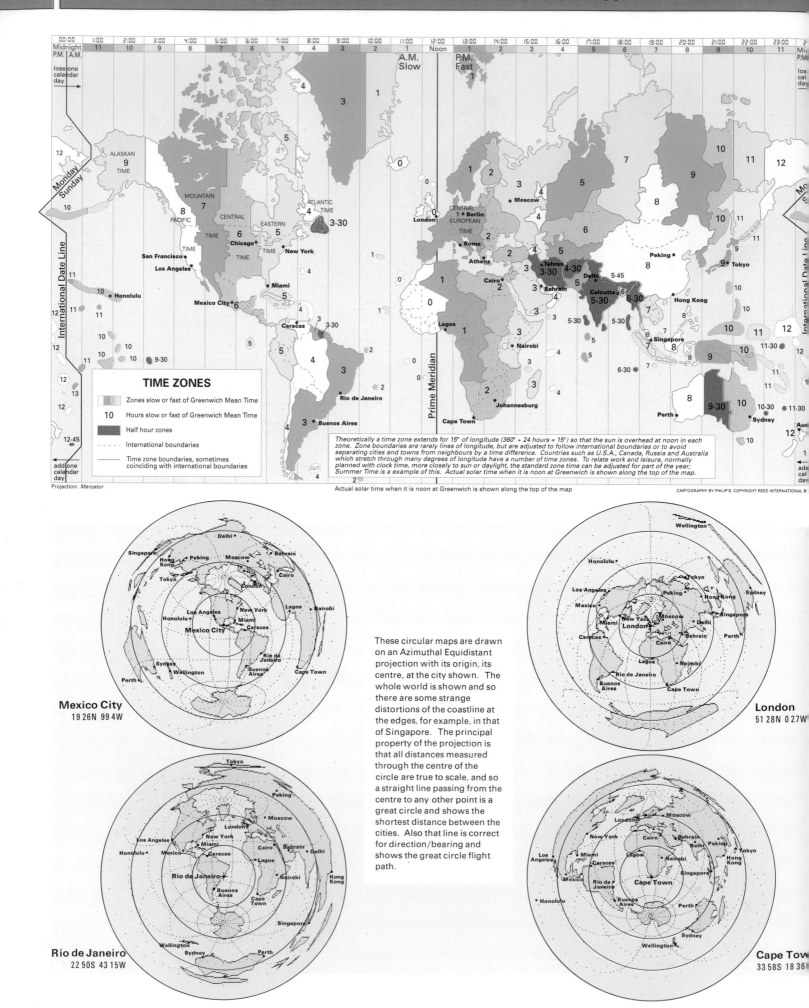

TIME ZONES

Zones slow or fast of Greenwich Mean Time

10 Hours slow or fast of Greenwich Mean Time

Half hour zones

International boundaries

Time zone boundaries, sometimes coinciding with international boundaries

Theoretically a time zone extends for 15° of longitude (360° ÷ 24 hours = 15°) so that the sun is overhead at noon in each zone. Zone boundaries are rarely lines of longitude, but are adjusted to follow international boundaries or to avoid separating cities and towns from neighbours by a time difference. Countries such as U.S.A., Canada, Russia and Australia which stretch through many degrees of longitude have a number of time zones. To relate work and leisure, normally planned with clock time, more closely to sun or daylight, the standard zone time can be adjusted for part of the year; Summer Time is a example of this. Actual solar time when it is noon at Greenwich is shown along the top of the map.

Projection: *Mercator*

Actual solar time when it is noon at Greenwich is shown along the top of the map

CARTOGRAPHY BY PHILIP'S. COPYRIGHT REED INTERNATIONAL B

Mexico City
19 26N 99 4W

London
51 28N 0 27W

Rio de Janeiro
22 50S 43 15W

Cape Tow
33 58S 18 36

These circular maps are drawn on an Azimuthal Equidistant projection with its origin, its centre, at the city shown. The whole world is shown and so there are some strange distortions of the coastline at the edges, for example, in that of Singapore. The principal property of the projection is that all distances measured through the centre of the circle are true to scale, and so a straight line passing from the centre to any other point is a great circle and shows the shortest distance between the cities. Also that line is correct for direction/bearing and shows the great circle flight path.

These distances are in kilometres and are the great circle distances between the cities (international airports). Great circle distances are the shortest distances between two points on the globe. They are the normal flight paths for aircraft where they are free from the restrictions of air corridors or national airspace.

	Bahrain	Buenos Aires	Cairo	Cape Town	Caracas	Delhi	Hong Kong	Honolulu	Lagos	London	Los Angeles	Mexico	Miami	Moscow	Nairobi	New York	Peking	Perth	Rio de Janeiro	Singapore	Sydney	Tokyo
Buenos Aires	13 291																					
Cairo	1 927	11 845																				
Cape Town	7 496	6 880	7 246																			
Caracas	12 121	5 124	10 200	10 254																		
Delhi	2 618	15 784	4 400	9 278	14 186																	
Hong Kong	6 387	18 442	8 121	11 852	16 340	3 768																
Honolulu	13 882	12 158	14 195	18 555	9 671	11 984	8 911															
Lagos	5 454	7 932	3 926	4 783	7 722	8 071	11 832	16 286														
London	5 089	11 128	3 528	9 672	7 465	6 726	9 637	11 617	4 998													
Los Angeles	13 210	9 854	12 206	16 067	5 813	12 863	11 634	4 105	12 408	8 752												
Mexico	13 962	7 391	12 360	13 701	3 572	14 651	12 121	6 096	11 043	8 898	2 498											
Miami	12 182	7 113	10 441	12 334	2 190	13 495	14 430	7 806	9 045	7 102	3 759	2 050										
Moscow	3 466	13 488	2 909	10 150	9 900	4 359	7 148	11 289	6 250	2 505	9 748	10 682	9 191									
Nairobi	3 398	10 413	3 542	4 096	11 545	5 413	8 750	17 255	3 828	6 835	15 560	14 812	12 771	6 365								
New York	10 613	8 526	9 009	12 551	3 402	11 747	12 956	8 000	8 437	5 535	3 968	3 361	1 751	7 476	11 828							
Peking	6 180	19 273	7 526	12 956	14 356	3 804	1 985	8 124	11 452	8 146	10 030	12 426	12 475	5 789	9 217	10 971						
Perth	9 467	12 562	11 256	8 684	17 610	7 874	6 030	10 886	12 517	14 495	14 986	16 247	18 281	12 236	8 889	18 699	8 000					
Rio de Janeiro	11 462	1 990	9 897	6 080	4 522	14 054	17 688	13 330	6 022	9 248	10 132	7 659	6 713	11 528	8 937	7 724	17 306	13 527				
Singapore	6 319	15 860	8 246	9 650	18 332	4 148	2 581	10 789	11 149	10 867	14 099	16 593	16 951	8 437	7 446	15 330	4 489	3 909	15 729			
Sydney	12 502	11 760	14 391	10 982	15 341	10 424	7 370	8 163	15 514	17 005	12 052	12 973	15 012	14 501	12 125	16 001	8 956	3 274	13 512	6 294		
Tokyo	8 271	18 338	9 552	14 710	14 154	5 852	2 874	6 185	13 475	9 584	8 806	11 304	11 991	7 487	11 243	10 869	2 089	7 896	18 557	5 300	7 809	
Wellington	14 678	9 943	16 503	11 287	13 119	12 647	9 424	7 508	16 047	18 816	10 787	11 099	13 054	16 547	13 643	14 406	10 782	5 246	11 865	8 521	2 226	9 258

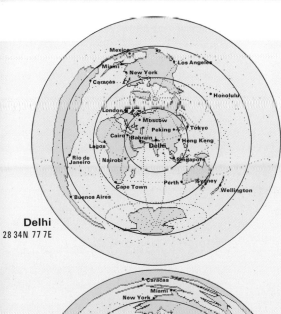

Delhi
28 34N 77 7E

Tokyo
35 33N 139 46E

Singapore
1 21N 103 54E

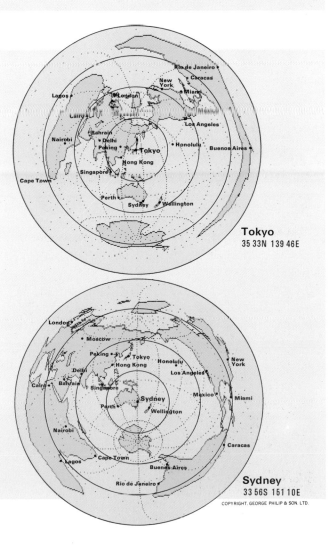

Sydney
33 56S 151 10E

The three circles are drawn at radius 5 000, 10 000 and 15 000 km from the central city

• Cities shown on the distance table

The co-ordinates given are for the airport of each city

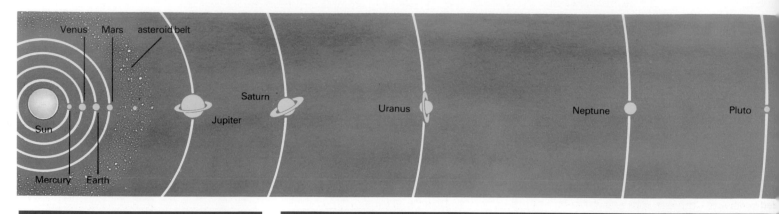

THE SOLAR SYSTEM

A minute part of one of the billions of galaxies (collections of stars) that comprise the Universe, the Solar System lies some 27,000 light-years from the centre of our own galaxy, the 'Milky Way'. Thought to be over 4,700 million years old, it consists of a central sun with nine planets and their moons revolving around it, attracted by its gravitational pull. The planets orbit the Sun in the same direction – anti-clockwise when viewed from the Northern Heavens – and almost in the same plane. Their orbital paths, however, vary enormously.

The Sun's diameter is 109 times that of Earth, and the temperature at its core – caused by continuous thermonuclear fusions of hydrogen into helium – is estimated to be 15 million degrees Celsius. It is the Solar System's only source of light and heat.

PROFILE OF THE PLANETS

	Mean distance from Sun (million km)	Mass (Earth = 1)	Period of orbit	Period of rotation (in days)	Diameter (km)	Number of known satellites
Mercury	58.3	0.06	88 days	58.67	4,878	0
Venus	107.7	0.8	224.7 days	243.0	12,104	0
Earth	149.6	1.0	365.24 days	0.99	12,756	1
Mars	227.3	0.1	1.88 years	1.02	6,794	2
Jupiter	777.9	317.8	11.86 years	0.41	142,800	16
Saturn	1427.1	95.2	29.63 years	0.42	120,000	17
Uranus	2872.3	14.5	83.97 years	0.45	52,000	15
Neptune	4502.7	17.2	164.8 years	0.67	48,400	8
Pluto	5894.2	0.002	248.63 years	6.38	2,400	1

All planetary orbits are elliptical in form, but only Pluto and Mercury follow paths that deviate noticeably from a circular one. Near Perihelion - its closest approach to the Sun - Pluto actually passes inside the orbit of Neptune, an event that last occurred in 1983. Pluto will not regain its station as outermost planet until February 1999.

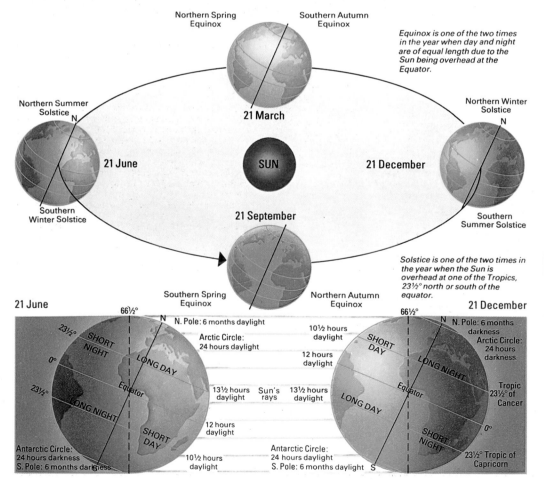

Equinox is one of the two times in the year when day and night are of equal length due to the Sun being overhead at the Equator.

Solstice is one of the two times in the year when the Sun is overhead at one of the Tropics, 23½° north or south of the equator.

THE SEASONS

The Earth revolves around the Sun once a year in an 'anti-clockwise' direction, tilted at constant angle 66½°. In June, the northern hemisphere is tilted towards the Sun: as a result it receives more hours of sunshine in a day and therefore has its warmest season, summer. In December, the Earth has rotated halfway round the Sun so that the southern hemisphere is tilted towards the Sun and has its summer; the hemisphere that is tilted away from the Sun has winter. On 21 June the Sun is directly overhead at the Tropic of Cancer (23½° N), and this is midsummer in the northern hemisphere. Midsummer in the southern hemisphere occurs on 21 December, when the Sun is overhead at the Tropic of Capricorn (23½° S).

DAY & NIGHT

The Sun appears to rise in the east, reach its highest point at noon, and then set in the west to be followed by night. In reality it is not the Sun that is moving but the Earth revolving from west to east. Due to the tilting of the Earth the length of day and night varies from place to place and month to month.

At the summer solstice in the northern hemisphere (21 June), the Arctic has total daylight and the Antarctic total darkness. The opposite occurs at the winter solstice (21 December). At the equator, the length of day and night are almost equal all year, at latitude 30° the length of day varies from about 14 hours to 10 hours, and at latitude 50° from about 16 hours to about 8 hours.

TIME

[Year]: the time taken by the Earth to revolve around [the] Sun, or 365.24 days.

[Mon]th: the approximate time taken by the Moon to [revo]lve around the Earth. The 12 months of the [year] in fact vary from 28 (29 in a Leap Year) to 31 [days].

[Wee]k: an artificial period of 7 days, not based on [astr]onomical time.

[Day]: the time taken by the Earth to complete one [rota]tion on its axis.

[Hour]: 24 hours make one day. Usually the day is [divi]ded into hours AM (ante meridiem or before [noon]) and PM (post meridiem or after noon), [thou]gh most timetables now use the 24-hour [syst]em, from midnight to midnight.

SUNRISE
SUNSET

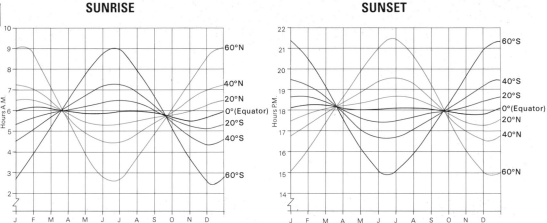

THE MOON

Distance from Earth: 356,410 km - 406,685 km; Mean diameter: 3,475.1 km; Mass: approx. 1/81 that of Earth; Surface gravity: one sixth of Earth's; Daily range of temperature at lunar equator: 200°C; Average orbital speed: 3,683 km/h

PHASES OF THE MOON

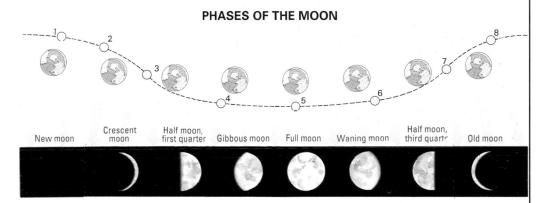

| New moon | Crescent moon | Half moon, first quarter | Gibbous moon | Full moon | Waning moon | Half moon, third quarter | Old moon |

[Th]e Moon rotates more slowly than the Earth, making [o]ne complete turn on its axis in just over 27 days. [Si]nce this corresponds to its period of revolution [ar]ound the Earth, the Moon always presents the same hemisphere or face to us, and we never see 'the dark side'. The interval between one full Moon and the next (and between new Moons) is about 29½ days - a lunar month. The apparent changes in the shape of the Moon are caused by its changing position in relation to the Earth; like the planets, it produces no light of its own and shines only by reflecting the rays of the Sun.

Partial eclipse (1)

Total eclipse (2)

Lunar eclipse

ECLIPSES

When the Moon passes between the Sun and the Earth it causes a partial eclipse of the Sun (1) if the Earth passes through the Moon's outer shadow (P), or a total eclipse (2) if the inner cone shadow crosses the Earth's surface. In a lunar eclipse, the Earth's shadow crosses the Moon and, again, provides either a partial or total eclipse. Eclipses of the Sun and the Moon do not occur every month because of the 5° difference between the plane of the Moon's orbit and the plane in which the Earth moves. In the 1990s only 14 lunar eclipses are possible, for example, seven partial and seven total; each is visible only from certain, and variable, parts of the world. The same period witnesses 13 solar eclipses - six partial (or annular) and seven total.

TIDES

[Th]e daily rise and fall of the ocean's tides are the [re]sult of the gravitational pull of the Moon and [th]at of the Sun, though the effect of the latter is [on]ly 46.6% as strong as that of the Moon. This [eff]ect is greatest on the hemisphere facing the [Mo]on and causes a tidal 'bulge'. When lunar and [sol]ar forces pull together, with Sun, Earth and [Mo]on in line (near new and full Moons), higher ['sp]ring tides' (and lower low tides) occur; when [lun]ar and solar forces are least coincidental with [th]e Sun and Moon at an angle (near the Moon's [fir]st and third quarters), 'neap tides' occur, which [ha]ve a small tidal range.

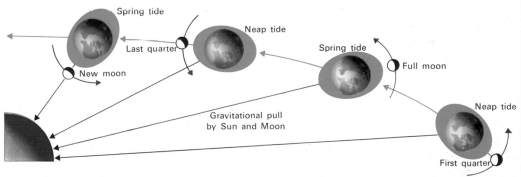

Spring tide

Neap tide

Last quarter

Spring tide

New moon

Full moon

Neap tide

Gravitational pull by Sun and Moon

First quarter

MAP PROJECTIONS

A map projection is the systematic depiction on a plane surface of the imaginary lines of latitude or longitude from a globe of the earth. This network of lines is called the graticule and forms the framework upon which an accurate depiction of the earth is made. The map graticule, which is the basis of any map, is constructed sometimes by graphical means, but often by using mathematical formulae to give the intersections of the graticule plotted as x and y co-ordinates. The choice between projections is based upon which properties the cartographer wishes the map to possess, the map scale and also the extent of the area to be mapped. Since the globe is three dimensional, it is not possible to depict its surface on a two dimensional plane without distortion. Preservation of one of the basic properties listed below can only be secured at the expense of the others and the choice of projection is often a compromise solution.

Correct Area

In these projections the areas from the globe are to scale on the map. For example, if you look at the diagram at the top right, areas of 10° x 10° are shown from the equator to the poles. The proportion of this area at the extremities are approximately 11:1. An equal area projection will retain that proportion in its portrayal of those areas. This is particularly useful in the mapping of densities and distributions. Projections with this property are termed **Equal Area, Equivalent or Homolographic.**

Correct Distance

In these projections the scale is correct along the meridians, or in the case of the Azimuthal Equidistant scale is true along any line drawn from the centre of the projection. They are called **Equidistant.**

Correct Shape

This property can only be true within small areas as it is achieved only by having a uniform scale distortion along both x and y axes of the projection. The projections are called **Conformal** or **Orthomorphic.**

In order to minimise the distortions at the edges of some projections, central portions of them are often selected for atlas maps. Below are listed some of the major types of projection.

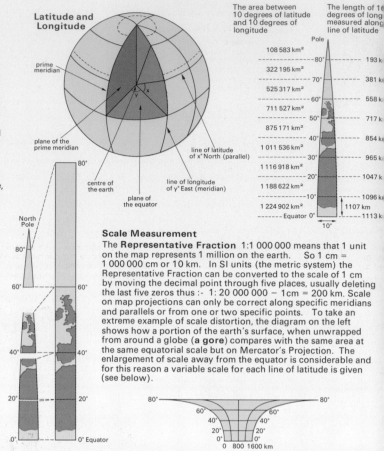

Latitude and Longitude

prime meridian

plane of the prime meridian

centre of the earth

plane of the equator

line of latitude of x° North (parallel)

line of longitude of y° East (meridian)

North Pole

The area between 10 degrees of latitude and 10 degrees of longitude		The length of 10 degrees of longitude measured along a line of latitude
	Pole	
108 583 km²	80°	193 k
322 195 km²	70°	381 k
525 317 km²	60°	558 k
711 527 km²	50°	717 k
875 171 km²	40°	854 k
1 011 536 km²	30°	965 k
1 116 918 km²	20°	1047 k
1 188 622 km²	10°	1096 k
1 224 902 km²		1107 km
Equator 0°		1113 k

Scale Measurement

The **Representative Fraction** 1:1 000 000 means that 1 unit on the map represents 1 million on the earth. So 1 cm = 1 000 000 cm or 10 km. In SI units (the metric system) the Representative Fraction can be converted to the scale of 1 cm by moving the decimal point through five places, usually deleting the last five zeros thus :- 1: 20 000 000 − 1cm = 200 km. Scale on map projections can only be correct along specific meridians and parallels or from one or two specific points. To take an extreme example of scale distortion, the diagram on the left shows how a portion of the earth's surface, when unwrapped from around a globe (**a gore**) compares with the same area at the same equatorial scale but on Mercator's Projection. The enlargement of scale away from the equator is considerable and for this reason a variable scale for each line of latitude is given (see below).

0   800 1600 km

AZIMUTHAL OR ZENITHAL PROJECTIONS

These are constructed by the projection of part of the graticule from the globe onto a plane tangential to any single point on it. This plane may be tangential to the equator (**equatorial case**), the poles (**polar case**) or any other point (**oblique case**). Any straight line drawn from the point at which the plane touches the globe is the shortest distance from that point and is known as a **great circle**. In its **Gnomonic** construction *any* straight line on the map is a great circle, but there is great exaggeration towards the edges and this reduces its general uses. There are five different ways of transferring the graticule onto the plane and these are shown on the right. The central diagram below shows how the graticules vary, using the polar case as the example.

| Equidistant | Equal-Area | Orthographic | Gnomonic | Stereographic (conformal) |

Oblique Case

The plane touches the globe at any point between the equator and poles. The oblique orthographic uses the distortion in azimuthal projections away from the centre to give a graphic depiction of the earth as seen from any desired point in space. It can also be used in both Polar and Equatorial cases. It is used not only for the earth but also for the moon and planets.

Polar Case

The polar case is the simplest to construct and the diagram below shows the differing effects of all five methods of construction comparing their coverage, distortion etc., using North America as the example.

Equatorial Case

The example shown here is Lambert's Equivalent Azimuthal. It is the only projection which is both equal area and where bearing is true from the centre.

Stereographic

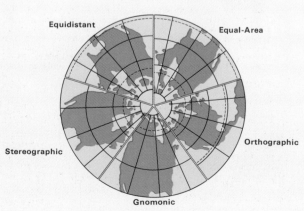

Equidistant

Equal-Area

Orthographic

Gnomonic

CONICAL PROJECTIONS

These use the projection of the graticule from the globe onto a cone which is tangential to a line of latitude (termed the **standard parallel**). This line is always an arc and scale is always true along it. Because of its method of construction it is used mainly for depicting the temperate latitudes around the standard parallel i.e. where there is least distortion. To reduce the distortion and include a larger range of latitudes, the projection may be constructed with the cone bisecting the surface of the globe so that there are two standard parallels each of which is true to scale. The distortion is thus spread more evenly between the two chosen parallels.

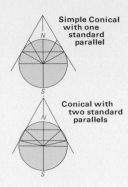

Simple Conical with one standard parallel

Conical with two standard parallels

Bonne

This is a modification of the simple conic whereby the true scale along the meridians is sacrificed to enable the accurate representation of areas. However scale is true along each parallel but shapes are distorted at the edges.

mple Conic

ale is correct not only along the standard parallel t also along all meridians. The selection of the ndard parallel used is crucial because of the tortion away from it. The projection is usually ed to portray regions or continents at small scales.

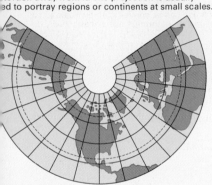

Lambert's Conformal Conic

This projection uses two standard parallels but instead of being equal area as Albers, it is Conformal. Because it has comparatively small distortion, direction and distances can be readily measured and it is therefore used for some navigational charts.

Albers Conical Equal Area

This projection uses two standard parallels and once again the selection of the two specific ones relative to the land area to be mapped is very important. It is equal area and is especially useful for large land masses oriented East-West, for example the U.S.A.

CYLINDRICAL AND OTHER WORLD PROJECTIONS

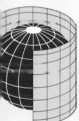

This group of projections are those which permit the whole of the Earth's surface to be depicted on one map. They are a very large group of projections and the following are only a few of them. Cylindrical projections are constructed by the projection of the graticule from the globe onto a cylinder tangential to the globe. In the examples shown here the cylinder touches the equator, but it can be moved through 90° so it touches the poles - this is called the **Transverse Aspect**. If the cylinder is twisted so that it touches anywhere between the equator and poles it is called the **Oblique Aspect**. Although cylindrical projections can depict all the main land masses, there is considerable distortion of shape and area towards the poles. One cylindrical projection, **Mercator** overcomes this shortcoming by possessing the unique navigational property that any straight drawn on it is a line of constant bearing (**loxodrome**), i.e. a straight line route on the globe crosses the parallels and meridians on the map at the same angles as on the globe. It is used for maps and charts between 15° either side of the equator. Beyond this enlargement of area is a serious drawback, although it is used for navigational charts at all latitudes.

Cylindrical with two standard parallels

Simple Cylindrical

Mercator

Mollweide

Sanson Flamsteed

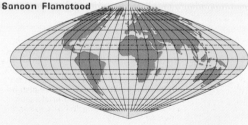

mmer

s is not a cylindrical projection, but is developed m the Lambert Azimuthal Equal Area by doubling the East-West distances along the parallels from central meridian. Like both Sanson—Flamsteed d Mollweide it is distorted towards its edges but s curved parallels to lessen the distortion.

Mollweide and Sanson-Flamsteed

Both of these projections are termed **pseudo-cylindrical**. They are basically cylindrical projections where parallels have been progressively shortened and drawn to scale towards the poles. This allows them to overcome the gross distortions exhibited by the ordinary cylindrical projections and they are in fact Equal Area, Mollweide's giving a slightly better shape. To improve the shape of the continents still further they, like some other projections can be **Interrupted** as can be seen below, but this is at the expense of contiguous sea areas. These projections can have any central meridian and so can be 'centred' on the Atlantic, Pacific, Asia, America etc. In this form both projections are suitable for any form of mapping statistical distributions.

Interrupted Mollweide

Interrupted Sanson-Flamsteed

	Population									Land and Agriculture					Energy	Trade	
	Population Total 1991	Population Density 1991	Change 1970-80	Change 1980-90	Birth Rate	Death Rate	Fertility Rate	Life Expectancy	Urban Population	Land Area	Arable and Permanent Crops	Permanent grassland	Forest	Agric. Population	Comm. Consumpt. 1989	Imports per capita	Exports per capita
	millions	persons per km²	%	%	births per thousand	deaths per thousand	children	years	%	thousand km²	% of land area	% of land area	% of land area	% of active pop.	gigajoules	US $	US $
Afghanistan	17.7	27	18	3	52	22	6.8	44	22	652	12	46	3	55	7	58	15
Albania	3.3	122	25	21	22	6	2.7	73	35	27	26	15	38	48	37	...	...
Algeria	25.7	11	36	33	35	7	4.9	66	45	2,382	3	13	2	24	27	313	345
Angola	10.3	8.3	38	30	47	10	6.3	47	28	1,247	3	23	42	70	3	48	233
Argentina	32.7	12	18	14	20	9	2.8	71	86	2,737	13	52	22	10	57	126	380
Australia	17.1	2.2	17	15	14	8	1.8	77	86	7,618	6	55	14	5	211	2,223	2,410
Austria	7.6	93	1	0	12	12	1.5	75	58	82	19	24	39	6	117	6,488	5,254
Bahamas	0.26	26	23	20	19	5	2.2	69	59	10	1	0	32	6	76	12,004	11,144
Bangladesh	119	914	32	31	41	14	5.1	53	14	130	71	5	15	69	2	27	13
Barbados	0.26	593	4	2	16	9	1.8	75	45	0.43	77	9	0	7	47	2,692	804
Belgium	9.8	321	2	0	12	12	1.7	76	97	31	25	21	21	2	168	11,875	11,602
Benin	4.9	44	28	34	49	18	7.1	48	42	111	17	4	32	61	1	103	20
Bolivia	7.6	7.0	29	31	41	12	5.8	56	51	1,084	3	25	51	42	11	124	113
Botswana	1.4	2.5	45	45	44	10	6.4	61	24	567	2	58	19	63	...	...	...
Brazil	153	18	27	24	26	8	3.2	66	77	8,457	9	20	65	24	23	134	209
Bulgaria	9	81	4	2	12	12	1.8	73	70	111	38	18	35	12	144	1,434	1,485
Burkina Faso	9.3	34	25	29	47	17	6.5	49	9	274	13	37	24	84	1	57	17
Burma	42.6	65	27	20	30	9	3.7	63	25	658	15	1	49	47	2	14	10
Burundi	5.6	218	17	32	47	16	6.8	50	7	26	52	36	3	91	1	43	14
Cambodia	8.5	48	-8	29	37	15	4.4	51	12	177	17	3	76	70	1	...	...
Cameroon	12.2	26	31	37	47	13	6.9	55	49	465	15	18	53	61	7	115	84
Canada	26.7	2.9	13	10	13	8	1.7	77	76	9,221	5	4	39	3	321	4,376	4,699
Central Africa	3.1	5.0	25	31	45	16	6.2	51	47	623	3	5	57	63	1	51	45
Chad	5.8	4.6	23	27	43	18	5.8	48	33	1,259	3	36	10	75	1	78	26
Chile	13.4	18	17	18	23	6	2.7	72	86	749	6	18	12	13	35	552	652
China	1,131	121	20	14	21	7	2.3	71	21	9,326	10	34	14	68	23	55	63
Colombia	33.6	32	26	23	26	6	2.9	69	70	1,039	5	39	49	27	24	169	205
Congo	2.3	6.73	32	36	46	13	6.3	55	42	342	0	29	62	60	10	238	414
Costa Rica	3.1	61	32	32	26	4	3.0	75	54	51	10	45	32	24	16	684	466
Cuba	10.7	97	14	10	17	7	1.9	76	75	110	30	27	25	19	45	728	530
Cyprus	0.71	77	2	11	17	8	2.2	77	53	9.2	17	1	13	21	74	3,664	1,356
Czechoslovakia	15.7	126	7	2	14	11	2.0	72	69	125	41	13	37	9	175	837	759
Denmark	5.1	121	4	0	11	11	1.5	76	86	42	60	5	12	5	130	6,276	6,967
Dominican Republic	7.3	152	29	26	26	6	3.3	68	60	48	30	43	13	36	12	249	102
Ecuador	10.9	39	34	30	31	7	3.9	67	57	277	10	18	40	30	19	249	295
Egypt	53.6	54	24	30	31	9	4.0	62	49	995	3	0	0	41	22	173	49
El Salvador	5.4	270	26	16	36	7	4.5	66	44	20	35	29	5	37	7	172	79
Ethiopia	50.7	46	27	27	48	18	6.8	47	13	1,101	13	41	25	75	1	21	6
Finland	5	16	4	4	12	10	1.7	76	68	305	8	0	76	8	169	4,257	4,532
France	56.3	102	6	4	13	10	1.8	77	74	550	35	21	27	5	115	4,075	3,767
Gabon	1.2	4.7	60	45	43	16	5.3	54	46	258	2	18	78	68	37	691	1,215
Gambia	0.88	88	38	34	45	20	6.2	45	23	10	18	9	16	81	4	233	48
Germany	79.5	228	1	2	11	12	1.5	75	84	349	35	16	30	5	200	4,734	4,849
Ghana	15.5	67	25	40	44	12	6.3	56	33	230	12	22	35	50	3	64	72
Greece	10.1	77	10	4	12	10	1.7	77	63	131	30	40	20	24	91	1,954	792
Guatemala	9.5	88	32	33	39	8	5.4	65	42	108	17	13	35	51	6	177	130
Guinea	5.9	24	14	29	51	20	7.0	45	26	246	3	25	60	74	3	...	...
Guinea-Bissau	0.98	35	51	21	43	21	5.8	44	20	28	12	38	38	79	2	69	14
Guyana	0.80	4.1	7	5	24	7	2.4	65	34	197	3	6	83	22	11	640	319
Haiti	6.6	244	18	21	35	12	4.8	57	30	27	33	18	1	64	2	56	16
Honduras	5.3	47	39	40	37	7	4.9	66	44	112	16	23	30	55	5	198	184
Hong Kong	5.9	5,960	28	16	12	6	1.4	78	93	0.99	7	1	12	1	58	16,992	16,708
Hungary	10.5	114	4	-1	12	13	1.8	72	60	92	57	13	18	12	107	831	920
Iceland	0.26	2.6	12	11	15	7	1.9	78	91	100	0	23	1	7	165	6,615	5,977
India	871	293	24	20	31	10	4.1	60	28	2,973	57	4	22	67	9	28	22
Indonesia	188	104	26	19	27	9	3.1	63	29	1,812	12	7	63	49	8	122	143
Iran	55.8	34	37	40	33	7	4.7	67	55	1,636	9	27	11	28	45	306	353
Iraq	19.6	45	42	42	41	7	5.9	66	74	437	12	9	4	21	31	670	2,021

Wealth							Social Indicators						Aid		
GNP 1990	GNP per capita 1990	Rate of change 1980-90	GDP share agriculture	GDP share industry	GDP share services	Real GDP per capita 1989	Human Development Index	Food Intake	Population per doctor 1984	% of GNP spent on education 1989	% of age-group in secondary education	Adult Illiteracy	Per capita 1989	% of GNP 1990	
million US $	US $	%	%	%	%	US $		calories per day	persons	%	%	%	US $	%	
7,200	450	2.6	65	20	15	710	0.065	2,000	5,200	1.8	8	71	10	...	Afghanistan
3,255	1,000	1.8	60	28	12	4,270	0.791	2,500	1,230	...	...	15	3	...	Albania
51,585	2,060	-0.3	16	44	40	3,088	0.533	2,818	2,340	9.4	61	43	9	0.3	Algeria
6,207	620	6.1	75	10	15	1,225	0.169	2,000	17,790	3.4	11	58	21	3.5	Angola
76,491	2,370	-1.8	14	33	53	4,310	0.833	3,110	370	1.5	74	5	6.7	0.4	Argentina
290,522	17,080	1.7	4	32	64	15,266	0.971	3,186	440	5.7	79	1	*59.6	*0.38	Australia
147,016	19,240	2	3	37	60	13,063	0.95	3,496	390	6	...	1	*37.2	*0.23	Austria
2,913	11,510	1.7	...	...	...	11,293	0.875	2,791	1,100	6.2	...	1	12	0.1	Bahamas
22,579	200	1	44	14	42	820	0.185	1,996	6,730	2.2	17	65	16.2	8.9	Bangladesh
1,680	6,540	1.4	7	15	78	8,351	0.927	3,247	1,150	6.9	93	1	12	0.2	Barbados
154,688	15,440	1.2	2	31	67	13,313	0.95	3,947	330	5.4	89	1	*71.7	*0.46	Belgium
1,716	360	-1	46	12	42	1,030	0.111	2,245	15,940	3.5	16	77	53.8	14.7	Benin
4,526	620	-2.6	24	30	46	1,531	0.394	1,968	1,540	2.3	34	22	60.8	9.6	Bolivia
2,561	2,040	6.3	3	57	40	3,180	0.534	2,368	6,900	8.2	37	26	116	6.5	Botswana
402,788	2,680	0.6	9	43	48	4,951	0.739	2,722	1,080	3.7	38	19	1.3	0.05	Brazil
19,875	2,210	2.3	11	59	30	5,064	0.865	3,683	280	3.5	59	7	...	...	Bulgaria
2,955	330	1.4	32	26	42	617	0.074	2,286	57,220	2.3	7	82	32.4	11.1	Burkina Faso
20,805	500	2.1	51	10	39	595	0.385	2,474	3,740	2.2	24	19	5.4	1.1	Burma
1,151	210	1.3	56	15	29	611	0.165	1,995	21,120	3.2	4	50	37.3	18.6	Burundi
2,475	300	2.5	75	10	15	1,000	0.178	2,500		...	...	65	4	...	Cambodia
11,233	940	-0.3	27	27	46	1,699	0.313	2,195	14,000	3.3	26	46	40.7	4.2	Cameroon
542,774	20,450	2.4	3	21	76	18,635	0.982	3,462	510	7.2	93	1	*86.9	*0.44	Canada
1,194	390	-1.3	42	15	43	770	0.159	2,004	23,530	2.9	11	62	75	17.1	Central Africa
1,074	190	3.3	36	20	44	582	0.088	1,800	38,360	2	7	70	55	30.3	Chad
25,504	1,940	1.1	8	30	62	4,987	0.863	2,553	1,230	3.6	75	7	7	0.2	Chile
415,884	370	7.9	32	48	20	2,656	0.612	2,634	1,000	2.4	44	27	2	0.5	China
40,805	1,240	1.1	17	36	47	4,068	0.758	2,571	1,240	2.9	52	13	3	0.2	Colombia
2,296	1,010	-0.2	14	35	51	2,382	0.372	2,603	8,320	5.1	...	43	92	10.2	Congo
5,342	1,910	0.6	18	27	55	4,413	0.842	2,791	960	4.4	41	7	76	4.3	Costa Rica
21,250	2,000	1.1	12	36	52	2,500	0.732	3,153	560	6.6	89	6	3	0.1	Cuba
5,633	8,040	4.9	7	27	66	9,368	0.912	3,250	1,100	3.6	88	6	49	0.7	Cyprus
49,225	3,140	1.3	6	57	37	7,420	0.807	3,609	280	4	86	1	...	...	Czechoslovakia
113,515	22,090	2.1	5	29	66	13,751	0.953	3,622	400	7.3	84	1	*183.7	*0.94	Denmark
5,847	820	-0.4	15	26	59	2,537	0.595	2,342	1,760	1.5	74	17	13	2.1	Dominican Republic
10,112	960	-0.8	15	39	46	3,012	0.641	2,518	820	2.6	56	14	15.7	1.6	Ecuador
31,381	600	2.1	19	30	51	1,934	0.385	3,326	770	6.8	81	52	107	17.2	Egypt
5,707	1,100	-0.6	21	21	58	1,897	0.498	2,200	2,830	2	26	27	65	7.6	El Salvador
6,041	120	-1.2	42	16	42	392	0.173	1,750	60,000	4.4	15	34	18	11.6	Ethiopia
129,823	26,070	3.1	7	36	57	14,598	0.953	3,144	440	5.7	83	1	*141.2	*0.63	Finland
1,099,750	19,480	1.7	4	29	67	14,164	0.969	3,449	320	6.6	83	1	*132.3	*0.78	France
3,654	3,220	-2.6	11	47	42	4,735	0.545	2,500	2,790	5.6	...	39	121.3	3.9	Gabon
229	260	-0.3	34	12	54	886	0.083	2,351	11,600	4	16	73	109	48	Gambia
1,468,871	22,730	2.2	3	37	60	14,507	0.955	3,650	380	4.5	85	1	*62.3	*0.41	Germany
5,824	390	-0.6	50	17	33	1,005	0.31	2,246	14,890	3.4	39	40	37.6	10.3	Ghana
60,245	6,000	0.8	16	29	55	6,764	0.901	3,793	350	3.1	85	7	3.3	0.1	Greece
8,309	900	-2.1	18	26	56	2,531	0.485	2,229	2,180	1.8	21	45	21	3.1	Guatemala
2,756	480	2.5	30	33	37	602	0.052	2,193	46,420	3	9	76	48	12.6	Guinea
176	180	1.7	47	16	37	820	0.088	2,500	7,500	2.8	7	63	122	68.2	Guinea-Bissau
293	370	-3.2	25	31	44	1,453	0.539	2,736	6,200	8.8	64	4	133	42.7	Guyana
2,400	370	-2.3	31	38	31	962	0.276	2,011	7,180	1.8	19	47	31.1	8.4	Haiti
3,023	590	-1.2	21	25	54	1,504	0.473	2,229	1,510	4.9	32	27	87	9.9	Honduras
66,666	11,540	5.5	0	28	72	15,180	0.913	2,817	1,070	2.8	73	10	8	0.03	Hong Kong
30,047	2,780	1.5	14	36	50	6,245	0.893	3,638	310	4	73	3	...	...	Hungary
5,456	21,150	1.2	10	15	75	14,210	0.958	3,518	460	3.7	85	1	...	...	Iceland
294,816	350	3.2	32	29	39	910	0.297	2,196	2,520	3.2	43	52	2.3	0.7	India
101,151	560	4.1	24	37	39	2,034	0.491	2,708	9,460	0.9	47	23	10.3	1.9	Indonesia
139,120	2,450	-0.8	25	15	60	3,120	0.547	3,300	2,690	3.1	53	46	1.7	0.1	Iran
37,828	2,000	3.6	25	20	55	3,510	0.589	3,000	1,740	3.7	47	40	3	0.01	Iraq

	Population									Land and Agriculture					Energy	Trade	
	Population Total 1991	Population Density 1991	Change 1970-80	Change 1980-90	Birth Rate	Death Rate	Fertility Rate	Life Expectancy	Urban Population	Land Area	Arable and Permanent Crops	Permanent grassland	Forest	Agric. Population	Comm. Consumpt. 1989	Imports per capita	Exports per capita
	millions	persons per km²	%	%	births per thousand	deaths per thousand	children	years	%	thousand km²	% of land area	% of land area	% of land area	% of active pop.	gigajoules	US $	US $
Ireland	3.8	56	15	9	18	8	2.4	75	59	68	14	68	5	14	112	5,922	6,797
Israel	4.7	235	30	19	21	7	2.8	76	92	20	21	7	5	4	89	3,241	2,484
Italy	57.1	194	5	1	11	11	1.4	76	69	294	41	17	23	7	111	3,113	2,931
Ivory Coast	12.5	39	49	46	50	13	7.4	55	47	318	12	41	24	56	5	189	251
Jamaica	2.5	231	14	15	22	6	2.4	74	52	11	25	18	17	27	25	770	461
Japan	124	329	12	6	12	8	1.7	79	77	377	12	2	67	6	118	1,901	2,538
Jordan	4.2	48	27	37	39	5	5.5	68	68	88	4	9	1	6	29	649	230
Kenya	24.9	44	45	44	47	10	6.8	61	24	570	4	67	4	77	3	93	44
Korea, North	22.2	185	25	19	25	5	2.4	71	67	120	17	0	74	34	83	...	...
Korea, South	43.2	441	19	12	15	6	1.7	71	72	98	22	1	66	25	65	1,629	1,517
Laos	4.3	19	18	29	44	15	6.7	51	19	231	4	3	55	72	1	...	...
Lebanon	2.8	280	8	1	30	8	3.4	67	84	10	29	1	8	9	42	846	197
Lesotho	1.8	59	26	32	40	11	5.8	59	20	30	11	66	0	80	...	...	...
Liberia	2.7	28	35	37	47	14	6.7	56	44	96	4	59	18	70	4	131	163
Libya	4.7	2.7	53	49	43	8	6.7	63	70	1,760	1	8	0	14	117	1,559	1,773
Luxembourg	0.40	155	7	2	12	11	1.5	75	84	2.6	...	...	...	...	361	...	...
Madagascar	12.4	21	30	37	45	13	6.5	56	25	582	5	58	27	77	1	29	27
Malawi	9.1	97	37	42	55	19	7.6	49	15	94	26	20	40	75	1	69	50
Malaysia	18.3	56	27	30	28	5	3.5	71	42	329	15	0	58	32	41	2,028	1,899
Mali	9.5	7.8	25	19	51	19	7.1	46	19	1,220	2	25	6	81	1	70	33
Malta	0.40	1,333	12	-3	13	9	1.9	74	87	0.30	41	0	0	4	60	5,580	3,217
Mauritania	2.1	2.0	27	30	46	18	6.5	48	42	1,025	0	38	5	64	21	178	229
Mexico	90.5	47	33	22	27	5	3.1	70	73	1,909	13	39	23	30	51	348	308
Mongolia	2.3	1.5	32	32	34	8	4.7	64	51	1,567	1	79	9	30	57	...	...
Morocco	25.7	58	27	29	33	8	4.2	63	49	446	21	47	18	37	11	276	170
Mozambique	16.1	21	29	29	44	17	6.2	49	27	782	4	49	23	82	1	48	7
Namibia	1.8	2.2	29	36	42	11	5.7	59	57	823	1	64	22	35	...		
Nepal	19.6	143	29	29	36	13	5.5	54	10	137	19	15	18	92	1	36	11
Netherlands	15.1	458	9	6	13	9	1.6	78	89	33	28	32	9	4	195	8,360	8,868
New Zealand	3.4	13	10	9	16	8	2.0	76	84	268	2	51	27	9	151	2,514	2,867
Nicaragua	4	34	35	40	39	7	5.0	66	60	119	11	45	29	38	8	264	86
Niger	8	6.3	34	38	51	19	7.1	47	20	1,267	3	7	2	87	2	52	32
Nigeria	88.5	97	39	38	47	14	6.6	53	35	911	34	44	13	65	6	40	95
Norway	4.2	14	5	3	13	11	1.7	78	74	307	3	0	27	5	209	5,954	8,027
Pakistan	126	164	30	31	42	11	5.9	59	32	771	27	6	5	50	8	73	56
Panama	2.5	33	28	24	25	5	2.9	73	55	76	8	20	44	25	17	615	133
Papua New Guinea	3.96	8.7	27	26	33	11	4.8	56	16	453	1	0	84	67	9	348	308
Paraguay	4.4	11	34	36	33	6	4.3	67	48	397	6	52	36	46	6	167	280
Peru	22	17	31	29	29	8	3.6	65	70	1,280	3	21	54	35	15	134	152
Philippines	63.9	214	29	29	30	7	3.9	65	42	298	27	4	35	47	9	212	133
Poland	38.6	127	9	8	15	10	2.1	72	63	304	48	13	29	21	134	373	378
Portugal	10.6	115	8	5	13	10	1.7	74	33	92	41	8	32	16	53	2,380	1,552
Puerto Rico	3.6	406	18	9	18	8	2.1	76	74	8.9	14	38	20	3	82	...	...
Romania	23.4	102	10	5	15	11	2.0	72	50	230	45	19	28	20	132	241	177
Rwanda	7.5	313	38	40	50	16	8.0	51	8	24	47	19	23	91	1	55	15
Saudi Arabia	14.7	6.8	63	51	42	7	7.1	66	77	2,150	1	40	1	39	186	1,466	1,967
Senegal	7.5	39	33	32	44	16	6.2	49	38	193	27	30	31	78	6	148	88
Sierra Leone	4.3	61	23	27	48	22	6.5	43	32	71	25	31	29	62	2	40	35
Singapore	2.8	4,667	16	24	16	6	1.8	75	100	0.60	2	0	5	1	146	20,262	17,580
Somalia	7.7	12	46	40	47	18	6.6	47	36	627	2	69	14	71	2	19	15
South Africa	36.1	30	26	25	31	9	4.2	63	59	1,221	11	67	4	14	77	484	538
Spain	39.3	79	11	4	13	9	1.7	77	78	499	41	20	31	11	73	2,391	1,542
Sri Lanka	17.4	272	18	16	21	6	2.5	72	21	64	29	7	27	52	3	155	113
Sudan	25.9	11	35	35	43	14	6.3	52	22	2,376	6	6	6	60	2	45	21
Surinam	0.43	2.8	-5	20	25	6	2.6	70	48	156	0	0	95	16	35	735	753
Swaziland	0.82	48	34	40	47	11	6.5	58	33	17	10	69	6	66	...	...	...
Sweden	8.5	21	3	2	13	12	1.9	78	84	412	7	1	68	4	147	5,759	6,381
Switzerland	6.6	169	2	5	12	10	1.6	78	60	39	10	40	26	4	107	9,796	9,063

Wealth							Social Indicators						Aid		
GNP 1990	GNP per capita 1990	Rate of change 1980-90	GDP share agriculture	GDP share industry	GDP share services	Real GDP per capita 1989	Human Development Index	Food Intake	Population per doctor 1984	% of GNP spent on education 1989	% of age-group in secondary education	Adult Illiteracy	Per capita 1989	% of GNP 1990	
million US $	US $	%	%	%	%	US $		calories per day	persons	%	%	%	US $	%	
33,467	9,550	1.1	10	10	80	7,481	0.921	3,779	680	6.2	79	1	*12.9	*0.17	Ireland
50,866	10,970	1.5	5	22	73	10,448	0.939	3,150	350	...	83	4	264.4	2.6	Israel
970,619	16,850	2.2	4	34	62	13,608	0.922	3,508	230	3.9	77	3	*62.3	*0.42	Italy
8,920	730	-3.7	46	24	30	1,381	0.289	2,580	15,000	7	20	46	56	7.2	Ivory Coast
3,606	1,510	-0.4	6	45	49	2,787	0.722	2,622	2,040	6.6	61	2	113	9.2	Jamaica
3,140,948	25,430	3.5	3	41	56	14,311	0.981	2,909	660	6.5	96	1	*72.2	*0.32	Japan
3,924	1,240	-3.9	6	29	65	2,415	0.586	3,000	1,140	5.9	46	20	221	16.7	Jordan
8,958	370	0.3	31	20	49	1,023	0.366	2,159	9,970	6.5	23	31	41.1	11.7	Kenya
50,000	2,000	1.8	...	...	...	2,172	0.654	2,909	500	...	87	4	5	1	Korea, North
231,132	5,400	8.9	10	44	46	6,117	0.871	2,853	1,160	3.6	87	4	1	1	Korea, South
848	200	0.7	70	10	20	1,025	0.24	2,400	1,360	1.2	27	46	34.8	22.5	Laos
5,400	2,000	0.3	8	35	57	2,250	0.561	3,000	680	...	67	20	50	...	Lebanon
832	470	-0.9	24	30	46	1,646	0.423	2,326	18,610	4	26	22	78	16.9	Lesotho
1,280	500	3.2	37	28	35	937	0.227	2,404	9,340	5.7	17	60	37	4.5	Liberia
26,367	5,800	-9.2	5	50	45	4,927	0.659	3,350	690	10.1	...	36	2	0.52	Libya
10,875	28,770	3.9	3	41	56	16,537	0.929	...	570	2.8	60	1	...	...	Luxembourg
2,710	230	-2.3	31	14	55	690	0.325	2,177	9,780	1.8	19	20	28.4	12.6	Madagascar
1,662	200	-0.1	35	19	46	620	0.166	2,098	11,330	3.3	4	53	47.9	30.5	Malawi
41,524	2,340	2.5	23	42	35	5,649	0.789	2,754	1,930	5.6	59	22	26	1.3	Malaysia
2,292	270	1.2	50	12	38	576	0.081	2,234	25,390	3.3	6	68	50	22.6	Mali
2,342	6,630	3.6	4	41	55	8,231	0.854	3,238	850	3.6	75	13	15	0.2	Malta
987	500	-1.8	37	24	39	1,092	0.141	2,599	12,120	6	16	66	101.8	19.4	Mauritania
214,500	2,490	-0.9	9	32	59	5,691	0.804	3,048	1,240	3.8	53	13	1.1	0.1	Mexico
850	400	2.7	40	25	35	2,000	0.574	2,449	570	...	92	7	5	0.05	Mongolia
23,788	950	1.6	16	34	50	2,298	0.429	3,005	15,580	7.3	36	50	39	4.4	Morocco
1,208	80	-4.1	64	22	14	1,060	0.153	1,665	37,960	...	5	67	59	77.4	Mozambique
1,780	1,000	3.1	11	38	51	1,500	0.295	2,200	...	1.9	...	60	35	2.3	Namibia
3,289	170	1.8	58	14	28	896	0.168	2,074	32,710	2.8	30	74	20	11.9	Nepal
258,804	17,330	1.4	5	31	64	13,351	0.968	3,163	450	6.8	82	1	*138.7	*0.94	Netherlands
43,185	12,680	0.6	10	28	62	11,155	0.947	3,389	580	4.9	86	1	*25.6	*0.22	New Zealand
3,082	800	-1.4	29	23	48	1,463	0.496	2,500	1,500	3.9	37	19	81	7.4	Nicaragua
2,365	310	-4.5	35	13	52	634	0.078	2,297	39,730	3.1	6	72	39.8	14.5	Niger
31,285	270	-3	31	44	25	1,160	0.241	2,306	7,990	1.5	19	49	3	1.1	Nigeria
98,079	23,120	2.7	4	34	62	16,838	0.978	3,338	450	6.7	85	1	*218.3	*1.04	Norway
42,649	380	2.9	27	24	49	1,789	0.305	2,197	2,910	2.6	20	65	10.2	2.8	Pakistan
4,414	1,030	-2	10	15	75	3,231	0.731	2,537	980	6.2	59	12	38	2.2	Panama
3,372	860	-0.5	28	30	42	1,834	0.321	...	6,070	5	13	48	97	9.5	Papua New Guinea
4,796	1,110	-1.3	29	22	49	2,742	0.637	2,755	1,460	1.5	29	10	12	2.2	Paraguay
25,149	1,160	-2	8	30	62	2,731	0.6	2,244	1,040	3.5	70	15	14.2	1	Peru
43,954	730	-1.5	23	33	44	2,269	0.6	2,342	6,700	2.9	73	10	20	3	Philippines
64,480	1,700	1.2	14	50	36	4,770	0.874	3,464	490	3.6	76	3	...	...	Poland
50,692	4,890	2.4	9	37	54	6,259	0.85	3,414	410	4.1	37	15	7.6	0.2	Portugal
21,346	6,470	2.1	2	40	58	...	...	...	...	...	...	...	...	...	Puerto Rico
38,025	1,640	1.1	14	53	33	3,000	0.733	3,252	570	2.7	79	4	...	...	Romania
2,214	310	-2.2	37	23	40	680	0.186	1,945	34,680	4.2	7	50	34.5	11	Rwanda
92,839	6,230	-5.6	8	45	47	10,330	0.687	2,842	690	7.6	46	38	81.2	1.46	Saudi Arabia
5,260	710	0	22	31	47	1,208	0.178	2,374	13,060	4.6	16	62	90.5	14	Senegal
981	240	-1.5	46	11	43	1,061	0.062	1,841	13,630	3.8	18	79	16	10.5	Sierra Leone
33,512	12,310	5.7	0	37	63	15,108	0.848	3,249	1,310	3.4	69	12	35.4	0.3	Singapore
946	150	-1.8	65	10	25	861	0.088	1,932	16,080	0.4	10	76	58	38.9	Somalia
90,410	2,520	-0.9	6	44	50	4,958	0.674	3,104	2,000	4.6	...	30	...	...	South Africa
429,404	10,920	2.7	6	9	85	8,723	0.916	3,567	320	3.2	79	6	*6	*0.1	Spain
7,971	470	2.4	26	27	47	2,253	0.651	2,299	5,520	3	74	12	33.2	9.1	Sri Lanka
11,300	450	1.1	36	15	49	1,042	0.157	2,028	10,100	4.8	20	73	31		Sudan
1,365	3,050	-5	11	26	63	3,907	0.749	2,908	1,400	9.5	53	5	135	4.3	Surinam
645	820	1.1	23	40	37	2,405	0.458	2,612	23,000	6.2	50	28	69	7.9	Swaziland
202,498	23,680	1.8	4	34	62	14,817	0.976	2,945	390	7.5	86	1	*211.6	*0.97	Sweden
219,337	32,790	1.7	4	42	54	18,590	0.977	3,565	700	5.2	86	1	*84.5	*0.3	Switzerland

	Population									Land and Agriculture					Energy	Trade	
	Population Total 1991	Population Density 1991	Change 1970-80	Change 1980-90	Birth Rate	Death Rate	Fertility Rate	Life Expectancy	Urban Population	Land Area	Arable and Permanent Crops	Permanent grassland	Forest	Agric. Population	Comm. Consumpt. 1989	Imports per capita	Exports per capita
	millions	persons per km²	%	%	births per thousand	deaths per thousand	children	years	%	thousand km²	% of land area	% of land area	% of land area	% of active pop.	gigajoules	US $	US $
Syria	12.8	70	41	42	43	6	6.3	67	52	184	30	43	4	24	28	208	335
Taiwan	20.5	569	21	13	17	5	1.7	70	76	36	13	11	52		...	...	...
Tanzania	28.4	32	40	36	50	13	7.1	55	33	886	6	40	46	81	1	62	14
Thailand	56.5	111	31	22	20	7	2.2	67	23	511	43	2	28	64	18	584	403
Togo	3.6	67	29	35	45	13	6.6	55	26	54	27	33	30	70	2	161	85
Trinidad & Tobago	1.3	253	11	18	23	6	2.7	72	69	5.1	23	2	43	8	165	994	1,666
Tunisia	8.4	54	25	28	27	6	3.4	68	54	155	30	19	4	24	21	641	458
Turkey	58.5	76	26	32	27	8	3.3	66	48	770	36	11	26	48	28	396	230
Uganda	19.5	98	34	43	52	14	7.3	53	10	200	34	9	28	81	1	31	16
USSR (CIS)	282	13	9	9	17	10	2.3	71	66	22,098	10	17		13	191	417	360
United Kingdom	57.6	238	1	2	14	12	1.8	76	93	242	28	46	10	2	147	3,659	3,227
United States	251	27	11	9	14	9	1.9	76	74	9,167	21	26	32	2	295	20,293	16,792
Uruguay	3.1	18	4	6	17	10	2.3	73	86	175	7	77	4	14	23	433	546
Venezuela	20.2	23	42	31	28	5	3.5	70	91	882	4	20	35	11	83	323	891
Vietnam	65.2	201	26	24	30	8	3.7	64	22	325	20	1	30	61	3	...	...
Yemen	12.1	23	21	47	51	14	7.6	52	32	528	3	30	8	56	20	2	...
Yugoslavia	23.9	94	9	7	14	9	1.9	73	50	255	30	25	37	22	75	793	601
Zaïre	36.7	16	33	36	45	13	6.1	54	40	2,267	3	7	77	66	2	25	28
Zambia	8.8	12	37	47	50	12	7.2	55	56	743	7	40	39	69	6	154	111
Zimbabwe	10	26	35	36	40	9	5.3	61	28	387	7	13	50	68	20	197	184

As yet, for the new divisions of Czechoslovakia, Ethiopia, USSR and Yugoslavia, many of the statistics shown in the main table are not available. The area and population of the new republics are shown in the second table, opposite, which lists the area and population of the smaller countries and territories.

Many figures for Luxembourg are included in those for Belgium.

For trade and energy the figures for South Africa include those for Botswana, Lesotho, Swaziland and Namibia.

The sign ... means that figures are not available.

Population Total. This is the UN estimate for the mid-year, 1991.

Population Density. This is the total population divided by the land area, both quoted in the table.

Population Change. This shows the percentage change over ten years 1970-80 and 1980-90.

Birth and Death Rates and Life Expectancy. These are UN estimates for the current period. The Birth and Death rates are the number of these occurrences per year, per thousand population. Life Expectancy is the number of years that a child born today can expect to live if the levels of mortality of today last throughout its life. The figure is the average of that for men and women.

Fertility Rate. This is the average number of children born to a woman in her lifetime.

Urban Population. This is the percentage of the total population living in urban areas. The definition of urban is that of the individual nations and often includes quite small towns.

Land Area. This is the total area of the country less the area covered by major lakes and rivers.

Arable Land and Permanent Crops. This excludes fallow land but includes temporary pasture.

Forest and Woodland. This includes natural and planted woodland and land recently cleared of timber which will be replanted.

Agricultural Population. This is the percentage of the economically active population working in agriculture. It includes those working in forestry, hunting and fishing.

Energy. All forms of energy have been expressed in gigajoules, which is a measure of their calorific value. A gigajoule = 24 kg of oil equivalent.

Trade. The trade figures are for 1991 or 1990. In a few cases the figure is older than this but is the latest available. The total Import and Export figures have been divided by the population to give a figure in US $ per capita.

Gross National Product (GNP). This figure is an estimate of the value of a country's production and the average production per person for 1990, in US $. The GNP measures the value of goods and services produced in a country, plus the balance, positive or negative, of income from abroad, for example, from investments, interest on capital, money returned from workers abroad, etc. The average annual rate of change is for the GNP per capita during the period 1980-90. The

GDP, the Gross Domestic Product, is the GNP less the foreign balances. The adjoining three columns show the percentage contribution to the GDP made by the agricultural, mining and manufacturing and service sectors of the economy.

Real GDP per capita. Using exchange rates to convert national currencies into $ US makes no attempt to reflect the varying domestic purchasing powers of the local currency. The UN has made these estimates of Real GDP taking into account these local purchasing values.

Human Development Index. This is a calculation made by the UN Development Programme, using 1990 data, and takes into account not only national income, but also life expectancy, adult literacy and the years in education. It is a measure of national human progress. The wealthy developed countries have an index approaching 1, and the figures range down to some of the poorer with an index of less than 0.100.

Food Intake. The figures are the average intake per person in calories per day.

Adult Illiteracy. This is the percentage of the population aged 15 and over who cannot read or write a simple sentence.

Aid. The bulk of the table is concerned with aid received but aid given is shown by an asterisk.

To convert square kilometres to square miles multiply by 0.39.

Wealth							Social Indicators						Aid		
GNP 1990	GNP per capita 1990	Rate of change 1980-90	GDP share agriculture	GDP share industry	GDP share services	Real GDP per capita 1989	Human Development Index	Food Intake	Population per doctor 1984	% of GNP spent on education 1989	% of age-group in secondary education	Adult Illiteracy	Per capita 1989	% of GNP 1990	
million US $	US $	%	%	%	%	US $		calories per day	persons	%	%	%	US $	%	
12,404	990	-2.1	38	23	39	4,348	0.665	3,074	1,260	4.1	54	35	51	5.2	Syria
132,660	6,600	6.4	6	46	48	...	...	3,000	1,000	...	...	...	...	...	Taiwan
2,779	120	-0.7	66	7	27	557	0.268	2,209	26,200	3.7	4	35	38.5	32	Tanzania
79,044	1,420	5.6	17	38	45	3,569	0.685	2,312	6,290	...	28	7	12.6	1	Thailand
1,474	410	-1.7	34	23	43	752	0.218	2,141	8,700	5.2	22	57	58	13.6	Togo
4,458	3,470	-6	3	41	56	6,266	0.876	2,913	950	4.9	83	4	8	0.3	Trinidad & Tobago
11,592	1,420	0.9	13	33	54	3,329	0.582	3,081	2,150	6.3	44	35	30.9	2.5	Tunisia
91,742	1,630	3	17	35	48	4,002	0.671	3,170	1,380	1.8	51	19	23	1.7	Turkey
3,814	220	0.8	17	7	76	499	0.192	2,136	21,900	3.4	13	52	30	13.2	Uganda
1,435,000	5,000	0.8	23	42	35	6,270	0.873	3,380	250	...	...	1	14	...	USSR (CIS)
923,959	16,070	2.5	2	37	61	13,732	0.962	3,181	620	5	79	1	*44.9	*0.31	United Kingdom
5,445,825	21,700	2.2	2	29	69	20,998	0.976	3,676	470	6.8	88	1	*30.6	*0.15	United States
7,929	2,560	-0.9	11	28	61	5,805	0.88	2,697	520	3.1	77	4	15	0.5	Uruguay
50,574	2,560	-2	6	46	48	5,908	0.824	2,620	700	4.2	56	12	4	0.2	Venezuela
19,942	300	2.1	70	20	10	1,000	0.464	2,250	1,000	...	42	12	2.1	...	Vietnam
6,432	640	3.4	24	25	51	1,560	0.232	2,300	5,639	6.1	21	61	33	5.4	Yemen
72,800	3,060	0.9	14	42	44	5,095	0.857	3,620	550	3.6	80	7	1.8	0.1	Yugoslavia
8,117	230	-1.5	30	32	38	380	0.262	2,061	12,940	0.9	24	28	23	6.6	Zaïre
3,391	420	2.9	14	47	39	767	0.315	2,054	7,150	5.5	20	27	49.6	14.1	Zambia
6,313	640	0.8	13	39	47	1,469	0.397	2,288	6,700	8.5	52	33	27.9	4.5	Zimbabwe

	Land Area thousand km²	Population 1991 millions
American Samoa	0.20	0.038
Andorra	0.49	0.050
Anguilla	0.096	0.007
Antigua & Barbuda	0.44	0.076
Armenia	30	3.3
Aruba	0.19	0.059
Ascension I.	0.090	0.002
Azerbaijan	87	7.1
Bahrain	0.70	0.53
Belize	22	0.19
Belorussia	208	10.3
Bermuda	0.050	0.058
Bhutan	47	1.6
Bosnia-Herzegovina	51	4.4
Brunei	5.3	0.27
Cape Verde Is.	4.0	0.38
Cayman Is.	0.26	0.030
Cocos Is.	0.014	0.001
Comoros	2.2	0.57
Cook Is.	0.24	0.020
Croatia	57	4.7
Czech Republic	79	10.4
Djibouti	23	0.42
Dominica	0.75	0.083
Equatorial Guinea	28	0.36
Eritrea	93.7	3.5
Estonia	45	1.6
Ethiopia	1,007.3	47.2
Falkland Is.	12	0.002
Faroe Is.	1.4	0.050
Fiji	18	0.78
French Guiana	88	0.10
French Polynesia	3.7	0.21

	Land Area thousand km²	Population 1991 millions
Georgia	70	5.5
Gibraltar	0.010	0.030
Greenland	342	0.056
Grenada	0.34	0.084
Guadeloupe	1.7	0.35
Guam	0.54	0.12
Kazakhstan	2,717	16.7
Kirghizia	199	4.4
Kiribati	0.73	0.066
Kuwait	17	2.2
Latvia	64	2.7
Liechtenstein	0.16	0.028
Lithuania	65	3.8
Macau	0.020	0.50
Macedonia	26	2.1
Maldives	0.30	0.22
Martinique	1.1	0.34
Mauritius	1.9	1.1
Micronesia	0.71	0.18
Moldavia	34	4.4
Monaco	0.002	0.030
Montenegro	14	0.63
Montserrat	0.100	0.012
Nauru	0.020	0.009
Netherlands Antilles	0.99	0.19
New Caledonia	18	0.17
Niue	0.26	0.003
Norfolk I.	0.036	0.002
Northern Marianas	0.48	0.020
Oman	212	1.6
Palau	0.46	0.015
Qatar	11	0.38
Reunion	2.5	0.61

	Land Area thousand km²	Population 1991 millions
Russia	17,068	147
St Christopher-Nevis	0.36	0.044
St Helena	0.122	0.007
St Lucia	0.61	0.15
St Pierre & Miquelon	0.24	0.006
St Vincent & the Grenadines	0.39	0.12
San Marino	0.060	0.020
São Tomé & Principe	0.96	0.12
Serbia	88	9.8
Seychelles	0.30	0.069
Slovenia	20	1.9
Slovak Republic	49	5.3
Solomon Is.	28	0.33
Svalbard	62	0.004
Tajikistan	143	5.3
Tokelau	0.010	0.002
Tonga	0.75	0.094
Tristan da Cunha	0.104	0.0003
Turkmenistan	488	3.6
Turks & Caicos Is.	0.43	0.010
Tuvalu	0.030	0.009
Ukraine	604	51.8
United Arab Emirates	83	1.6
Uzbekistan	447	20.3
Vanuatu	12	0.16
Vatican	0.0004	0.001
Virgin Is. [Br.]	0.150	0.010
Virgin Is. [US]	0.34	0.12
Wallis & Futuna	0.20	0.018
Western Sahara	266	0.18
Western Samoa	2.8	0.17

This list shows the principal cities with more than 500,000 inhabitants (for Brazil, China, India, Japan and USA only cities with more than 1 million are included). The figures are taken from the most recent census or estimate available, and as far as possible are the population of the metropolitan area, eg greater New York, Mexico or London. All the figures are in thousands. The top 20 world cities are indicated with their rank in brackets following the name.

Population in Thousands

Afghanistan
Kabul 1,127
Algeria
Algiers 1,722
Oran 664
Angola
Luanda 1,200
Argentina
Buenos Aires [8] 10,728
Cordoba 1,055
Rosario 1,016
Mendoza 668
La Plata 611
San Miguel de Tucuman 571
Armenia
Yerevan 1,199
Australia
Sydney 3,531
Melbourne 2,965
Brisbane 1,215
Perth 1,083
Adelaide 1,013
Austria
Vienna 1,483
Azerbaijan
Baku 1,757
Bangladesh
Dacca 4,770
Chittagong 1,840
Khulna 860
Rajshahi 430
Belgium
Brussels 970
Antwerp 500
Belorussia
Minsk 1,589
Gomel 500
Bolivia
La Paz 993
Brazil
São Paulo [3] 16,832
Rio de Janeiro [7] 11,141
Belo Horizonte 3,446
Recife 2,945
Pôrto Alegre 2,924
Salvador 2,362
Fortaleza 2,169
Çuritiba 1,926
Brasília 1,557
Nova Iguaçu 1,325
Belem 1,296
Santos 1,200
Bulgaria
Sofia 1,129
Burma
Rangoon 2,459
Mandalay 533
Cambodia
Phnom Penh 500
Cameroon
Douala 1,030
Yaoundé 654
Central African Rep.
Bangui 597
Chad
Ndjamena 512
Canada
Toronto 3,427
Montréal 2,921
Vancouver 1,381
Ottawa-Hull 819
Edmonton 785
Calgary 671
Winnipeg 623
Québec 603
Hamilton 557
Chile
Santiago 4,858
China
Shanghai [5] 12,320

Peking [10] 9,750
Tientsin 5,459
Shenyang 4,285
Wuhan 3,493
Canton 3,359
Chungking 2,832
Harbin 2,668
Chengdu 2,642
Sian 2,387
Zibo 2,329
Nanking 2,290
Nanchang 2,289
Lupanshui 2,247
Taiyuan 1,929
Changchun 1,908
Dalian 1,682
Zhaozhuang 1,612
Zhengzhou 1,610
Kunming 1,516
Jinan 1,464
Tangshan 1,410
Guiyang 1,403
Lanzhou 1,391
Linyi 1,385
Pingxiang 1,305
Qiqihar 1,301
Anshan 1,298
Qingdao 1,273
Xintao 1,272
Hangzhou 1,271
Fushun 1,270
Yangcheng 1,265
Yulin 1,255
Dongguan 1,230
Chao'an 1,227
Xiaogan 1,219
Fuzhou 1,205
Suining 1,195
Changsha 1,193
Shijiazhuang 1,187
Jilin 1,169
Xintai 1,167
Puyang 1,125
Baotou 1,119
Bozhou 1,112
Zhongshan 1,073
Luoyang 1,063
Laiwu 1,054
Leshan 1,039
Urumqi 1,038
Ningbo 1,033
Datong 1,020
Huainan 1,019
Heze 1,017
Handan 1,014
Linhai 1,012
Macheng 1,010
Changshu 1,004
Colombia
Bogotá 4,185
Medellin 1,506
Cali 1,397
Barranquilla 920
Cartagena 560
Congo
Brazzaville 596
Croatia
Zagreb 1,175
Cuba
Havana 2,059
Czech Republic
Prague 1,194
Denmark
Copenhagen 1,339
Dominican Rep.
Santo Domingo 1,313
Ecuador
Guayaquil 1,301
Quito 1,110
Egypt
Cairo [18] 6,325
Alexandria 2,893

El Giza 1,858
Shubra el Kheima 711
El Salvador
San Salvador 973
Ethiopia
Addis Ababa 1,686
Finland
Helsinki 987
France
Paris [13] 8,510
Lyons 1,170
Marseilles 1,080
Lille 935
Bordeaux 628
Toulouse 523
Georgia
Tbilisi 1,194
Germany
Berlin 3,301
Hamburg 1,594
Munich 1,189
Cologne 928
Essen 623
Frankfurt 619
Dortmund 584
Düsseldorf 563
Stuttgart 552
Leipzig 545
Bremen 533
Duisburg 525
Dresden 518
Hanover 500
Ghana
Accra 965
Greece
Athens 3,027
Thessalonika 872
Guatemala
Guatemala 2,000
Guinea
Conakry 705
Haiti
Port-au-Prince 1,144
Honduras
Tegucigalpa 605
Hong Kong
Kowloon 2,302
Hong Kong 1,176
Tsuen Wan 690
Hungary
Budapest 2,115
India
Calcutta [11] 9,194
Bombay [14] 8,243
Delhi 5,729
Madras 4,289
Bangalore 2,922
Ahmadabad 2,548
Hyderabad 2,546
Poona 1,686
Kanpur 1,639
Nagpur 1,302
Jaipur 1,015
Lucknow 1,008
Indonesia
Jakarta [17] 7,348
Surabaya 2,224
Medan 1,806
Bandung 1,567
Semarang 1,026
Palembang 787
Ujung Pandang 709
Malang 512
Iran
Tehran [19] 6,043
Mashhad 1,464
Esfahan 987
Tabriz 971
Shiraz 848
Ahvaz 580
Bakhtaran 561
Qom 543

Iraq
Baghdad 4,649
Basra 617
Mosul 571
Ireland
Dublin 921
Italy
Rome 2,817
Milan 1,464
Naples 1,203
Turin 1,012
Palermo 731
Genoa 712
Ivory Coast
Abidjan 1,850
Bouaké 640
Jamaica
Kingston 525
Japan
Tokyo [6] 11,829
Yokohama 2,993
Osaka 2,636
Nagoya 2,116
Sapporo 1,543
Kyoto 1,479
Kobe 1,411
Fukuoka 1,160
Kawasaki 1,089
Kitakyushu 1,056
Hiroshima 1,044
Jordan
Amman 1,160
Irbid 680
Kazakhstan
Alma Ata 1,108
Karaganda 614
Astrakhan 509
Kenya
Nairobi 1,429
Mombasa 500
Kirghizia
Bishkek 616
Korea, North
Pyongyang 2,639
Hamhung 775
Chongjin 754
Chinnampo 691
Sinuiju 500
Korea, South
Seoul [9] 10,513
Pusan 3,754
Taegu 2,206
Inchon 1,604
Kwangju 1,165
Taejon 866
Ulsan 551
Latvia
Riga 915
Lebanon
Beirut 702
Libya
Tripoli 980
Benghazi 650
Lithuania
Vilnius 582
Macedonia
Skopje 505
Madagascar
Antananarivo 703
Malaysia
Kuala Lumpur 1,103
Mali
Bamako 646
Mauritania
Nouakchott 500
Mexico
Mexico City [1] 18,748
Guadalajara 2,587
Monterrey 2,335
Puebla 1,218
León 947
Torreón 730

San Luis Potosi 602
Ciudad Juárez 596
Mérida 580
Culiacán Rosales 560
Mexicali 511
Moldavia
Kishinev 565
Mongolia
Ulan Bator 500
Morocco
Casablanca 2,158
Rabat-Salé 893
Fès 548
Mozambique
Maputo 1,070
Netherlands
Rotterdam 1,040
Amsterdam 1,038
The Hague 684
Utrecht 526
New Zealand
Auckland 851
Nicaragua
Managua 682
Nigeria
Lagos 1,097
Ibadan 1,060
Ogbomosho 527
Norway
Oslo 643
Pakistan
Karachi 5,208
Lahore 2,953
Faisalabad 1,104
Rawalpindi 795
Hyderabad 752
Multan 722
Gujranwala 659
Peshawar 556
Panama
Panama City 625
Paraguay
Asunción 708
Peru
Lima-Callao 4,605
Arequipa 592
Philippines
Manila 1,728
Quezon City 1,326
Cebu 552
Caloocan 524
Poland
Warsaw 1,671
Lodz 852
Krakow 744
Wroclaw 640
Poznan 586
Portugal
Lisbon 1,612
Oporto 1,315
Puerto Rico
San Juan 1,816
Romania
Bucharest 2,014
Russia
Moscow [12] 8,967
St Petersburg 5,020
Nizhniy Novgorod 1,438
Novosibirsk 1,436
Yekaterinburg 1,367
Samara 1,257
Chelyabinsk 1,179
Omsk 1,148
Kazan 1,094
Perm 1,091
Ufa 1,083
Rostov 1,020
Volgograd 999
Krasnoyarsk 912
Saratov 905
Voronezh 887
Vladivostok 648

Izhevsk 635
Yaroslavl 633
Togliatti 630
Irkutsk 626
Simbirsk 625
Krasnodar 620
Barnaul 602
Khabarovsk 601
Novokuznetsk 600
Orenburg 547
Penza 543
Tula 540
Kemerovo 520
Ryazan 515
Tomsk 502
Naberezhniye-Chelni 501
Saudi Arabia
Riyadh 2,000
Jedda 1,400
Mecca 618
Medina 500
Senegal
Dakar 1,382
Serbia
Belgrade 1,470
Singapore
Singapore 2,600
Somali Rep.
Mogadishu 1,000
South Africa
Cape Town 1,912
Johannesburg 1,762
East Rand 1,038
Durban 982
Pretoria 823
Port Elizabeth 652
West Rand 647
Vereeniging 540
Spain
Madrid 3,123
Barcelona 1,694
Valencia 739
Seville 668
Zaragoza 596
Malaga 595
Sri Lanka
Colombo 1,412
Sudan
Omdurman 600
Khartoum 510
Sweden
Stockholm 1,471
Gothenburg 720
Malmö 500
Switzerland
Zurich 839
Syria
Damascus 1,361
Aleppo 1,308
Taiwan
Taipei 2,680
Kaohsiung 1,343
Taichung 715
Tainan 657
Panchiao 506
Tajikistan
Dushanbe 595
Tanzania
Dar es Salaam 1,100
Thailand
Bangkok 5,609
Tunisia
Tunis 774
Turkey
Istanbul 5,495
Ankara 2,252
Izmir 1,490
Adana 776
Bursa 614
Uganda
Kampala 500

Ukraine
Kiev 2,587
Kharkhov 1,611
Dnepropetrovsk 1,179
Odessa 1,115
Donetsk 1,110
Zaporozhye 884
Lvov 790
Krivoy Rog 713
Mariupol 529
Lugansk 509
Nikolayev 503
United Kingdom
London [17] 6,378
Manchester 1,669
Birmingham 1,400
Liverpool 1,060
Glasgow 730
Newcastle 617
Uruguay
Montevideo 1,248
United States
New York [2] 18,120
Los Angeles [4] 13,770
Chicago [15] 8,181
San Francisco [20] 6,042
Philadelphia 5,963
Detroit 4,620
Dallas 3,766
Boston 3,736
Washington 3,734
Houston 3,642
Miami 3,001
Cleveland 2,769
Atlanta 2,737
Saint Louis 2,467
Seattle 2,421
Minneapolis-SP. 2,388
San Diego 2,370
Baltimore 2,343
Pittsburgh 2,284
Phoenix 2,030
Tampa 1,995
Denver 1,858
Cincinnati 1,729
Kansas City 1,575
Milwaukee 1,572
Portland 1,414
Sacramento 1,385
Norfolk 1,380
Columbus 1,344
San Antonio 1,323
New Orleans 1,307
Indianapolis 1,237
Buffalo 1,176
Providence 1,118
Charlotte 1,112
Hartford 1,108
Salt Lake City 1,065
Uzbekistan
Tashkent 2,073
Venezuela
Caracas 3,247
Maracaibo 1,295
Valencia 1,135
Maracay 857
Barquisimeto 718
Vietnam
Ho Chi Minh 3,900
Hanoi 3,100
Haiphong 1,279
Da-Nang 500
Yemen
San'a 500
Zaïre
Kinshasa 2,654
Lubumbashi 543
Zambia
Lusaka 900
Zimbabwe
Harare 681
Bulawayo 500

INDEX TO
WORLD MAPS

The index contains the names of all the principal places and features shown on the World Maps. Each name is followed by an additional entry in italics giving the country or region within which it is located. The alphabetical order of names composed of two or more words is governed primarily by the first word and then by the second. This is an example of the rule:

New South Wales □, *Australia*.. **34 G8**　33 0S　　146 0E
New York □, *U.S.A.* .... **43 D10**　42 40N　　76 0W
New York City, *U.S.A.* .... **43 E11**　40 45N　　74 0W
New Zealand ■, *Oceania*............. **35 J13**　40 0S　　176 0E
Newark, *U.S.A.* .... **43 F10**　39 42N　75 45W

Physical features composed of a proper name (Erie) and a description (Lake) are positioned alphabetically by the proper name. The description is positioned after the proper name and is usually abbreviated:

Erie, L., *N. Amer.* ....　**42 D7**　42 15N　81 0W

Where a description forms part of a settlement or administrative name, however, it is always written in full and put in its true alphabetical position.

Mount Isa, *Australia*...................... **34 E6**　20 42S　139 26E

Names beginning with M' and Mc are indexed as if they were spelt Mac. Names beginning St. are alphabetized under Saint, but Santa and San are all spelt in full and are alphabetized accordingly. If the same placename occurs two or more times in the index and all are in the same country, each is followed by the name of the administrative subdivision in which it is located. The names are placed in the alphabetical order of the subdivision. For example:

Columbus, Ga., *U.S.A.* .... **41 D10**　32 30N　84 58W
Columbus, Ind., *U.S.A.* .... **42 F5**　39 14N　85 55W
Columbus, Ohio, *U.S.A.* ....**42 F6**　39 57N　83 1W

The number in bold type which follows each name in the index refers to the number of the map page where that feature or place will be found. This is usually the largest scale at which the place or feature appears.

The letter and figure which are in bold type immediately after the page number give the grid square on the map page, within which the feature is situated. The letter represents the latitude and the figure the longitude. In some cases the feature itself may fall within the specified square, while the name is outside.

For a more precise location, the geographical co-ordinates which follow the letter-figure references give the latitude and the longitude of each place. The first set of figures represent the latitude, which is the distance north or south of the Equator measured as an angle at the centre of the Earth. The Equator is latitude 0°, the North Pole is 90°N, and the South Pole 90°S.

The second set of figures represent the longitude, which is the distance east or west of the prime meridian, which runs through Greenwich, England. Longitude is also measured as an angle at the centre of the Earth and is given east or west of the prime meridian, from 0° to 180° in either direction.

The unit of measurement for latitude and longitude is the degree, which is subdivided into 60 minutes. Each index entry states the position of a place in degrees and minutes, a space being left between the degrees and the minutes. The latitude is followed by N(orth) or S(outh) and the longitude by E(ast) or W(est).

Rivers are indexed to their mouths or confluences, and carry the symbol → after their names. A solid square ■ follows the name of a country, while an open square □ refers to a first order administrative area.

ABBREVIATIONS USED IN THE INDEX

Afghan. – Afghanistan	Conn. – Connecticut	Isla, Island, Isle(s)	Mo. – Missouri	Nebr. – Nebraska	Provincial	Sib. – Siberia
Ala. – Alabama	Cord. – Cordillera	Ill. – Illinois	Mont. – Montana	Neths. – Netherlands	Pt. – Point	St. – Saint, Sankt, Sint
Alta. – Alberta	Cr. – Creek	Ind. – Indiana	Mozam.– Mozambique	Nev. – Nevada	Pta. – Ponta, Punta	Str. – Strait, Stretto
Amer. – America(n)	D.C. – District of	Ind. Oc. – Indian Ocean	Mt.(s).– Mont, Monte,	Nfld. – Newfoundland	Pte. – Pointe	Switz. – Switzerland
Arch. – Archipelago	Columbia	Ivory C. – Ivory Coast	Monti, Montaña,	Nic. – Nicaragua	Qué. – Québec	Tas. – Tasmania
Ariz. – Arizona	Del. – Delaware	Kans. – Kansas	Mountain	O.F.S. – Orange Free	Queens. – Queensland	Tenn. – Tennessee
Ark. – Arkansas	Domin. – Dominica	Ky. – Kentucky	N. – Nord, Norte, North,	State	R. – Rio, River	Tex. – Texas
Atl. Oc. – Atlantic Ocean	Dom. Rep. – Dominican	L. – Lac, Lacul, Lago,	Northern	Okla. – Oklahoma	R.I. – Rhode Island	Trin. & Tob. – Trinidad
B. – Baie, Bahia, Bay,	Republic	Lagoa, Lake, Limni,	N.B. – New Brunswick	Ont. – Ontario	Ra.(s). – Range(s)	& Tobago
Bucht, Bugt	E. – East	Loch, Lough	N.C. – North Carolina	Oreg. – Oregon	Reg. – Region	U.A.E. – United Arab
B.C. – British Columbia	El Salv. – El Salvador	La. – Louisiana	N. Cal. – New Caledonia	P.E.I. – Prince Edward	Rep. – Republic	Emirates
Bangla. – Bangladesh	Eq. Guin. – Equatorial	Lux. – Luxembourg	N. Dak. – North Dakota	Island	Res. – Reserve,	U.K. – United Kingdom
C. – Cabo, Cap, Cape,	Guinea	Madag. – Madagascar	N.H. – New Hampshire	Pa. – Pennsylvania	Reservoir	U.S.A. – United States
Coast	Fla. – Florida	Man. – Manitoba	N.J. – New Jersey	Pac. Oc. – Pacific Ocean	S. – San, South	of America
C.A.R. – Central African	Falk. Is. – Falkland Is.	Mass.– Massachusetts	N. Mex. – New Mexico	Papua N.G. – Papua	Si. Arabia – Saudi Arabia	Va. – Virginia
Republic	G. – Golfe, Golfo, Gulf	Md. – Maryland	N.S. – Nova Scotia	New Guinea	S.C. – South Carolina	Vic. – Victoria
C. Prov. – Cape	Ga. – Georgia	Me. – Maine	N.S.W. – New South	Pen. – Peninsula,	S. Dak. – South Dakota	Vol. – Volcano
Province	Guinea–Biss. –	Medit. S. –	Wales	Peninsule	S. Leone – Sierra Leone	Vt. – Vermont
Calif. – California	Guinea–Bissau	Mediterranean Sea	N.W.T. – North West	Phil. – Philippines	Sa. – Serra, Sierra	W. – West
Cent. – Central	Hd. – Head	Mich. – Michigan	Territory	Pk. – Park, Peak	Sask. – Saskatchewan	W. Va. – West Virginia
Chan. – Channel	Hts. – Heights	Minn. – Minnesota	N.Y. – New York	Plat. – Plateau	Scot. – Scotland	Wash. – Washington
Colo. – Colorado	I.(s). – Ile, Ilha, Insel,	Miss. – Mississippi	N.Z. – New Zealand	Prov. – Province,	Sd. – Sound	Wis. – Wisconsin

106 INDEX TO WORLD MAPS

Aachen Balkhash, L.

A

Aachen, *Germany* **10 C2** 50 47N 6 4 E
Aalborg, *Denmark* **6 G9** 57 2N 9 54 E
Aalst, *Belgium* **8 B6** 50 56N 4 2 E
Aarau, *Switz.* **10 E3** 47 23N 8 4 E
Aare →, *Switz.* **10 E3** 47 33N 8 14 E
Aarhus, *Denmark* **6 G10** 56 8N 10 11 E
Abadan, *Iran* **24 B3** 30 22N 48 20 E
Abbeville, *France* **8 B4** 50 6N 1 49 E
Abéché, *Chad* **29 G11** 13 50N 20 35 E
Abeokuta, *Nigeria* **30 C2** 7 3N 3 19 E
Aberdeen, *U.K.* **7 D5** 57 9N 2 6W
Aberystwyth, *U.K.* **7 F4** 52 25N 4 6W
Abidjan, *Ivory C.* **28 H6** 5 26N 3 58W
Abitibi, L., *Canada* **42 A8** 48 40N 79 40W
Abkhaz Republic □, *Georgia* **15 F7** 43 0N 41 0 E
Abohar, *India* **23 D5** 30 10N 74 10 E
Abu Dhabi, *U.A.E.* **24 C4** 24 28N 54 22 E
Abuja, *Nigeria* **30 C3** 9 16N 7 2 E
Acapulco, *Mexico* **44 D5** 16 51N 99 56W
Accomac, *U.S.A.* **43 G10** 37 43N 75 40W
Accra, *Ghana* **30 C1** 5 35N 0 6W
Achill I., *Ireland* **7 F1** 53 58N 10 5W
Acklins I., *Bahamas* **45 C10** 22 30N 74 0W
Aconcagua, *Argentina* **47 F3** 32 39S 70 0W
Acre, *Israel* **29 N21** 32 55N 35 4 E
Acre □, *Brazil* **46 C2** 9 1S 71 0W
Adamawa Highlands, *Cameroon* **28 H9** 7 20N 12 20 E
Adana, *Turkey* **15 G6** 37 0N 35 16 E
Adapazarı, *Turkey* **15 F5** 40 48N 30 25 E
Adare, C., *Antarctica* **48 C19** 71 0S 171 0 E
Addis Ababa, *Ethiopia* **29 H14** 9 2N 38 42 E
Adelaide, *Australia* **34 G6** 34 52S 138 30 E
Adelaide, *S. Africa* **31 C4** 32 42S 26 20 E
Adelaide I., *Antarctica* **48 C23** 67 15S 68 30W
Adélie Land, *Antarctica* **48 C18** 68 0S 140 0 E
Aden, *Yemen* **24 D3** 12 45N 45 0 E
Aden, G. of, *Asia* **24 D3** 12 30N 47 30 E
Adirondack Mts., *U.S.A.* **43 D10** 44 0N 74 15W
Admiralty Is., *Papua N. G.* **36 H6** 2 0S 147 0 E
Ado Ekiti, *Nigeria* **30 C3** 7 38N 5 12 E
Adoni, *India* **25 D6** 15 33N 77 18 E
Adour →, *France* **9 F3** 43 32N 1 32W
Adrar, *Algeria* **28 D6** 27 51N 0 11W
Adrian, *U.S.A.* **42 E5** 41 55N 84 5W
Adriatic Sea, *Europe* **12 C6** 43 0N 16 0 E
Adzhar Republic □, *Georgia* **15 F7** 41 30N 42 0 E
Ægean Sea, *Europe* **13 E11** 38 30N 25 0 E
Afghanistan ■, *Asia* **24 B5** 33 0N 65 0 E
'Afif, *Si. Arabia* **24 C3** 23 53N 42 56 E
Agadès, *Niger* **30 A3** 16 58N 7 59 E
Agadir, *Morocco* **28 C5** 30 28N 9 55W
Agartala, *India* **23 H13** 23 50N 91 23 E
Agen, *France* **9 E4** 44 12N 0 38 E
Agra, *India* **23 F6** 27 17N 77 58 E
Agrigento, *Italy* **12 F5** 37 19N 13 33 E
Aguascalientes, *Mexico* **44 C4** 21 53N 102 12W
Agulhas, C., *S. Africa* **31 C3** 34 52S 20 0 E
Ahmadabad, *India* **23 H4** 23 0N 72 40 E
Ahmadnagar, *India* **25 D6** 19 7N 74 46 E
Ahmadpur, *Pakistan* **23 E3** 29 12N 71 10 E
Ahvaz, *Iran* **24 B3** 31 20N 48 40 E
Ahvenanmaa Is., *Finland* **6 F11** 60 15N 20 0 E
Aigoual, Mt., *France* **9 E5** 44 8N 3 35 E
Ain →, *France* **9 E6** 45 45N 5 11 E
Aïr, *Niger* **28 F8** 18 30N 8 0 E
Aisne →, *France* **8 C5** 49 26N 2 50 E
Aix-en-Provence, *France* **9 F6** 43 32N 5 27 E
Aix-les-Bains, *France* **9 E6** 45 41N 5 53 E
Ajaccio, *France* **9 G8** 41 55N 8 40 E
Ajanta Ra., *India* **23 J5** 20 28N 75 50 E
Ajmer, *India* **23 F5** 26 28N 74 37 E
Akashi, *Japan* **19 B4** 34 45N 134 58 E
Akita, *Japan* **19 G12** 39 45N 140 7 E
Akola, *India* **23 J6** 20 42N 77 2 E
Akranes, *Iceland* **6 B2** 64 19N 22 5W
Akron, *U.S.A.* **42 E7** 41 7N 81 31W
Aksai Chih, *India* **23 B7** 35 15N 79 55 E
Aktyubinsk, *Kazakhstan* **15 D10** 50 17N 57 10 E
Akure, *Nigeria* **30 C3** 7 15N 5 5 E
Akureyri, *Iceland* **6 B4** 65 40N 18 6W
Akyab, *Burma* **25 C8** 20 18N 92 45 E
Al Ḥudaydah, *Yemen* **24 D3** 14 50N 43 0 E
Al Hufūf, *Si. Arabia* **24 C3** 25 25N 49 45 E
Al Jawf, *Si. Arabia* **24 C2** 29 55N 39 40 E
Al Kut, *Iraq* **24 B3** 32 30N 46 0 E
Al Qatif, *Si. Arabia* **24 C3** 26 35N 50 0 E
Al 'Ula, *Si. Arabia* **24 C2** 26 35N 38 0 E
Alabama □, *U.S.A.* **41 D9** 33 0N 87 0W
Aland Is., *Sweden* **6 G11** 60 0N 19 30 E
Alaska □, *U.S.A.* **38 B5** 65 0N 150 0W
Alaska, G. of, *Pac. Oc.* **38 C5** 58 0N 145 0W
Alaska Pen., *U.S.A.* **38 C4** 56 0N 160 0W
Alaska Range, *U.S.A.* **38 B4** 62 50N 151 0W
Alba Iulia, *Romania* **13 A10** 46 8N 23 39 E
Albacete, *Spain* **11 C5** 39 0N 1 50W
Albania ■, *Europe* **13 D9** 41 0N 20 0 E
Albany, *Australia* **34 H2** 35 1S 117 58 E
Albany, *Ga., U.S.A.* **41 D10** 31 40N 84 10W
Albany, *N.Y., U.S.A.* **43 D11** 42 35N 73 47W
Albany →, *Canada* **39 C11** 52 17N 81 31W
Alberta □, *Canada* **38 C8** 54 40N 115 0W
Albertville, *France* **9 E7** 45 40N 6 22 E
Albi, *France* **9 F5** 43 56N 2 9 E
Albion, *U.S.A.* **42 D5** 42 15N 84 45W
Albuquerque, *U.S.A.* **40 C5** 35 5N 106 47W
Albury, *Australia* **34 H8** 36 3S 146 56 E
Alcalá de Henares, *Spain* **11 B4** 40 28N 3 22W
Aldabra Is., *Seychelles* **27 G8** 9 22S 46 28 E
Aldan →, *Russia* **18 C14** 63 28N 129 35 E
Alderney, *Chan. Is.* **8 C2** 49 42N 2 12W
Aleksandrovsk-Sakhalinskiy, *Russia* **18 D16** 50 50N 142 20 E
Alençon, *France* **8 C4** 48 27N 0 4 E
Aleppo, *Syria* **24 B2** 36 10N 37 15 E
Alès, *France* **9 E6** 44 9N 4 5 E
Alessandria, *Italy* **12 B3** 44 54N 8 37 E
Ålesund, *Norway* **6 F9** 62 28N 6 12 E
Aleutian Is., *Pac. Oc.* **36 B10** 52 0N 175 0W
Alexander Arch., *U.S.A.* **38 C6** 57 0N 135 0W
Alexander I., *Antarctica* **48 C23** 69 0S 70 0W
Alexandria, *Egypt* **29 C13** 31 0N 30 0 E
Alexandria, *La., U.S.A.* **41 D8** 31 20N 92 30W
Alexandria, *Va., U.S.A.* **42 F9** 38 47N 77 1W
Algarve, *Portugal* **11 D1** 36 58N 8 20W
Algeciras, *Spain* **11 D3** 36 9N 5 28W
Algeria ■, *Africa* **28 D7** 28 30N 2 0 E
Algiers, *Algeria* **28 B7** 36 42N 3 8 E
Alicante, *Spain* **11 C5** 38 23N 0 30W
Alice Springs, *Australia* **34 E5** 23 40S 133 50 E
Aligarh, *India* **23 F7** 27 55N 78 10 E
Alipur Duar, *India* **23 F12** 26 30N 89 35 E
Aliquippa, *U.S.A.* **42 E7** 40 38N 80 18W
Aliwal North, *S. Africa* **31 C4** 30 45S 26 45 E
Alkmaar, *Neths.* **8 A6** 52 37N 4 45 E
Allahabad, *India* **23 G8** 25 25N 81 58 E
Allegan, *U.S.A.* **42 D5** 42 32N 85 52W
Allegheny →, *U.S.A.* **42 E8** 40 27N 80 0W
Allegheny Plateau, *U.S.A.* **42 G7** 38 0N 80 0W
Allentown, *U.S.A.* **43 E10** 40 36N 75 30W
Alleppey, *India* **25 E6** 9 30N 76 28 E
Allier →, *France* **8 D5** 46 57N 3 4 E
Alma, *U.S.A.* **42 D5** 43 25N 84 40W
Alma Ata, *Kazakhstan* **18 E9** 43 15N 76 57 E
Almelo, *Neths.* **8 A7** 52 22N 6 42 E
Almería, *Spain* **11 D4** 36 52N 2 27W
Alor, *Indonesia* **22 D4** 8 15S 124 30 E
Alpena, *U.S.A.* **42 C6** 45 6N 83 24W
Alps, *Europe* **4 F7** 46 30N 9 30 E
Alsace, *France* **8 C7** 48 15N 7 25 E
Altai, *Mongolia* **20 B4** 46 40N 92 45 E
Altay, *China* **20 B3** 47 48N 88 10 E
Altoona, *U.S.A.* **42 E8** 40 32N 78 24W
Altun Shan, *China* **20 C3** 38 30N 88 0 E
Alwar, *India* **23 F6** 27 38N 76 34 E
Amadjuak L., *Canada* **39 B12** 65 0N 71 8W
Amagasaki, *Japan* **19 B4** 34 42N 135 20 E
Amarillo, *U.S.A.* **40 C6** 35 14N 101 46W
Amazon →, *S. Amer.* **46 C5** 0 5S 50 0W
Ambala, *India* **23 D6** 30 23N 76 56 E
Ambert, *France* **9 E5** 45 33N 3 44 E
Ambikapur, *India* **23 H9** 23 15N 83 15 E
Ambon, *Indonesia* **22 D4** 3 35S 128 20 E
American Highland, *Antarctica* **48 C16** 73 0S 75 0 E
American Samoa ■, *Pac. Oc.* **35 C17** 14 20S 170 40W
Amersfoort, *Neths.* **8 A6** 52 9N 5 23 E
Amiens, *France* **8 C5** 49 54N 2 16 E
Amman, *Jordan* **24 B2** 31 57N 35 52 E
Amos, *Canada* **42 A8** 48 35N 78 5W
Amravati, *India* **23 J6** 20 55N 77 45 E
Amreli, *India* **23 J3** 21 35N 71 17 E
Amritsar, *India* **23 D5** 31 35N 74 57 E
Amroha, *India* **23 E7** 28 53N 78 30 E
Amsterdam, *Neths.* **8 A6** 52 23N 4 54 E
Amsterdam, *U.S.A.* **43 D10** 42 58N 74 10W
Amu Darya →, *Uzbekistan* **18 E7** 43 40N 59 0 E
Amundsen Gulf, *Canada* **38 A7** 71 0N 124 0W
Amundsen Sea, *Antarctica* **48 C22** 72 0S 115 0W
Amur →, *Russia* **18 D16** 52 56N 141 10 E
An Najaf, *Iraq* **24 B3** 32 3N 44 15 E
An Nasiriyah, *Iraq* **24 B3** 31 0N 46 15 E
An Nhon, *Vietnam* **22 B2** 13 55N 109 7 E
Anadyr, *Russia* **18 C19** 64 35N 177 20 E
Anadyr, G. of, *Russia* **18 C20** 64 0N 180 0 E
Anaheim, *U.S.A.* **40 D3** 33 50N 118 0W
Anambas Is., *Indonesia* **22 C2** 3 20N 106 30 E
Anantnag, *India* **23 C5** 33 45N 75 10 E
Anar, *Iran* **24 B4** 30 55N 55 13 E
Anatolia, *Turkey* **15 G5** 39 0N 30 0 E
Ancenis, *France* **8 D3** 47 21N 1 10W
Anchorage, *U.S.A.* **38 B5** 61 10N 149 50W
Ancona, *Italy* **12 C5** 43 37N 13 30 E
Anda, *China* **21 B7** 46 24N 125 19 E
Andalusia □, *Spain* **11 D3** 37 35N 5 0W
Andaman Is., *Ind. Oc.* **25 D8** 12 30N 92 30 E
Anderson, *U.S.A.* **42 E5** 40 5N 85 40W
Andes, *S. Amer.* **46 E3** 20 0S 68 0W
Andhra Pradesh □, *India* **25 D6** 18 0N 79 0 E
Andorra ■, *Europe* **11 A6** 42 30N 1 30 E
Andreanof Is., *U.S.A.* **38 C2** 52 0N 178 0W
Andria, *Italy* **12 D7** 41 13N 16 17 E
Andros I., *Bahamas* **45 C9** 24 30N 78 0W
Angara →, *Russia* **18 D11** 58 5N 94 20 E
Ånge, *Sweden* **6 F11** 62 31N 15 35 E
Angel Falls, *Venezuela* **46 B3** 5 57N 62 30W
Angerman →, *Sweden* **6 F11** 62 40N 18 0 E
Angers, *France* **8 D3** 47 30N 0 35W
Anglesey, *U.K.* **7 F4** 53 17N 4 20W
Angola ■, *Africa* **33 G3** 12 0S 18 0 E
Angoulême, *France* **9 E4** 45 39N 0 10 E
Angoumois, *France* **9 E4** 45 50N 0 25 E
Anguilla, *W. Indies* **44 J18** 18 14N 63 5W
Anhui □, *China* **21 C6** 32 0N 117 0 E
Anjou, *France* **8 D3** 47 20N 0 15W
Ankara, *Turkey* **15 G5** 39 57N 32 54 E
Ann, C., *U.S.A.* **43 D12** 42 39N 70 37W
Ann Arbor, *U.S.A.* **42 D6** 42 17N 83 45W
Annaba, *Algeria* **28 B8** 36 50N 7 46 E
Annapolis, *U.S.A.* **42 F9** 39 0N 76 30W
Annecy, *France* **9 E7** 45 55N 6 8 E
Annemasse, *France* **9 D7** 46 12N 6 16 E
Annobón, *Atl. Oc.* **28 K8** 1 25S 5 36 E
Anshan, *China* **21 B7** 41 5N 122 58 E
Anshun, *China* **20 D5** 26 18N 105 57 E
Antalya, *Turkey* **15 G5** 36 52N 30 45 E
Antananarivo, *Madag.* **33 H9** 18 55S 47 31 E
Antarctic Pen., *Antarctica* **48 C24** 67 0S 60 0W
Antarctica **48 C24** 90 0S 0 0 E
Antibes, *France* **9 F7** 43 34N 7 6 E
Anticosti I., *Canada* **43 A16** 49 30N 63 0W
Antigua & Barbuda ■, *W. Indies* **44 K20** 17 20N 61 48W
Antofagasta, *Chile* **47 E2** 23 50S 70 30W
Antrim, *U.K.* **7 E3** 54 43N 6 13W
Antrim, Mts. of, *U.K.* **7 E3** 54 57N 6 8W
Antsiranana, *Madag.* **33 G9** 12 25S 49 20 E
Antwerp, *Belgium* **8 B6** 51 13N 4 25 E
Anyang, *China* **21 C6** 36 5N 114 21 E
Aomori, *Japan* **19 F12** 40 45N 140 45 E
Aparri, *Phil.* **22 B4** 18 22N 121 38 E
Apeldoorn, *Neths.* **8 A6** 52 13N 5 57 E
Apennines, *Italy* **12 C4** 44 0N 10 0 E
Apia, *W. Samoa* **35 C16** 13 50S 171 50W
Appalachian Mts., *U.S.A.* **42 G7** 38 0N 80 0W
Appleton, *U.S.A.* **42 C3** 44 17N 88 25W
Ar Ramadi, *Iraq* **24 B3** 33 25N 43 20 E
Arabia, *Asia* **16 G8** 25 0N 45 0 E
Arabian Gulf = Gulf, The, *Asia* **24 C4** 27 0N 50 0 E
Arabian Sea, *Ind. Oc.* **24 D5** 16 0N 65 0 E
Aracaju, *Brazil* **46 D6** 10 55S 37 4W
Arad, *Romania* **10 E9** 46 10N 21 20 E
Arafura Sea, *E. Indies* **22 D5** 9 0S 135 0 E
Aragón □, *Spain* **11 B5** 41 25N 0 40W
Araguaia →, *Brazil* **46 C5** 5 21S 48 41W
Arakan Yoma, *Burma* **25 C8** 20 0N 94 40 E
Aral Sea, *Asia* **18 E8** 44 30N 60 0 E
Aralsk, *Kazakhstan* **18 E8** 46 50N 61 20 E
Aran I., *Ireland* **7 E2** 55 0N 8 30W
Araq, *Iran* **24 B3** 34 0N 49 40 E
Arbroath, *U.K.* **7 D5** 56 34N 2 35W
Arcachon, *France* **9 E3** 44 40N 1 10W
Archangel = Arkhangelsk, *Russia* **14 B7** 64 40N 41 0 E
Arctic Ocean, *Arctic* **48 A1** 78 0N 160 0W
Arctic Red River, *Canada* **38 B6** 67 15N 134 0W
Ardebil, *Iran* **24 B3** 38 15N 48 18 E
Ardennes, *Belgium* **8 C6** 49 50N 5 5 E
Arendal, *Norway* **6 G9** 58 28N 8 46 E
Arequipa, *Peru* **46 D2** 16 20S 71 30W
Argentan, *France* **8 C3** 48 45N 0 1W
Argentina ■, *S. Amer.* **47 F3** 35 0S 66 0W
Arima, *Trin. & Tob.* **44 S20** 10 38N 61 17W
Arizona □, *U.S.A.* **40 D4** 34 20N 111 30W
Arkansas □, *U.S.A.* **41 D8** 35 0N 92 30W
Arkansas →, *U.S.A.* **41 D8** 33 48N 91 4W
Arkhangelsk, *Russia* **14 B7** 64 40N 41 0 E
Arklow, *Ireland* **7 F3** 52 48N 6 10W
Arlberg Pass, *Austria* **10 E4** 47 9N 10 12 E
Arles, *France* **9 F6** 43 41N 4 40 E
Arlington, *U.S.A.* **42 F9** 38 52N 77 5W
Arlon, *Belgium* **8 C6** 49 42N 5 49 E
Armagh, *U.K.* **7 E3** 54 22N 6 40W
Armançon →, *France* **8 D5** 47 59N 3 30 E
Armenia ■, *Asia* **15 F7** 40 20N 45 0 E
Arnhem, *Neths.* **8 B6** 51 58N 5 55 E
Arnhem Land, *Australia* **34 C5** 13 10S 134 30 E
Arnprior, *Canada* **42 C9** 45 26N 76 21W
Arrah, *India* **23 G10** 25 35N 84 32 E
Arran, *U.K.* **7 E4** 55 34N 5 12W
Arras, *France* **8 B5** 50 17N 2 46 E
Artois, *France* **8 B5** 50 20N 2 30 E
Aru Is., *Indonesia* **22 D5** 6 0S 134 30 E
Arunachal Pradesh □, *India* **25 C8** 28 0N 95 0 E
Arusha, *Tanzania* **32 E7** 3 20S 36 40 E
As Salt, *Jordan* **29 P22** 32 2N 35 43 E
Asab, *Namibia* **31 B2** 25 30S 18 0 E
Asahigawa, *Japan* **19 F12** 43 46N 142 22 E
Asansol, *India* **23 H11** 23 40N 87 1 E
Asbestos, *Canada* **43 C12** 45 47N 71 58W
Asbury Park, *U.S.A.* **43 E10** 40 15N 74 1W
Ascension I., *Atl. Oc.* **2 E9** 8 0S 14 15W
Ashford, *U.K.* **7 G7** 51 8N 0 53 E
Ashkhabad, *Turkmenistan* **18 F7** 38 0N 57 50 E
Ashland, *Ky., U.S.A.* **42 F6** 38 25N 82 40W
Ashland, *Ohio, U.S.A.* **42 E6** 40 52N 82 20W
Ashqelon, *Israel* **29 Q20** 31 42N 34 35 E
Ashtabula, *U.S.A.* **42 E7** 41 52N 80 50W
Asifabad, *India* **23 K7** 19 20N 79 24 E
Asir □, *Si. Arabia* **29 F15** 18 40N 42 30 E
Asir, Ras, *Somali Rep.* **29 G17** 11 55N 51 10 E
Asmara, *Eritrea* **29 F14** 15 19N 38 55 E
Assam □, *India* **23 F13** 26 0N 93 0 E
Assen, *Neths.* **8 A7** 53 0N 6 35 E
Asti, *Italy* **12 B3** 44 54N 8 11 E
Astrakhan, *Russia* **15 E8** 46 25N 48 5 E
Asturias □, *Spain* **11 A2** 43 15N 6 0W
Asunción, *Paraguay* **47 E4** 25 10S 57 30W
Aswân, *Egypt* **29 E13** 24 4N 32 57 E
Atacama Desert, *Chile* **47 E3** 24 0S 69 20W
Atbara →, *Sudan* **29 F13** 17 40N 33 56 E
Athabasca, L., *Canada* **38 C9** 59 15N 109 15W
Athens, *Greece* **13 F10** 37 58N 23 46 E
Athens, *U.S.A.* **42 F6** 39 25N 82 6W
Athlone, *Ireland* **7 F3** 53 26N 7 57W
Atikokan, *Canada* **42 A2** 48 45N 91 37W
Atlanta, *U.S.A.* **41 D10** 33 50N 84 24W
Atlantic City, *U.S.A.* **43 F10** 39 25N 74 25W
Atlantic Ocean **2 E9** 0 0 20 0W
Au Sable →, *U.S.A.* **42 C6** 44 25N 83 20W
Aube →, *France* **8 C5** 48 34N 3 43 E
Auburn, *Ind., U.S.A.* **42 E5** 41 20N 85 5W
Auburn, *N.Y., U.S.A.* **42 D9** 42 57N 76 39W
Aubusson, *France* **9 E5** 45 57N 2 11 E
Auch, *France* **9 F4** 43 39N 0 36 E
Auckland, *N.Z.* **35 H13** 36 52S 174 46 E
Aude →, *France* **9 F5** 43 13N 3 14 E
Augrabies Falls, *S. Africa* **31 B3** 28 35S 20 20 E
Augsburg, *Germany* **10 D4** 48 22N 10 54 E
Augusta, *Ga., U.S.A.* **41 D10** 33 29N 81 59W
Augusta, *Maine, U.S.A.* **43 C13** 44 20N 69 46W
Aunis, *France* **9 D3** 46 5N 0 50W
Aurangabad, *Bihar, India* **23 G10** 24 45N 84 18 E
Aurangabad, *Maharashtra, India* **23 K5** 19 50N 75 23 E
Aurillac, *France* **9 E5** 44 55N 2 26 E
Aurora, *U.S.A.* **42 E3** 41 42N 88 12W
Austin, *U.S.A.* **40 D7** 30 20N 97 45W
Australia ■, *Oceania* **34 E5** 23 0S 135 0 E
Australian Alps, *Australia* **34 H8** 36 30S 148 30 E
Australian Capital Territory □, *Australia* **34 H8** 35 30S 149 0 E
Austria ■, *Europe* **10 E6** 47 0N 14 0 E
Autun, *France* **8 D6** 46 58N 4 17 E
Auvergne, *France* **9 E5** 45 20N 3 15 E
Auxerre, *France* **8 D5** 47 48N 3 32 E
Avallon, *France* **8 D5** 47 30N 3 53 E
Avellino, *Italy* **12 D6** 40 54N 14 46 E
Avesnes-sur-Helpe, *France* **8 B5** 50 8N 3 55 E
Aveyron →, *France* **9 E4** 44 5N 1 16 E
Avignon, *France* **9 F6** 43 57N 4 50 E
Ávila, *Spain* **11 B3** 40 39N 4 43W
Avranches, *France* **8 C3** 48 40N 1 20W
Ayers Rock, *Australia* **34 F5** 25 23S 131 5 E
Aylesbury, *U.K.* **7 G6** 51 48N 0 49W
Ayr, *U.K.* **7 E4** 55 28N 4 37W
Azamgarh, *India* **23 F9** 26 5N 83 13 E
Azerbaijan ■, *Asia* **15 F8** 40 20N 48 0 E
Azores, *Atl. Oc.* **28 B1** 38 44N 29 0W
Azov, Sea of, *Europe* **15 E6** 46 0N 36 30 E
Azuero, Pen., *Panama* **45 F8** 7 30N 80 30W

B

Babol, *Iran* **24 B4** 36 40N 52 50 E
Babuyan Chan., *Phil.* **22 B4** 18 40N 121 30 E
Bacolod, *Phil.* **22 B4** 10 40N 122 57 E
Bad Axe, *U.S.A.* **42 D6** 43 48N 82 59W
Badajoz, *Spain* **11 C2** 38 50N 6 59W
Badalona, *Spain* **11 B7** 41 26N 2 15 E
Baden-Württemberg □, *Germany* **10 D3** 48 40N 9 0 E
Baffin B., *Canada* **48 A10** 72 0N 64 0W
Baffin I., *Canada* **39 B12** 68 0N 75 0W
Baghdad, *Iraq* **24 B3** 33 20N 44 30 E
Bagnères-de-Bigorre, *France* **9 F4** 43 5N 0 9 E
Baguio, *Phil.* **22 B4** 16 26N 120 34 E
Bahamas ■, *N. Amer.* **45 C10** 24 0N 75 0W
Bahawalpur, *Pakistan* **23 E3** 29 24N 71 40 E
Bahía = Salvador, *Brazil* **46 D6** 13 0S 38 30W
Bahía □, *Brazil* **46 D5** 12 0S 42 0W
Bahía Blanca, *Argentina* **47 F3** 38 35S 62 13W
Bahraich, *India* **23 F8** 27 38N 81 37 E
Bahrain ■, *Asia* **24 C4** 26 0N 50 35 E
Baie-St-Paul, *Canada* **43 B12** 47 28N 70 32W
Baikal, L., *Russia* **18 D12** 53 0N 108 0 E
Baile Atha Cliath = Dublin, *Ireland* **7 F3** 53 20N 6 18W
Baja California = Lower California, *Mexico* **44 B2** 31 10N 115 12W
Bakersfield, *U.S.A.* **40 C3** 35 25N 119 0W
Bakhtaran, *Iran* **24 B3** 34 23N 47 0 E
Bakony Forest, *Hungary* **10 E7** 47 10N 17 30 E
Baku, *Azerbaijan* **15 F8** 40 25N 49 45 E
Balabac Str., *E. Indies* **22 C3** 7 53N 117 5 E
Balaghat, *India* **23 J8** 21 49N 80 12 E
Balasore, *India* **23 J11** 21 35N 87 3 E
Balaton, L., *Hungary* **10 E7** 46 50N 17 40 E
Balboa, *Panama* **44 H14** 9 0N 79 30W
Baldwin, *U.S.A.* **42 D5** 43 54N 85 53W
Balearic Is., *Spain* **11 C7** 39 30N 3 0 E
Bali, *Indonesia* **22 D3** 8 20S 115 0 E
Balikeşir, *Turkey* **15 G4** 39 35N 27 58 E
Balikpapan, *Indonesia* **22 D3** 1 10S 116 55 E
Balkan Mts., *Bulgaria* **13 C10** 43 15N 23 0 E
Balkan Peninsula, *Europe* **4 G10** 42 0N 23 0 E
Balkhash, *Kazakhstan* **18 E9** 46 50N 74 50 E
Balkhash, L., *Kazakhstan* **18 E9** 46 0N 74 50 E

Bruges Colorado Springs

Elgin

Great Barrier Reef

Great Basin

112 INDEX TO WORLD MAPS

Istres — Kuala Terengganu

Istres, *France* . . . . **9 F6** 43 31N 4 59 E
Itaipu Dam, *Brazil* **47 E4** 25 30S 54 30W
Italy ■, *Europe* . . . . . . **12 D5** 42 0N 13 0 E
Ithaca, *U.S.A.* **42 D9** 42 25N 76 30W
Ivanovo, *Russia* . . . . . . **14 C7** 57 5N 41 0 E
Ivory Coast ■, *Africa* . . **28 H6** 7 30N 5 0W
Ivugivik, *Canada* **39 B12** 62 24N 77 55W
Iwaki, *Japan* . . . . **19 G12** 37 3N 140 55 E
Iwo, *Nigeria* . . . . **30 C2** 7 39N 4 9 E
Ixopo, *S. Africa* . . . . . . **31 C5** 30 11S 30 5 E
Izhevsk, *Russia* . . . . . . **14 C9** 56 51N 53 14 E
İzmir, *Turkey* . . . . **15 G4** 38 25N 27 8 E

J

Jabalpur, *India* . . . . **23 H7** 23 9N 79 58 E
Jackson, *Ky., U.S.A.* . . **42 G6** 37 35N 83 22W
Jackson, *Mich., U.S.A.* **42 D5** 42 18N 84 25W
Jackson, *Miss., U.S.A.* **41 D8** 32 20N 90 10W
Jacksonville, *U.S.A.* . . . **41 D10** 30 15N 81 38W
Jacobabad, *Pakistan* . . **23 E2** 28 20N 68 29 E
Jaén, *Spain* **11 D4** 37 44N 3 43W
Jaffna, *Sri Lanka* . . . . . **25 E7** 9 45N 80 2 E
Jagersfontein, *S. Africa* **31 B4** 29 44S 25 27 E
Jahrom, *Iran* . . . . **24 C4** 28 30N 53 31 E
Jaipur, *India* . . . . **23 F5** 27 0N 75 50 E
Jakarta, *Indonesia* . . . . **22 D2** 6 9S 106 49 E
Jalalabad, *Afghan.* . . . . **23 B3** 34 30N 70 29 E
Jalgaon, *India* . . . . **23 J5** 21 0N 75 42 E
Jalna, *India* . . . . **23 K5** 19 48N 75 38 E
Jalpaiguri, *India* . . . . . **23 F12** 26 32N 88 46 E
Jamaica ■, *W. Indies* . **44 J16** 18 10N 77 30W
Jamalpur, *Bangla.* . . . . **23 G12** 24 52N 89 56 E
Jamalpur, *India* . . . . . . **23 G11** 25 18N 86 28 E
Jambi, *Indonesia* . . . . . **22 D2** 1 38S 103 30 E
James B., *Canada* **39 C11** 51 30N 80 0W
Jamestown, *Ky., U.S.A.* **42 G5** 37 0N 85 5W
Jamestown, *N.Y., U.S.A.* **42 D8** 42 5N 79 18W
Jammu, *India* . . . . **23 C5** 32 43N 74 54 E
Jammu & Kashmir □, *India* . . . . **23 B6** 34 25N 77 0 E
Jamnagar, *India* . . . . . . **23 H3** 22 30N 70 6 E
Jamshedpur, *India* . . . . **23 H11** 22 44N 86 12 E
Jan Mayen, *Arctic* **48 A8** 71 0N 9 0W
Jaora, *India* . . . . **23 H5** 23 40N 75 10 E
Japan ■, *Asia* . . . . **19 B5** 36 0N 136 0 E
Japan, Sea of, *Asia* . . . **19 G11** 40 0N 135 0 E
Japurá →, *Brazil* **46 C3** 3 8S 65 46W
Jask, *Iran* . . . . **24 C4** 25 38N 57 45 E
Jaunpur, *India* . . . . **23 G9** 25 46N 82 44 E
Java, *Indonesia* . . . . . . **22 D3** 7 0S 110 0 E
Java Sea, *Indonesia* . . . **22 D2** 4 35S 107 15 E
Jedburgh, *U.K.* **7 E5** 55 28N 2 33W
Jedda = Jidda, *Si. Arabia* . . . . **24 C2** 21 29N 39 10 E
Jeffersonville, *U.S.A.* . . **42 F5** 38 20N 85 42W
Jelenia Góra, *Poland* . . **10 C6** 50 50N 15 45 E
Jena, *Germany* . . . . . . **10 C4** 50 56N 11 33 E
Jerez de la Frontera, *Spain* **11 D2** 36 41N 6 7W
Jersey, *Chan. Is.* **8 C2** 49 13N 2 7W
Jersey City, *U.S.A.* . . . **43 E10** 40 41N 74 8W
Jerusalem, *Israel* . . . . . **29 Q21** 31 47N 35 10 E
Jessore, *Bangla.* . . . . . **23 H12** 23 10N 89 10 E
Jhang Maghiana, *Pakistan* . . . . **23 D4** 31 15N 72 22 E
Jhansi, *India* . . . . **23 G7** 25 30N 78 36 E
Jhelum, *Pakistan* . . . . . **23 C4** 33 0N 73 45 E
Jhelum →, *Pakistan* . **23 D4** 31 20N 72 10 E
Jiamusi, *China* . . . . **21 B8** 46 40N 130 26 E
Jian, *China* . . . . **21 D6** 27 6N 114 59 E
Jiangsu □, *China* . . . . . **21 C7** 33 0N 120 0 E
Jiangxi □, *China* . . . . . **21 D6** 27 30N 116 0 E
Jidda, *Si. Arabia* . . . . . **24 C2** 21 29N 39 10 E
Jihlava →, *Czech.* . . . . **10 D7** 48 55N 16 36 E
Jilin, *China* . . . . **21 B7** 43 44N 126 30 E
Jilin □, *China* . . . . **21 B7** 44 0N 127 0 E
Jima, *Ethiopia* . . . . **29 H14** 7 40N 36 47 E
Jinan, *China* . . . . **21 C6** 36 38N 117 1 E
Jinja, *Uganda* . . . . **32 D6** 0 25N 33 12 E
Jinzhou, *China* . . . . **21 B7** 41 5N 121 3 E
Jixi, *China* . . . . **21 B8** 45 20N 130 50 E
João Pessoa, *Brazil* . . . **46 C6** 7 10S 34 52W
Jodhpur, *India* . . . . **23 F4** 26 23N 73 8 E
Johannesburg, *S. Africa* **31 B4** 26 10S 28 2 E
Johnson City, *U.S.A.* . . **43 D10** 42 7N 75 57W
Johnstown, *U.S.A.* **42 E8** 40 19N 78 53W
Johor Baharu, *Malaysia* **22 C2** 1 28N 103 46 E
Joliet, *U.S.A.* **42 E3** 41 30N 88 5W
Joliette, *Canada* **43 B11** 46 3N 73 24W
Jolo, *Phil.* . . . . **22 C4** 6 0N 121 0 E
Jönköping, *Sweden* . . . **6 G10** 57 45N 14 10 E
Jonquière, *Canada* **43 A12** 48 27N 71 14W
Jonzac, *France* **9 E3** 45 27N 0 28W
Jordan ■, *Asia* . . . . **24 B2** 31 0N 36 0 E
Jordan →, *Asia* . . . . . **29 Q22** 31 48N 35 32 E
Jos, *Nigeria* . . . . **30 C3** 9 53N 8 51 E
Juan de Fuca Str., *Canada* **40 A2** 48 15N 124 0W
Juiz de Fora, *Brazil* . . . **46 E5** 21 43S 43 19W
Jullundur, *India* . . . . . . **23 D5** 31 20N 75 40 E
Junagadh, *India* . . . . . . **23 J3** 21 30N 70 30 E
Juneau, *U.S.A.* **38 C6** 58 20N 134 20W
Jupiter →, *Canada* . . . **43 A16** 49 29N 63 37W
Jura, *France* . . . . **8 D7** 46 35N 6 5 E
Jura, *Germany* . . . . **10 D3** 48 30N 9 30 E
Jura, *U.K.* **7 E4** 56 0N 5 50W
Jutland, *Denmark* . . . . **6 G9** 56 25N 9 30 E
Jyväskylä, *Finland* . . . . **6 F13** 62 14N 25 50 E

K

K2, *Pakistan* . . . . **23 B6** 35 58N 76 32 E
Kabardino-Balkar Republic □, *Russia* . **15 F7** 43 30N 43 30 E
Kābul, *Afghan.* . . . . **23 B2** 34 28N 69 11 E
Kabwe, *Zambia* . . . . . . **33 G5** 14 30S 28 29 E
Kachin □, *Burma* . . . . . **25 C8** 26 0N 97 30 E
Kaduna, *Nigeria* . . . . . **30 B3** 10 30N 7 21 E
Kaesong, *N. Korea* . . . **21 C7** 37 58N 126 35 E
Kagoshima, *Japan* . . . . **19 D2** 31 35N 130 33 E
Kai Is., *Indonesia* . . . . . **22 D5** 5 55S 132 45 E
Kaifeng, *China* . . . . **21 C6** 34 48N 114 21 E
Kaiserslautern, *Germany* **10 D2** 49 30N 7 43 E
Kaitaia, *N.Z.* . . . . **35 H13** 35 8S 173 17 E
Kajaani, *Finland* . . . . . . **6 F13** 64 17N 27 46 E
Kakinada, *India* . . . . . . **25 D7** 16 57N 82 11 E
Kalahari, *Africa* . . . . . . **31 A3** 24 0S 21 30 E
Kalamazoo, *U.S.A.* **42 D5** 42 20N 85 35W
Kalamazoo →, *U.S.A.* . **42 D4** 42 40N 86 12W
Kalemie, *Zaïre* . . . . **32 F5** 5 55S 29 9 E
Kalgoorlie-Boulder, *Australia* . . . . **34 G3** 30 40S 121 22 E
Kalimantan, *Indonesia* . **22 D3** 0 0 114 0 E
Kaliningrad, *Russia* . . . **14 D3** 54 42N 20 32 E
Kalisz, *Poland* . . . . **10 C8** 51 45N 18 8 E
Kalkaska, *U.S.A.* **42 C5** 44 44N 85 11W
Kalmar, *Sweden* . . . . . . **6 G11** 56 40N 16 20 E
Kalmyk Republic □, *Russia* . . . . **15 E8** 46 5N 46 1 E
Kaluga, *Russia* . . . . **14 D6** 54 35N 36 10 E
Kamchatka Pen., *Russia* **18 D18** 57 0N 160 0 E
Kamina, *Zaïre* . . . . **32 F5** 8 45S 25 0 E
Kamloops, *Canada* **38 C7** 50 40N 120 20W
Kampala, *Uganda* . . . . **32 D6** 0 20N 32 30 E
Kampuchea = Cambodia ■, *Asia* . . **22 B2** 12 15N 105 0 E
Kananga, *Zaïre* . . . . . . **32 F4** 5 55S 22 18 E
Kanawha →, *U.S.A.* . . **42 F6** 38 50N 82 8W
Kanazawa, *Japan* . . . . **19 A5** 36 30N 136 38 E
Kanchenjunga, *Nepal* . **23 F12** 27 50N 88 10 E
Kanchipuram, *India* . . . **25 D6** 12 52N 79 45 E
Kandy, *Sri Lanka* . . . . . **25 E7** 7 18N 80 43 E
Kane, *U.S.A.* **42 E8** 41 39N 78 53W
Kangean Is., *Indonesia* **22 D3** 6 55S 115 23 E
Kanin Pen., *Russia* . . . **14 A8** 68 0N 45 0 E
Kankakee, *U.S.A.* **42 E4** 41 6N 87 50W
Kankakee →, *U.S.A.* . **42 E3** 41 23N 88 16W
Kankan, *Guinea* **28 G5** 10 23N 9 15W
Kano, *Nigeria* . . . . **30 B3** 12 2N 8 30 E
Kanpur, *India* . . . . **23 F8** 26 28N 80 20 E
Kansas □, *U.S.A.* **40 C7** 38 40N 98 0W
Kansas City, *Kans., U.S.A.* **41 C8** 39 5N 94 40W
Kansas City, *Mo., U.S.A.* **41 C8** 39 3N 94 30W
Kanye, *Botswana* . . . . . **31 A4** 24 55S 25 28 E
Kaohsiung, *Taiwan* . . . **21 D7** 22 35N 120 16 E
Kaolack, *Senegal* **28 G3** 14 5N 16 8W
Kaposvár, *Hungary* . . . **10 E7** 46 25N 17 47 E
Kapuas →, *Indonesia* . **22 D2** 0 25S 109 20 E
Kapuas Hulu Ra., *Malaysia* . . . . **22 C3** 1 30N 113 30 E
Kapuskasing, *Canada* . **42 A6** 49 25N 82 30W
Kara Bogaz Gol, *Turkmenistan* . . . . . . **15 F9** 41 0N 53 30 E
Kara Kum, *Turkmenistan* **18 F8** 39 30N 60 0 E
Kara Sea, *Russia* . . . . . **18 B8** 75 0N 70 0 E
Karachi, *Pakistan* . . . . . **23 G1** 24 53N 67 0 E
Karaganda, *Kazakhstan* **18 E9** 49 50N 73 10 E
Karakoram Pass, *Pakistan* . . . . **23 B6** 35 33N 77 50 E
Karakoram Ra., *Pakistan* **23 B6** 35 30N 77 0 E
Karasburg, *Namibia* . . . **31 B2** 28 0S 18 44 E
Karbala, *Iraq* . . . . **24 B3** 32 36N 44 3 E
Karelian Republic □, *Russia* . . . . **14 A5** 65 30N 32 30 E
Karimata Is., *Indonesia* **22 D2** 1 25S 109 0 E
Karimunjawa Is., *Indonesia* . . . . **22 D3** 5 50S 110 30 E
Karl-Marx-Stadt = Chemnitz, *Germany* . **10 C5** 50 50N 12 55 E
Karlskrona, *Sweden* . . . **6 G11** 56 10N 15 35 E
Karlsruhe, *Germany* . . . **10 D3** 49 3N 8 23 E
Karlstad, *Sweden* . . . . . **6 G10** 59 23N 13 30 E
Karnal, *India* . . . . **23 E6** 29 42N 77 2 E
Karnataka □, *India* . . . . **25 D6** 13 15N 77 0 E
Karsakpay, *Kazakhstan* **18 E8** 47 55N 66 40 E
Kasai →, *Zaïre* . . . . . . **32 E3** 3 30S 16 10 E
Kashan, *Iran* . . . . **24 B4** 34 5N 51 30 E
Kashi, *China* . . . . **20 C2** 39 30N 76 2 E
Kassala, *Sudan* . . . . . . **29 F14** 15 30N 36 0 E
Kassel, *Germany* . . . . . **10 C3** 51 19N 9 32 E
Kasur, *Pakistan* . . . . . . **23 D5** 31 5N 74 25 E
Katha, *Burma* . . . . **25 C8** 24 10N 96 30 E
Katihar, *India* . . . . **23 G11** 25 34N 87 36 E
Katmandu, *Nepal* . . . . . **23 F10** 27 45N 85 20 E
Katowice, *Poland* . . . . . **10 C8** 50 17N 19 5 E
Katsina, *Nigeria* . . . . . . **30 B3** 13 0N 7 32 E
Kattegatt, *Denmark* . . . . **6 G10** 57 0N 11 20 E
Kauai, *U.S.A.* **40 H15** 22 0N 159 30W
Kaukauna, *U.S.A.* **42 C3** 44 20N 88 13W
Kaunas, *Lithuania* . . . . **14 D3** 54 54N 23 54 E
Kavålla, *Greece* . . . . . . **13 D11** 40 57N 24 28 E
Kawagoe, *Japan* . . . . . . **19 B6** 35 55N 139 29 E
Kawardha, *India* . . . . . . **23 J8** 22 0N 81 17 E
Kawasaki, *Japan* . . . . . . **19 B6** 35 35N 139 42 E
Kayes, *Mali* **28 G4** 14 25N 11 30W
Kayseri, *Turkey* . . . . . . **15 G6** 38 45N 35 30 E
Kazakhstan ■, *Asia* . . . **18 E9** 50 0N 70 0 E
Kazan, *Russia* . . . . **14 C8** 55 48N 49 3 E
Kazerun, *Iran* . . . . **24 C4** 29 38N 51 40 E
Kebnekaise, *Sweden* . . **6 E11** 67 53N 18 33 E
Kecskemét, *Hungary* . . **10 E8** 46 57N 19 42 E
Kediri, *Indonesia* . . . . . **22 D3** 7 51S 112 1 E
Keene, *U.S.A.* **43 D11** 42 57N 72 17W
Keetmanshoop, *Namibia* **31 B2** 26 35S 18 8 E
Kefallinía, *Greece* . . . . **13 E9** 38 20N 20 30 E
Keflavík, *Iceland* **6 B2** 64 2N 22 35W
Keighley, *U.K.* **7 F6** 53 52N 1 54W
Kelang, *Malaysia* . . . . . **22 C2** 3 2N 101 26 E
Kelowna, *Canada* **38 D8** 49 50N 119 25W
Kemerovo, *Russia* . . . . **18 D10** 55 20N 86 5 E
Kemi, *Finland* . . . . **6 E12** 65 44N 24 34 E
Kemi →, *Finland* . . . . **6 E12** 65 47N 24 32 E
Kemp Land, *Antarctica* **48 C15** 69 0S 55 0 E
Kendari, *Indonesia* . . . . **22 D4** 3 50S 122 30 E
Kenhardt, *S. Africa* . . . **31 B3** 29 19S 21 12 E
Kenitra, *Morocco* **28 C5** 34 15N 6 40W
Kenosha, *U.S.A.* **42 D4** 42 33N 87 48W
Kent, *U.S.A.* **42 E7** 41 8N 81 20W
Kenton, *U.S.A.* **42 E6** 40 40N 83 35W
Kentucky □, *U.S.A.* . . . **42 G5** 37 20N 85 0W
Kentucky →, *U.S.A.* . . **42 F5** 38 41N 85 11W
Kentville, *Canada* **43 C15** 45 6N 64 29W
Kenya ■, *Africa* . . . . . . **32 D7** 1 0N 38 0 E
Kenya, Mt., *Kenya* . . . . **32 E7** 0 10S 37 18 E
Kerala □, *India* . . . . **25 D6** 11 0N 76 15 E
Kerch, *Ukraine* . . . . **15 E6** 45 20N 36 20 E
Kerinci, *Indonesia* . . . . **22 D2** 1 40S 101 15 E
Kérkira, *Greece* . . . . . . **13 E8** 39 38N 19 50 E
Kermadec Trench, *Pac. Oc.* **35 G15** 30 30S 176 0W
Kerman, *Iran* . . . . **24 B4** 30 15N 57 1 E
Kestell, *S. Africa* . . . . . **31 B4** 28 17S 28 42 E
Ketchikan, *U.S.A.* **38 C6** 55 25N 131 40W
Kewaunee, *U.S.A.* **42 C4** 44 27N 87 30W
Keweenaw B., *U.S.A.* . . **42 B3** 46 56N 88 23W
Keweenaw Pen., *U.S.A.* **42 B3** 47 30N 88 0W
Keweenaw Pt., *U.S.A.* . **42 B4** 47 26N 87 40W
Key West, *U.S.A.* **41 F10** 24 33N 82 0W
Keyser, *U.S.A.* **42 F8** 39 26N 79 0W
Khabarovsk, *Russia* . . . **18 E15** 48 30N 135 5 E
Khairpur, *Pakistan* . . . . **23 F2** 27 32N 68 49 E
Khamas Country, *Botswana* . . . . **31 A4** 21 45S 26 30 E
Khandwa, *India* . . . . **23 J6** 21 49N 76 22 E
Khanewal, *Pakistan* . . . **23 D3** 30 20N 71 55 E
Khaniá, *Greece* . . . . . . **13 G11** 35 30N 24 4 E
Kharagpur, *India* . . . . . **23 H11** 22 20N 87 25 E
Khargon, *India* . . . . **23 J5** 21 45N 75 40 E
Kharkov, *Ukraine* . . . . . **15 E6** 49 58N 36 20 E
Khartoum, *Sudan* . . . . . **29 F13** 15 31N 32 35 E
Khaskovo, *Bulgaria* . . . **13 D11** 41 56N 25 30 E
Khatanga, *Russia* . . . . . **18 B12** 72 0N 102 20 E
Kherson, *Ukraine* . . . . . **15 E5** 46 35N 32 35 E
Khíos, *Greece* . . . . **13 E12** 38 27N 26 9 E
Khorixas, *Namibia* . . . . **31 A1** 20 16S 14 59 E
Khorramshahr, *Iran* . . . **24 B3** 30 29N 48 15 E
Khulna, *Bangla.* . . . . . . **23 H12** 22 45N 89 34 E
Khulna □, *Bangla.* . . . . **23 H12** 22 25N 89 35 E
Khumago, *Botswana* . . . **31 A3** 20 26S 24 32 E
Khushab, *Pakistan* . . . . **23 C4** 32 20N 72 20 E
Khuzdar, *Pakistan* . . . . **23 F1** 27 52N 66 30 E
Kicking Horse Pass, *Canada* **38 C8** 51 28N 116 16W
Kidderminster, *U.K.* . . . **7 F5** 52 24N 2 13W
Kiel, *Germany* . . . . **10 A4** 54 16N 10 8 E
Kiel B., *Germany* . . . . . **10 A4** 54 30N 10 30 E
Kiel Canal, *Germany* . . **10 A3** 54 15N 9 40 E
Kielce, *Poland* . . . . **10 C9** 50 52N 20 42 E
Kiev, *Ukraine* . . . . **15 D5** 50 30N 30 28 E
Kigali, *Rwanda* . . . . **32 E6** 1 59S 30 4 E
Kigoma-Ujiji, *Tanzania* . **32 E5** 4 55S 29 36 E
Kikládhes, *Greece* . . . . **13 F11** 37 20N 24 30 E
Kikwit, *Zaïre* . . . . **32 E3** 5 0S 18 45 E
Kilimanjaro, *Tanzania* . **32 E7** 3 7S 37 20 E
Kilkenny, *Ireland* **7 F3** 52 40N 7 17W
Kilmarnock, *U.K.* **7 E4** 55 36N 4 30W
Kimberley, *S. Africa* . . . **31 B3** 28 43S 24 46 E
Kimberley Plateau, *Australia* . . . . **34 D4** 16 20S 127 0 E
Kincardine, *Canada* . . . **42 C7** 44 10N 81 40W
Kindu, *Zaïre* . . . . **32 E5** 2 55S 25 50 E
King George I., *Antarctica* **48 C24** 60 0S 60 0W
King William's Town, *S. Africa* . . . . **31 C4** 32 51S 27 22 E
King's Lynn, *U.K.* . . . . . **7 F7** 52 45N 0 25 E
Kingston, *Canada* **42 C9** 44 14N 76 30W
Kingston, *Jamaica* **44 K17** 18 0N 76 50W
Kingston, *N.Y., U.S.A.* . **43 E10** 41 55N 74 0W
Kingston, *Pa., U.S.A.* . . **43 E10** 41 19N 75 58W
Kingston upon Hull, *U.K.* **7 F6** 53 45N 0 20W
Kingstown, *St. Vincent* **44 P20** 13 10N 61 10W
Kinross, *U.K.* **7 D5** 56 13N 3 25W
Kinshasa, *Zaïre* . . . . . . **32 E3** 4 20S 15 15 E
Kintyre, *U.K.* **7 E4** 55 30N 5 35W
Kirensk, *Russia* . . . . . . **18 D12** 57 50N 107 55 E
Kirghizia ■, *Asia* . . . . . **18 E9** 42 0N 75 0 E
Kirgiz Steppe, *Kazakhstan* . . . . **15 D10** 50 0N 55 0 E
Kiribati ■, *Pac. Oc.* . . . **36 H10** 5 0S 176 0W
Kirkcaldy, *U.K.* **7 D5** 56 7N 3 10W
Kirkenes, *Norway* . . . . . **6 E14** 69 40N 30 5 E
Kirkland Lake, *Canada* **42 A7** 48 9N 80 2W
Kirkuk, *Iraq* . . . . **24 B3** 35 30N 44 21 E
Kirkwall, *U.K.* **7 C5** 58 59N 2 59W
Kirkwood, *S. Africa* . . . **31 C4** 33 22S 25 15 E
Kirthar Range, *Pakistan* **23 F1** 27 0N 67 0 E
Kiruna, *Sweden* . . . . . . **6 E12** 67 52N 20 15 E
Kisangani, *Zaïre* . . . . . **32 D5** 0 35N 25 15 E
Kishanganj, *India* . . . . . **23 F12** 26 3N 88 14 E
Kishinev, *Moldavia* . . . . **15 E4** 47 0N 28 50 E
Kismayu, *Somali Rep.* . . **29 K15** 0 22S 42 32 E
Kisumu, *Kenya* . . . . **32 E6** 0 3S 34 45 E
Kitakyūshū, *Japan* . . . . **19 C2** 33 50N 130 50 E
Kitchener, *Canada* **42 D7** 43 27N 80 29W
Kíthira, *Greece* . . . . **13 F11** 36 9N 23 12 E
Kitikmeot □, *Canada* . . **38 B9** 70 0N 110 0W
Kitimat, *Canada* **38 C7** 54 3N 128 38W
Kittanning, *U.S.A.* **42 E8** 40 49N 79 30W
Kitwe, *Zambia* . . . . **33 G5** 12 54S 28 13 E
Kivu, L., *Zaïre* . . . . **32 E5** 1 48S 29 0 E
Kiyev = Kiev, *Ukraine* . **15 D5** 50 30N 30 28 E
Kladno, *Czech.* . . . . **10 C6** 50 10N 14 7 E
Klagenfurt, *Austria* . . . . **10 E6** 46 38N 14 20 E
Klar →, *Sweden* . . . . . **6 G10** 59 23N 13 32 E
Klawer, *S. Africa* . . . . . **31 C2** 31 44S 18 36 E
Klerksdorp, *S. Africa* . . **31 B4** 26 53S 26 38 E
Klipplaat, *S. Africa* . . . . **31 C3** 33 1S 24 22 E
Klondike, *Canada* **38 B6** 64 0N 139 26W
Klyuchevsk Vol., *Russia* **18 D18** 55 50N 160 30 E
Knossos, *Greece* . . . . . . **13 G11** 35 16N 25 10 E
Knoxville, *U.S.A.* **41 C10** 35 58N 83 57W
Knysna, *S. Africa* . . . . . **31 C3** 34 2S 23 2 E
Kōbe, *Japan* . . . . **19 B4** 34 45N 135 10 E
København = Copenhagen, *Denmark* . . . . **6 G10** 55 41N 12 34 E
Koblenz, *Germany* . . . . **10 C2** 50 21N 7 36 E
Kobroor, *Indonesia* . . . . **22 D5** 6 10S 134 30 E
Kodiak I., *U.S.A.* **38 C4** 57 30N 152 45W
Koffiefontein, *S. Africa* **31 B4** 29 30S 25 0 E
Koforidua, *Ghana* **30 C1** 6 3N 0 17W
Koh-i-Bābā, *Afghan.* . . . **23 B1** 34 30N 67 0 E
Kohat, *Pakistan* . . . . . . **23 C3** 33 40N 71 29 E
Kokchetav, *Kazakhstan* **18 D8** 53 20N 69 25 E
Kokomo, *U.S.A.* **42 E4** 40 30N 86 6W
Kokstad, *S. Africa* . . . . . **31 C4** 30 32S 29 29 E
Kola Pen., *Russia* . . . . . **14 A6** 67 30N 38 0 E
Kolar, *India* . . . . **25 D6** 13 12N 78 15 E
Kolguyev, I., *Russia* . . . **14 A8** 69 20N 48 30 E
Kolhapur, *India* . . . . **25 D6** 16 43N 74 15 E
Köln = Cologne, *Germany* . . . . **10 C2** 50 56N 6 58 E
Kolomna, *Russia* . . . . . . **14 C6** 55 8N 38 45 E
Kolwezi, *Zaïre* . . . . **32 G5** 10 40S 25 25 E
Kolyma →, *Russia* . . . **18 C18** 69 30N 161 0 E
Kolyma Ra., *Russia* . . . **18 C17** 63 0N 157 0 E
Komandorskiye Is., *Russia* . . . . **18 D18** 55 0N 167 0 E
Komatipoort, *S. Africa* . **31 B5** 25 25S 31 55 E
Komi Republic □, *Russia* . . . . **14 B10** 64 0N 55 0 E
Kompong Cham, *Cambodia* . . . . **22 B2** 12 0N 105 30 E
Kompong Chhnang, *Cambodia* . . . . **22 B2** 12 20N 104 35 E
Kompong Som, *Cambodia* . . . . **22 B2** 10 38N 103 30 E
Komsomolets I., *Russia* **18 A11** 80 30N 95 0 E
Komsomolsk, *Russia* . . **18 D15** 50 30N 137 0 E
Konin, *Poland* . . . . **10 B8** 52 12N 18 15 E
Konya, *Turkey* . . . . **15 G5** 37 52N 32 35 E
Korce, *Albania* . . . . **13 D9** 40 37N 20 50 E
Korea, North ■, *Asia* . . **21 C7** 40 0N 127 0 E
Korea, South ■, *Asia* . . **21 C7** 36 0N 128 0 E
Korea Strait, *Asia* . . . . **21 C7** 34 0N 129 30 E
Kōriyama, *Japan* . . . . . . **19 G12** 37 24N 140 23 E
Korla, *China* . . . . **20 B3** 41 45N 86 4 E
Körös →, *Hungary* . . . **10 E9** 46 43N 20 12 E
Kortrijk, *Belgium* . . . . . . **8 B5** 50 50N 3 17 E
Kos, *Greece* . . . . **13 F12** 36 50N 27 15 E
Košice, *Slovakia* . . . . . **10 D9** 48 42N 21 15 E
Kosti, *Sudan* . . . . **29 G13** 13 8N 32 43 E
Kostroma, *Russia* . . . . . **14 C7** 57 50N 40 58 E
Koszalin, *Poland* . . . . . . **10 A7** 54 11N 16 8 E
Kota, *India* . . . . **23 G5** 25 14N 75 49 E
Kota Baharu, *Malaysia* **22 C2** 6 7N 102 14 E
Kota Kinabalu, *Malaysia* **22 C3** 6 0N 116 4 E
Kotka, *Finland* . . . . **6 F13** 60 28N 26 58 E
Kotri, *Pakistan* . . . . **23 G2** 25 22N 68 22 E
Kotuy →, *Russia* . . . . **18 B12** 71 54N 102 6 E
Kounradskiy, *Kazakhstan* . . . . **18 E9** 46 59N 75 0 E
Kra, Isthmus of, *Thailand* . . . . **22 B1** 10 15N 99 30 E
Kragujevac, *Serbia, Yug.* **13 B9** 44 2N 20 56 E
Kraków, *Poland* . . . . **10 C8** 50 4N 19 57 E
Krasnodar, *Russia* . . . . **15 E6** 45 5N 39 0 E
Krasnoturinsk, *Russia* . **14 C11** 59 46N 60 12 E
Krasnovodsk, *Turkmenistan* . . . . **15 F9** 40 0N 52 52 E
Krasnoyarsk, *Russia* . . . **18 D11** 56 8N 93 0 E
Kratie, *Cambodia* . . . . . . **22 B2** 12 32N 106 10 E
Krefeld, *Germany* . . . . . **10 C2** 51 20N 6 32 E
Kremenchug, *Ukraine* . . **15 E5** 49 5N 33 25 E
Krishna →, *India* . . . . **25 D7** 15 57N 80 59 E
Krishnanagar, *India* . . . **23 H12** 23 24N 88 33 E
Kristiansand, *Norway* . . **6 G9** 58 9N 8 1 E
Kristiansund, *Norway* . . **6 F9** 63 7N 7 45 E
Kríti = Crete, *Greece* . . **13 G11** 35 15N 25 0 E
Krivoy Rog, *Ukraine* . . . **15 E5** 47 51N 33 20 E
Kroonstad, *S. Africa* . . . **31 B4** 27 43S 27 19 E
Krosno, *Poland* . . . . **10 D9** 49 42N 21 46 E
Kruger Nat. Park, *S. Africa* . . . . **31 A5** 23 30S 31 40 E
Krugersdorp, *S. Africa* . **31 B4** 26 5S 27 46 E
Kruisfontein, *S. Africa* . **31 C3** 33 59S 24 43 E
Kruševac, *Serbia, Yug.* **13 C9** 43 35N 21 28 E
Kuala Lumpur, *Malaysia* **22 C2** 3 9N 101 41 E
Kuala Terengganu, *Malaysia* . . . . **22 C2** 5 20N 103 8 E

113

Kualakapuas — Malacca, Str. of

Kualakapuas, *Indonesia* **22 D3** 2 55S 114 20 E
Kuching, *Malaysia* **22 C3** 1 33N 110 25 E
Kudat, *Malaysia* **22 C3** 6 55N 116 55 E
Kumanovo,
Macedonia, Yug. **13 C9** 42 9N 21 42 E
Kumasi, *Ghana* **30 C1** 6 41N 1 38W
Kumayri, *Armenia* **15 F7** 40 47N 43 50 E
Kumbakonam, *India* **25 D6** 10 58N 79 25 E
Kunlun Shan, *Asia* **20 C3** 36 0N 86 30 E
Kunming, *China* **20 D5** 25 1N 102 41 E
Kuopio, *Finland* **6 F13** 62 53N 27 35 E
Kupang, *Indonesia* **22 E4** 10 19S 123 39 E
Kura →, *Azerbaijan* **15 G8** 39 50N 49 20 E
Kurashiki, *Japan* **19 B3** 34 40N 133 50 E
Kurdistan, *Asia* **24 B3** 37 20N 43 30 E
Kure, *Japan* **19 B3** 34 14N 132 32 E
Kurgan, *Russia* **18 D8** 55 26N 65 18 E
Kuril Is., *Russia* **18 E17** 45 0N 150 0 E
Kurnool, *India* **25 D6** 15 45N 78 0 E
Kursk, *Russia* **14 D6** 51 42N 36 11 E
Kuruman, *S. Africa* **31 B3** 27 28S 23 28 E
Kuruman →, *S. Africa* **31 B3** 26 56S 20 39 E
Kurume, *Japan* **19 C2** 33 15N 130 30 E
Kushiro, *Japan* **19 F12** 43 0N 144 25 E
Kushtia, *Bangla.* **23 H12** 23 55N 89 5 E
Kütahya, *Turkey* **15 G5** 39 30N 30 2 E
Kutaisi, *Georgia* **15 F7** 42 19N 42 40 E
Kutch, Gulf of, *India* **23 H2** 22 50N 69 15 E
Kutch, Rann of, *India* **23 G2** 24 0N 70 0 E
Kuwait, *Kuwait* **24 C3** 29 30N 48 0 E
Kuwait ■, *Asia* **24 C3** 29 30N 47 30 E
Kuybyshev = Samara,
Russia **14 D9** 53 8N 50 6 E
KwaMashu, *S. Africa* **31 B5** 29 45S 30 58 E
Kwangju, *S. Korea* **21 C7** 35 9N 126 54 E
Kyōto, *Japan* **19 B4** 35 0N 135 45 E
Kyūshū, *Japan* **19 C2** 33 0N 131 0 E
Kyzyl Kum, *Uzbekistan* **18 E8** 42 30N 65 0 E
Kzyl-Orda, *Kazakhstan* **18 E8** 44 48N 65 28 E

L

La Chorrera, *Panama* **44 H14** 8 50N 79 50W
La Ciotat, *France* **9 F6** 43 10N 5 37 E
La Coruña, *Spain* **11 A1** 43 20N 8 25W
La Flèche, *France* **8 D3** 47 42N 0 4W
La Habana = Havana,
Cuba **45 C8** 23 8N 82 22W
La Mancha, *Spain* **11 C4** 39 10N 2 54W
La Paz, *Bolivia* **46 D3** 16 20S 68 10W
La Perouse Str., *Asia* **16 E18** 45 40N 142 0 E
La Plata, *Argentina* **47 F4** 35 0S 57 55W
La Porte, *U.S.A.* **42 E4** 41 36N 86 43W
La Roche-sur-Yon,
France **8 D3** 46 40N 1 25W
La Sarre, *Canada* **42 A8** 48 45N 79 15W
La Spezia, *Italy* **12 B3** 44 8N 9 50 E
La Tour-du-Pin, *France* **9 E6** 45 33N 5 27 E
La Tuque, *Canada* **43 B11** 47 30N 72 50W
Labrador, Coast of,
Canada **39 C13** 53 20N 61 0W
Labuk B., *Malaysia* **22 C3** 6 10N 117 50 E
Lac-Mégantic, *Canada* **43 C12** 45 35N 70 53W
Laccadive Is. =
Lakshadweep Is.,
Ind. Oc. **25 D6** 10 0N 72 30 E
Lachine, *Canada* **43 C11** 45 30N 73 40W
Laconia, *U.S.A.* **43 D12** 43 32N 71 30W
Ladakh Ra., *India* **23 B6** 34 0N 78 0 E
Ladoga, L., *Russia* **14 B5** 61 15N 30 30 E
Ladybrand, *S. Africa* **31 B4** 29 9S 27 29 E
Ladysmith, *S. Africa* **31 B4** 28 32S 29 46 E
Lae, *Papua N. G.* **34 B8** 6 40S 147 2 E
Lafayette, *Ind., U.S.A.* **42 E4** 40 25N 86 54W
Lafayette, *La., U.S.A.* **41 D8** 30 18N 92 0W
Lagos, *Nigeria* **30 C2** 6 25N 3 27 E
Lagos, *Portugal* **11 D1** 37 5N 8 41W
Lahn →, *Germany* **10 C2** 50 17N 7 38 E
Lahore, *Pakistan* **23 D5** 31 32N 74 22 E
Lahti, *Finland* **6 F13** 60 58N 25 40 E
Laingsburg, *S. Africa* **31 C3** 33 9S 20 52 E
Lake Charles, *U.S.A.* **41 D8** 30 15N 93 10W
Lakewood, *U.S.A.* **42 E7** 41 28N 81 50W
Lakshadweep Is.,
Ind. Oc. **25 D6** 10 0N 72 30 E
Lalitapur, *Nepal* **23 F10** 27 40N 85 20 E
Lamon Bay, *Phil.* **22 B4** 14 30N 122 20 E
Lancaster, *U.K.* **7 E5** 54 3N 2 48W
Lancaster, *N.H., U.S.A.* **43 C12** 44 27N 71 33W
Lancaster, *Pa., U.S.A.* **42 E9** 40 4N 76 19W
Lancaster Sd., *Canada* **39 A11** 74 13N 84 0W
Landes, *France* **9 E3** 44 0N 1 0W
Land's End, *U.K.* **7 G4** 50 4N 5 43W
Langon, *France* **9 E3** 44 33N 0 16W
Langres, *France* **8 D6** 47 52N 5 20 E
Langres, Plateau de,
France **8 D6** 47 45N 5 3 E
Lannion, *France* **8 C2** 48 46N 3 29W
L'Annonciation, *Canada* **43 B10** 46 25N 74 55W
L'Anse, *U.S.A.* **42 B3** 46 47N 88 28W
Lansing, *U.S.A.* **42 D5** 42 47N 84 40W
Lanzhou, *China* **20 C5** 36 1N 103 52 E
Laoag, *Phil.* **22 B4** 18 7N 120 34 E
Laon, *France* **8 C5** 49 33N 3 35 E
Laos ■, *Asia* **22 B2** 17 45N 105 0 E
Lapeer, *U.S.A.* **42 D6** 43 3N 83 20W
Lapland, *Europe* **6 E12** 68 7N 24 0 E
Laptev Sea, *Russia* **18 B14** 76 0N 125 0 E
Laredo, *U.S.A.* **40 E7** 27 34N 99 29W
Largentière, *France* **9 E6** 44 34N 4 18 E
Larisa, *Greece* **13 E10** 39 49N 22 28 E
Larne, *U.K.* **7 E4** 54 52N 5 50W
Larvik, *Norway* **6 G10** 59 4N 10 4 E
Las Palmas, *Canary Is.* **28 D3** 28 7N 15 26W
Las Vegas, *U.S.A.* **40 C3** 36 10N 115 5W
Lashio, *Burma* **25 C8** 22 56N 97 45 E
Latakia, *Syria* **24 B2** 35 30N 35 45 E
Latina, *Italy* **12 D5** 41 26N 12 53 E
Latvia ■, *Europe* **14 C3** 56 50N 24 0 E
Launceston, *Australia* **34 J8** 41 24S 147 8 E
Laurentian Plateau,
Canada **39 C13** 52 0N 70 0W
Lausanne, *Switz.* **8 D7** 46 32N 6 38 E
Laut, *Indonesia* **22 C2** 4 45N 108 0 E
Lauzon, *Canada* **43 B12** 46 48N 71 10W
Laval, *France* **8 C3** 48 4N 0 48W
Lawrence, *U.S.A.* **43 D12** 42 40N 71 9W
Layla, *Si. Arabia* **24 C3** 22 10N 46 40 E
Le Creusot, *France* **8 D6** 46 48N 4 24 E
Le Havre, *France* **8 C4** 49 30N 0 5 E
Le Mans, *France* **8 D4** 48 0N 0 10 E
Le Puy, *France* **9 E5** 45 3N 3 52 E
Leamington, *Canada* **42 D6** 42 3N 82 36W
Lebanon, *Ind., U.S.A.* **42 E4** 40 3N 86 28W
Lebanon, *Ky., U.S.A.* **42 G5** 37 35N 85 15W
Lebanon, *Pa., U.S.A.* **42 E9** 40 20N 76 28W
Lebanon ■, *Asia* **24 B2** 34 0N 36 0 E
Lecce, *Italy* **13 D8** 40 20N 18 10 E
Leduc, *Canada* **38 C8** 53 15N 113 30W
Leeds, *U.K.* **7 F6** 53 48N 1 34W
Leeuwarden, *Neths.* **8 A6** 53 15N 5 48 E
Leeuwin, C., *Australia* **34 G2** 34 20S 115 9 E
Leeward Is., *Atl. Oc.* **44 L18** 16 30N 63 30W
Leghorn, *Italy* **12 C4** 43 32N 10 18 E
Legnica, *Poland* **10 C7** 51 12N 16 10 E
Leh, *India* **23 B6** 34 9N 77 35 E
Lehututu, *Botswana* **31 A3** 23 54S 21 55 E
Leicester, *U.K.* **7 F6** 52 39N 1 9W
Leiden, *Neths.* **8 A6** 52 9N 4 30 E
Leine →, *Germany* **10 B3** 52 20N 9 50 E
Leipzig, *Germany* **10 C5** 51 20N 12 23 E
Leith, *U.K.* **7 E5** 55 59N 3 10W
Leitrim, *Ireland* **7 F2** 54 0N 8 5W
Lena →, *Russia* **18 B14** 72 52N 126 40 E
Leningrad = St.
Petersburg, *Russia* **14 C5** 59 55N 30 20 E
Leninsk-Kuznetskiy,
Russia **18 D10** 54 44N 86 10 E
Lens, *France* **8 B5** 50 26N 2 50 E
Leominster, *U.S.A.* **43 D12** 42 32N 71 45W
León, *Mexico* **44 C4** 21 7N 101 30W
León, *Guanajuato,*
Mexico **44 C4** 21 7N 101 40W
León, *Spain* **11 A3** 42 38N 5 34W
Lérida, *Spain* **11 B6** 41 37N 0 39 E
Lerwick, *U.K.* **7 A6** 60 10N 1 10W
Les Andelys, *France* **8 C4** 49 15N 1 25 E
Les Sables-d'Olonne,
France **9 D3** 46 30N 1 45W
Leskovac, *Serbia, Yug.* **13 C9** 43 0N 21 58 E
Lesotho ■, *Africa* **31 B4** 29 40S 28 0 E
Lesparre-Médoc, *France* **9 E3** 45 18N 0 57W
Lesvos, *Greece* **13 E12** 39 10N 26 20 E
Leszno, *Poland* **10 C7** 51 50N 16 30 E
Lethbridge, *Canada* **38 D8** 49 45N 112 45W
Leti Is., *Indonesia* **22 D4** 8 10S 128 0 E
Letiahau →, *Botswana* **31 A3** 21 16S 24 0 E
Leuven, *Belgium* **8 B6** 50 52N 4 42 E
Lévis, *Canada* **43 B12** 46 48N 71 9W
Lewes, *U.K.* **7 G7** 50 53N 0 2 E
Lewis, *U.K.* **7 C3** 58 10N 6 40W
Lewiston, *U.S.A.* **43 C12** 44 3N 70 10W
Lewistown, *U.S.A.* **42 E9** 40 37N 77 33W
Lexington, *U.S.A.* **42 F5** 38 6N 84 30W
Lexington Park, *U.S.A.* **42 F9** 38 16N 76 27W
Leyte, *Phil.* **22 B4** 11 0N 125 0 E
Lhasa, *China* **20 D4** 29 25N 90 58 E
Liaoning □, *China* **21 B7** 41 40N 122 30 E
Liaoyang, *China* **21 B7** 41 15N 122 58 E
Liaoyüan, *China* **21 B7** 42 58N 125 2 E
Liberec, *Czech.* **10 C6** 50 47N 15 7 E
Liberia ■, *W. Afr.* **28 H5** 6 30N 9 30W
Libourne, *France* **9 E3** 44 55N 0 14W
Libreville, *Gabon* **32 D1** 0 25N 9 26 E
Libya ■, *N. Afr.* **28 D10** 27 0N 17 0 E
Lichinga, *Mozam.* **33 G7** 13 13S 35 11 E
Lichtenburg, *S. Africa* **31 B4** 26 8S 26 8 E
Liechtenstein ■, *Europe* **10 E3** 47 8N 9 35 E
Liège, *Belgium* **8 B6** 50 38N 5 35 E
Liepāja, *Latvia* **14 C3** 56 30N 21 0 E
Ligurian Sea, *Italy* **12 C3** 43 20N 9 0 E
Likasi, *Zaïre* **32 G5** 10 55S 26 48 E
Lille, *France* **8 B5** 50 38N 3 3 E
Lillehammer, *Norway* **6 F10** 61 8N 10 30 E
Lilongwe, *Malawi* **33 G6** 14 0S 33 48 E
Lim Fjord, *Denmark* **6 G9** 56 55N 9 0 E
Lima, *Peru* **46 D2** 12 0S 77 0W
Lima, *U.S.A.* **42 E5** 40 42N 84 5W
Limerick, *Ireland* **7 F2** 52 40N 8 38W
Límnos, *Greece* **13 E11** 39 50N 25 5 E
Limoges, *France* **9 E4** 45 50N 1 15 E
Limousin, *France* **9 E4** 45 30N 1 30 E
Limoux, *France* **9 F5** 43 4N 2 12 E
Limpopo →, *Africa* **33 K6** 25 5S 33 30 E
Linares, *Spain* **11 C4** 38 10N 3 40W
Lincoln, *U.K.* **7 F6** 53 14N 0 32W
Lincoln, *Maine, U.S.A.* **43 C13** 45 27N 68 29W
Lincoln, *Nebr., U.S.A.* **41 B7** 40 50N 96 42W
Lindsay, *Canada* **42 C8** 44 22N 78 43W
Lingga Arch., *Indonesia* **22 D2** 0 10S 104 30 E
Linköping, *Sweden* **6 G11** 58 28N 15 36 E
Linton, *U.S.A.* **42 F4** 39 0N 87 10W
Linxia, *China* **20 C5** 35 36N 103 10 E
Linz, *Austria* **10 D6** 48 18N 14 18 E
Lions, G. of, *France* **9 F5** 43 10N 4 0 E
Lipari Is., *Italy* **12 E6** 38 30N 14 50 E
Lipetsk, *Russia* **14 D6** 52 37N 39 35 E
Lippe →, *Germany* **10 C2** 51 39N 6 38 E
Lisbon, *Portugal* **11 C1** 38 42N 9 10W
Lisburn, *U.K.* **7 E3** 54 30N 6 9W
Lisieux, *France* **8 C4** 49 10N 0 12 E
Lismore, *Australia* **34 F9** 28 44S 153 21 E
Listowel, *Canada* **42 D7** 43 44N 80 58W
Lithuania ■, *Europe* **14 C3** 55 30N 24 0 E
Little Current, *Canada* **42 C7** 45 55N 82 0W
Little Karoo, *S. Africa* **31 C3** 33 45S 21 0 E
Little Laut Is., *Indonesia* **22 D3** 4 45S 115 40 E
Little Rock, *U.S.A.* **41 D8** 34 41N 92 10W
Liuzhou, *China* **21 D5** 24 22N 109 22 E
Liverpool, *U.K.* **7 F5** 53 25N 3 0W
Livingstone, *Zambia* **33 H5** 17 46S 25 52 E
Livonia, *U.S.A.* **42 D6** 42 25N 83 23W
Livorno = Leghorn, *Italy* **12 C4** 43 32N 10 18 E
Ljubljana, *Slovenia* **12 A6** 46 4N 14 33 E
Ljusnan →, *Sweden* **6 F11** 61 12N 17 8 E
Llandudno, *U.K.* **7 F5** 53 19N 3 51W
Llanelli, *U.K.* **7 G4** 51 41N 4 11W
Llanos, *S. Amer.* **46 B2** 5 0N 71 35W
Lobatse, *Botswana* **31 B4** 25 12S 25 40 E
Lobito, *Angola* **33 G2** 12 18S 13 35 E
Loches, *France* **8 D4** 47 7N 1 0 E
Lock Haven, *U.S.A.* **42 E9** 41 7N 77 31W
Lodève, *France* **9 F5** 43 44N 3 19 E
Łódź, *Poland* **10 C8** 51 45N 19 27 E
Lofoten, *Norway* **6 E10** 68 30N 15 0 E
Logan, *Ohio, U.S.A.* **42 F6** 39 25N 82 22W
Logan, *W. Va., U.S.A.* **42 G7** 37 51N 81 59W
Logan, Mt., *Canada* **38 B5** 60 31N 140 22W
Logansport, *U.S.A.* **42 E4** 40 45N 86 21W
Logroño, *Spain* **11 A4** 42 28N 2 27W
Lohardaga, *India* **23 H10** 23 27N 84 45 E
Loir →, *France* **8 D3** 47 33N 0 32W
Loire →, *France* **8 D2** 47 16N 2 10W
Lombardy □, *Italy* **12 B3** 45 35N 9 45 E
Lomblen, *Indonesia* **22 D4** 8 30S 123 32 E
Lombok, *Indonesia* **22 D3** 8 45S 116 30 E
Lomé, *Togo* **30 C2** 6 9N 1 20 E
Lomond, L., *U.K.* **7 D4** 56 8N 4 38W
Łomza, *Poland* **10 B10** 53 10N 22 2 E
London, *Canada* **42 D7** 42 59N 81 15W
London, *U.K.* **7 G6** 51 30N 0 5W
Londrina, *Brazil* **47 E4** 23 18S 51 10W
Long Beach, *U.S.A.* **40 D3** 33 46N 118 12W
Long Branch, *U.S.A.* **43 E11** 40 19N 74 0W
Long I., *Bahamas* **45 C9** 23 20N 75 10W
Long I., *U.S.A.* **43 E11** 40 50N 73 20W
Long Xuyen, *Vietnam* **22 B2** 10 19N 105 28 E
Longlac, *Canada* **42 A4** 49 45N 86 25W
Lons-le-Saunier, *France* **8 D6** 46 40N 5 31 E
Lop Nor, *China* **20 B4** 40 20N 90 10 E
Lorain, *U.S.A.* **42 E6** 41 28N 82 55W
Loralai, *Pakistan* **23 D2** 30 20N 68 41 E
Lorca, *Spain* **11 D5** 37 41N 1 42W
Lorient, *France* **8 D2** 47 45N 3 23W
Lorn, Firth of, *U.K.* **7 D4** 56 20N 5 40W
Lorraine, *France* **8 C6** 48 53N 6 0 E
Los Angeles, *Chile* **47 F2** 37 28S 72 23W
Los Angeles, *U.S.A.* **40 D3** 34 0N 118 10W
Los Mochis, *Mexico* **44 B3** 25 45N 108 57W
Lot →, *France* **9 E4** 44 18N 0 20 E
Louis Trichardt, *S. Africa* **31 A4** 23 1S 29 43 E
Louisa, *U.S.A.* **42 F6** 38 5N 82 40W
Louiseville, *Canada* **43 B11** 46 20N 72 56W
Louisiana □, *U.S.A.* **41 D8** 30 50N 92 0W
Louisville, *U.S.A.* **42 F5** 38 15N 85 45W
Lourdes, *France* **9 F3** 43 6N 0 3W
Low Tatra, *Slovakia* **10 D8** 48 55N 19 30 E
Lowell, *U.S.A.* **43 D12** 42 38N 71 19W
Lower California, *Mexico* **44 B2** 31 10N 115 12W
Lower Tunguska →,
Russia **18 C10** 65 48N 88 4 E
Lowestoft, *U.K.* **7 F7** 52 29N 1 44 E
Lowville, *U.S.A.* **43 D10** 43 48N 75 30W
Luanda, *Angola* **32 F2** 8 50S 13 15 E
Luanshya, *Zambia* **33 G5** 13 3S 28 28 E
Lubbock, *U.S.A.* **40 D6** 33 40N 101 53W
Lübeck, *Germany* **10 B4** 53 52N 10 41 E
Lublin, *Poland* **10 C10** 51 12N 22 38 E
Lubumbashi, *Zaïre* **33 G5** 11 40S 27 28 E
Lucknow, *India* **23 F8** 26 50N 81 0 E
Lüda = Dalian, *China* **21 C7** 38 50N 121 40 E
Lüderitz, *Namibia* **31 B2** 26 41S 15 8 E
Ludhiana, *India* **23 D5** 30 57N 75 56 E
Ludington, *U.S.A.* **42 D4** 43 58N 86 27W
Ludwigshafen, *Germany* **10 D3** 49 27N 8 27 E
Lugano, *Switz.* **10 F3** 46 0N 8 57 E
Lugansk, *Ukraine* **15 E6** 48 38N 39 15 E
Lugo, *Spain* **11 A2** 43 2N 7 35W
Lule →, *Sweden* **6 E12** 65 35N 22 10 E
Luleå, *Sweden* **6 E12** 65 35N 22 10 E
Lüneburg Heath,
Germany **10 B4** 53 0N 10 0 E
Lunéville, *France* **8 C7** 48 36N 6 30 E
Luni →, *India* **23 G3** 24 41N 71 14 E
Luoyang, *China* **21 C6** 34 40N 112 26 E
Luray, *U.S.A.* **42 F8** 38 39N 78 26W
Lusaka, *Zambia* **33 H5** 15 28S 28 16 E
Luton, *U.K.* **7 G6** 51 53N 0 24W
Luxembourg, *Lux.* **8 C7** 49 37N 6 9 E
Luxembourg ■, *Europe* **8 C7** 49 45N 6 0 E
Luzern, *Switz.* **10 E3** 47 3N 8 18 E
Luzhou, *China* **20 D5** 28 52N 105 20 E
Luzon, *Phil.* **22 B4** 16 0N 121 0 E
Lvov, *Ukraine* **15 E3** 49 50N 24 0 E
Lyakhov Is., *Russia* **18 B16** 73 40N 141 0 E
Lydda, *Israel* **29 C13** 31 57N 34 54 E
Lydenburg, *S. Africa* **31 B5** 25 10S 30 29 E
Lynchburg, *U.S.A.* **42 G8** 37 23N 79 10W
Lynn Lake, *Canada* **38 C9** 56 51N 101 3W
Lyonnais, *France* **9 E6** 45 45N 4 15 E
Lyons, *France* **9 E6** 45 46N 4 50 E

M

Ma'an, *Jordan* **24 B2** 30 12N 35 44 E
Maastricht, *Neths.* **8 B6** 50 50N 5 40 E
Macapá, *Brazil* **46 B4** 0 5N 51 4W
Macau ■, *China* **21 D6** 22 16N 113 35 E
Macclesfield, *U.K.* **7 F5** 53 16N 2 9W
M'Clure Str., *Canada* **48 A11** 75 0N 119 0W
Macdonnell Ras.,
Australia **34 E5** 23 40S 133 0 E
Macedonia □, *Greece* **13 D10** 40 39N 22 0 E
Macedonia ■,
Macedonia, Yug. **13 D9** 41 53N 21 40 E
Maceió, *Brazil* **46 C6** 9 40S 35 41W
Macgillycuddy's Reeks,
Ireland **7 F2** 52 2N 9 45W
Mach, *Pakistan* **23 E1** 29 50N 67 20 E
Machakos, *Kenya* **32 E7** 1 30S 37 15 E
Machias, *U.S.A.* **43 C14** 44 40N 67 28W
Machilipatnam, *India* **25 D7** 16 12N 81 8 E
Mackay, *Australia* **34 E8** 21 8S 149 11 E
Mackay, L., *Australia* **34 E4** 22 30S 129 0 E
McKeesport, *U.S.A.* **42 E8** 40 21N 79 50W
Mackenzie →, *Canada* **38 B6** 69 10N 134 20W
Mackenzie Mts., *Canada* **38 B7** 64 0N 130 0W
Mackinaw City, *U.S.A.* **42 C5** 45 47N 84 44W
McKinley, Mt., *U.S.A.* **38 B4** 63 2N 151 0W
Maclear, *S. Africa* **31 C4** 31 2S 28 23 E
M'Clintock Chan.,
Canada **38 A9** 72 0N 102 0W
McMurdo Sd.,
Antarctica **48 C19** 77 0S 170 0 E
Mâcon, *France* **9 D6** 46 19N 4 50 E
Macon, *U.S.A.* **41 D10** 32 50N 83 37W
Macquarie Is., *Pac. Oc.* **36 N7** 54 36S 158 55 E
Madadeni, *S. Africa* **31 B5** 27 43S 30 3 E
Madagascar ■, *Africa* **33 J9** 20 0S 47 0 E
Madaripur, *Bangla.* **23 H13** 23 19N 90 15 E
Madeira, *Atl. Oc.* **28 C3** 32 50N 17 0W
Madeira →, *Brazil* **46 C4** 3 22S 58 45W
Madhya Pradesh □,
India **23 H7** 21 50N 78 0 E
Madinat al Shaab,
Yemen **29 G16** 12 50N 45 0 E
Madison, *Ind., U.S.A.* **42 F5** 38 42N 85 20W
Madison, *Wis., U.S.A.* **41 B9** 43 5N 89 25W
Madisonville, *U.S.A.* **42 G4** 37 20N 87 30W
Madiun, *Indonesia* **22 D3** 7 38S 111 32 E
Madras, *India* **25 D7** 13 8N 80 19 E
Madrid, *Spain* **11 B4** 40 25N 3 45W
Madurai, *India* **25 E6** 9 55N 78 10 E
Mafeking, *S. Africa* **31 B4** 25 50S 25 38 E
Mafeteng, *Lesotho* **31 B4** 29 51S 27 15 E
Magadan, *Russia* **18 D17** 59 38N 150 50 E
Magdalen Is., *Canada* **43 B17** 47 30N 61 40W
Magdalena →,
Colombia **40 A2** 11 0N 74 51W
Magdeburg, *Germany* **10 B4** 52 8N 11 36 E
Magelang, *Indonesia* **22 D3** 7 29S 110 13 E
Magellan's Str., *Chile* **47 H2** 52 30S 75 0W
Maggiore, L., *Italy* **12 A3** 46 0N 8 35 E
Magnetic Pole (North),
Canada **48 A4** 77 58N 102 8W
Magnetic Pole (South),
Antarctica **48 C18** 64 8S 138 8 E
Magnitogorsk, *Russia* **14 D10** 53 27N 59 4 E
Magog, *Canada* **43 C11** 45 18N 72 9W
Mahakam →,
Indonesia **22 D3** 0 35S 117 17 E
Mahalapye, *Botswana* **31 A4** 23 1S 26 51 E
Mahanadi →, *India* **23 J11** 20 20N 86 25 E
Maharashtra □, *India* **23 J5** 20 30N 75 30 E
Mahesana, *India* **23 H4** 23 39N 72 26 E
Maidstone, *U.K.* **7 G7** 51 16N 0 31 E
Maiduguri, *Nigeria* **30 B4** 12 0N 13 20 E
Maijdi, *Bangla.* **23 H13** 22 48N 91 10 E
Maikala Ra., *India* **23 J8** 22 0N 81 0 E
Maimana, *Afghan.* **24 B5** 35 53N 64 38 E
Main →, *Germany* **10 D3** 50 0N 8 18 E
Maine, *France* **8 D3** 47 55N 0 25W
Maine □, *U.S.A.* **43 C13** 45 20N 69 0W
Mainz, *Germany* **10 D3** 50 0N 8 17 E
Majorca = Mallorca,
Spain **11 C7** 39 30N 3 0 E
Makasar, Str. of,
Indonesia **22 D3** 1 0S 118 20 E
Makeyevka, *Ukraine* **15 E6** 48 0N 38 0 E
Makgadikgadi Salt
Pans, *Botswana* **31 A4** 20 40S 25 45 E
Makhachkala, *Russia* **15 F8** 43 0N 47 30 E
Makkah = Mecca,
Si. Arabia **24 C2** 21 30N 39 54 E
Makunda, *Botswana* **31 A3** 22 30S 20 7 E
Malabar Coast, *India* **25 D6** 11 0N 75 0 E
Malacca, Str. of,
Indonesia **22 C2** 3 0N 101 0 E

Málaga — **Mzimkulu**

115

Naab — Ostrava

N

Naab →, *Germany* **10 D5** 49 1N 12 2 E
Nābulus, *Jordan* **29 P21** 32 14N 35 15 E
Nadiad, *India* **23 H4** 22 41N 72 56 E
Nafud Desert, *Si. Arabia* **24 C3** 28 15N 41 0 E
Nagaland □, *India* **25 C8** 26 0N 94 30 E
Nagano, *Japan* **19 A6** 36 40N 138 10 E
Nagaoka, *Japan* **19 G11** 37 27N 138 51 E
Nagasaki, *Japan* **19 C1** 32 47N 129 50 E
Nagaur, *India* **23 F4** 27 15N 73 45 E
Nagercoil, *India* **25 E6** 8 12N 77 26 E
Nagoya, *Japan* **19 B5** 35 10N 136 50 E
Nagpur, *India* **23 J7** 21 8N 79 10 E
Nairn, *U.K.* **7 D5** 57 35N 3 54W
Nairobi, *Kenya* **32 E7** 1 17S 36 48 E
Najibabad, *India* **23 E7** 29 40N 78 20 E
Nakhichevan Republic □, *Azerbaijan* **15 G8** 39 14N 45 30 E
Nakhon Ratchasima, *Thailand* **22 B2** 14 59N 102 12 E
Nakhon Si Thammarat, *Thailand* **22 C2** 8 29N 100 0 E
Nakina, *Canada* **42 A4** 50 10N 86 40W
Nakuru, *Kenya* **32 E7** 0 15S 36 4 E
Nalchik, *Russia* **15 F7** 43 30N 43 33 E
Nam Co, *China* **20 C4** 30 30N 90 45 E
Namaland, *Namibia* **31 A2** 24 30S 17 0 E
Namaqualand, *S. Africa* **31 B2** 30 0S 17 25 E
Namib Desert, *Namibia* **31 A1** 22 30S 15 0 E
Namibe, *Angola* **33 H2** 15 7S 12 11 E
Namibia ■, *Africa* **31 A2** 22 0S 18 9 E
Namlea, *Indonesia* **22 D4** 3 18S 127 5 E
Nampula, *Mozam.* **33 H7** 15 6S 39 15 E
Namur, *Belgium* **8 B6** 50 27N 4 52 E
Nan Shan, *China* **20 C4** 38 30N 96 0 E
Nanaimo, *Canada* **38 D7** 49 10N 124 0W
Nanchang, *China* **21 D6** 28 42N 115 55 E
Nanchong, *China* **20 C5** 30 43N 106 2 E
Nancy, *France* **8 C7** 48 42N 6 12 E
Nanda Devi, *India* **23 D7** 30 23N 79 59 E
Nanded, *India* **25 D6** 19 10N 77 20 E
Nandurbar, *India* **23 J5** 21 20N 74 15 E
Nanga Parbat, *Pakistan* **23 B5** 35 10N 74 35 E
Nanking, *China* **21 C6** 32 2N 118 47 E
Nanning, *China* **20 D5** 22 48N 108 20 E
Nanp'ing, *China* **21 D6** 26 38N 118 10 E
Nantes, *France* **8 D3** 47 12N 1 33W
Nanticoke, *U.S.A.* **42 E9** 41 12N 76 1W
Nantong, *China* **21 C7** 32 1N 120 52 E
Nantua, *France* **9 D6** 46 10N 5 35 E
Napier, *N.Z.* **35 H14** 39 30S 176 56 E
Naples, *Italy* **12 D6** 40 50N 14 17 E
Nara, *Japan* **19 B4** 34 40N 135 49 E
Narayanganj, *Bangla.* **23 H13** 23 40N 90 33 E
Narbonne, *France* **9 F5** 43 11N 3 0 E
Narmada →, *India* **23 J4** 21 38N 72 36 E
Narvik, *Norway* **6 E11** 68 28N 17 26 E
Nashua, *U.S.A.* **43 D12** 42 50N 71 25W
Nashville, *U.S.A.* **41 C9** 36 12N 86 46W
Nasik, *India* **23 K4** 19 58N 73 50 E
Nasirabad, *India* **23 F5** 26 15N 74 45 E
Nassau, *Bahamas* [illegible] 25 0N 77 20W
Nasser, L., *Egypt* **29 E13** 23 0N 32 30 E
Nata, *Botswana* **31 A4** 20 12S 26 12 E
Natal, *Brazil* **46 C6** 5 47S 35 13W
Natal □, *S. Africa* **31 B5** 28 30S 30 30 E
Nathdwara, *India* **23 G4** 24 55N 73 50 E
Natuna Is., *Indonesia* **22 C2** 4 0N 108 15 E
Nauru ■, *Pac. Oc.* **36 H8** 1 0S 166 0 E
Navarra □, *Spain* **11 A5** 42 40N 1 40W
Navsari, *India* **23 J4** 20 57N 72 59 E
Nawabshah, *Pakistan* **23 F2** 26 15N 68 25 E
Náxos, *Greece* **13 F11** 37 8N 25 25 E
Nazareth, *Israel* **29 N21** 32 42N 35 17 E
Ndjamena, *Chad* **28 G9** 12 10N 14 59 E
Ndola, *Zambia* **33 G5** 13 0S 28 34 E
Neagh, L., *U.K.* **7 E3** 54 35N 6 25W
Nebraska □, *U.S.A.* **40 B7** 41 30N 100 0W
Neckar →, *Germany* **10 D3** 49 31N 8 26 E
Neemuch, *India* **23 G5** 24 30N 74 56 E
Neenah, *U.S.A.* **42 C3** 44 10N 88 30W
Negaunee, *U.S.A.* **42 B4** 46 30N 87 36W
Negrais, C., *Burma* **25 D8** 16 0N 94 30 E
Negro →, *Argentina* **47 G3** 41 2S 62 47W
Negro →, *Brazil* **46 C4** 3 0S 60 0W
Negros, *Phil.* **22 C4** 9 30N 122 40 E
Neijiang, *China* **20 D5** 29 35N 104 55 E
Neiva, *Colombia* **46 B2** 2 56N 75 18W
Nejd, *Si. Arabia* **24 C3** 26 30N 42 0 E
Nellore, *India* **25 D6** 14 27N 79 59 E
Nelson, *N.Z.* **35 J13** 41 18S 173 16 E
Nelson →, *Canada* **38 C10** 54 33N 98 2W
Nelspruit, *S. Africa* **31 B5** 25 29S 30 59 E
Nemunas →, *Lithuania* **14 C3** 55 25N 21 10 E
Nepal ■, *Asia* **23 F10** 28 0N 84 30 E
Nérac, *France* **9 E4** 44 8N 0 21 E
Ness, L., *U.K.* **7 D4** 57 15N 4 30W
Netherlands ■, *Europe* **8 B6** 52 0N 5 30 E
Netherlands Antilles ■, *S. Amer.* **45 E11** 12 15N 69 0W
Neuchâtel, *Switz.* **10 E2** 47 0N 6 55 E
Neuchâtel, L., *Switz.* **10 E2** 46 53N 6 50 E
Neufchâteau, *France* **8 C6** 48 21N 5 40 E
Neusiedl, L., *Austria* **10 E7** 47 50N 16 47 E
Nevada □, *U.S.A.* **40 C3** 39 20N 117 0W
Nevada, Sierra, *Spain* **11 D4** 37 3N 3 15W
Nevada, Sierra, *U.S.A.* **40 C2** 39 0N 120 30W
Nevers, *France* **8 D5** 47 0N 3 9 E
New Albany, *U.S.A.* **42 F5** 38 20N 85 50W
New Bedford, *U.S.A.* **43 E12** 41 40N 70 52W
New Britain, *Papua N. G.* **34 B9** 5 50S 150 20 E
New Britain, *U.S.A.* **43 E11** 41 41N 72 47W
New Brunswick, *U.S.A.* **43 E10** 40 30N 74 28W
New Brunswick □, *Canada* **43 B14** 46 50N 66 30W
New Caledonia, *Pac. Oc.* **35 E12** 21 0S 165 0 E
New Castle, *Ind., U.S.A.* **42 F5** 39 55N 85 23W
New Castle, *Pa., U.S.A.* **42 E7** 41 0N 80 20W
New Glasgow, *Canada* **43 C16** 45 35N 62 36W
New Guinea, *Oceania* **36 H5** 4 0S 136 0 E
New Hampshire □, *U.S.A.* **43 D12** 43 40N 71 40W
New Haven, *U.S.A.* **43 E11** 41 20N 72 54W
New Jersey □, *U.S.A.* **43 E10** 40 30N 74 10W
New Lexington, *U.S.A.* **42 F6** 39 40N 82 15W
New Liskeard, *Canada* **42 B8** 47 31N 79 41W
New London, *U.S.A.* **43 E11** 41 23N 72 8W
New Mexico □, *U.S.A.* **40 D5** 34 30N 106 0W
New Orleans, *U.S.A.* **41 E9** 30 0N 90 5W
New Philadelphia, *U.S.A.* **42 E7** 40 29N 81 25W
New Plymouth, *N.Z.* **35 H13** 39 4S 174 5 E
New Siberian Is., *Russia* **18 B15** 75 10N 150 0 E
New South Wales □, *Australia* **34 G8** 33 0S 146 0 E
New York □, *U.S.A.* **43 D9** 42 40N 76 0W
New York City, *U.S.A.* **43 E11** 40 45N 74 0W
New Zealand ■, *Oceania* **35 J13** 40 0S 176 0 E
Newark, *Del., U.S.A.* **43 F10** 39 42N 75 45W
Newark, *N.J., U.S.A.* **43 E10** 40 41N 74 12W
Newark, *N.Y., U.S.A.* **42 D9** 43 2N 77 10W
Newark, *Ohio, U.S.A.* **42 E6** 40 5N 82 24W
Newaygo, *U.S.A.* **42 D5** 43 25N 85 48W
Newberry, *U.S.A.* **42 B5** 46 20N 85 32W
Newburgh, *U.S.A.* **43 E10** 41 30N 74 1W
Newburyport, *U.S.A.* **43 D12** 42 48N 70 50W
Newcastle, *Australia* **34 G9** 33 0S 151 46 E
Newcastle, *Canada* **43 B15** 47 1N 65 38W
Newcastle, *S. Africa* **31 B4** 27 45S 29 58 E
Newcastle-upon-Tyne, *U.K.* **7 E6** 54 59N 1 37W
Newfoundland □, *Canada* **39 C14** 53 0N 58 0W
Newman, *Australia* **34 E2** 23 18S 119 45 E
Newport, *Gwent, U.K.* **7 G5** 51 35N 3 0W
Newport, *I. of W., U.K.* **7 G6** 50 42N 1 18W
Newport, *Ky., U.S.A.* **42 F5** 39 5N 84 23W
Newport, *R.I., U.S.A.* **43 E12** 41 13N 71 19W
Newport, *Vt., U.S.A.* **43 C11** 44 57N 72 17W
Newport News, *U.S.A.* **41 C11** 37 2N 76 30W
Newry, *U.K.* **7 E3** 54 10N 6 20W
Nganglong Kangri, *China* **23 C8** 33 0N 81 0 E
Nha Trang, *Vietnam* [illegible] 12 10N 109 10 E
Niagara, *U.S.A.* **42 C3** 45 45N 88 0W
Niagara Falls, *Canada* **42 D8** 43 7N 79 5W
Niagara Falls, *U.S.A.* **42 D8** 43 5N 79 0W
Niamey, *Niger* **30 B2** 13 27N 2 6 E
Nias, *Indonesia* **22 C1** 1 0N 97 30 E
Nicaragua ■, *Cent. Amer.* **44 E7** 11 40N 85 30W
Nicaragua, L. of, *Nic.* **44 E7** 12 0N 85 30W
Nice, *France* **9 F7** 43 42N 7 14 E
Nicholasville, *U.S.A.* **42 G5** 37 54N 84 31W
Nicobar Is., *Ind. Oc.* **25 E8** 9 0N 93 0 E
Nicosia, *Cyprus* **24 B2** 35 10N 33 25 E
Nicoya, Pen., *Costa Rica* **44 F7** 9 45N 85 40W
Niger ■, *W. Afr.* **28 F9** 17 30N 10 0 E
Niger →, *W. Afr.* **30 C3** 5 33N 6 33 E
Nigeria ■, *W. Afr.* **30 C3** 8 30N 8 0 E
Niigata, *Japan* **19 G11** 37 58N 139 0 E
Niihau, *U.S.A.* **40 H14** 21 55N 160 10W
Nijmegen, *Neths.* **8 B6** 51 50N 5 52 E
Nikolayev, *Ukraine* **15 E5** 46 58N 32 0 E
Nikolayevsk-na-Amur, *Russia* **18 D16** 53 8N 140 44 E
Nile →, *Africa* **29 C13** 30 10N 31 6 E
Nîmes, *France* **9 F6** 43 50N 4 23 E
Ningbo, *China* **21 D7** 29 51N 121 28 E
Ningxia Huizu Zizhiqu □, *China* **20 C5** 38 0N 106 0 E
Niort, *France* **9 D3** 46 19N 0 29W
Nipigon, *Canada* **42 A3** 49 0N 88 17W
Nipigon, L., *Canada* **42 A3** 49 50N 88 30W
Nipissing L., *Canada* **42 B8** 46 20N 80 0W
Niš, *Serbia, Yug.* **13 C9** 43 19N 21 58 E
Niterói, *Brazil* **47 E5** 22 52S 43 0W
Nitra, *Slovakia* **10 D8** 48 19N 18 4 E
Nitra →, *Slovakia* **10 E8** 47 46N 18 10 E
Niue, *Cook Is.* **35 D17** 19 2S 169 54W
Nivernais, *France* **8 D5** 47 15N 3 30 E
Nizamabad, *India* **25 D6** 18 45N 78 7 E
Nizhniy Novgorod, *Russia* **14 C7** 56 20N 44 0 E
Nizhniy Tagil, *Russia* **14 C10** 57 55N 59 57 E
Nkongsamba, *Cameroon* **30 D3** 4 55N 9 55 E
Nobeoka, *Japan* **19 C2** 32 36N 131 41 E
Noblesville, *U.S.A.* **42 E5** 40 1N 85 59W
Nogales, *Mexico* **44 A2** 31 20N 110 56W
Nogent-le-Rotrou, *France* **8 C4** 48 20N 0 50 E
Noirmoutier, I. de, *France* **8 D2** 46 58N 2 10W
Noranda, *Canada* **42 A8** 48 20N 79 0W
Norfolk, *U.S.A.* **41 C11** 36 40N 76 15W
Norfolk I., *Pac. Oc.* **35 F12** 28 58S 168 3 E
Norilsk, *Russia* **18 C10** 69 20N 88 6 E
Normandy, *France* **8 C4** 48 45N 0 10 E
Norristown, *U.S.A.* **43 E10** 40 9N 75 21W
Norrköping, *Sweden* **6 G11** 58 37N 16 11 E
Norrland, *Sweden* **6 F11** 62 15N 15 45 E
Norseman, *Australia* **34 G3** 32 8S 121 43 E
North Battleford, *Canada* **38 C9** 52 50N 108 17W
North Bay, *Canada* **42 B8** 46 20N 79 30W
North C., *Canada* **43 B17** 47 2N 60 20W
North Cape, *Norway* **6 D13** 71 10N 25 44 E
North Carolina □, *U.S.A.* **41 C11** 35 30N 80 0W
North Channel, *Canada* **42 B6** 46 0N 83 0W
North Channel, *U.K.* **7 E4** 55 0N 5 30W
North Dakota □, *U.S.A.* **40 A7** 47 30N 100 0W
North Downs, *U.K.* **7 G7** 51 17N 0 30 E
North European Plain, *Europe* **4 D11** 55 0N 25 0 E
North I., *N.Z.* **35 H14** 38 0S 175 0 E
North Ossetian Republic □, *Russia* **15 F7** 43 30N 44 30 E
North Pt., *Canada* **43 B15** 47 5N 64 0W
North Pole, *Arctic* **48 A1** 90 0N 0 0 E
North Rhine Westphalia □, *Germany* **10 C2** 51 45N 7 30 E
North Sea, *Europe* **4 D6** 56 0N 4 0 E
North Vernon, *U.S.A.* **42 F5** 39 0N 85 35W
North West Frontier □, *Pakistan* **23 C3** 34 0N 71 0 E
North West Highlands, *U.K.* **7 D4** 57 35N 5 2W
North West Territories □, *Canada* **38 B9** 67 0N 110 0W
North York Moors, *U.K.* **7 E6** 54 25N 0 50W
Northampton, *U.K.* **7 F6** 52 14N 0 54W
Northampton, *U.S.A.* **43 D11** 42 22N 72 31W
Northern Ireland □, *U.K.* **7 E3** 54 45N 7 0W
Northern Marianas □, *Pac. Oc.* **36 F6** 17 0N 145 0 E
Northern Territory □, *Australia* **34 E5** 20 0S 133 0 E
Northumberland Str., *Canada* **43 B15** 46 20N 64 0W
Norwalk, *U.S.A.* **42 E6** 41 13N 82 38W
Norway ■, *Europe* **6 F10** 63 0N 11 0 E
Norwegian Sea, *Atl. Oc.* **48 A7** 66 0N 1 0 E
Norwich, *U.K.* **7 F7** 52 38N 1 17 E
Norwich, *U.S.A.* **43 D10** 42 32N 75 30W
Nossob →, *S. Africa* **31 B3** 26 55S 20 45 E
Nottingham, *U.K.* **7 F6** 52 57N 1 10W
Nouâdhibou, *Mauritania* **28 E3** 20 54N 17 0W
Nouakchott, *Mauritania* **28 F3** 18 9N 15 58W
Nouméa, *N. Cal.* **35 E12** 22 17S 166 30 E
Noupoort, *S. Africa* **31 C3** 31 10S 24 57 E
Nova Scotia □, *Canada* **43 C16** 45 10N 63 0W
Novara, *Italy* **12 B3** 45 27N 8 36 E
Novaya Zemlya, *Russia* **18 B7** 75 0N 56 0 E
Novi Sad, *Serbia, Yug.* **13 B8** 45 18N 19 52 E
Novocherkassk, *Russia* **15 E7** 47 27N 40 15 E
Novokuznetsk, *Russia* **18 D10** 53 45N 87 10 E
Novomoskovsk, *Russia* **14 D6** 54 5N 38 15 E
Novorossiysk, *Russia* **15 F6** 44 43N 37 46 E
Novoshakhtinsk, *Russia* **15 E6** 47 46N 39 58 E
Novosibirsk, *Russia* **18 D10** 55 0N 83 5 E
Nowy Sącz, *Poland* **10 D9** 49 40N 20 41 E
Nubian Desert, *Sudan* **29 E13** 21 30N 33 30 E
Nuevo Laredo, *Mexico* **44 B5** 27 30N 99 30W
Nuku'alofa, *Tonga* **35 E16** 21 10S 174 0W
Nullarbor Plain, *Australia* [illegible] 31 10S 129 0 E
Nuremburg, *Germany* **10 D4** 49 26N 11 5 E
Nuuk = Godthåb, *Greenland* **48 A9** 64 10N 51 35W
Nuweveldberge, *S. Africa* **31 C3** 32 10S 21 45 E
Nyasa, L., *Africa* **33 G6** 12 30S 34 30 E
Nyíregyháza, *Hungary* **10 E9** 47 58N 21 47 E
Nylstroom, *S. Africa* **31 A4** 24 42S 28 22 E
Nysa, *Poland* **10 C7** 50 30N 17 22 E
Nysa →, *Europe* **10 B6** 52 4N 14 46 E

O

Oahe L., *U.S.A.* **40 A6** 45 30N 100 25W
Oahu, *U.S.A.* **40 H16** 21 30N 158 0W
Oak Hill, *U.S.A.* **42 G7** 38 0N 81 7W
Oakland, *U.S.A.* **40 C2** 37 50N 122 18W
Oates Land, *Antarctica* **48 C19** 69 0S 160 0 E
Oaxaca, *Mexico* **44 D5** 17 2N 96 40W
Ob →, *Russia* **18 C8** 66 45N 69 30 E
Ob, G. of, *Russia* **18 C9** 69 0N 73 0 E
Oba, *Canada* **42 A5** 49 4N 84 7W
Oban, *U.K.* **7 D4** 56 25N 5 30W
Oberhausen, *Germany* **10 C2** 51 28N 6 50 E
Obi Is., *Indonesia* **22 D4** 1 23S 127 45 E
Ocean City, *U.S.A.* **43 F10** 39 18N 74 34W
Oconto, *U.S.A.* **42 C4** 44 52N 87 53W
October Revolution I., *Russia* **18 B11** 79 30N 97 0 E
Odendaalsrus, *S. Africa* **31 B4** 27 48S 26 45 E
Odense, *Denmark* **6 G10** 55 22N 10 23 E
Odessa, *Ukraine* **15 E5** 46 30N 30 45 E
Odessa, *U.S.A.* **40 D6** 31 51N 102 23W
Odra →, *Poland* **10 B6** 53 33N 14 38 E
Offa, *Nigeria* **30 C2** 8 13N 4 42 E
Ogbomosho, *Nigeria* **30 C2** 8 1N 4 11 E
Ogden, *U.S.A.* **40 B4** 41 13N 112 1W
Ogdensburg, *U.S.A.* **43 C10** 44 40N 75 27W
Ohio □, *U.S.A.* **42 E5** 40 20N 84 10W
Ohio →, *U.S.A.* **41 C9** 36 59N 89 8W
Ohre →, *Czech.* **10 C6** 50 30N 14 10 E
Oil City, *U.S.A.* **42 E8** 41 26N 79 40W
Oise →, *France* **8 C5** 49 0N 2 4 E
Ōita, *Japan* **19 C2** 33 14N 131 36 E
Ojos del Salado, Cerro, *Argentina* **47 E3** 27 0S 68 40W
Okahandja, *Namibia* **31 A2** 22 0S 16 59 E
Okaputa, *Namibia* **31 A2** 20 5S 17 0 E
Okara, *Pakistan* **23 D4** 30 50N 73 31 E
Okavango Swamps, *Botswana* **33 H4** 18 45S 22 45 E
Okayama, *Japan* **19 B3** 34 40N 133 54 E
Okazaki, *Japan* **19 B5** 34 57N 137 10 E
Okha, *Russia* **18 D16** 53 40N 143 0 E
Okhotsk, *Russia* **18 D16** 59 20N 143 10 E
Okhotsk, Sea of, *Asia* **18 D16** 55 0N 145 0 E
Oklahoma □, *U.S.A.* **40 C7** 35 20N 97 30W
Oklahoma City, *U.S.A.* **40 C7** 35 25N 97 30W
Okwa →, *Botswana* **31 A3** 22 30S 23 0 E
Öland, *Sweden* **6 G11** 56 45N 16 38 E
Old Town, *U.S.A.* **43 C13** 45 0N 68 41W
Oldenburg, *Germany* **10 B3** 53 10N 8 10 E
Oldham, *U.K.* **7 F5** 53 33N 2 8W
Olean, *U.S.A.* **42 D8** 42 8N 78 25W
Olekminsk, *Russia* **18 C14** 60 25N 120 30 E
Olenek →, *Russia* **18 B14** 73 0N 120 10 E
Oléron, I. d', *France* **9 E3** 45 55N 1 15W
Olney, *U.S.A.* **42 F3** 38 40N 88 5W
Olomouc, *Czech.* **10 D7** 49 38N 17 12 E
Oloron-Ste.-Marie, *France* **9 F3** 43 11N 0 38W
Olsztyn, *Poland* **10 B9** 53 48N 20 29 E
Olt →, *Romania* **13 C11** 43 43N 24 51 E
Olympia, *Greece* **13 F9** 37 39N 21 39 E
Olympus, Mt., *Greece* **13 D10** 40 6N 22 23 E
Omaha, *U.S.A.* **41 B7** 41 15N 95 55W
Oman ■, *Asia* **17 G9** 23 0N 58 0 E
Oman, G. of, *Asia* **24 C4** 24 30N 58 30 E
Omaruru, *Namibia* **31 A2** 21 26S 16 0 E
Ombai Str., *Indonesia* **22 D4** 8 30S 124 50 E
Omdurman, *Sudan* **29 F13** 15 40N 32 28 E
Ōmiya, *Japan* **19 B6** 35 54N 139 38 E
Omsk, *Russia* **18 D9** 55 0N 73 12 E
Ōmuta, *Japan* **19 C2** 33 5N 130 26 E
Ondo, *Nigeria* **30 C2** 7 4N 4 47 E
Onega →, *Russia* **4 C13** 63 58N 37 55 E
Onega, G. of, *Russia* **14 B6** 64 30N 37 0 E
Onega, L., *Russia* **14 B6** 62 0N 35 30 E
Oneida, *U.S.A.* **43 D10** 43 5N 75 40W
Oneida L., *U.S.A.* **42 D10** 43 12N 76 0W
Oneonta, *U.S.A.* **43 D10** 42 26N 75 5W
Onitsha, *Nigeria* **30 C3** 6 6N 6 42 E
Ontario □, *Canada* **42 A2** 48 0N 83 0W
Ontario, L., *N. Amer.* **42 D8** 43 40N 78 0W
Ontonagon, *U.S.A.* **42 B3** 46 52N 89 19W
Oostende = Ostend, *Belgium* **8 B5** 51 15N 2 54 E
Opava, *Czech.* **10 D7** 49 57N 17 58 E
Opole, *Poland* **10 C7** 50 42N 17 58 E
Oporto, *Portugal* **11 B1** 41 8N 8 40W
Oradea, *Romania* **10 E9** 47 2N 21 58 E
Orai, *India* **23 G7** 25 58N 79 30 E
Oran, *Algeria* **28 B6** 35 45N 0 39W
Orange, *Australia* **34 G8** 33 15S 149 7 E
Orange, *France* **9 E6** 44 8N 4 47 E
Orange, *U.S.A.* **42 F8** 38 17N 78 5W
Orange →, *S. Africa* **31 B2** 28 41S 16 28 E
Orange Free State □, *S. Africa* **31 B4** 28 30S 27 0 E
Orangeville, *Canada* **42 D7** 43 55N 80 5W
Oranjemund, *Namibia* **31 B2** 28 38S 16 29 E
Ordos, *China* **21 C5** 39 0N 109 0 E
Örebro, *Sweden* **6 G11** 59 20N 15 18 E
Oregon □, *U.S.A.* **40 B2** 44 0N 121 0W
Orekhovo-Zuyevo, *Russia* **14 C6** 55 50N 38 55 E
Orel, *Russia* **14 D6** 52 57N 36 3 E
Orenburg, *Russia* **14 D10** 51 45N 55 6 E
Orense, *Spain* **11 A2** 42 19N 7 55W
Orinoco →, *Venezuela* **46 B3** 9 15N 61 30W
Orissa □, *India* **23 J9** 20 0N 84 0 E
Oristano, *Italy* **12 E3** 39 54N 8 35 E
Orizaba, *Mexico* **44 D5** 18 51N 97 6W
Orkney Is., *U.K.* **7 C5** 59 0N 3 0W
Orlando, *U.S.A.* **41 E10** 28 30N 81 25W
Orléanais, *France* **8 D4** 48 0N 2 0 E
Orléans, *France* **8 D4** 47 54N 1 52 E
Orléans, I. d', *Canada* **43 B12** 46 54N 70 58W
Ormara, *Pakistan* **24 C5** 25 16N 64 33 E
Ormoc, *Phil.* **22 B4** 11 0N 124 37 E
Örnsköldsvik, *Sweden* **6 F11** 63 17N 18 40 E
Orsk, *Russia* **14 D10** 51 12N 58 34 E
Orumiyeh, *Iran* **24 B3** 37 50N 45 30 E
Oruro, *Bolivia* **46 D3** 18 0S 67 9W
Ōsaka, *Japan* **19 B4** 34 40N 135 30 E
Oshawa, *Canada* **42 D8** 43 50N 78 50W
Oshogbo, *Nigeria* **30 C2** 7 48N 4 37 E
Osijek, *Croatia* **13 B8** 45 34N 18 41 E
Osizweni, *S. Africa* **31 B5** 27 49S 30 7 E
Oskarshamn, *Sweden* **6 G11** 57 15N 16 27 E
Oslo, *Norway* **6 G10** 59 55N 10 45 E
Oslo Fjord, *Norway* **6 G10** 59 20N 10 35 E
Osnabrück, *Germany* **10 B3** 52 16N 8 2 E
Osorno, *Chile* **47 G2** 40 25S 73 0W
Ostend, *Belgium* **8 B5** 51 15N 2 54 E
Östersund, *Sweden* **6 F10** 63 10N 14 38 E
Ostrava, *Czech.* **10 D8** 49 51N 18 18 E

117

Rainier, Mt.

Sault Ste. Marie

Rainier, Mt., *U.S.A.*	**40 A2**	46 50N	121 50W
Raipur, *India*	**23 J8**	21 17N	81 45 E
Raj Nandgaon, *India*	**23 J8**	21 5N	81 5 E
Rajahmundry, *India*	**25 D7**	17 1N	81 48 E
Rajasthan □, *India*	**23 F4**	26 45N	73 30 E
Rajasthan Canal, *India*	**23 F3**	28 0N	72 0 E
Rajkot, *India*	**23 H3**	22 15N	70 56 E
Rajshahi, *Bangla.*	**23 G12**	24 22N	88 39 E
Rajshahi □, *Bangla.*	**23 G12**	25 0N	89 0 E
Rakaposhi, *Pakistan*	**23 A5**	36 10N	74 25 E
Rakops, *Botswana*	**31 A3**	21 1S	24 28 E
Raleigh, *U.S.A.*	**41 C11**	35 47N	78 39W
Ramgarh, *India*	**23 H10**	23 40N	85 35 E
Ramotswa, *Botswana*	**31 A4**	24 50S	25 52 E
Rampur, *India*	**23 E7**	28 50N	79 5 E
Rancagua, *Chile*	**47 F2**	34 10S	70 50W
Ranchi, *India*	**23 H10**	23 19N	85 27 E
Randers, *Denmark*	**6 G10**	56 29N	10 1 E
Rangoon, *Burma*	**25 D8**	16 45N	96 20 E
Rangpur, *Bangla.*	**23 G12**	25 42N	89 22 E
Rantoul, *U.S.A.*	**42 E3**	40 18N	88 10W
Rasht, *Iran*	**24 B3**	37 20N	49 40 E
Ratangarh, *India*	**23 E5**	28 5N	74 35 E
Ratlam, *India*	**23 H5**	23 20N	75 0 E
Raurkela, *India*	**23 H10**	22 14N	84 50 E
Ravenna, *Italy*	**12 B5**	44 28N	12 15 E
Ravi →, *Pakistan*	**23 D3**	30 35N	71 49 E
Rawalpindi, *Pakistan*	**23 C4**	33 38N	73 8 E
Raz, Pte. du, *France*	**8 C1**	48 2N	4 47W
Ré, I. de, *France*	**9 D3**	46 12N	1 30W
Reading, *U.K.*	**7 G6**	51 27N	0 57W
Reading, *U.S.A.*	**43 E10**	40 20N	75 53W
Recife, *Brazil*	**46 C6**	8 0S	35 0W
Red →, *U.S.A.*	**41 D8**	31 0N	91 40W
Red Deer, *Canada*	**38 C8**	52 20N	113 50W
Red Sea, *Asia*	**29 E14**	25 0N	36 0 E
Redon, *France*	**8 D2**	47 40N	2 6W
Ree, L., *Ireland*	**7 F3**	53 35N	8 0W
Regensburg, *Germany*	**10 D5**	49 1N	12 7 E
Reggio di Calabria, *Italy*	**12 E6**	38 7N	15 38 E
Reggio nell' Emilia, *Italy*	**12 B4**	44 42N	10 38 E
Regina, *Canada*	**38 C9**	50 27N	104 35W
Rehoboth, *Namibia*	**31 A2**	23 15S	17 4 E
Reichenbach, *Germany*	**10 C5**	50 36N	12 19 E
Reigate, *U.K.*	**7 G6**	51 14N	0 11W
Reims, *France*	**8 C6**	49 15N	4 1 E
Reindeer L., *Canada*	**38 C9**	57 15N	102 15W
Reitz, *S. Africa*	**31 B4**	27 48S	28 29 E
Remscheid, *Germany*	**10 C2**	51 11N	7 12 E
Renfrew, *Canada*	**42 C9**	45 30N	76 40W
Rennes, *France*	**8 C3**	48 7N	1 41W
Reno, *U.S.A.*	**40 C3**	39 30N	119 50W
Resistencia, *Argentina*	**47 E4**	27 30S	59 0W
Rethel, *France*	**8 C6**	49 30N	4 20 E
Réthímnon, *Greece*	**13 G11**	35 18N	24 30 E
Réunion ■, *Ind. Oc.*	**27 J9**	21 0S	56 0 E
Revilla Gigedo, Is., *Pac. Oc.*	**37 F16**	18 40N	112 0W
Rewa, *India*	**23 G8**	24 33N	81 25 E
Rewari, *India*	**23 E6**	28 15N	76 40 E
Reykjavík, *Iceland*	**6 B3**	64 10N	21 57W
Reynosa, *Mexico*	[illegible]	[illegible]	[illegible]
Rhine →, *Europe*	**8 B7**	51 52N	6 2 E
Rhineland-Palatinate □, *Germany*	**10 D2**	50 0N	7 0 E
Rhode Island □, *U.S.A.*	**43 E12**	41 38N	71 37W
Rhodes = Ródhos, *Greece*	**13 F13**	36 15N	28 10 E
Rhodope Mts., *Bulgaria*	**13 D11**	41 40N	24 20 E
Rhön, *Germany*	**10 C3**	50 24N	9 58 E
Rhône →, *France*	**9 F6**	43 28N	4 42 E
Rhyl, *U.K.*	**7 F5**	53 19N	3 29W
Riau Arch., *Indonesia*	**22 C2**	0 30N	104 20 E
Ribeirão Prêto, *Brazil*	**46 E5**	21 10S	47 50W
Richards Bay, *S. Africa*	**31 B5**	28 48S	32 6 E
Richlands, *U.S.A.*	**42 G7**	37 7N	81 49W
Richmond, *Ind., U.S.A.*	**42 F5**	39 50N	84 50W
Richmond, *Ky., U.S.A.*	**42 G5**	37 40N	84 20W
Richmond, *Va., U.S.A.*	**42 G9**	37 33N	77 27W
Ridder, *Kazakhstan*	**18 D10**	50 20N	83 30 E
Ridgway, *U.S.A.*	**42 E8**	41 25N	78 43W
Riet →, *S. Africa*	**31 B3**	29 0S	23 54 E
Riga, *Latvia*	**14 C3**	56 53N	24 8 E
Riga, G. of, *Latvia*	**14 C3**	57 40N	23 45 E
Rijeka, *Croatia*	**12 B6**	45 20N	14 21 E
Rimini, *Italy*	**12 B5**	44 3N	12 33 E
Rîmnicu Vîlcea, *Romania*	**13 B11**	45 9N	24 21 E
Rimouski, *Canada*	**43 A13**	48 27N	68 30W
Rio de Janeiro, *Brazil*	**47 E5**	23 0S	43 12W
Río Gallegos, *Argentina*	**47 H3**	51 35S	69 15W
Rio Grande →, *U.S.A.*	**41 E7**	25 57N	97 9W
Ripon, *U.S.A.*	**42 D3**	43 51N	88 50W
Riverhead, *U.S.A.*	**43 E11**	40 53N	72 40W
Riversdale, *S. Africa*	**31 C3**	34 7S	21 15 E
Riverside, *U.S.A.*	**40 D3**	33 58N	117 22W
Rivière-du-Loup, *Canada*	**43 B13**	47 50N	69 30W
Riyadh, *Si. Arabia*	**24 C3**	24 41N	46 42 E
Roanne, *France*	**9 D6**	46 3N	4 4 E
Roanoke, *U.S.A.*	**42 G8**	37 19N	79 55W
Roberval, *Canada*	**43 A11**	48 32N	72 15W
Robson, Mt., *Canada*	**38 C8**	53 10N	119 10W
Rochechouart, *France*	**9 E4**	45 50N	0 49 E
Rochefort, *France*	**9 E3**	45 56N	0 57W
Rochester, *Ind., U.S.A.*	**42 E4**	41 5N	86 15W
Rochester, *Minn., U.S.A.*	**41 B8**	44 1N	92 28W
Rochester, *N.H., U.S.A.*	**43 D12**	43 19N	70 57W
Rochester, *N.Y., U.S.A.*	**42 D9**	43 10N	77 40W
Rockall, *Atl. Oc.*	**4 D3**	57 37N	13 42W
Rockford, *U.S.A.*	**41 B9**	42 20N	89 7W
Rockhampton, *Australia*	**34 E9**	23 22S	150 32 E
Rockland, *U.S.A.*	**43 C13**	44 6N	69 6W
Rocky Mts., *N. Amer.*	**38 C7**	55 0N	121 0W
Rodez, *France*	**9 E5**	44 21N	2 33 E
Ródhos, *Greece*	**13 F13**	36 15N	28 10 E
Roermond, *Neths.*	**8 B6**	51 12N	6 0 E
Roeselare, *Belgium*	**8 B5**	50 57N	3 7 E
Rogers City, *U.S.A.*	**42 C6**	45 25N	83 49W
Rohtak, *India*	**23 E6**	28 55N	76 43 E
Roma, *Australia*	**34 F8**	26 32S	148 49 E
Romania ■, *Europe*	**13 B11**	46 0N	25 0 E
Romans-sur-Isère, *France*	**9 E6**	45 3N	5 3 E
Rome, *Italy*	**12 D5**	41 54N	12 30 E
Rome, *U.S.A.*	**43 D10**	43 14N	75 29W
Romney, *U.S.A.*	**42 F8**	39 21N	78 45W
Romorantin-Lanthenay, *France*	**8 D4**	47 21N	1 45 E
Rondônia □, *Brazil*	**46 D3**	11 0S	63 0W
Ronne Ice Shelf, *Antarctica*	**48 C23**	78 0S	60 0W
Roodepoort, *S. Africa*	**31 B4**	26 11S	27 54 E
Roosevelt I., *Antarctica*	**48 C20**	79 30S	162 0W
Roquefort, *France*	**9 E3**	44 2N	0 20W
Roraima □, *Brazil*	**46 B3**	2 0N	61 30W
Rosario, *Argentina*	**47 F3**	33 0S	60 40W
Roscommon, *U.S.A.*	**42 C5**	44 27N	84 35W
Roseau, *Domin.*	**44 M20**	15 20N	61 24W
Rosenheim, *Germany*	**10 E5**	47 51N	12 9 E
Ross Ice Shelf, *Antarctica*	**48 C20**	80 0S	180 0 E
Ross Sea, *Antarctica*	**48 C19**	74 0S	178 0 E
Rossignol, L., *Canada*	**43 C15**	44 12N	65 10W
Rosslare, *Ireland*	**7 F3**	52 17N	6 23W
Rostock, *Germany*	**10 A5**	54 4N	12 9 E
Rostov, *Russia*	**15 E6**	47 15N	39 45 E
Rothaar Gebirge, *Germany*	**10 C3**	51 0N	8 5 E
Rotherham, *U.K.*	**7 F6**	53 26N	1 21W
Rothesay, *U.K.*	**7 E4**	55 50N	5 3W
Rotorua, *N.Z.*	**35 H14**	38 9S	176 16 E
Rotterdam, *Neths.*	**8 B6**	51 55N	4 30 E
Roubaix, *France*	**8 B5**	50 40N	3 10 E
Rouen, *France*	**8 C4**	49 27N	1 4 E
Roussillon, *France*	**9 F5**	42 30N	2 35 E
Rouxville, *S. Africa*	**31 C4**	30 25S	26 50 E
Rouyn, *Canada*	**42 A8**	48 20N	79 0W
Rovaniemi, *Finland*	**6 E13**	66 29N	25 41 E
Royal Leamington Spa, *U.K.*	**7 F6**	52 18N	1 32W
Royan, *France*	**9 E3**	45 37N	1 2W
Rub' al Khali, *Si. Arabia*	**24 D3**	18 0N	48 0 E
Rugby, *U.K.*	**7 F6**	52 23N	1 16W
Rügen, *Germany*	**10 A5**	54 22N	13 25 E
Ruhr →, *Germany*	**10 C2**	51 25N	6 44 E
Rumania = Romania ■, *Europe*	**13 B11**	46 0N	25 0 E
Rumford, *U.S.A.*	**43 C12**	44 30N	70 30W
Rupat, *Indonesia*	**22 C2**	1 45N	101 40 E
Ruse, *Bulgaria*	**13 C11**	43 48N	25 59 E
Rushville, *U.S.A.*	**42 F5**	39 38N	85 22W
Russia ■, *Eurasia*	**18 C12**	62 0N	105 0 E
Rustenburg, *S. Africa*	**31 B4**	25 41S	27 14 E
Ruteng, *Indonesia*	**22 D4**	8 35S	120 30 E
Ruwenzori, *Africa*	**32 D5**	0 30N	29 55 E
Rwanda ■, *Africa*	**32 E5**	2 0S	30 0 E
Ryazan, *Russia*	**14 D6**	54 40N	39 40 E
Rybinsk, *Russia*	**14 C6**	58 5N	38 50 E
Rybinsk Res., *Russia*	**14 C6**	58 30N	38 25 E
Ryūkyū Is., *Japan*	**21 D7**	26 0N	126 0 E
Rzeszów, *Poland*	**10 C9**	50 5N	21 58 E

S

Saale →, *Germany*	**10 C4**	51 57N	11 56 E
Saar →, *Europe*	**10 D2**	49 41N	6 32 E
Saarbrücken, *Germany*	**10 D2**	49 15N	6 58 E
Saaremaa, *Estonia*	**14 C3**	58 30N	22 30 E
Saba, *W. Indies*	**44 K18**	17 42N	63 26W
Sabadell, *Spain*	**11 B7**	41 28N	2 7 E
Sabah □, *Malaysia*	**22 C3**	6 0N	117 0 E
Sabhah, *Libya*	**28 D9**	27 9N	14 29 E
Sabie, *S. Africa*	**31 B5**	25 10S	30 48 E
Sable, C., *Canada*	**43 D15**	43 29N	65 38W
Saco, *U.S.A.*	**43 D12**	43 30N	70 27W
Sacramento, *U.S.A.*	**40 C2**	38 33N	121 30W
Safi, *Morocco*	**28 C5**	32 18N	9 20W
Saginaw, *U.S.A.*	**42 D6**	43 26N	83 55W
Saginaw B., *U.S.A.*	**42 D6**	43 50N	83 40W
Saguenay →, *Canada*	**43 A12**	48 22N	71 0W
Sahara, *Africa*	**26 D4**	23 0N	5 0 E
Saharanpur, *India*	**23 E6**	29 58N	77 33 E
Sahiwal, *Pakistan*	**23 D4**	30 45N	73 8 E
Saidabad, *Iran*	**24 C4**	29 30N	55 45 E
Saidpur, *Bangla.*	**23 G12**	25 48N	89 0 E
St. Albans, *U.K.*	**7 G6**	51 44N	0 19W
St. Albans, *Vt., U.S.A.*	**43 C11**	44 49N	73 7W
St. Albans, *W. Va., U.S.A.*	**42 F7**	38 21N	81 50W
St.-Amand-Mont-Rond, *France*	**9 D5**	46 43N	2 30 E
St. Andrews, *U.K.*	**7 D5**	56 20N	2 48W
St. Boniface, *Canada*	**38 D10**	49 53N	97 5W
St.-Brieuc, *France*	**8 C2**	48 30N	2 46W
St. Catharines, *Canada*	**42 D8**	43 10N	79 15W
St. Christopher-Nevis ■, *W. Indies*	**44 K19**	17 20N	62 40W
St. Clair, L., *Canada*	**42 D6**	42 30N	82 45W
St.-Claude, *France*	**9 D6**	46 22N	5 52 E
St.-Dié, *France*	**8 C7**	48 17N	6 56 E
St.-Dizier, *France*	**8 C6**	48 38N	4 56 E
St.-Étienne, *France*	**9 E6**	45 27N	4 22 E
St.-Félicien, *Canada*	**43 A11**	48 40N	72 25W
St.-Flour, *France*	**9 E5**	45 2N	3 6 E
St. Gallen, *Switz.*	**10 E3**	47 26N	9 22 E
St.-Gaudens, *France*	**9 F4**	43 6N	0 44 E
St-Georges, *Canada*	**43 B12**	46 8N	70 40W
St. George's, *Grenada*	**44 Q20**	12 5N	61 43W
St. George's Channel, *U.K.*	**7 G4**	52 0N	6 0W
St.-Girons, *France*	**9 F4**	42 59N	1 8 E
St. Gotthard P., *Switz.*	**10 E3**	46 33N	8 33 E
St. Helena, *Atl. Oc.*	**2 E9**	15 55S	5 44W
St. Helena B., *S. Africa*	**33 L3**	32 40S	18 10 E
St. Helens, *U.K.*	**7 F5**	53 28N	2 44W
St. Helier, *U.K.*	**8 C2**	49 11N	2 6W
St-Hyacinthe, *Canada*	**43 C11**	45 40N	72 58W
St. Ignace, *U.S.A.*	**42 C5**	45 53N	84 43W
St-Jean, *Canada*	**43 C11**	45 20N	73 20W
St-Jean, L., *Canada*	**43 A11**	48 40N	72 0W
St.-Jean-d'Angély, *France*	**9 E3**	45 57N	0 31W
St-Jérôme, *Canada*	**43 C11**	45 47N	74 0W
St. John, *Canada*	**43 C14**	45 20N	66 8W
St. John's, *Antigua*	**44 K20**	17 6N	61 51W
St. John's, *Canada*	**39 D14**	47 35N	52 40W
St. Johns, *U.S.A.*	**42 D5**	43 0N	84 31W
St. Johnsbury, *U.S.A.*	**43 C11**	44 25N	72 1W
St. Joseph, *Mich., U.S.A.*	**42 D4**	42 5N	86 30W
St. Joseph, *Mo., U.S.A.*	**41 C8**	39 46N	94 50W
St. Lawrence →, *Canada*	**43 A13**	49 30N	66 0W
St. Lawrence, Gulf of, *Canada*	**43 A16**	48 25N	62 0W
St.-Lô, *France*	**8 C3**	49 7N	1 5W
St-Louis, *Senegal*	**28 F3**	16 8N	16 27W
St. Louis, *U.S.A.*	**41 C8**	38 40N	90 12W
St. Lucia ■, *W. Indies*	**44 P21**	14 0N	60 50W
St. Lucia, L., *S. Africa*	**31 B5**	28 5S	32 30 E
St. Malo, *France*	**8 C2**	48 39N	2 1W
St.-Malo, G. de, *France*	**8 C2**	48 50N	2 30W
St-Martin, *W. Indies*	**44 K19**	18 0N	63 0W
St. Marys, *U.S.A.*	**42 E8**	41 27N	78 33W
St.-Nazaire, *France*	**8 D2**	47 17N	2 12W
St. Niklass, *Belgium*	**8 B6**	51 10N	4 9 E
St.-Omer, *France*	**8 B5**	50 45N	2 15 E
St. Paul, *U.S.A.*	**41 B8**	44 54N	93 5W
St. Peter Port, *Chan. Is.*	**8 C2**	49 27N	2 31W
St. Petersburg, *Russia*	**14 C5**	59 55N	30 20 E
St. Petersburg, *U.S.A.*	**41 E10**	27 45N	82 40W
St.-Pierre et Miquelon □, *St- P. & M.*	**39 D14**	46 55N	56 10W
St.-Quentin, *France*	**8 C5**	49 50N	3 16 E
St.-Raphaël, *France*	**9 F7**	43 25N	6 46 E
St. Stephen, *Canada*	**43 C14**	45 16N	67 17W
St. Thomas, *Canada*	**42 D7**	42 45N	81 10W
St.-Tropez, *France*	**9 F7**	43 17N	6 38 E
St. Vincent and the Grenadines ■, *W. Indies*	**44 Q20**	13 0N	61 10W
Ste-Marie de la Madeleine, *Canada*	**43 B12**	46 26N	71 0W
Ste.-Menehould, *France*	**8 C6**	49 5N	4 54 E
Saintes, *France*	**9 E3**	45 45N	0 37W
Saintonge, *France*	**9 E3**	45 40N	0 50W
Sak →, *S. Africa*	**31 C3**	30 52S	20 25 E
Sakai, *Japan*	**19 B4**	34 30N	135 30 E
Sakhalin, *Russia*	**18 D16**	51 0N	143 0 E
Sala, *Sweden*	**6 G11**	59 58N	16 35 E
Salado →, *Argentina*	**47 F3**	31 40S	60 41W
Salamanca, *Spain*	**11 B3**	40 58N	5 39W
Salamanca, *U.S.A.*	**42 D8**	42 10N	78 42W
Salayar, *Indonesia*	**22 D4**	6 7S	120 30 E
Saldanha, *S. Africa*	**31 C2**	33 0S	17 58 E
Salekhard, *Russia*	**18 C8**	66 30N	66 35 E
Salem, *India*	**25 D6**	11 40N	78 11 E
Salem, *Ind., U.S.A.*	**42 F4**	38 38N	86 6W
Salem, *Mass., U.S.A.*	**43 D12**	42 29N	70 53W
Salem, *Ohio, U.S.A.*	**42 E7**	40 52N	80 50W
Salem, *Va., U.S.A.*	**42 G7**	37 19N	80 8W
Salerno, *Italy*	**12 D6**	40 40N	14 44 E
Salford, *U.K.*	**7 F5**	53 30N	2 17W
Salisbury, *U.K.*	**7 G6**	51 4N	1 48W
Salisbury, *U.S.A.*	**43 F10**	38 20N	75 38W
Salisbury Plain, *U.K.*	**7 G6**	51 13N	1 50W
Salon-de-Provence, *France*	**9 F6**	43 39N	5 6 E
Salonica = Thessaloníki, *Greece*	**13 D10**	40 38N	22 58 E
Salt Lake City, *U.S.A.*	**40 B4**	40 45N	111 58W
Salta, *Argentina*	**47 E3**	24 57S	65 25W
Saltcoats, *U.K.*	**7 E4**	55 38N	4 47W
Saltillo, *Mexico*	**44 B4**	25 30N	100 57W
Saltillo, *Coahuila, Mexico*	**44 B4**	25 25N	101 0W
Salto, *Uruguay*	**47 F4**	31 27S	57 50W
Salvador, *Brazil*	**46 D6**	13 0S	38 30W
Salween →, *Burma*	**25 D8**	16 31N	97 37 E
Salyersville, *U.S.A.*	**42 G6**	37 45N	83 4W
Salzburg, *Austria*	**10 E5**	47 48N	13 2 E
Salzgitter, *Germany*	**10 B4**	52 13N	10 22 E
Samar, *Phil.*	**22 B4**	12 0N	125 0 E
Samara, *Russia*	**14 D9**	53 8N	50 6 E
Samarkand, *Uzbekistan*	**18 F8**	39 40N	66 55 E
Sambalpur, *India*	**23 J10**	21 28N	84 4 E
Sambhal, *India*	**23 E7**	28 35N	78 37 E
Sambhar, *India*	**23 F5**	26 52N	75 6 E
Sámos, *Greece*	**13 F12**	37 45N	26 50 E
Samsun, *Turkey*	**15 F6**	41 15N	36 22 E
San →, *Poland*	**10 C9**	50 45N	21 51 E
San Agustin, C., *Phil.*	**22 C4**	6 20N	126 13 E
San Angelo, *U.S.A.*	**40 D6**	31 30N	100 30W
San Antonio, *U.S.A.*	**40 E7**	29 30N	98 30W
San Bernardino, *U.S.A.*	**40 D3**	34 7N	117 18W
San Bernardino Str., *Phil.*	**22 B4**	13 0N	125 0 E
San Diego, *U.S.A.*	**40 D3**	32 43N	117 10W
San Francisco, *U.S.A.*	**40 C2**	37 47N	122 30W
San Jorge, G., *Argentina*	**47 G3**	46 0S	66 0W
San José, *Costa Rica*	**45 F8**	9 55N	84 2W
San Jose, *U.S.A.*	**40 C2**	37 20N	121 53W
San Juan, *Argentina*	**47 F3**	31 30S	68 30W
San Juan, *Puerto Rico*	**45 D11**	18 28N	66 8W
San Lucas, C., *Mexico*	**44 C3**	22 50N	110 0W
San Luis Potosí, *Mexico*	**44 C4**	22 9N	100 59W
San Marino ■, *Europe*	**12 C5**	43 56N	12 25 E
San Miguel de Tucumán, *Argentina*	**47 E3**	26 50S	65 20W
San Pedro Sula, *Honduras*	**44 D7**	15 30N	88 0W
San Salvador, *El Salv.*	**44 E7**	13 40N	89 10W
San Salvador de Jujuy, *Argentina*	**47 E3**	24 10S	64 48W
San Sebastián, *Spain*	**11 A5**	43 17N	1 58W
Sana', *Yemen*	**24 D3**	15 27N	44 12 E
Sancy, Puy de, *France*	**9 E5**	45 32N	2 50 E
Sand →, *S. Africa*	**31 A5**	22 25S	30 5 E
Sandakan, *Malaysia*	**22 C3**	5 53N	118 4 E
Sandusky, *U.S.A.*	**42 E6**	41 25N	82 40W
Sangli, *India*	**25 D6**	16 55N	74 33 E
Santa Ana, *U.S.A.*	**40 D3**	33 48N	117 55W
Santa Clara, *Cuba*	**45 C9**	22 20N	80 0W
Santa Cruz, *Bolivia*	**46 D3**	17 43S	63 10W
Santa Cruz de Tenerife, *Canary Is.*	**28 D3**	28 28N	16 15W
Santa Fe, *Argentina*	**47 F3**	31 35S	60 41W
Santa Fe, *U.S.A.*	**40 C5**	35 40N	106 0W
Santa Maria, *Brazil*	**47 E4**	29 40S	53 48W
Santa Marta, *Colombia*	**46 A2**	11 15N	74 13W
Santander, *Spain*	**11 A4**	43 27N	3 51W
Santarém, *Brazil*	**46 C4**	2 25S	54 42W
Santarém, *Portugal*	**11 C1**	39 12N	8 42W
Santiago, *Chile*	**47 F2**	33 24S	70 40W
Santiago de Compostela, *Spain*	**11 A1**	42 52N	8 37W
Santiago de Cuba, *Cuba*	**45 D9**	20 0N	75 49W
Santiago de los Caballeros, *Dom. Rep.*	**45 D10**	19 30N	70 40W
Santo André, *Brazil*	**47 E5**	23 39S	46 29W
Santo Domingo, *Dom. Rep.*	**45 D11**	18 30N	69 59W
Santos, *Brazil*	**47 E5**	24 0S	46 20W
São Francisco →, *Brazil*	**46 D6**	10 30S	36 24W
São José do Rio Prêto, *Brazil*	**46 E5**	20 50S	49 20W
São Luís, *Brazil*	**46 C5**	2 39S	44 15W
São Paulo, *Brazil*	**47 E5**	23 32S	46 37W
São Roque, C. de, *Brazil*	**46 C6**	5 30S	35 16W
São Tomé & Principe ■, *Africa*	**28 J8**	0 12N	6 39 E
Saône →, *France*	**9 E6**	45 44N	4 50 E
Sapporo, *Japan*	**19 F12**	43 0N	141 21 E
Saragossa = Zaragoza, *Spain*	**11 B5**	41 39N	0 53W
Sarajevo, *Bos.-H., Yug.*	**13 C8**	43 52N	18 26 E
Saranac Lakes, *U.S.A.*	**43 C10**	44 20N	74 10W
Sarangani B., *Phil.*	**22 C4**	6 0N	125 13 E
Saransk, *Russia*	**14 D8**	54 10N	45 10 E
Saratoga Springs, *U.S.A.*	**43 D11**	43 5N	73 47W
Saratov, *Russia*	**14 D8**	51 30N	46 2 E
Sarawak □, *Malaysia*	**22 C3**	2 0N	113 0 E
Sarda →, *India*	**23 F8**	27 21N	81 23 E
Sardinia, *Italy*	**12 E3**	39 57N	9 0 E
Sargodha, *Pakistan*	**23 C4**	32 10N	72 40 E
Sarh, *Chad*	**28 H10**	9 5N	18 23 E
Sarlat-la-Canéda, *France*	**9 E4**	44 54N	1 13 E
Sarnia, *Canada*	**42 D6**	42 58N	82 23W
Sarrebourg, *France*	**8 C7**	48 43N	7 3 E
Sarreguemines, *France*	**8 C7**	49 5N	7 4 E
Sartène, *France*	**9 G8**	41 38N	8 58 E
Sarthe →, *France*	**8 D3**	47 33N	0 31W
Sasebo, *Japan*	**19 C1**	33 10N	129 43 E
Saser, *India*	**23 B6**	34 50N	77 50 E
Saskatchewan □, *Canada*	**38 C9**	54 40N	106 0W
Saskatchewan →, *Canada*	**38 C9**	53 37N	100 40W
Saskatoon, *Canada*	**38 C9**	52 10N	106 38W
Sasolburg, *S. Africa*	**31 B4**	26 46S	27 49 E
Sassari, *Italy*	**12 D3**	40 44N	8 33 E
Sassnitz, *Germany*	**10 A5**	54 29N	13 39 E
Satmala Hills, *India*	**23 J5**	20 15N	74 40 E
Satna, *India*	**23 G8**	24 35N	80 50 E
Satpura Ra., *India*	**23 J6**	21 25N	76 10 E
Satu Mare, *Romania*	**10 E10**	47 46N	22 55 E
Sauðarkrókur, *Iceland*	**6 B4**	65 45N	19 40W
Saudi Arabia ■, *Asia*	**24 C3**	26 0N	44 0 E
Sault Ste. Marie, *Canada*	**42 B5**	46 30N	84 20W
Sault Ste. Marie, *U.S.A.*	**42 B5**	46 27N	84 22W

Saumur, France	8 D3	47 15N	0 5W
Sava →, Serbia, Yug.	13 B9	44 50N	20 26 E
Savanna la Mar, Jamaica	44 J15	18 10N	78 10W
Savannah, U.S.A.	41 D10	32 4N	81 4W
Saverne, France	8 C7	48 43N	7 20 E
Savona, Italy	12 B3	44 19N	8 29 E
Savonlinna, Finland	14 B4	61 52N	28 53 E
Sawahlunto, Indonesia	22 D2	0 40S	100 52 E
Sawu, Indonesia	22 D4	9 35S	121 50 E
Sawu Sea, Indonesia	22 D4	9 30S	121 50 E
Sayda, Lebanon	29 L21	33 35N	35 25 E
Sayre, U.S.A.	42 E9	42 0N	76 30W
Sázava →, Czech.	10 D6	49 53N	14 24 E
Sca Fell, U.K.	7 E5	54 27N	3 14W
Scandinavia, Europe	4 C8	64 0N	12 0 E
Scarborough, U.K.	7 E6	54 17N	0 24W
Schaffhausen, Switz.	10 E3	47 42N	8 39 E
Schefferville, Canada	39 C13	54 48N	66 50W
Schelde →, Belgium	8 B6	51 15N	4 16 E
Schenectady, U.S.A.	43 D11	42 50N	73 58W
Schleswig, Germany	10 A3	54 32N	9 34 E
Schleswig-Holstein □, Germany	10 A3	54 10N	9 40 E
Schouten Is., Indonesia	22 D5	1 0S	136 0 E
Schreiber, Canada	42 A4	48 45N	87 20W
Schwaner Ra., Indonesia	22 D3	1 0S	112 30 E
Schwarzwald = Black Forest, Germany	10 E3	48 0N	8 0 E
Schweizer-Reneke, S. Africa	31 B4	27 11S	25 18 E
Schwerin, Germany	10 B4	53 37N	11 22 E
Schwyz, Switz.	10 E3	47 2N	8 39 E
Scilly, Isles of, U.K.	7 H3	49 55N	6 15W
Scioto →, U.S.A.	42 F6	38 44N	83 0W
Scotland □, U.K.	7 D5	57 0N	4 0W
Scott I., Antarctica	48 C19	67 0S	179 0 E
Scottsburg, U.S.A.	42 F5	38 40N	85 46W
Scranton, U.S.A.	43 E10	41 22N	75 41W
Scunthorpe, U.K.	7 F6	53 35N	0 38W
Seaford, U.S.A.	43 F10	38 37N	75 36W
Seattle, U.S.A.	40 A2	47 41N	122 15W
Sedan, France	8 C6	49 43N	4 57 E
Seeheim, Namibia	31 B2	26 50S	17 45 E
Segovia, Spain	11 B3	40 57N	4 10W
Sehore, India	23 H6	23 10N	77 5 E
Seine →, France	8 C4	49 26N	0 26 E
Seine, B. de la, France	8 C3	49 40N	0 40W
Sekondi-Takoradi, Ghana	30 D1	4 58N	1 45W
Sekuma, Botswana	31 A3	24 36S	23 50 E
Selaru, Indonesia	22 D5	8 9S	131 0 E
Sélestat, France	8 C7	48 16N	7 26 E
Selkirk, U.K.	7 E5	55 33N	2 50W
Selkirk Mts., Canada	38 C8	51 15N	117 40W
Selvas, Brazil	46 C3	6 30S	67 0W
Semarang, Indonesia	22 D3	7 0S	110 26 E
Semipalatinsk, Kazakhstan	18 D10	50 30N	80 10 E
Semmering Pass, Austria	10 E6	47 41N	15 45 E
Sendai, Japan	19 G12	38 15N	140 53 E
Seneca L., U.S.A.	42 D9	42 40N	76 58W
Senegal ■, W. Afr.	28 G4	14 30N	14 30W
Senegal →, W. Afr.	28 F3	15 48N	16 32W
Senekal, S. Africa	31 B4	28 20S	27 36 E
Senja, Norway	6 E11	69 25N	17 30 E
Senlis, France	8 C5	49 13N	2 35 E
Sens, France	8 C5	48 11N	3 15 E
Seoul, S. Korea	21 C7	37 31N	126 58 E
Sequoia Nat. Park, U.S.A.	40 C3	36 30N	118 30W
Seram, Indonesia	22 D4	3 10S	129 0 E
Serbia □, Serbia, Yug.	13 C9	43 30N	21 0 E
Seremban, Malaysia	22 C2	2 43N	101 53 E
Sergiyev Posad, Russia	14 C6	56 20N	38 10 E
Serowe, Botswana	31 A4	22 25S	26 43 E
Serpukhov, Russia	14 D6	54 55N	37 28 E
Sète, France	9 F5	43 25N	3 42 E
Sétif, Algeria	28 B8	36 9N	5 26 E
Setúbal, Portugal	11 C1	38 30N	8 58W
Sevan, L., Armenia	15 F8	40 30N	45 20 E
Sevastopol, Ukraine	15 F5	44 35N	33 30 E
Severn →, U.K.	7 G5	51 35N	2 38W
Severnaya Zemlya, Russia	18 B11	79 0N	100 0 E
Seville, Spain	11 D3	37 23N	6 0W
Seward Pen., U.S.A.	38 B3	65 0N	164 0W
Seychelles ■, Ind. Oc.	17 K9	5 0S	56 0 E
Seyðisfjörður, Iceland	6 B7	65 16N	13 57W
Seymour, U.S.A.	42 F5	38 55N	85 50W
Sfax, Tunisia	28 C9	34 49N	10 48 E
Sfîntu Gheorghe, Romania	13 B11	45 52N	25 48 E
Shaanxi □, China	21 C5	35 0N	109 0 E
Shaba □, Zaïre	32 F4	8 0S	25 0 E
Shache, China	20 C2	38 20N	77 10 E
Shahjahanpur, India	23 F7	27 54N	79 57 E
Shajapur, India	23 H6	23 27N	76 21 E
Shakhty, Russia	15 E7	47 40N	40 16 E
Shaki, Nigeria	30 C2	8 41N	3 21 E
Shan □, Burma	25 C8	21 30N	98 30 E
Shandong □, China	21 C6	36 0N	118 0 E
Shanghai, China	21 C7	31 15N	121 26 E
Shangrao, China	21 D6	28 25N	117 59 E
Shannon →, Ireland	7 F2	52 35N	9 30W
Shantar Is., Russia	18 D15	55 9N	137 40 E
Shantou, China	21 D6	23 18N	116 40 E
Shanxi □, China	21 C6	37 0N	112 0 E
Shaoguan, China	21 D6	24 48N	113 35 E
Shaoyang, China	21 D6	27 14N	111 25 E
Sharjah, U.A.E.	24 C4	25 23N	55 26 E
Sharon, U.S.A.	42 E7	41 18N	80 30W
Shatt al'Arab →, Iraq	24 C3	29 57N	48 34 E
Shawano, U.S.A.	42 C3	44 45N	88 38W
Shawinigan, Canada	43 B11	46 35N	72 50W
Sheboygan, U.S.A.	42 D4	43 46N	87 45W
Sheffield, U.K.	7 F6	53 23N	1 28W
Shelburne, Canada	43 D15	43 47N	65 20W
Shelbyville, U.S.A.	42 F5	39 30N	85 42W
Shelekhov G., Russia	18 D17	59 30N	157 0 E
Shellharbour, Australia	34 G9	34 31S	150 51 E
Shenandoah, U.S.A.	43 E9	40 49N	76 13W
Shenandoah →, U.S.A.	42 F9	39 19N	77 44W
Shenyang, China	21 B7	41 48N	123 27 E
Shepparton, Australia	34 H8	36 23S	145 26 E
Sherbrooke, Canada	43 C12	45 28N	71 57W
Shetland Is., U.K.	7 A6	60 30N	1 30W
Shickshock Mts., Canada	43 A14	48 55N	66 0W
Shijiazhuang, China	21 C6	38 2N	114 28 E
Shikarpur, Pakistan	23 F2	27 57N	68 39 E
Shikoku, Japan	19 C3	33 30N	133 30 E
Shillong, India	23 G13	25 35N	91 53 E
Shimoga, India	25 D6	13 57N	75 32 E
Shimonoseki, Japan	19 C2	33 58N	130 55 E
Shipki La, India	23 D7	31 45N	78 40 E
Shiraz, Iran	24 C4	29 42N	52 30 E
Shire →, Africa	33 H7	17 42S	35 19 E
Shivpuri, India	23 G6	25 26N	77 42 E
Shizuoka, Japan	19 B6	34 57N	138 24 E
Shkoder, Albania	13 C8	42 6N	19 20 E
Shoshong, Botswana	31 A4	22 56S	26 31 E
Shreveport, U.S.A.	41 D8	32 30N	93 50W
Shrewsbury, U.K.	7 F5	52 42N	2 45W
Shuangyashan, China	21 B8	46 28N	131 5 E
Shwebo, Burma	25 C8	22 30N	95 45 E
Shyok, India	23 B7	34 15N	78 12 E
Sialkot, Pakistan	23 C5	32 32N	74 30 E
Sian, China	21 C5	34 15N	109 0 E
Siberia, Russia	16 D14	60 0N	100 0 E
Siberut, Indonesia	22 D1	1 30S	99 0 E
Sibi, Pakistan	23 E1	29 30N	67 54 E
Sibiu, Romania	13 B11	45 45N	24 9 E
Sibolga, Indonesia	22 C1	1 42N	98 45 E
Sibu, Malaysia	22 C3	2 18N	111 49 E
Sibuyan, Phil.	22 B4	12 25N	122 40 E
Sichuan □, China	20 C5	31 0N	104 0 E
Sicily, Italy	12 F6	37 30N	14 30 E
Sidney, U.S.A.	42 E5	40 18N	84 6W
Siedlce, Poland	10 B10	52 10N	22 20 E
Siegen, Germany	10 C3	50 52N	8 2 E
Siena, Italy	12 C4	43 20N	11 20 E
Sierra Leone ■, W. Afr.	28 H4	9 0N	12 0W
Siglufjörður, Iceland	6 A4	66 12N	18 55W
Sikar, India	23 F5	27 33N	75 10 E
Sikhote Alin Ra., Russia	18 E17	45 0N	136 0 E
Sikkim □, India	23 F12	27 50N	88 30 E
Silesia, Poland	10 C7	51 0N	16 30 E
Siliguri, India	23 F12	26 45N	88 25 E
Simbirsk, Russia	14 D8	54 20N	48 25 E
Simcoe, Canada	42 D7	42 50N	80 20W
Simcoe, L., Canada	42 C8	44 25N	79 20W
Simeulue, Indonesia	22 C1	2 45N	95 45 E
Simferopol, Ukraine	15 F5	44 55N	34 3 E
Simla, India	23 D6	31 2N	77 9 E
Simplon Pass, Switz.	10 E3	46 15N	8 3 E
Simpson Desert, Australia	34 F6	25 0S	137 0 E
Sind □, Pakistan	23 F2	26 0N	69 0 E
Sind Sagar Doab, Pakistan	23 D3	32 0N	71 30 E
Singapore ■, Asia	22 C2	1 17N	103 51 E
Sinkiang Uighur = Xinjiang Uygur Zizhiqu □, China	20 B3	42 0N	86 0 E
Sion, Switz.	10 E2	46 14N	7 20 E
Sioux Falls, U.S.A.	41 B7	43 35N	96 40W
Siping, China	21 B7	43 8N	124 21 E
Sipora, Indonesia	22 D1	2 18S	99 40 E
Siracusa, Italy	12 F6	37 4N	15 17 E
Sirajganj, Bangla.	23 G12	24 25N	89 47 E
Sirohi, India	23 G4	24 52N	72 53 E
Sirsa, India	23 E5	29 33N	75 4 E
Sishen, S. Africa	31 B3	27 47S	22 59 E
Sitapur, India	23 F8	27 38N	80 45 E
Sivas, Turkey	15 G6	39 43N	36 58 E
Siwan, India	23 F10	26 13N	84 21 E
Sjælland, Denmark	6 G10	55 30N	11 30 E
Skagerrak, Denmark	6 G9	57 30N	9 0 E
Skagway, U.S.A.	38 C6	59 23N	135 20W
Skardu, Pakistan	23 B5	35 20N	75 44 E
Skeena →, Canada	38 C6	54 9N	130 5W
Skellefte →, Sweden	6 F12	64 45N	21 10 E
Skellefteå, Sweden	6 F12	64 45N	20 50 E
Skien, Norway	6 G9	59 12N	9 35 E
Skikda, Algeria	28 B8	36 50N	6 58 E
Skopje, Macedonia, Yug.	13 C9	42 1N	21 32 E
Skowhegan, U.S.A.	43 C13	44 49N	69 40W
Skye, U.K.	7 D3	57 15N	6 10W
Slamet, Indonesia	22 D2	7 16S	109 8 E
Slatina, Romania	13 B11	44 28N	24 22 E
Sligo, Ireland	7 E2	54 17N	8 28W
Sliven, Bulgaria	13 C12	42 42N	26 19 E
Slough, U.K.	7 G6	51 30N	0 35W
Slovak Rep. ■, Europe	10 D8	48 30N	20 0 E
Slovakian Ore Mts., Slovakia	10 D8	48 45N	20 0 E
Slovenia ■, Europe	12 B6	45 58N	14 30 E
Slurry, S. Africa	31 B4	25 49S	25 42 E
Smederevo, Serbia, Yug.	13 B9	44 40N	20 57 E
Smith Sd., Greenland	48 A10	78 30N	74 0W
Smiths Falls, Canada	43 C9	44 55N	76 0W
Smolensk, Russia	14 D5	54 45N	32 5 E
Snake →, U.S.A.	40 A3	46 12N	119 2W
Sneeuberge, S. Africa	31 C3	31 46S	24 20 E
Snøhetta, Norway	6 F9	62 19N	9 16 E
Snow Hill, U.S.A.	43 F10	38 10N	75 21W
Snowdon, U.K.	7 F4	53 4N	4 8W
Sochi, Russia	15 F6	43 35N	39 40 E
Society Is., Pac. Oc.	37 J12	17 0S	151 0W
Socotra, Ind. Oc.	24 D4	12 30N	54 0 E
Söderhamn, Sweden	6 F11	61 18N	17 10 E
Soekmekaar, S. Africa	31 A4	23 30S	29 55 E
Sofia, Bulgaria	13 C10	42 45N	23 20 E
Sogne Fjord, Norway	6 F9	61 10N	5 50 E
Sohâg, Egypt	29 D13	26 33N	31 43 E
Soissons, France	8 C5	49 25N	3 19 E
Sokoto, Nigeria	30 B3	13 2N	5 16 E
Solapur, India	25 D6	17 43N	75 56 E
Solomon Is. ■, Pac. Oc.	35 B10	6 0S	155 0 E
Solothurn, Switz.	10 E2	47 13N	7 32 E
Solway Firth, U.K.	7 E5	54 45N	3 38W
Somali Rep. ■, Africa	24 E3	7 0N	47 0 E
Somerset, U.S.A.	42 G5	37 5N	84 40W
Somerset East, S. Africa	31 C4	32 42S	25 35 E
Somerset I., Canada	38 A10	73 30N	93 0W
Somme →, France	8 B4	50 11N	1 38 E
Sondags →, S. Africa	31 C4	33 44S	25 51 E
Søndre Strømfjord, Greenland	39 B14	66 59N	50 40W
Songkhla, Thailand	22 C2	7 13N	100 37 E
Sopot, Poland	10 A8	54 27N	18 31 E
Sorel, Canada	43 C11	46 0N	73 10W
Soria, Spain	11 B4	41 43N	2 32W
Sorong, Indonesia	22 D5	0 55S	131 15 E
Sørøya, Norway	6 D12	70 40N	22 30 E
Sorsogon, Phil.	22 B4	13 0N	124 0 E
Sosnowiec, Poland	10 C8	50 20N	19 10 E
Sŏul = Seoul, S. Korea	21 C7	37 31N	126 58 E
Sound, The, Europe	6 G10	55 45N	12 45 E
Sousse, Tunisia	28 B9	35 50N	10 38 E
South Africa ■, Africa	31 C3	32 0S	23 0 E
South Australia □, Australia	34 G6	32 0S	139 0 E
South Bend, U.S.A.	42 E4	41 38N	86 20W
South Carolina □, U.S.A.	41 D10	33 45N	81 0W
South Charleston, U.S.A.	42 F7	38 20N	81 40W
South China Sea, Asia	22 B3	10 0N	113 0 E
South Dakota □, U.S.A.	40 B7	45 0N	100 0W
South Downs, U.K.	7 G6	50 53N	0 10W
South Georgia, Antarctica	48 D24	54 30S	37 0W
South I., N.Z.	35 J13	44 0S	170 0 E
South Natuna Is., Indonesia	22 C2	2 45N	109 0 E
South Orkney Is., Antarctica	48 C24	63 0S	45 0W
South Platte →, U.S.A.	40 B6	41 7N	100 42W
South Pole, Antarctica	48 C14	90 0S	0 0 E
South Sandwich Is., Antarctica	48 D13	57 0S	27 0W
South Shetland Is., Antarctica	48 C24	62 0S	59 0W
South Shields, U.K.	7 E6	54 59N	1 26W
Southampton, U.K.	7 G6	50 54N	1 23W
Southampton I., Canada	39 B11	64 30N	84 0W
Southend-on-Sea, U.K.	7 G7	51 32N	0 42 E
Southern Alps, N.Z.	35 J13	43 41S	170 11 E
Sovetskaya Gavan, Russia	18 E16	48 50N	140 5 E
Soweto, S. Africa	31 B4	26 14S	27 54 E
Spain ■, Europe	11 C4	39 0N	4 0W
Spanish, Canada	42 B6	46 12N	82 20W
Spanish Town, Jamaica	44 K17	18 0N	76 57W
Spencer, U.S.A.	42 F7	38 47N	81 24W
Spencer G., Australia	34 G6	34 0S	137 20 E
Spessart, Germany	10 C3	50 10N	9 20 E
Spey →, U.K.	7 D5	57 40N	3 25W
Spitzbergen = Svalbard, Arctic	48 A7	78 0N	17 0 E
Split, Croatia	12 C7	43 31N	16 26 E
Spokane, U.S.A.	40 A3	47 45N	117 25W
Spree →, Germany	10 B5	52 32N	13 13 E
Springbok, S. Africa	31 B2	29 42S	17 54 E
Springfield, Ill., U.S.A.	41 C9	39 48N	89 40W
Springfield, Mass., U.S.A.	43 D11	42 8N	72 37W
Springfield, Mo., U.S.A.	41 C8	37 15N	93 20W
Springfield, Ohio, U.S.A.	42 F6	39 58N	83 48W
Springfontein, S. Africa	31 C4	30 15S	25 40 E
Springhill, Canada	43 C15	45 40N	64 4W
Springs, S. Africa	31 B4	26 13S	28 25 E
Sredinny Ra., Russia	18 D18	57 0N	160 0 E
Sri Lanka ■, Asia	25 E7	7 30N	80 50 E
Srikakulam, India	25 D7	18 14N	83 58 E
Srinagar, India	23 B5	34 5N	74 50 E
Stadlandet, Norway	6 F9	62 10N	5 10 E
Staffa, U.K.	7 D3	56 26N	6 21W
Stafford, U.K.	7 F5	52 49N	2 9W
Stamford, U.S.A.	43 E11	41 5N	73 30W
Standerton, S. Africa	31 B4	26 55S	29 7 E
Standish, U.S.A.	42 D6	43 58N	83 57W
Stanger, S. Africa	31 B5	29 27S	31 14 E
Stanovoy Ra., Russia	18 D14	55 0N	130 0 E
Stara Zagora, Bulgaria	13 C11	42 26N	25 39 E
Start Pt., U.K.	7 G5	50 13N	3 38W
State College, U.S.A.	42 E9	40 47N	77 1W
Staunton, U.S.A.	42 F8	38 7N	79 4W
Stavanger, Norway	6 G9	58 57N	5 40 E
Stavropol, Russia	15 E7	45 5N	42 0 E
Steinkjer, Norway	6 F10	63 59N	11 31 E
Steinkopf, S. Africa	31 B2	29 18S	17 43 E
Stellarton, Canada	43 C16	45 32N	62 30W
Stellenbosch, S. Africa	31 C2	33 58S	18 50 E
Sterlitamak, Russia	14 D10	53 40N	56 0 E
Steubenville, U.S.A.	42 E7	40 21N	80 39W
Stewart I., N.Z.	35 K12	46 58S	167 54 E
Steynsburg, S. Africa	31 C4	31 15S	25 49 E
Steyr, Austria	10 D6	48 3N	14 25 E
Stirling, U.K.	7 D5	56 7N	3 57W
Stockholm, Sweden	6 G11	59 20N	18 3 E
Stockport, U.K.	7 F5	53 25N	2 11W
Stockton, U.S.A.	40 C2	37 58N	121 20W
Stockton-on-Tees, U.K.	7 E6	54 34N	1 20W
Stoke on Trent, U.K.	7 F5	53 1N	2 11W
Stonehaven, U.K.	7 D5	56 58N	2 11W
Storavan, Sweden	6 E11	65 45N	18 10 E
Storlulea, Sweden	6 E11	67 10N	19 30 E
Stornoway, U.K.	7 C3	58 12N	6 23W
Storsjön, Sweden	6 F10	62 50N	13 8 E
Storuman, Sweden	6 E11	65 5N	17 10 E
Stralsund, Germany	10 A5	54 17N	13 5 E
Strand, S. Africa	31 C2	34 9S	18 48 E
Stranraer, U.K.	7 E4	54 54N	5 0W
Strasbourg, France	8 C7	48 35N	7 42 E
Stratford, Canada	42 D7	43 23N	81 0W
Stratford-upon-Avon, U.K.	7 F6	52 12N	1 42W
Strathroy, Canada	42 D7	42 58N	81 38W
Sturgeon Bay, U.S.A.	42 C4	44 52N	87 20W
Sturgeon Falls, Canada	42 B8	46 25N	79 57W
Stutterheim, S. Africa	31 C4	32 33S	27 28 E
Stuttgart, Germany	10 D3	48 46N	9 10 E
Subotica, Serbia, Yug.	13 A8	46 6N	19 39 E
Sucre, Bolivia	46 D3	19 0S	65 15W
Sudan ■, Africa	29 G13	15 0N	30 0 E
Sudbury, Canada	42 B7	46 30N	81 0W
Sudeten Highlands, Europe	10 C7	50 20N	16 45 E
Suez, Egypt	29 D13	29 58N	32 31 E
Sukkur, Pakistan	23 F2	27 42N	68 54 E
Sulaiman Range, Pakistan	23 D2	30 30N	69 50 E
Sulawesi □, Indonesia	22 D3	2 0S	120 0 E
Sulawesi Sea, Indonesia	22 C4	3 0N	123 0 E
Sulitjelma, Norway	6 E11	67 9N	16 3 E
Sulu Arch., Phil.	22 C4	6 0N	121 0 E
Sulu Sea, E. Indies	22 C4	8 0N	120 0 E
Sumatera □, Indonesia	22 C2	0 40N	100 20 E
Sumba, Indonesia	22 D3	9 45S	119 35 E
Sumbawa, Indonesia	22 D3	8 26S	117 30 E
Summerside, Canada	43 B16	46 24N	63 47W
Sumy, Ukraine	15 D5	50 57N	34 50 E
Sunbury, U.S.A.	42 E9	40 50N	76 46W
Sunda Is., Indonesia	16 K14	5 0S	105 0 E
Sunda Str., Indonesia	22 D2	6 20S	105 30 E
Sundarbans, The, Asia	23 J12	22 0N	89 0 E
Sunderland, U.K.	7 E6	54 54N	1 22W
Sundsvall, Sweden	6 F11	62 23N	17 17 E
Superior, L., N. Amer.	42 B4	47 40N	87 0W
Sür, Lebanon	29 M21	33 19N	35 16 E
Surabaya, Indonesia	22 D3	7 17S	112 45 E
Surakarta, Indonesia	22 D3	7 35S	110 48 E
Surat, India	23 J4	21 12N	72 55 E
Surinam ■, S. Amer.	46 B4	4 0N	56 0W
Susquehanna →, U.S.A.	42 F9	39 33N	76 5W
Sussex, Canada	43 C15	45 45N	65 37W
Sutherland, S. Africa	31 C3	32 24S	20 40 E
Sutlej →, Pakistan	23 E3	29 23N	71 3 E
Suva, Fiji	35 D14	18 6S	178 30 E
Suwałki, Poland	10 A10	54 8N	22 59 E
Suzhou, China	21 C7	31 19N	120 38 E
Svalbard, Arctic	48 A7	78 0N	17 0 E
Svealand □, Sweden	6 F10	59 55N	15 0 E
Sverdlovsk = Yekaterinburg, Russia	14 C11	56 50N	60 30 E
Sverdrup Is., Canada	48 A11	79 0N	97 0W
Swakopmund, Namibia	31 A1	22 37S	14 30 E
Swansea, U.K.	7 G5	51 37N	3 57W
Swaziland ■, Africa	31 B5	26 30S	31 30 E
Sweden ■, Europe	6 G10	57 0N	15 0 E
Swellendam, S. Africa	31 C3	34 1S	20 26 E
Swift Current, Canada	38 C9	50 20N	107 45W
Swindon, U.K.	7 G6	51 33N	1 47W
Switzerland ■, Europe	10 E3	46 30N	8 0 E
Sydney, Australia	34 G9	33 53S	151 10 E
Sydney, Canada	43 B17	46 7N	60 7W
Syktyvkar, Russia	14 B9	61 45N	50 40 E
Sylhet, Bangla.	23 G13	24 54N	91 52 E
Syr Darya →, Kazakhstan	18 E8	46 3N	61 0 E
Syracuse, U.S.A.	43 D9	43 4N	76 11W
Syria ■, Asia	24 B2	35 0N	38 0 E
Syrian Desert, Asia	24 B2	32 0N	40 0 E
Syzran, Russia	14 D8	53 12N	48 30 E
Szczecin, Poland	10 B6	53 27N	14 27 E
Szechwan = Sichuan □, China	20 C5	31 0N	104 0 E
Szeged, Hungary	10 E9	46 16N	20 10 E
Székesfehérvár, Hungary	10 E8	47 15N	18 25 E
Szekszárd, Hungary	10 E8	46 22N	18 42 E
Szolnok, Hungary	10 E9	47 10N	20 15 E
Szombathely, Hungary	10 E7	47 14N	16 38 E

T

Tabas, Iran	24 B4	33 35N	56 55 E
Tablas, Phil.	22 B4	12 25N	122 2 E
Table Mt., S. Africa	31 C2	34 0S	18 22 E
Tabora, Tanzania	32 F6	5 2S	32 50 E
Tabriz, Iran	24 B3	38 7N	46 20 E
Tacloban, Phil.	22 B4	11 15N	124 58 E
Tacna, Peru	46 D2	18 0S	70 20W
Tacoma, U.S.A.	40 A2	47 15N	122 30W
Tacuarembó, Uruguay	47 F4	31 45S	56 0W
Tadzhikistan = Tajikistan ■, Asia	18 F8	38 30N	70 0 E
Taegu, S. Korea	21 C7	35 50N	128 37 E
Taejon, S. Korea	21 C7	36 20N	127 28 E
Taganrog, Russia	15 E6	47 12N	38 50 E
Tagus →, Europe	11 C1	38 40N	9 24W
Tahiti, Pac. Oc.	37 J13	17 37S	149 27W
Taichung, Taiwan	21 D7	24 12N	120 35 E
Taimyr Peninsula, Russia	18 B11	75 0N	100 0 E
Tainan, Taiwan	21 D7	23 17N	120 18 E
T'aipei, Taiwan	21 D7	25 2N	121 30 E
Taiping, Malaysia	22 C2	4 51N	100 44 E
Taiwan ■, Asia	21 D7	23 30N	121 0 E
Taiyuan, China	21 C6	37 52N	112 33 E
Ta'izz, Yemen	24 D3	13 35N	44 2 E
Tajikistan ■, Asia	18 F8	38 30N	70 0 E
Tak, Thailand	22 B1	16 52N	99 8 E
Takamatsu, Japan	19 B4	34 20N	134 5 E
Takaoka, Japan	19 A5	36 47N	137 0 E
Takasaki, Japan	19 A6	36 20N	139 0 E
Takla Makan, China	16 F12	38 0N	83 0 E
Talaud Is., Indonesia	22 C4	4 30N	127 10 E
Talca, Chile	47 F2	35 28S	71 40W
Talcahuano, Chile	47 F2	36 40S	73 10W
Taliabu, Indonesia	22 D4	1 45S	124 55 E
Tallahassee, U.S.A.	41 D10	30 25N	84 15W
Tallinn, Estonia	14 C3	59 22N	24 48 E
Tamale, Ghana	30 C1	9 22N	0 50W
Tambov, Russia	14 D7	52 45N	41 28 E
Tamil Nadu □, India	25 D6	11 0N	77 0 E
Tamo Abu Ra., Malaysia	22 C3	3 10N	115 5 E
Tampa, U.S.A.	41 E10	27 57N	82 38W
Tampere, Finland	6 F12	61 30N	23 50 E
Tampico, Mexico	44 C5	22 20N	97 50W
Tamworth, Australia	34 G9	31 7S	150 58 E
Tana →, Norway	6 D13	70 30N	28 23 E
Tana, L., Ethiopia	29 G14	13 5N	37 30 E
Tanami Desert, Australia	34 D5	18 50S	132 0 E
Tananarive = Antananarivo, Madag.	33 H9	18 55S	47 31 E
Tando Adam, Pakistan	23 G2	25 45N	68 40 E
Tanga, Tanzania	32 F7	5 5S	39 2 E
Tanganyika, L., Africa	32 F6	6 40S	30 0 E
Tangier, Morocco	28 B5	35 50N	5 49W
Tangshan, China	21 C6	39 38N	118 10 E
Tanimbar Is., Indonesia	22 D5	7 30S	131 30 E
Tanjungbalai, Indonesia	22 C1	2 55N	99 44 E
Tanzania ■, Africa	32 F6	6 0S	34 0 E
Tapajós →, Brazil	46 C4	2 24S	54 41W
Tapti →, India	20 J4	21 0N	70 11 E
Tappahannock, U.S.A.	42 G9	37 56N	76 50W
Tarābulus = Tripoli, Lebanon	24 B2	34 31N	35 50 E
Tarābulus = Tripoli, Libya	28 C9	32 49N	13 7 E
Tarakan, Indonesia	22 C3	3 20N	117 35 E
Taranto, Italy	12 D7	40 30N	17 11 E
Táranto, G. di, Italy	12 D7	40 0N	17 15 E
Tarbagatai Ra., Kazakhstan	18 E10	48 0N	83 0 E
Tarbes, France	9 F4	43 15N	0 3 E
Tarim Basin, China	20 B3	40 0N	84 0 E
Tarkastad, S. Africa	31 C4	32 0S	26 16 E
Tarnów, Poland	10 C9	50 3N	21 0 E
Tarragona, Spain	11 B6	41 5N	1 17 E
Tarrasa, Spain	11 B7	41 34N	2 1 E
Tashkent, Uzbekistan	18 E8	41 20N	69 10 E
Tasman Sea, Pac. Oc.	36 L8	36 0S	160 0 E
Tasmania □, Australia	34 J8	42 0S	146 30 E
Tatar Republic □, Russia	14 C9	55 30N	51 30 E
Tatarsk, Russia	18 D9	55 14N	76 0 E
Tatta, Pakistan	23 G1	24 42N	67 55 E
Tauern, Austria	10 E5	47 15N	12 40 E
Taung, S. Africa	31 B3	27 33S	24 47 E
Taunton, U.K.	7 G5	51 1N	3 7W
Taunton, U.S.A.	43 E12	41 54N	71 6W
Taunus, Germany	10 C3	50 15N	8 20 E
Taurus Mts., Turkey	15 G5	37 0N	32 30 E
Tawas City, U.S.A.	42 C6	44 16N	83 31W
Tawau, Malaysia	22 C3	4 20N	117 55 E
Tay →, U.K.	7 D5	56 37N	3 38W
Tay, Firth of, U.K.	7 D5	56 25N	3 8W
Tbilisi, Georgia	15 F7	41 43N	44 50 E
Tchad, L. = Chad, L., Chad	28 G9	13 30N	14 30 E
Tebingtinggi, Indonesia	22 C1	3 20N	99 9 E
Tegal, Indonesia	22 D2	6 52S	109 8 E
Tegucigalpa, Honduras	44 E7	14 5N	87 14W
Tehran, Iran	24 B4	35 44N	51 30 E
Tehuantepec, Gulf of, Mexico	44 D5	15 50N	95 12W
Tehuantepec, Isthmus of, Mexico	44 D6	17 0N	94 30W
Tel Aviv-Jaffa, Israel	29 P20	32 4N	34 48 E
Telford, U.K.	7 F5	52 42N	2 31W
Tell City, U.S.A.	42 G4	37 55N	86 44W
Teluk Betung, Indonesia	22 C2	4 13N	108 12 E

Tema, Ghana	30 C2	5 41N	0 0 E
Temba, S. Africa	31 B4	25 20S	28 17 E
Témiscaming, Canada	42 B8	46 44N	79 5W
Tenerife, Canary Is.	28 D3	28 15N	16 35W
Tennessee □, U.S.A.	41 C9	36 0N	86 30W
Tennessee →, U.S.A.	41 C9	37 4N	88 34W
Tepic, Mexico	44 C4	21 30N	104 54W
Teramo, Italy	12 C5	42 40N	13 40 E
Teresina, Brazil	46 C5	5 9S	42 45W
Ternate, Indonesia	22 C4	0 45N	127 25 E
Terni, Italy	12 C5	42 34N	12 38 E
Terre Haute, U.S.A.	42 F4	39 28N	87 24W
Teruel, Spain	11 B5	40 22N	1 8W
Tetouan, Morocco	28 B5	35 35N	5 21W
Tetovo, Macedonia, Yug.	13 C9	42 1N	21 2 E
Teutoburger Wald, Germany	10 B3	52 5N	8 20 E
Texas □, U.S.A.	40 D7	31 40N	98 30W
Texel, Neths.	8 A6	53 5N	4 50 E
Tezpur, India	23 F14	26 40N	92 45 E
Thabana Ntlenyana, Lesotho	31 B4	29 30S	29 16 E
Thabazimbi, S. Africa	31 A4	24 40S	27 21 E
Thailand ■, Asia	22 B2	16 0N	102 0 E
Thailand, G. of, Asia	22 B2	11 30N	101 0 E
Thal, Pakistan	23 C3	33 28N	70 33 E
Thal Desert, Pakistan	23 D3	31 10N	71 30 E
Thames →, Canada	42 D6	42 20N	82 25W
Thames →, U.K.	7 G7	51 30N	0 35 E
Thane, India	23 K4	19 12N	72 59 E
Thar Desert, India	23 E4	28 0N	72 0 E
The Hague, Neths.	8 A6	52 7N	4 17 E
The Pas, Canada	38 C9	53 45N	101 15W
Thessalon, Canada	42 B6	46 20N	83 30W
Thessaloníki, Greece	13 D10	40 38N	22 58 E
Thessaloníki, Gulf of, Greece	13 D10	40 15N	22 45 E
Thessaly □, Greece	13 E9	38 25N	21 50 E
Thetford Mines, Canada	43 B12	46 8N	71 18W
Thiers, France	9 E5	45 52N	3 33 E
Thies, Senegal	28 G3	14 50N	16 51W
Thimphu, Bhutan	23 F12	27 31N	89 45 E
Thionville, France	8 C7	49 20N	6 10 E
Thonon-les-Bains, France	9 D7	46 22N	6 29 E
Thrace □, Greece	13 D11	41 9N	25 30 E
Thule, Greenland	48 A10	77 40N	69 0W
Thunder B., U.S.A.	42 C6	45 0N	83 20W
Thunder Bay, Canada	42 A3	48 20N	89 15W
Thuringian Forest, Germany	10 C4	50 35N	11 0 E
Thurso, U.K.	7 C5	58 34N	3 31W
Tianjin = Tientsin, China	21 C6	39 8N	117 10 E
Tianshui, China	20 C5	34 32N	105 40 E
Tiber →, Italy	12 D5	41 44N	12 14 E
Tiberias, Israel	N21	32 47N	00 02 C
Tibesti, Chad	28 E10	21 0N	17 30 E
Tibet = Xizang □, China	20 C3	32 0N	88 0 E
Ticino →, Italy	12 B3	45 9N	9 14 E
Ticonderoga, U.S.A.	43 D11	43 50N	73 28W
Tien Shan, Asia	16 F11	42 0N	76 0 E
Tientsin, China	21 C6	39 8N	117 10 E
Tierra del Fuego, I. Gr. de, Argentina	47 H3	54 0S	69 0W
Tiffin, U.S.A.	42 E6	41 7N	83 10W
Tignish, Canada	43 B15	46 58N	64 2W
Tigris →, Asia	24 D5	31 0N	47 25 E
Tijuana, Mexico	44 A1	32 30N	117 10W
Tiksi, Russia	18 B14	71 40N	128 45 E
Tilburg, Neths.	8 B6	51 31N	5 6 E
Timaru, N.Z.	35 J13	44 23S	171 14 E
Timbuktu = Tombouctou, Mali	30 A1	16 50N	3 0W
Timişoara, Romania	13 B9	45 43N	21 15 E
Timmins, Canada	42 A7	48 28N	81 25W
Timor, Indonesia	22 D4	9 0S	125 0 E
Tinaca Pt., Phil.	22 C4	5 30N	125 25 E
Tipperary, Ireland	7 F2	52 28N	8 10W
Tiranë, Albania	13 D8	41 18N	19 49 E
Tîrgovişte, Romania	13 B11	44 55N	25 27 E
Tîrgu-Jiu, Romania	13 B10	45 5N	23 19 E
Tirich Mir, Pakistan	23 A3	36 15N	71 55 E
Tiruchchirappalli, India	25 D6	10 45N	78 45 E
Tirunelveli, India	25 E6	8 45N	77 45 E
Tisa →, Serbia, Yug.	10 F9	46 8N	20 2 E
Tisza →, Serbia, Yug.	10 F9	46 8N	20 17 E
Titicaca, L., S. Amer.	46 D3	15 30S	69 30W
Titusville, U.S.A.	42 E8	41 38N	79 39W
Tizi-Ouzou, Algeria	28 B7	36 42N	4 3 E
Toba Kakar Hills, Pakistan	23 D2	31 30N	69 0 E
Tobago, W. Indies	44 R21	11 10N	60 30W
Tobermory, Canada	42 C7	45 12N	81 40W
Tocantins →, Brazil	46 C5	1 45S	49 10W
Togliatti, Russia	14 D8	53 32N	49 24 E
Togo ■, W. Afr.	30 C2	8 30N	1 35 E
Tokelau Is., Pac. Oc.	35 B16	9 0S	171 45W
Tōkyō, Japan	19 B6	35 45N	139 45 E
Tolbukhin, Bulgaria	13 C12	43 37N	27 49 E
Toledo, Spain	11 C3	39 50N	4 2W
Toledo, U.S.A.	42 E6	41 39N	83 33W
Toliara, Madag.	33 J8	23 21S	43 40 E
Toluca, Mexico	44 D5	19 20N	99 40W
Tomaszów Mazowiecki, Poland	10 C8	51 30N	19 57 E
Tombouctou, Mali	30 A1	16 50N	3 0W
Tomini, G. of, Indonesia	22 D4	0 10S	122 0 E
Tomsk, Russia	18 D10	56 30N	85 5 E

Tonga ■, Pac. Oc.	35 D16	19 50S	174 30W
Tonga Trench, Pac. Oc.	35 E16	18 0S	173 0W
Tongaat, S. Africa	31 B5	29 33S	31 9 E
Tongking, G. of, Asia	20 E5	20 0N	108 0 E
Tonk, India	23 F5	26 6N	75 54 E
Tonlé Sap, Cambodia	22 B2	13 0N	104 0 E
Toowoomba, Australia	34 F9	27 32S	151 56 E
Topeka, U.S.A.	41 C7	39 3N	95 40W
Torino = Turin, Italy	12 B2	45 4N	7 40 E
Torne →, Sweden	6 E12	65 50N	24 12 E
Torne, L., Sweden	6 E11	68 24N	19 15 E
Tornio, Finland	6 E12	65 50N	24 12 E
Toronto, Canada	42 D8	43 39N	79 20W
Torquay, U.K.	7 G5	50 27N	3 31W
Torreón, Mexico	44 B4	25 33N	103 26W
Tortosa, Spain	11 B6	40 49N	0 31 E
Toruń, Poland	10 B8	53 2N	18 39 E
Toteng, Botswana	31 A3	20 22S	22 58 E
Toul, France	8 C6	48 40N	5 53 E
Toulon, France	9 F6	43 10N	5 55 E
Toulouse, France	9 F4	43 37N	1 27 E
Touraine, France	8 D4	47 20N	0 30 E
Tournai, Belgium	8 B5	50 35N	3 25 E
Tournon, France	9 E6	45 4N	4 50 E
Tours, France	8 D4	47 22N	0 40 E
Touwsrivier, S. Africa	31 C3	33 20S	20 2 E
Towanda, U.S.A.	42 E9	41 46N	76 30W
Townsville, Australia	34 D8	19 15S	146 45 E
Towson, U.S.A.	42 F9	39 26N	76 34W
Toyama, Japan	19 A5	36 40N	137 15 E
Toyohashi, Japan	19 B5	34 45N	137 25 E
Trabzon, Turkey	15 F6	41 0N	39 45 E
Trafalgar, C., Spain	11 D2	36 10N	6 2W
Trail, Canada	38 D8	49 5N	117 40W
Tralee, Ireland	7 F2	52 16N	9 42W
Trang, Thailand	22 C1	7 33N	99 38 E
Trangan, Indonesia	22 D5	6 40S	134 20 E
Transkei □, S. Africa	31 C4	32 15S	28 15 E
Transvaal □, S. Africa	31 A4	25 0S	29 0 E
Transylvania, Romania	13 B11	45 19N	25 0 E
Transylvanian Alps, Romania	4 F10	45 30N	25 0 E
Trapani, Italy	12 E5	38 1N	12 30 E
Traverse City, U.S.A.	42 C5	44 45N	85 39W
Trent →, U.K.	7 F6	53 33N	0 44W
Trentino-Alto Adige □, Italy	12 A4	46 30N	11 0 E
Trento, Italy	12 A4	46 5N	11 8 E
Trenton, Canada	42 C9	44 10N	77 34W
Trenton, U.S.A.	43 E10	40 15N	74 41W
Trier, Germany	10 D2	49 45N	6 37 E
Trieste, Italy	12 B5	45 39N	13 45 E
Trincomalee, Sri Lanka	25 E7	8 38N	81 15 E
Trinidad & Tobago , W. Indies	44 S20	10 30N	61 20W
Tripoli, Lebanon	24 B2	34 31N	35 50 E
Tripoli, Libya	28 C9	32 49N	13 7 E
Tripura □, India	23 H13	24 0N	92 0 E
Tristan da Cunha, Atl. Oc.	2 F9	37 6S	12 20W
Trivandrum, India	25 E6	8 41N	77 0 E
Trnava, Slovakia	10 D7	48 23N	17 35 E
Trois-Rivières, Canada	43 B11	46 25N	72 34W
Trollhättan, Sweden	6 G10	58 17N	12 20 E
Trondheim, Norway	6 F10	63 36N	10 25 E
Trondheim Fjord, Norway	6 F10	63 35N	10 30 E
Troy, N.Y., U.S.A.	43 D11	42 45N	73 39W
Troy, Ohio, U.S.A.	42 E5	40 3N	84 10W
Troyes, France	8 C6	48 19N	4 3 E
Trujillo, Peru	46 C2	8 6S	79 0W
Truk, Pac. Oc.	36 G7	7 25N	151 46 E
Truro, Canada	43 C16	45 21N	63 14W
Truro, U.K.	7 G4	50 17N	5 2W
Tsau, Botswana	31 A3	20 8S	22 22 E
Tselinograd, Kazakhstan	18 D9	51 10N	71 30 E
Tshabong, Botswana	31 B3	26 2S	22 29 E
Tshane, Botswana	31 A3	24 5S	21 54 E
Tshwane, Botswana	31 A3	22 24S	22 1 E
Tsimlyansk Res., Russia	15 E7	48 0N	43 0 E
Tsu, Japan	19 B5	34 45N	136 25 E
Tsumeb, Namibia	31 A2	19 9S	17 44 E
Tsumis, Namibia	31 A2	23 39S	17 29 E
Tuamotu Arch., Pac. Oc.	37 J13	17 0S	144 0W
Tubuai Is., Pac. Oc.	37 K12	25 0S	150 0W
Tucson, U.S.A.	40 D4	32 14N	110 59W
Tugela →, S. Africa	31 B5	29 14S	31 30 E
Tula, Russia	14 D6	54 13N	37 38 E
Tulcea, Romania	13 B13	45 13N	28 46 E
Tulle, France	9 E4	45 16N	1 46 E
Tulsa, U.S.A.	41 C7	36 10N	96 0W
Tunis, Tunisia	28 B9	36 50N	10 11 E
Tunisia ■, Africa	28 C8	33 30N	9 10 E
Tunja, Colombia	46 B2	5 33N	73 25W
Tura, Russia	23 G13	25 30N	90 16 E
Turabah, Si. Arabia	24 C3	28 20N	43 15 E
Turin, Italy	12 B2	45 4N	7 40 E
Turkana, L., Africa	32 D7	3 30N	36 0 E
Turkey ■, Eurasia	15 G6	39 0N	36 0 E
Turkmenistan ■, Asia	18 F7	39 0N	59 0 E
Turks Is., W. Indies	45 C10	21 20N	71 20W
Turku, Finland	6 F12	60 30N	22 19 E
Tuticorin, India	25 E6	8 50N	78 12 E
Tuvalu ■, Pac. Oc.	35 B14	8 0S	178 0 E
Tuxtla Gutiérrez, Mexico	44 D6	16 50N	93 10W
Tuz Gölü, Turkey	15 G5	38 45N	33 30 E
Tuzla, Bos.-H., Yug.	13 B8	44 34N	18 41 E
Tver, Russia	14 C6	56 55N	35 55 E
Two Rivers, U.S.A.	42 C4	44 10N	87 31W
Tychy, Poland	10 C8	50 9N	18 59 E
Tynemouth, U.K.	7 E6	55 1N	1 27W
Tyre = Sūr, Lebanon	29 C14	33 19N	35 16 E

Tyrol □, Austria	10 E4	47 3N	10 43 E
Tyrrhenian Sea, Europe	12 E5	40 0N	12 30 E
Tyumen, Russia	18 D8	57 11N	65 29 E
Tzaneen, S. Africa	31 A5	23 47S	30 9 E

U

Ubangi = Oubangi →, Zaïre	32 E3	0 30S	17 50 E
Ube, Japan	19 C2	33 56N	131 15 E
Uberaba, Brazil	46 D5	19 50S	47 55W
Uberlândia, Brazil	46 D5	19 0S	48 20W
Ucayali →, Peru	46 C2	4 30S	73 30W
Udaipur, India	23 G4	24 36N	73 44 E
Udaipur Garhi, Nepal	23 F11	27 0N	86 35 E
Udine, Italy	12 A5	46 5N	13 10 E
Udmurt Republic □, Russia	14 C9	57 30N	52 30 E
Udon Thani, Thailand	22 B2	17 29N	102 46 E
Ufa, Russia	14 D10	54 45N	55 55 E
Uganda ■, Africa	32 D6	2 0N	32 0 E
Uitenhage, S. Africa	31 C4	33 40S	25 28 E
Ujjain, India	23 H5	23 9N	75 43 E
Ujung Pandang, Indonesia	22 D3	5 10S	119 20 E
Ukraine ■, Europe	15 E5	49 0N	32 0 E
Ulan Bator, Mongolia	20 B5	47 55N	106 53 E
Ulan Ude, Russia	18 D12	51 45N	107 40 E
Ulhasnagar, India	23 K4	19 15N	73 10 E
Ullapool, U.K.	7 D4	57 54N	5 10W
Ulm, Germany	10 D4	48 23N	10 0 E
Ulyasutay, Mongolia	20 B4	47 56N	97 28 E
Umbria □, Italy	12 C5	42 53N	12 30 E
Ume →, Sweden	6 F12	63 45N	20 20 E
Umeå, Sweden	6 F12	63 45N	20 20 E
Umtata, S. Africa	31 C4	31 36S	28 49 E
Umzimvubu, S. Africa	31 C4	31 38S	29 33 E
Umzinto, S. Africa	31 C5	30 15S	30 45 E
Ungava B., Canada	39 C13	59 30N	67 30W
Ungava Pen., Canada	39 C12	60 0N	74 0W
Uniontown, U.S.A.	42 F8	39 54N	79 45W
United Arab Emirates ■, Asia	24 C4	23 50N	54 0 E
United Kingdom ■, Europe	7 F5	53 0N	2 0W
United States of America ■, N. Amer.	40 C7	37 0N	96 0W
Upington, S. Africa	31 B3	28 25S	21 15 E
Uppsala, Sweden	6 G11	59 53N	17 38 E
Ural →, Kazakhstan	15 E9	47 0N	51 40 E
Ural Mts., Russia	14 C10	60 0N	59 0 E
Uralsk, Kazakhstan	14 D9	51 20N	51 20 E
Uranium City, Canada	38 C9	59 34N	108 37W
Urbana, Ill., U.S.A.	42 E3	40 7N	88 12W
Urbana, Ohio, U.S.A.	42 E6	40 9N	83 44W
Uruguay ■, S. Amer.	47 F4	32 30S	56 30W
Uruguay →, S. Amer.	47 F4	34 12S	58 18W
Ürümqi, China	20 B3	43 45N	87 45 E
Usakos, Namibia	31 A2	21 54S	15 31 E
Ushant = Ouessant, I. d', France	8 C1	48 28N	5 6W
Üsküdar, Turkey	13 D13	41 0N	29 5 E
Ussel, France	9 E5	45 32N	2 18 E
Ust Urt Plateau, Kazakhstan	18 E7	44 0N	55 0 E
Ústí nad Labem, Czech.	10 C6	50 41N	14 3 E
Utah □, U.S.A.	40 C4	39 30N	111 30W
Utica, U.S.A.	43 D10	43 5N	75 18W
Utrecht, Neths.	8 A6	52 5N	5 8 E
Utsunomiya, Japan	19 A6	36 30N	139 50 E
Uttar Pradesh □, India	23 F8	27 0N	80 0 E
Uttaradit, Thailand	22 B2	17 36N	100 5 E
Uusikaupunki, Finland	6 F12	60 47N	21 25 E
Uzbekistan ■, Asia	18 E8	41 30N	65 0 E

V

Vaal →, S. Africa	31 B3	29 4S	23 38 E
Vaal Dam, S. Africa	31 B4	27 0S	28 14 E
Vaasa, Finland	6 F12	63 6N	21 38 E
Vadodara, India	23 H4	22 20N	73 10 E
Vadsø, Norway	6 D13	70 3N	29 50 E
Váh →, Slovakia	10 E8	47 43N	18 7 E
Val d'Or, Canada	42 A9	48 7N	77 47W
Valdez, U.S.A.	38 B5	61 14N	146 17W
Valdivia, Chile	47 F2	39 50S	73 14W
Valence, France	9 E6	44 57N	4 54 E
Valencia, Spain	11 C5	39 27N	0 23W
Valencia, Venezuela	46 A3	10 11N	68 0W
Valenciennes, France	8 B5	50 20N	3 34 E
Valladolid, Spain	11 B3	41 38N	4 43W
Valletta, Malta	12 G6	35 54N	14 31 E
Valparaíso, Chile	47 F2	33 2S	71 40W
Van, L., Turkey	15 G7	38 30N	43 0 E
Van Buren, U.S.A.	43 B13	47 10N	68 1W
Van Wert, U.S.A.	42 E5	40 52N	84 31W
Vancouver, Canada	38 D7	49 15N	123 10W
Vancouver I., Canada	38 D7	49 50N	126 0W
Vanderbijlpark, S. Africa	31 B4	26 42S	27 54 E
Vänern, L., Sweden	6 G10	58 47N	13 30 E
Vännäs, Sweden	6 F11	63 58N	19 48 E
Vannes, France	8 D2	47 40N	2 47W
Vanrhynsdorp, S. Africa	31 C2	31 36S	18 44 E
Vanua Levu, Fiji	35 D14	16 33S	179 15 E
Vanuatu ■, Pac. Oc.	35 D12	15 0S	168 0 E

INDEX TO WORLD MAPS